THE DANCE HANDBOOK

Allen Robertson
Donald Hutera

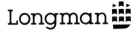

Longman

DV8 Physical Theatre (see entry on page 236)

Longman Group UK Limited,
Longman House, Burnt Mill, Harlow, Essex CM20 2JE, England
and Associated Companies throughout the world.

First published 1988

British Library Cataloguing in Publication Data

Robertson, Allen
    The dance handbook. – (Longman handbooks).
    1. Great Britain. Dancing
    I. Title II. Hutera, Donald
    793.3'0941

ISBN 0-582-00100-5

Picture research by Lesley Davy.
Design by Karen Osborne and Sue Rawkins.

Typeset in 8pt Rockwell by Chapterhouse, Formby L37 3PX,
Printed in Great Britain by The Bath Press, Avon.

CONTENTS

Introduction by Merce Cunningham	5
How To Use The Dance Handbook	6
Origins	8
Romantic Ballet	12
Classical Ballet	26
The Ballets Russes	38
The Birth of Modern Dance	60
Modern Ballet	86
The Ballet Boom	134
The Dance Explosion	192
Alternatives	224
Databank – Glossary	258
Dance Books	261
Dance Information	262
Index	268

Acknowledgements

TO THE MEMORY of Else Aschengreen, and for Erik Aschengreen in Copenhagen and William Mowat-Thomson in Edinburgh, first and still ideal European hosts.

A thank you to George Ashley, Linda Brandt, Fiona Dick, Marc Farre, Jane Pritchard, David Vaughan and all those who provided assistance in getting the information together and the facts right. Our editor Philip Dodd not only got the project underway by commissioning it in the first place, but also provided the dogged persistence and encouragement needed to get it finished. A special thank you is due Merce Cunningham for agreeing to write the introduction.

The publishers would like to thank Judith Mackrell for her editorial advice, and Caroline Shercliff and the staff at the London Contemporary Dance School Library for their time and expertise. And for their unselfish help, many thanks to Gertrude Bliss, Assis Carreiro, Beth Dean, Enrico Galli and staff at Computer Shop in Florence, Helma Klooss, Laura Kumin, Lee Adair Lawrence, David Leonard and staff at Dance Books, Rebecca Libermann, Daryl Ries, C. Raman Schlemmer, Dora Sowden, Yvette Stachowiak and Geof Wheelwright of Greenleaf Publishing, Lulli Svedin, Sako Ueno, Vladimir Vasut and Basilio Esteban S. Villaruz.

We are grateful to the following for permission to reproduce copyright photographs:

Catherine Ashmore for page 61; BBC Hulton Picture Library for pages 38-9, 41, 77, 99, 120 and 132; Gertrude Bliss for page 105; Andrew Cockrill for pages 90, 168 and 171; Jean Cocteau © DACS 1988 for page 39; Dee Conway for pages 21, 190, 214, 232 and 254; Bill Cooper for pages 13, 29, 124, 155 and 175; Costas for pages 86-7; Anthony Crickmay for pages 17, 185 and 211; Alan Cunliffe for page 135; Merce Cunningham Dance Company for page 5 (photo by Steven Mark Needham); Dancing Times for pages 74, 85 and 114-5; Chris Davis for page 226; Delahaye for pages 179, 197, 220, 225 and 246; Brigitte Enguerand for page 10; Lois Greenfield for pages 157, 201, 205, 231 and 250; Images Dance Company for page 242; Shuhei Iwamoto for pages 25 and 51; LWT for page 55; The Mansell Collection for page 64; Herbert Migdoll for pages 192-3; Morgan & Morgan Inc. for page 69; Chris Nash for the contents page and for page 238; The Pritchard Collection at Rambert Dance Company for pages 48, 59 and 112; Oskar Schlemmer Theatre Estate/Photo Archive C. Raman Schlemmer for page 81; Snowden for page 162; Donald Southern for page 109; Leslie E. Spatt for pages 26-7, 30, 34-5, 138, 146 and 151; Martha Swope for pages 95 and 143; Victoria and Albert Museum for page 9

THE PRESENT VIGOUR of dance, and the enthusiasm for it by a more general and larger public than previously, makes a Handbook handy, especially if it conveys information clearly and easily to anyone reading it. What it can convey further is a view of the wide variety and multiplicity of directions that dance has taken in recent decades.

Dance is of course for everyone to do, but since most people are less likely to do it than see it – and that section of the populace seems to be growing – if they can read about it (preferably *after* seeing a dance, from my point of view, but as many will prefer, before seeing it) in a form that straightforwardly describes dancers and dances and the different approaches choreographers have used, a Handbook, like the dictionary, can help.

Dance is an elusive art. It slips through your fingers and toes. But a formidable one, as evidenced by its influence on twentieth-century arts. It is also constantly around us in its various guises – folk, popular, serious, from strict traditional classical ballet and the myriad individual modern dance approaches to the most recent innovations of the young. The output is enormous; gives one pause to look at a Handbook.

Merce Cunningham

HOW TO USE
THE DANCE
═══ HANDBOOK ═══

The Dance Handbook is a compact guide offering a structured approach to the extensive – and sometimes daunting – range of ballet and dance currently on offer. It starts from a framework of major choreographers, companies, dancers and danceworks, and aims to encourage you, through a system of cross-references, to encounter as wide a variety of dance as possible.

The Handbook's role is to pre-pare the groundwork for building up an overall view of ballet and dance in the context of their history, and to encourage you to develop your own personal tastes. The different routes you can take are clearly marked; it is up to you whether or not you choose to pursue them.

Above all, the Handbook is in-tended to be an active reference book: it has been designed for ease of use, and ease of access. The ideal way to use it is to follow the recommendations and sug-gestions, and experience dance in performance whenever you have the chance.

To support you, the Handbook provides back-up facts and inform-ation; although compact, it is crammed with data.

The entries

At the core of the Handbook are the two hundred main entries. They have been deliberately chosen to cover a wide and relevant spread of starting-points. These range from Romantic ballets (for example *La Sylphide* and *Giselle*) and the great Imperial works (such as *Swan Lake* and *The Sleeping Beauty*) to contemporary innovators like Twyla Tharp and Pina Bausch. We have not intended to cover every choreographer, every ballet or every dancer. The Handbook is not a comprehensive

encyclopedia, but rather a stimulus and a springboard for further exploration. Omission is by no means meant to imply lack of importance. For the purposes of this book, we have taken dance to mean Western theatrical dance, as opposed to ethnic or social dance.

The entries have been grouped into eight broadly chronological sections to create an immediate framework, which helps when you are dealing with what may appear at first to be the amorphous world of dance. You should note that:

○ The Handbook opens with a brief chapter called Origins, which explains the development of what we now call ballet.

○ A two-page spread begins each chapter with a summary of the salient features and trends of each era.

○ Clearly some companies, dancers and choreographers will straddle one or more of the chapters, but we have placed them in the chapter where they had their first or most important impact.

○ Three major subjects have two entries, such is the length and consistency of their contri-butions: Frederick Ashton, George Balanchine and Ballet Rambert/Rambert Dance Company.

Within the chapters, choreo-graphers, companies and dancers are listed in alphabetical order. Individual works are grouped after the relevant choreographer in chronological order of first per-formance. For example:

FREDERICK ASHTON
　　Façade (1931)
　　Symphonic Variations (1946)
　　Cinderella (1948)
GEORGE BALANCHINE
　　Serenade (1934) etc.

Where a ballet or dancework has been choreographed in a number of different stagings, we have selected the first or the best known version. The alternative stagings are listed at the end of the entry.

Main entries contain the following elements:

1 A block of **factual information**. For choreographers/dancers this contains:
   - Date and place of birth and death

   For dance companies:
   - Year of formation

   For ballets and danceworks:
   - Number of acts
   - Choreographer, librettist, composer and designer
   - The date and place of first performance

2 The **main critique** sets the subject of the entry in context, identifying what is important and individual about it, and what to look for. References to other main entries are indicated in **bold**: people and works are always cross-referenced; companies are usually, but not necessarily cross-referenced. At the first appearance in the book of ballets which are not main entries, the year of production is also given.

3 **Lineage** is the part of the entry which actively suggests links and new directions to follow. These links can range from the straightforward to the adventurous, encouraging you to cut across the different styles of dance rather than getting locked into any particular one. References to other main entries are again picked out in **bold**.

4 The **Follow-up** section gives pointers to other background materials available which focus on the particular person, company or work: for example, books, films or videos (an increasingly important source) with date of publication/release where known.

5 Entries on specific works may also have a set of alternative **Stagings**. This may simply list companies with the year they took the work (in the version described by the entry) into their repertory, eg:

   1 New York City Ballet/1979
   2 Dance Theatre of Harlem/1986

   Alternatively, where the score or subject matter has been interpreted by a number of different choreographers, or where stagings have been remounted after the choreographer's death, the name of the person who staged the individual versions is also given, eg:

   1 Rudolf Nureyev/Vienna Ballet/1964
   2 Erik Bruhn/National Ballet of Canada/1966.

The Databank

Following the main chapters is a Databank of additional information, including:

○ A **glossary** listing dance-related terms in the Handbook which may require further clarification or amplification.

○ **Dance books**: includes titles which will give further background or detail on dance in general, and provide an additional entrée to the world of dance.

○ A country-by-country listing of **information sources**: magazines, festivals, dance companies and other bodies which can supply useful information and act as contact points.

○ **Index**: an A-Z of choreographers, dancers, composers, designers, librettists, entrepreneurs, companies and works mentioned in the Handbook.

The Dance Handbook is the third title in a series of Longman Handbooks on the arts; see the back cover for further details.

ORIGINS

It began as magic. Like his cave paintings and his stone circles, dance linked prehistoric man to the awesome realm beyond everyday existence where ritual could attempt to define and control what could not be explained. The urge to dance, one of the forces of nature buried deep in the human psyche, is a universal impulse.

Today we watch dance being performed by youthful, svelte and beautiful bodies who act as our surrogates. Most of us no longer feel free enough to express our emotions in maypole or morris dances – let alone fertility rites. We do not summon the gods with our dancing; instead, we sit watching in the dark where, on rare occasions, we are lucky enough to experience vicariously that core of true magic at the heart of dance.

What we call dancing was born in the courts of the Italian city states, where it was used as a political tool, as a show of splendour and an exhibition of wealth and power. These entertainments were something like an indoor parade, a refined and elaborate version of the popular public fairs and festivals.

Dance, as it began to be codified in the late sixteenth century, was a hobby for aristocratic amateurs happy and eager to take part in the glorification of their monarchs. Like all of the arts of the Renaissance, dancing expressed its political messages through allegories drawn from the ancient gods and goddesses of Greek and Roman mythology. In fact, the most ardent of all royal dancers, the French king Louis XIV, could trace his nickname of the Sun King to a performance where he played Apollo, the god of the sun. Four hundred years later, the great choreographer George Balanchine would depict the young Apollo infusing the muses with the divine spark of poetic inspiration. The Sun King would have been mightily pleased.

It was Catherine de Medici who had brought the Italian ballet with her from Florence to France. Her grandson Louis XIII was another enthusiast who knew the power of these court spectacles to impress foreign ambassadors, visiting monarchs and even his own mother. The 1617 *Ballet de la Délivrance de Renaud* used its allegorical story to inform his mother that Louis was now old enough (at sixteen) to do away with her regency and assume control of the kingdom himself.

In 1670, when his son Louis XIV retired from performing in court ballets, the age of the noble amateur came to an end. The ballets had become so elaborate that even the most ambitious of courtiers anxious to impress their Sun King were hard pressed to live up to the steps devised for them by the likes of dancer-composer Jean-Baptiste Lully. In any case, Louis XIV had already taken the momentous step of establishing the Académie Royale de Danse, which would become the first professional training school and lead in an unbroken lineage to today's Paris Opéra Ballet.

Women were not admitted into the Académie until 1681. Before that, all the female roles had been danced by boys in feminine disguise. Women had taken part in some of the court ballets, but when dance moved from the private to the public sphere, it was initially considered unseemly for them to continue performing.

With Lully now officially in command, and Molière working in collaboration with him, the ballet began to take on a more cohesive

'Danse Générale et Dernière', a scene from the 1617 *Ballet de la Délivrance de Renaud* performed at the court of Louis XIII

shape. All of these performances, both at the court and in public, involved much more than dancing. They were a mix of poetry, music, dialogue and sumptuous design as well. Modern opera-goers would be more immediately at home with these spectacles than the average dance fan.

The same could be said of the masque, the English version of the French court ballet. Its two most celebrated London exponents were playwright Ben Jonson and his designer, the architect Inigo Jones. The masque, like its Continental counterpart, was a court entertainment; it was abruptly cut off by Cromwell along with the head of Charles I. An indigenous ballet would not flower again in

British soil until the 1930s, although an important London figure, John Weaver, did have an impact with his pantomine ballets in the early 1700s, and the first female choreographer, Marie Sallé, came from Paris in 1734 to premiere her ballet *Pygmalion* in London. She created an uproar by choosing to appear in a diaphanous muslin tunic rather than in the voluminous gowns of the day. Sallé's penchant for loose garments, prefiguring Isadora Duncan by almost 175 years, caused the same sort of scandalised titillation as would Isadora

French ensemble Ris et Danceries in their
reconstruction of *Bal à la Cour de Louis XIV*

Marie Camargo, Sallé's great
rival, was a very different sort of
dancer. While Sallé in her 'Greek'
tunic was trying to bring some sort
of verisimilitude into ballet,
Camargo was busy exploiting her
own technical skill. She too
violated the dress code, but for
entirely different reasons.
Camargo shortened her skirts to
ankle length so she could show off
her dazzling footwork.

Until this point, women had
simply glided, posed and paraded
round the stage while men did all
the intricate steps. Camargo
(despite the weight of her fashionable gown) was strong enough to
match the men step for step and
wanted to make certain that
audiences could see this. To
improve her technique even
further, she began to take the same
class as the male dancers. Maya
Plisetskaya, who became one of
the powerhouse stars of the Bolshoi
Ballet in the 1940s and 50s, also
polished her technique by taking
classes designed for men.

Together, Sallé and Camargo
represent the two poles of ballet
thought. Camargo stood for
spectacle, for ballet as virtuoso
display. Sallé was a reformer
searching for an emotional depth
of expression. She and other in-

novators believed ballet was
capable of telling stories that could
be unified, even poetic, rather than
merely diverting. Both approaches
have continued to hold sway
throughout dance history.

Jean-Georges Noverre, chief
among those searching for a fuller
theatrical truth, published his influential treatise, *Lettres sur la
Danse*, in 1760, just at the time he
was appointed ballet master at the
court theatre of Württemberg (now
the Stuttgart Ballet). His theories
about dance led him to devise the
ballet d'action. The genre featured
a single, consistent story from
beginning to end and used pantomime (as had Weaver in London)
to further the plot. This differed
considerably from the dominant
approach found in the court ballets
with their loosely linked set pieces,
known as divertissements.

The oldest ballet that can still be
seen owes much to Noverre's
theories. Vincenzo Galeotti's *The
Whims of Cupid and the Ballet
Master* was choreographed in 1786
for the Royal Danish Ballet; the
company has continued to perform
this comic gem ever since. Another
Copenhagen attraction evoking
bygone eras can be seen on
summer evenings at Tivoli, where
pantomime ballets have been
performed in the outdoor theatre
since 1847.

A more majestic past is conjured

up in the historically accurate performances in the Court Theatre at Drottningholm, outside Stockholm. Built in 1766, this 350-seat theatre (abandoned throughout the nineteenth century) has, since 1922, given summer performances of ballets, pantomimes and operas from the eighteenth century. Members of the Royal Swedish Ballet often take part, and the Ingmar Bergman version of Mozart's *The Magic Flute* was filmed there.

What makes Drottningholm such a marvel are the theatre's original stage settings. These ingenious creations, operated by counterweights, are made up of sliding panels set in tracks in the stage floor; it takes less than ten seconds for the stage to change from a city street to a forest, from a palace interior to a rocky seascape complete with rolling waves and miniature sailing ships in the distance. Here, we get a wonderful glimpse of what pre-Romantic ballet looked like in court theatres throughout Europe.

The current interest in historically authentic performances of works by Lully, Rameau and others is matched by an equal interest in the appropriate dance styles of their times. Several companies who specialise in seventeenth and eighteenth-century dance are now meeting this demand. Their research is exhaustive and their performances illustrate the art which European monarchs fostered. Ris et Danceries, based in Paris, where professional dancing first began, and the American group known as the New York Baroque Dance Company are just two of the most popular of these troupes.

With the exception of *The Whims of Cupid*, all of their dances are modern reconstructions. It is only with the advent of the Romantic era that we begin to encounter ballets which have passed down in a continuous chain from one generation of dancers to the next.

One important work whose original choreography has been lost is *La Fille mal gardée*. This ballet's story was one of the very first to deal with real-life folk in everyday situations, a significant shift of emphasis away from the nobles and the Arcadian gods and goddesses who had until then been the chief characters of ballet. Choreographed by Jean Dauberval, *La Fille mal gardée* premiered in Bordeaux just two weeks before the outbreak of the French Revolution.

By the time Europe had finished with Napoleon and begun the Industrial Revolution, the artistic climate had switched to a new sort of otherworldliness. Leading creative artists no longer looked up to the classic gods on Mount Olympus; instead, they were plunging into the misty and mysterious forests of the Romantic era.

In the theatre this yearning for fantasy was aided by one of the Industrial Revolution's important inventions: gas lighting. The impact on ballet and theatre design in general began to be felt in 1822, when gas was installed at the Paris Opéra. Designers quickly discovered how helpful the new lighting could be in generating illusion. The most dramatic advantage over candle-power was that gas could simulate the eerie effects of moonlight in a manner never before imagined. Since midnight was the favoured hour of the Romantics, this proved to be a major turning point. It can still be seen (and felt) in the spell of moonlit magic which hovers over the Romantic ballet's first masterpiece, *La Sylphide*.

ROMANTIC
BALLET

12th March 1832. The premiere of *La Sylphide* marked the resounding capitulation of ballet to the ideals of Romanticism, and catapulted Marie Taglioni to fame. She became the luminary of the era, a woman who used all of her strength to convince audiences that she was an ethereal, evanescent vision from another world. Even today, her image of airy delicacy holds sway as a universal picture of ballet dancing. Taglioni was, in all senses, the first modern ballerina.

Taglioni's style, aided by her new-fangled toe shoes, ushered in an age where Woman, perfect and unattainable, was too good to be true, too good to love in the real world. Choreographers, composers, writers and painters including Berlioz, Byron, Scott and Delacroix led a host of hot-blooded dreamers who concocted visionary worlds populated with sylphs, ondines, dryads, naiads and all manner of unearthly creatures.

Alluring, amoral and (literally) soulless heroines dominated the Romantic stage. These enchant-resses gave each hero a taste of the sublime while destroying his ability to cope with real life and 'mere' mortal women. The basic duality of the Romantic ballet was of an absolute love devoid of sexual fulfilment. Sanctity of the kind reserved for mothers and sisters was subliminally sanctioned through a passion of enforced chastity. The ballets of the era accommodated this double standard to perfection.

The archetypal image of a creature in gauzy white, floating just out of reach in the moonlight, was reinforced by Taglioni's ability to hover on the tips of her toes. She was not the first dancer ever to balance on point, but she was the first to transform the feat from gimmick to artistry.

This illusion of lightness and freedom did not come easily; the stamina required of the Romantic ballerinas was prodigious. Today's toe shoes, built of alternating layers of fabric and glue, are actually small platforms on which to stand. Taglioni and her sister sylphs only darned the tips of their shoes for traction and padded the ends with cotton wool: they really were dancing on their toes.

Small wonder that a group of St Petersburg aristocrats celebrated the final night of Taglioni's first Russian tour by eating a pair of her shoes.

The excessive adulation poured upon dancers like Taglioni, Carlotta Grisi, Lucile Grahn and others initiated the cult of the ballerina. This was the first time in the history of dance that women had taken centre stage. Their prominence produced an excess of fervour in audiences, who showered them in affection, celebrity and diamonds. It was only with the advent of Rudolf Nureyev – over a century later – that they would find their male consorts beginning to achieve equal prominence.

The passions of Romanticism quickly burned themselves out. In less than twenty years, opera had become the dominant art in both London and Paris, although the French continued to demand that their operas include a ballet. In Copenhagen, August Bournonville rode over the decline of Romanticism with sunny equanimity, but hardly anyone outside Denmark was aware of his work. The Royal Danish Ballet was like *The Sleeping Beauty*. A hundred years of seclusion lay ahead before the company made its first international tour in 1956.

As European ballet slipped back towards secondary status, the

The scarf scene from a London City Ballet production of August Bournonville's *La Sylphide*

talents of the Romantic era and their successors travelled to Russia. Coddled, nurtured and cherished under the tsars, ballet steadily grew in expertise and magnificence. By the end of the century, the Imperial spectacles devised by the Frenchman Marius Petipa had become the most elaborate and lavish events the dance world has ever known.

August Bournonville

Born: 21st August 1805/ Copenhagen
Died: 30th November 1879/ Copenhagen

The son of a French dancer who was a member of the Royal Danish Ballet, August Bournonville made his debut there when still a child. As a young man he journeyed to Paris on a court scholarship to study with the greatest teacher of the day, Auguste Vestris (see **Konservatoriet**), and, after performing in Paris and London, returned to Denmark an exceptionally accomplished dancer. In 1830, he was appointed company director and also continued as leading dancer for the next twenty years. During the half century he was in charge of the Royal Danish Ballet, Bournonville was able to produce an unprecedented stream of works. Only a dozen of them survive, but they constitute our single largest legacy from the nineteenth century.

Bournonville was a staunchly bourgeois family man, and his ballets reflect his faith in the good things in life. A generous, at times cosy, sense of community pervades his ballets every step of the way. Like his close friend Hans Christian Andersen, Bournonville's works express a belief in man's essential goodness. He eventually turned his back on the excesses of French Romanticism and, working in Copenhagen away from the mainstream, fostered a style of dancing overflowing with warmth and a good-humoured optimism.

Bournonville single-handedly managed to preserve the role of the male dancer during the Romantic era's ballerina mania. Demanding the same standard of skills from all his dancers, he championed an (on-stage) equality of the sexes at the very time when audiences in Europe's major capitals were throwing themselves at the feet of Marie Taglioni and the other Romantic goddesses.

His style is noted for its fleet, fluid footwork. The choreography never stops moving: each phrase of dancing is linked up with the next in one long interwoven skein of unbroken steps. Rarely does a dancer stop to strike an impressive pose. Another Bournonville hallmark is the use of big, arcing leaps that come straight at the audience in bounding ebullience. The radiant enthusiasm infusing Bournonville's style is his unique and lasting contribution.

Lineage
Of all the companies in the world, the Royal Danish Ballet retains the most direct link to the past. In addition to its preservation of the Bournonville heritage, the company still performs the earliest of all extant ballets, Vincenzo Galeotti's *The Whims of Cupid and the Ballet Master* (1786). And while it is not unusual for a major dancer to become the director of a company, it is worth noting that three of the most exceptional dancer/directors of the twentieth century – **Erik Bruhn**, **Peter Martins** and **Peter Schaufuss** – are all Copenhagen-born performers who started life in the Bournonville school of the Royal Danish Ballet.

Follow-up
Bournonville's memoirs, *My Theatre Life*, were translated into English in 1977. A biography by Walter Terry, *The King's Ballet Master*, appeared in 1979 and Knud Arne Jürgensen's *The Bournonville Ballets: A Photographic Record 1844–1933* (1987) includes nearly five hundred photos of Copenhagen dancers in more than two dozen ballets. *The Royal Danish Ballet: 1902–1906* is a 1979 compilation of rare film footage including nine excerpts (five of which are still in the repertory) and offers an exceptional opportunity to see what dancers once looked like.

La Sylphide

Two acts
Choreography: August
Bournonville, based on the 1832
Paris version by Filippo Taglioni
Music: Herman Løvenskjold
Premiere: 28th November 1836/
Royal Theatre, Copenhagen

The earliest major ballet to survive
in anything like its original form, *La
Sylphide* helped kindle the vogue
for Romanticism that swept across
Europe. The Paris production
immediately established Marie
Taglioni (the original Sylph) as an
international personality. Idolised
from London to St Petersburg, her
unprecedented stardom marked
the frenzied beginnings of the
ballerina cults which persist even
today. Bournonville's 1836 version
(closely linked to the original,
which he had seen in Paris) led to
the same fame for his Sylph, Lucile
Grahn, and it is Bournonville's
staging which is most often seen
today.

The scene is set in the remote
Scottish highlands. For early
nineteenth-century cosmopolitans
this was foreign terrain, shrouded
in mists and magic. The curtain
rises on James asleep in a chair; a
winged Sylph, her white tulle skirts
billowing round her, is poised
beside him (this image, endlessly
reproduced as a lithograph,
achieved picture-postcard
popularity). Startled awake, James
is instantaneously captivated by
this otherworldly vision. Coyly
eluding his touch, she flies away –
up the chimney.

Villagers arrive for the wedding
of James and his fiancée Effie.
Among them is Gerd, her rejected
suitor. Their highland fling is
interrupted by Madge, an old
witch (traditionally performed by a
man). When James evicts her, she
hobbles away, swearing
vengeance. As the festivities
continue, the Sylph (visible to
James alone) returns to lure him off
to the forest. Unable to control his
irrational longings, he dashes after
her.

The second act opens with
Madge and her coven huddled
over a steaming cauldron. As
Madge draws an enchanted scarf
from the bubbling brew, the
witches hop round the fire in a
drunken stomping spree.
Meanwhile, in her forest glen, the
Sylph entrances James with her
delicate charms. Then she
presents her sister Sylphs who
perform a suite of charming
dances highlighted by some of the
first sustained examples of
ballerinas *en pointe*.

When the villagers come
searching for James, the Sylphs
vanish. He hides, and when they
are gone, Madge reappears to
tempt James with the scarf. The
Sylph, flying back to James, is
captivated by this pretty thing.
Hoping to please (and capture)
her, James winds the scarf around
her arms. Madge's spell works
instantly, and as her wings fall from
her back, the Sylph's immortality is
destroyed. She collapses into his
arms and dies – significantly, this is
the one and only time the two of
them actually touch. Her saddened
sisters assemble to bear her
heavenwards. This aerial tableau,
of the Sylph rising supine into the
skies, cradled by her mourning
sisters, was a stunning *coup de
théâtre* which helped ensure the
ballet's popularity.

As a wedding party for Effie and
Gerd passes in the distance,
Madge gloats over the prostrate
body of James, who has lost not
only his dream but also his claim to
human love.

Lineage

The most influential dancework of
the century, *La Sylphide* forever
altered the art form. Its
introduction of point work helped
the ballerina create a vision of a
spirit wafting across the earth. This
notion of an unobtainable feminine
ideal hovering just out of reach
was to become one of
Romanticism's most cherished
tenets.

Thanks to *La Sylphide* and its
many offshoots, ballet reached a

height of popularity that would remain unequalled until **Serge Diaghilev** brought his Russians to Paris in 1909. It was in honour of this Romantic classic that Diaghilev changed the name of **Michel Fokine**'s ballet from *Chopiniana* to **Les Sylphides**.

Follow-up

In 1972, following exhaustive excavations in the library of the Paris Opéra, Pierre Lacotte staged a historical reconstruction of the 1832 Taglioni version. This was originally commissioned by French television: the production features Ghislaine Thesmar (Mme Lacotte) and Michaël Denard, the Paris Opéra's most impressive star couple during the 1970s. Lacotte's reconstruction was also staged for the Kirov Ballet in 1981. Dances from the second act of the Bournonville version can be seen in Rudolf Nureyev's film *I Am a Dancer* (1972) with Carla Fracci as the Sylph.

Stagings

1 **Harald Lander**/American Ballet Theatre/1964
2 **Erik Bruhn**/National Ballet of Canada/1964
3 **Hans Brenaa**/Scottish Ballet/1973
4 **Peter Schaufuss**/London Festival Ballet/1979
4 **Pierre Lacotte**/Kirov Ballet/1981 (recreation of original 1832 version)

Napoli

Three acts
Choreography: August Bournonville
Music: Niels W. Gade, Edvard Helsted, Hans Christian Lumbye and Holger Simon Paulli
Premiere: 29th March 1842/Royal Theatre, Copenhagen

Subtitled 'The Fisherman and His Bride', *Napoli* is an ideal illustration of Bournonville's light approach to the darker aspects of Romanticism. This joyous travelogue of a ballet is designed in three distinct sections. The first act, set in the bustling Neapolitan harbour, is a comedy of local colour filled with inventive pantomime and clever characterisations, including a love-sick lemonade seller, a puppeteer, a buffoon who mimes a street song and even a priest to bless the fishermen's catch. The hero, Gennaro, and his love, Teresina, searching for a moment's privacy, set sail in his boat. A sudden storm sweeps her overboard.

The second act moves to the famous Blue Grotto on Capri, and brings in the otherworldly aspects so loved by all Romantic era audiences. Golfo, a sea god, has saved Teresina from drowning. Struck by her beauty, he turns her into one of his attendant naiads. This stage trick is a fine illustration of nineteenth-century theatricality. In the twinkling of an eye, Teresina's dress vanishes to reveal a new gown identical to that of the other naiads. (Actually, her first dress is pulled off by wires and disappears through a tiny trapdoor in the stage floor. If you aren't expecting it to happen, it really does seem to be magic.)

Gennaro, still searching for signs of Teresina, rows his boat into the grotto. At first she does not recognise him, but with the aid of a holy medallion she is brought back to her senses and the sea god is forced to release her from her watery living death.

Back on dry land, Act Three is a wedding celebration of dancing which includes the exhilarating Tarantella, complete with tambourines, handclaps and buoyant high-flying jumps, Bournonville's single most famed piece of choreography.

Napoli is a prime example of Bournonville's domestication of Romanticism's more exotic tendencies. His sense of community, his ideal of ballet as a microcosm for society, give his works an honest and earthy reality which many nineteenth-century ballets so conspicuously lacked. The mystical aspects of Romanticism are transformed in a harmony of high spirits and

wholesome charm.

A cornerstone of the Danish repertory ever since its creation, *Napoli* has had more than seven hundred Copenhagen performances. Many companies – both large and small – excerpt the festive third act dances as a showpiece, **London Festival Ballet**, **American Ballet Theatre**, Ballet West (Salt Lake City) and the **Royal Ballet** being among the most successful. The entire ballet is seen less frequently.

Lineage

In *Napoli* the scene is established in the first act, the conflict resolved in the second, leaving the third act free for celebration. This format was to be brought to perfection with **Marius Petipa**'s Russian ballets later in the century. Most full-length ballets are more smoothly integrated, although the entire story of **George Balanchine**'s *A Midsummer Night's Dream* (1962) is told in the first half, leaving the second part free for celebratory dancing. The third act of **Frederick Ashton**'s *Ondine* (1958) is made up almost entirely of display dancing inserted into a long pause in the plot.

Follow-up

A Royal Danish Ballet video production of *Napoli* (1985) features Linda Hindberg and Arne Villumsen.

Stagings

1 **Poul Gnatt**/Scottish Ballet/1978
2 **Peter Schaufuss**/National Ballet of Canada/1981
3 **Fergus Early**/Extemporary Dance Theatre/1982 (a contemporary one-act setting entitled *Naples*, loosely based on the Bournonville original)

Mona Vangsaae's 1973 production of *Konservatoriet* for London Festival Ballet

Konservatoriet

One act
Choreography: August Bournonville
Music: Holger Simon Paulli
Premiere: 6th May 1849/Royal Theatre, Copenhagen

Few ballets give us such an authentic glimpse into the past. Set in the 1820s, this is Bournonville's evocation of his student days in Paris, when he was a pupil of Auguste Vestris. Both Vestris and his father Gaetano had, in turn, been the most renowned dancers of their generations. Auguste followed his illustrious performance career by becoming a distinguished and influential teacher.

Konservatoriet (The Conservatory, or The Dancing School) depicts a group of dancers, from young children to established stars, practising their daily routine under the eagle eye of the autocratic ballet master. As was the norm until the end of the nineteenth century, the teacher accompanies the exercises on his own violin. All ballet classes begin at the barre: here dancers stretch their muscles, focus on balance and carefully adjust their alignment. These moments make exceptional demands on the dancers who are, after all, doing their homework in public. Gradually the class builds up speed and intricacy as travelling patterns (*enchaînements*) are introduced, in which the dancers strive for polish and precision as well as speed.

This was originally a two-act ballet; its subtitle, *A Proposal of Marriage Through a Newspaper*, refers to a puppyish love story essentially eliminated in 1941 when Harald Lander and former ballerina Valborg Borchsenius restaged the work as a single act.

Although this ballet is a tribute to the Franco-Italian style taught by Vestris, one of Bournonville's invaluable legacies was a codification of his own teaching methods. He devised a system of six daily classes which were repeated in weekly rotation (no class on Sunday). These classes are still taught today and, until the mid-1950s, were the sole teaching method used in Denmark.

Lineage

Other choreographers have utilised Bournonville's idea of staging a class as theatre. The best known comes from fellow Dane Harald Lander, whose *Etudes* (1948) traces the progress of technical mastery from children at the barre to the gloriously complex pyrotechnics of top performers. *Ballet School*, choreographed in 1962 for the Bolshoi Ballet, is Asaf Messerer's staging of the dances performed by graduating pupils of the Bolshoi Ballet School.

Another Dane, Flemming Flindt, draws on the relationship between pupil and teacher in his 1963 ballet adaptation of Ionesco's *La Leçon*, choreographed as *The Private Lesson*. **Jerome Robbins** set *The Afternoon of a Faun* (1953) in a dance studio: here the focus is quieter, more intimate and more dramatic than in *Konservatoriet*.

Martha Graham has used her modern dance technique for performance display on a number of occasions: *Adorations* (1975) is a Graham class amended only by settings and costumes; her thirty-minute film *A Dancer's World* (1957) is an illustration of class as quasi-performance; and *Acrobats of God* (1960) is set in a dance studio.

Follow-up

There is an excerpt from *Konservatoriet* in *Ballet For All: How Ballet Began* (Thames Television, 1972).

Stagings

1 **Hans Brenaa**/Joffrey Ballet/1969
2 **Mona Vangsaae**/London Festival Ballet/1973
3 **Fredbjörn Björnsson**/Royal Swedish Ballet/1973

A Folk Tale

Three acts
Choreography: August Bournonville
Music: Niels W. Gade and J.P.E. Hartmann
Premiere: 20th March 1854/Royal Theatre, Copenhagen

The choreographer himself cherished *A Folk Tale* as his favourite creation. Its magical medieval story has a 'once upon a time' atmosphere coupled with an underlying moral message about the redemptive powers of Christian love.

The ballet opens with a hunting party where Birthe, the lady of the manor (who is actually a troll changeling) unsuccessfully flirts with a young nobleman, Junker Ove. Rebuffed, she flounces off in a huff. Ove is then driven mad by a seductive night-time vision of elf maidens who rise up through the ground and try to lure him into the underworld. In their midst he sees Hilda, the true heiress of the manor, whom the trolls stole when they left Birthe in her place.

The second act is set in the troll caverns where Muri, the Queen, is forcing Hilda to wed her surly son. Their engagement is celebrated in a comedic drunken party of galumphing folk dance parodies. This gathering of the troll clans is Bournonville's sharpest satire on the baser aspects of human society. As the rowdy trolls collapse in a heap of inebriated disarray, Hilda manages to escape. Once above ground, with no knowledge of Christianity other than through her own purity, she restores Ove by innocently offering him a drink of water from a sacred spring.

Meanwhile, Birthe is trapped by her own mean-spirited self. As she primps in front of her mirror, her true troll origins burst out in eruptions of jagged, awkward movements that have Berthe clawing the air with her fingers and hopping around in grotesque, ungainly jumps. Several times she tries to control this Jekyll-and-Hyde split in her personality, but it is of no use. This startling sequence is one of the most intriguing character studies in the whole of nineteenth-century ballet. Birthe's mother, the troll queen, having discovered Hilda's escape, arrives to claim her real daughter, who happily abandons her attempts to be a respectable human.

The ballet ends with the Midsummer's Eve wedding of Hilda and Ove, celebrated to a tune that has become the standard wedding march in Danish churches. The finale includes a splendid suite of dances performed by the major characters with a troupe of travelling gipsies.

Lineage

Created more than a decade after **Giselle** and **La Sylphide**, *A Folk Tale* has only a cosy kinship with the supernatural Romantic tradition – the trolls are ultimately no threat, more comic than dangerous. Like **Napoli**, this ballet's aim is to celebrate the joys of communal harmony. Nor can Birthe, bizarre and complex though she may be, truly be seen as a precursor of such acute psychological creations as Hagar in **Antony Tudor**'s **Pillar of Fire** or the tormented **Kenneth MacMillan** heroines such as Anastasia. *A Folk Tale* is ultimately unique, a humane comedy that triumphs over its darkest moments.

Follow-up

Arlene Croce's analysis of the Royal Danish Ballet's infectious 1979 revival ('An Underground Classic?') is included in *Sight Lines* (1987).

Jules Perrot

Born: 18th August 1810/Lyon
Died: 24th August 1892/Paramé, near Saint-Malo

Frustratingly little remains from the works of the Romantic era's most prolific choreographer. First trained as an acrobat, Perrot made his stage debut at the age of nine. Three years later he had moved to Paris, where he quickly became a celebrity in the popular theatre. One of his early successes was as Jocko, a pantomime monkey who rescues a shipwrecked child and finds a cache of diamonds for his master before being murdered by pirates.

Perrot studied ballet with master teacher Auguste Vestris (who also trained **August Bournonville**). He was engaged by the Paris Opéra in 1830 and within a year was earning the maximum allowable salary. There he became Marie Taglioni's chief partner, but when his swift and athletic footwork began to usurp too much of her own limelight, she refused to share the stage with him. From that point on Perrot began to travel throughout Europe, and while working in Naples he met the seventeen-year-old Carlotta Grisi. She became his lover and Perrot set about grooming her for a career as one of the era's luminaries. They returned to Paris in 1840 and Perrot staged all of Grisi's solos for the premiere production of **Giselle** (although he received no programme credit for his work).

Perrot was appointed ballet master for Her Majesty's Theatre, London (from 1842 to 1848). During his stay in England he created some twenty ballets including *La Esmeralda* (based on Victor Hugo's *The Hunchback of Notre Dame*) and the famous showpiece **Pas de quatre**. His version of *Faust* was staged for La Scala, Milan in 1848, with Perrot himself as Mephistopheles. He then journeyed to Russia, where he served as Imperial Ballet Master from 1851 to 1858. It was here that Perrot's creativity had its most sustained impact. His large-scale productions served as a direct model for **Marius Petipa**, then a dancer, but soon to become the creator of the great style of Russian classicism which would dominate ballet in the later part of the nineteenth century. Perrot eventually married Capitoline Samovskaya, a minor Russian ballerina, and retired to Brittany in 1859.

Never forgetting his early training in the popular theatre, Perrot produced ballets of great audience appeal. He combined spectacle with elaborate stories which fully exploited the Romantic fascination with the exotic. His heroines were invariably ephemeral creatures – water sprites, wood nymphs or other creatures of the air such as the Arabian fairy known as La Péri. His special talent was an ability to mesh mood and character in a mix of mime and dance movement.

Lineage

Perrot could be called the P.T. Barnum of the Romantic Ballet. His sense of showmanship was unequalled and his ballets continued to enrapture Russian audiences long after the Romantic flame had died in both Paris and London. His elaborate story ballets paved the way for **Marius Petipa**'s innovations during the next generation, and his influence can be discerned in the grand stories told by such modern European choreographers as **Roland Petit** and **John Neumeier**. If Perrot had been born one hundred years later he would undoubtedly have had much in common with showman **Maurice Béjart**. **Frederick Ashton** used the story of *Ondine*, which Perrot first staged in London, as the basis for a 1958 three-act ballet with **Margot Fonteyn** in the title role.

Follow-up

Jules Perrot: Master of the Romantic Ballet (1984) is by Ivor Guest, the Romantic era's greatest authority.

Giselle

Two acts
Choreography: Jean Coralli and Jules Perrot
Libretto: Théophile Gautier and Jules Henri Vernoy de Saint-Georges
Music: Adolphe Adam
Premiere: 28th June 1841/Paris Opéra

The climax of the Romantic vision, *Giselle* is one of ballet's loftiest pinnacles. In only ninety minutes, it sums up the basic Romantic contradiction: the unbridgeable gap between belief in the simple happiness of long-ago places and the dark, brooding disasters of unattainable love.

The two choreographers worked in collaboration. Coralli was the official ballet master of the Paris Opéra, but Carlotta Grisi, the first Giselle, insisted that her lover Perrot design all her solos.

As the ballet opens, the grapes are being harvested in a medieval Rhineland village and the rollicking peasants have chosen Giselle to play the queen of the harvest festival. She is distracted by the handsome young stranger with whom she has fallen in love.

Hilarion, the village game-keeper, who in turn loves Giselle, exposes the stranger as Albrecht, a disguised nobleman. When it is also revealed that he is already engaged to a countess, the dispairing Giselle loses her reason: the ensuing 'mad scene' is one of the ultimate acting challenges for a ballerina. After attempting suicide, she dies of a broken heart.

The folkloric atmosphere is shattered with Giselle's death, and the ballet then moves to the supernatural realm of the Wilis. These glamorously dangerous phantoms are the lost souls of young women who died betrayed in love. They trap men in their forest and, in revenge, force them to dance to their deaths. As Giselle's spirit is summoned from her grave by Myrtha, Queen of the

Virginia Johnson (Giselle) and Eddie J. Shellman (Albrecht) in Arthur Mitchell's Creole version of *Giselle* for Dance Theatre of Harlem

Wilis, she is transformed from a dead creature into a dancing ghoul, wildly spinning on one foot like a dervish.

The first victim of the night is Hilarion. When the sadly repentant and chastened Albrecht arrives, Giselle attempts to shield him. Something of her ethereal quality is conveyed through the choreography: in one sequence of moves, Albrecht lifts Giselle above his head with an effortless ease that seems to indicate she is only a figment of his imagination. Her love, reaching from beyond the grave, gives him the strength to continue dancing until the dawn, when the Wilis must retreat to their tombs. His life is saved; but, ironically, he has lost Giselle all over again. In a desperate parting gesture of love, she tosses him a flower before sinking into her grave forever.

In creating the title role, Carlotta Grisi fashioned a Romantic icon which has endured as no other.

The poet Théophile Gautier, who was besotted with Grisi, came up with the brilliant notion of wedding the two contradictory aspects of the Romantic ideal into a single character. The result is the most fully-rounded portrait of the era.

Virtually every ballerina since 1841 has been drawn to the role. Acclaimed interpreters have included the Russian ballerinas Olga Spessivtseva, **Galina Ulanova**, Natalia Bessmertnova and **Natalia Makarova**, Britain's **Alicia Markova**, Paris Opéra star Yvette Chauviré, the Italian Carla Fracci and American ballerina **Gelsey Kirkland**.

As with the other Romantic ballets, Paris audiences soon found *Giselle* old-fashioned. Consequently it disappeared from the repertory in the early 1860s, and would have been lost forever but for preservation by the Russians. Ever since Fanny Elssler first danced there in 1848, *Giselle* has been a special Russian favourite, and it was **Serge Diaghilev** who re-introduced the ballet to the West in 1910 with Tamara Karsavina and **Vaslav Nijinsky**.

Lineage

An intriguing and successful re-interpretation of *Giselle* occurred in 1984 when Arthur Mitchell created an all-black version for his **Dance Theatre of Harlem**. Without modifying the choreography, Mitchell transferred the ballet to the Louisiana plantations and bayous of the 1850s. Here the barrier between Giselle and the Count Albrecht is no longer the traditional one of peasant and aristocrat, but is based on the elaborate Creole caste systems operating at that time. The *vendange* becomes a sugarcane harvest, the haunted woods of the Rhineland are transformed into the swamps of the Mississippi delta and Giselle emerges from one of the spooky raised mausoleums typical of Louisiana cemeteries. These resonances have provided a new immediacy and meaning for American audiences.

Follow-up

Film and video productions of *Giselle* include versions by the Bolshoi (with Galina Ulanova, 1956), American Ballet Theatre (Carla Fracci, Erik Bruhn, 1969) and The Royal Ballet (Lynn Seymour, Rudolf Nureyev, 1979). A 1987 film stars Alessandra Ferri partnered by Mikhail Baryshnikov. British historian Cyril Beaumont wrote *The Ballet Called Giselle* in 1944; Geoffrey Ashton's lavishly illustrated *Giselle* appeared in 1985. *Baryshnikov At Work* (1976) and Alicia Markova's 1979 *A Dance Autobiography* both discuss Giselle in detail.

Stagings

1 **Alicia Alonso**/National Ballet of Cuba/1959
2 **Mary Skeaping**/London Festival Ballet/1971
3 **Peter Darrell**/Scottish Ballet/1971
4 **Heinz Spoerli**/Basel Ballet/1976
5 **Arnold Spohr**/Royal Winnipeg Ballet/1982
6 **Arthur Mitchell**/Dance Theatre of Harlem/1984
7 **Peter Wright**/Royal Ballet/1985
8 **Mikhail Baryshnikov**/American Ballet Theatre/1987

Pas de quatre

One act
Choreography: Jules Perrot
Music: Cesare Pugni
Premiere: 12th July 1845/Her Majesty's Theatre, London

Box office economics led directly to the creation of *Pas de quatre*, an ingenious entrepreneurial showcase conceived by Benjamin Lumley, director of Her Majesty's Theatre. His idea was to assemble the great ballerinas of the day and have Jules Perrot, the finest choreographer, concoct a short ballet for them to perform before Queen Victoria and the Prince Consort.

Perrot's assignment was to arrange a suite of dances culminating in a solo variation tailored to display each ballerina's individual talents. A glimpse of his difficult task survives in a story of rehearsal conflicts amongst the dancers. Marie Taglioni, goddess of the age, was automatically awarded pride of place with the final variation, but bickering arose over the appropriate sequence for the other ballerinas: Lucile Grahn (**August Bournonville**'s Sylphide), Carlotta Grisi (the original **Giselle**) and the vivacious Fanny Cerrito. When things reached an icy impasse, Perrot threatened to abandon the project as an impossibility. Lumley, however, solved the problem. 'Let the oldest dance last', pronounced the wily producer. Hearing this, the ballerinas stumbled over one another in their gracious haste to give way to their 'elder sisters'. From that point on rehearsals ran smoothly and at the premiere, each of the solos – in the final order of Grahn, Grisi, Cerrito and Taglioni – ended in a showstopping cascade of flowers.

The ballet's opening pose, with the three younger dancers kneeling round a poised Taglioni, all in identical pink costumes with roses in their hair, quickly became a quintessential image of the age. Writers extolled the virtues of the dancers, the Queen was pleased and the performances (only four in all) were a huge financial success, as well as a shining summary of the delicate art of the Romantic ballerina.

Lineage

Celebratory ballets created for special occasions tend to vanish as soon as the event has passed, but *Pas de quatre* has retained its fascination for modern audiences. Several interpretations, all duplicating the original, continue to be performed; of these, the best known is **Anton Dolin**'s (1941). **Les Ballets Trockadero de Monte Carlo** present a clever travesty version that plays up the intense rivalry between the ballerinas.

Another gala ballet that continues to shine as a standard repertory piece is **Frederick Ashton**'s *Birthday Offering*. This was first devised for a gala on 5th May 1956, the twenty-fifth anniversary of the first full evening of ballet performed by the Vic-Wells (now Royal) Ballet. Like *Pas de quatre* it is a showpiece designed to display the dancers' talents. Here the style evoked is the grand Russian classicism of **Marius Petipa**.

There were many nineteenth-century variants on *Pas de quatre*, the most famous including Perrot's own *Le Jugement de Pâris* (1846) which featured a *Pas des Déesses*, reconstructed in 1954 by **Joffrey Ballet**.

August Bournonville's *Pas des trois cousines* (1849), still sometimes danced in Copenhagen, was created for three members of the Price family, one of the most illustrious of the nineteenth-century dance clans.

Follow-up

Perrot's original was reconstructed on film by Anton Dolin in 1968, and by the Kirov Ballet in their 1985 *Classic Ballet Night* video. Ivor Guest has written specifically about the work in *The Pas de quatre* (1970) and covers it in detail in his definitive 1984 biography of Perrot.

Arthur Saint-Léon

Born: 17th September 1821/Paris
Died: 2nd September 1870/Paris

No matter how talented a dancer may be, his or her body may not be ideally suited to mirror the pure perfection of movement that marks out the ballerina or her male counterpart, the *premier danseur*. Arthur Saint-Léon made capital out of this by becoming an exceptional character dancer instead. An accomplished musician as well, his first stage appearance found him both dancing and playing in the same performance. In later years, when his interest shifted to choreography, Saint-Léon expanded the range of character dancing. His final, most enduring ballet, the comedy **Coppélia**, is credited as the first theatrical use of national dances such as the Hungarian czardas and the Polish mazurka.

Saint-Léon was married to the famed Romantic ballerina Fanny Cerrito for six years from 1845. Together they created the leading roles in **Jules Perrot**'s *Ondine* and *La Esmeralda*. He succeeded Perrot as ballet master in St Petersburg (1859 to 1869), but from 1863 began travelling back and forth to Paris where he was working for part of each season.

His 1864 ballet *The Humpbacked Horse* was the first to incorporate Russian themes, and included a grand series of dances representing the various ethnic nationalities living in Russia. Saint-Léon's choreography is now lost, but modern versions remain popular in the Soviet Union.

Lineage

August Bournonville also featured character dances in many of his ballets, such as **Napoli**, but it was **Marius Petipa** who integrated, even formalised, the idea of inserting set pieces of national dances into each of his ballets. The tradition extends to **George Balanchine** who choreographed *Cortège Hongrois* (1973) as a suite of classical dances in the Hungarian style.

Follow-up

Saint-Léon's correspondence – *Letters of a Ballet Master* – has been edited by Ivor Guest (1981).

Coppélia

Three acts
Choreography: Arthur Saint-Léon
Libretto: Charles Nuitter and Arthur Saint-Léon, after E.T.A. Hoffman
Music: Léo Delibes
Premiere: 25th May 1870/Paris Opéra

The last and sunniest ballet of the then waning Romantic era, *Coppélia* is a comedy infused with a comfortable, even quaint, charm. Its bustling village square atmosphere is vividly created through large ensemble moments built on authentic folk dances.

In this story, Saint-Léon only plays with the supernatural; rather than luxuriating in the powers of darkness, he pokes fun at them. The title character is actually a doll: Coppélia, the crowning achievement of the eccentric toymaker Dr Coppelius, is so lifelike that the hero, Franz, falls in love with her at first sight. Subtitled *La Fille aux yeux d'émail* (The Girl with Enamel Eyes), the ballet is based on a story by E.T.A. Hoffman, who also wrote the original tale of **The Nutcracker**.

Franz's fiancée, the feisty village girl Swanilda, decides to confront her new rival. When she discovers that Coppélia is only a clockwork automaton, she disguises herself as the doll and pretends to come to life. This impersonation is her playful revenge on Dr Coppelius for having fooled her fiancé; the poor doctor, a bumbling 'mad scientist', is completely taken in. He believes he has finally achieved his goal of creating a waxwork with a soul, but soon discovers that a real girl is not as easy to manipulate as a doll.

Coppélia pretends to be distracted by his gifts – a fan leads to a Spanish solo, a tam o'shanter becomes the excuse for a Scottish jig – but all the while she is actually wreaking havoc on the doctor's workroom. Swanilda finally drops her disguise and Franz is forced to admit that he was the dupe of Coppelius's mechanical devices. The last act is devoted to the wedding festivities of the reunited couple.

Saint-Léon's final ballet opened just a week before Paris was plunged into the Franco-Prussian War. Both the choreographer and Giuseppina Bozzacchi, the sixteen-year-old creator of Swanilda, died during the ensuing siege. Preserved in several versions around the world (notably the **Marius Petipa** adaptation of 1884), *Coppélia* has always remained a Parisian favourite. Much of its lasting fame is also due to its superb, lilting score, which Tchaikovsky considered ideal and used as a direct model for his own ballet creations.

Ironically, *Coppélia* is also an example of how both the aesthetics and the ethics of French Romanticism had degenerated. At this point in history, most female dancers at the Opéra were notorious for their liaisons with rich gentlemen protectors. This upper-class male audience was pandered to in outrageous ways. Their obsession with the female form even led to the practice of casting male roles with women in drag (*en travesti*). Astonishingly, the role of Franz remained a victim of this gender gimmick at the Opéra as late as 1958. Noted historian Pierre Lacotte mounted a meticulously researched revival of the original in 1973; but now, of course, Franz is performed by a man.

Lineage

Swanilda, the only classically demanding role in this ballet, has

Eva Evdokimova as Swanilda and Niels Bjørn Larsen as Doctor Coppelius in the production of *Coppélia* staged by Ronald Hynd for London Festival Ballet

been a showcase for the comic talents of countless ballerinas (**Anna Pavlova** chose it for her American debut in 1910). Since the classical dancing is limited to the single star ballerina, *Coppélia* has become a favourite choice of companies whose resources do not extend to the challenges of **Swan Lake** or **The Sleeping Beauty**. Couple this ease of staging with the straightforward plot and it becomes clear why *Coppélia* is second only to **The Nutcracker** as an ideal introductory ballet for children.

The notion of a dancer impersonating a toy is often an excuse for bravura technical display. *The Nutcracker*, **Léonide Massine**'s *La Boutique fantasque* (1919) and **George Balanchine**'s

The Steadfast Tin Soldier (1975) all use the toy/doll motif. **Oskar Schlemmer**'s 1922 *Triadic Ballet* and the anthropomorphic creations of **Alwin Nikolais** take these impersonations several steps further towards abstraction.

Follow-up

Live from Lincoln Center: Coppélia (1978) features the New York City Ballet.

Stagings

1 **Pierre Lacotte**/Paris Opéra/1973 (recreation of the original)
2 **George Balanchine and Alexandra Danilova**/New York City Ballet/1974
3 **Roland Petit**/Ballet de Marseille/1975
4 **Erik Bruhn**/National Ballet of Canada/1975
5 **Peter Clegg**/Northern Ballet Theatre/1977
6 **Ronald Hynd**/London Festival Ballet/1985

CLASSICAL
BALLET

4th March 1877. For the first time, Odette, a princess magicked into a swan, would fling herself between her fellow swan-maidens and the threatening young man with a crossbow. 'Please', she gestures, 'you not shoot big birds'. Later, the same ballerina, now impersonating the wicked black swan Odile, will lure the young man to his doom in a spectacular sequence of thirty-two fouettés, a rapid series of spins that pulls him magnetically into her snare. Both of these moments from *Swan Lake* are in code. The first is the code of mime, the second the code of dance. Each has its own validity.

We do not know what the lost 1877 version of *Swan Lake* looked like, but the 'don't shoot' gesture is a part of the written scenario. The fouettés were definitely *not* there. They were only added when a Milanese ballerina, Pierina Legnani, the star of La Scala, arrived in Russia. Choreographer

Marius Petipa turned her party trick into metaphor in his 1895 revival of *Swan Lake*. Here, the fouettés are transformed into an insidious maelstrom of glittering brilliance. The young man, Prince Siegfried, captivated by their power, immediately answers her fouettés with spins of his own. In

that moment we see that Odile has won. Here, Petipa has used a dance code to emotionally heighten the technical demands inherent in the steps.

Petipa, a Frenchman who had first come to St Petersburg as a dancer in 1847, was the most important, but by no means the only foreigner to play a major role in nineteenth-century Russian ballet. During the second half of the century, all the principal choreographers and ballerinas from the Romantic era were to visit Russia, where ballet was kept alive and gradually transformed into a new, highly polished art which would outshine everything on offer in the European capitals.

It is thanks to the Russian Imperial Ballet that key Romantic ballets such as *Giselle* and *Coppélia* were not lost forever. The work we call *Giselle* is based on a staging by Petipa, an adaptation and expansion of a Jules Perrot

version, itself a substantial reworking of the original Paris Opéra production.

In his own original choreography, Petipa evolved a grand ballet format which reached its peak in the trio of ballets created with Tchaikovsky. His ballets shaped both the tastes of his audience and the talents of his dancers (who included a succession of Italian ballerinas like the spinning Legnani). The most technically advanced dancers of the day were being trained in Italy, but it was Petipa who converted their expertise into artistry.

Mime was just one aspect of Petipa's spectacles which developed a code of its own. Much of the language of dance is self-evident (hands on heart for love), but there are many more arcane gestures which have come to be a part of the mime code. Like any other foreign language, they can only be learned by rote. How should anyone who does not already know the meaning be able to recognise a rising circling of the hands above the 'speaker's' head as 'Let's all dance'? Other gestures must have been clearer to the original nineteenth-century audiences: for example, an arm sweeping out from the body and down towards the floor indicated an aristocratic lady, symbolised by the flowing train of her gown.

Mime has become something of a dirty word to many modern producers of the classical ballets. They fear it slows down the action; but without the mime the stories lose much of their resonance and even the dancing suffers a loss of definition. Well-executed mime can be as joyous or as moving as the silent film comedies of Charlie Chaplin or the melodramas of D.W. Griffith.

The Sadler's Wells Royal Ballet corps de ballet in the second act of *Swan Lake*

27

Lev Ivanov

Born: 18th February 1834/Moscow
Died: 24th December 1901/St
Petersburg

Although he choreographed half of
Swan Lake and all of **The
Nutcracker**, Ivanov the man has
become one of the insubstantial
ghosts of ballet history. After
joining the Maryinsky Theatre as a
dancer in 1850, his first big break
came in 1858, when (ironically, as it
would turn out) he replaced the
injured **Marius Petipa** at short
notice. Ivanov substituted for him
in one ballet with only a single
rehearsal and went on in a second
work without any rehearsals at all.
In 1869, when Petipa took over as
Director of the Imperial Theatres,
Ivanov was promoted to a *premier
danseur*. Subsequently he became
a rehearsal director in 1882 and
was made Petipa's official second-
in-command in 1885.
    His sensitivity to music can be
seen in both the Tchaikovsky
ballets, but beyond these none of
Ivanov's choreography has
survived. There have been various
explanations: that he was
complacent, even lazy; that he was
a drinker; or that he was a
misunderstood visionary who
lacked the requisite zeal to try and
put his ideas to the reactionary St
Petersburg audiences. What *is*
undeniable is that throughout their
joint careers, Ivanov lived in
Petipa's shadow (and under his
thumb), and that having devoted
nearly all his life to the Imperial
Ballet, he died in virtual poverty in
1901.

Lineage

Ivanov's symphonic approach to
group movement created a softer
and more pliable sense of ebb and
flow than **Marius Petipa**'s
technically brilliant but formulaic
regimentations. His masterly
manipulation of the corps de ballet
prefigures **Léonide Massine**'s
symphonic ballets of the 1930s, as

well as the plotless ballets of
George Balanchine. The
unfortunate example of the
Petipa/Ivanov relationship may
well explain why Balanchine
insisted that **Jerome Robbins**
become co-ballet master of **New
York City Ballet** rather than
working as his assistant.

The Nutcracker

Two acts
Choreography: Lev Ivanov
Libretto: Marius Petipa, after
E.T.A. Hoffman
Music: Pyotr Ilyich Tchaikovsky
Premiere: 18th December 1892/
Maryinsky Theatre, St Petersburg

Thanks to a supremely melodic
score coupled with an idealised
celebration of childhood
Christmases past, *The Nutcracker*
lives on. Although first seen in the
West in London during the 1934
season of the Vic-Wells (now
Royal) Ballet, it was not until the
1958 version by **George
Balanchine** that *The Nutcracker*
began its inexorable climb towards
its current popularity as an annual
holiday treat.
    Considering how flimsy (but
complicated) the storyline is, this is
actually a far from ideal ballet. In
the first act, based on a macabre
little tale by E.T.A. Hoffman (who
also wrote the **Coppélia** story), a
young heroine – Clara or Marie
depending on whose version you
see – is given a nutcracker doll on
Christmas Eve. That night she
dreams that the doll comes to life
to defend her in a toyland battle
against an army of mice. When
Clara tosses her shoe at the Mouse
King, she distracts him from his
duel with the Nutcracker, and the
mouse is killed.
    The wounded Nutcracker is then
transformed into a handsome
prince who whisks Clara off
through a kingdom of snows. The
Waltz of the Snowflakes is the most

The Royal Ballet production of *The Nutcracker* —
a perennial children's favourite

inventive choreography of the
entire ballet and the section of the
work that remains the closest to
Ivanov's original. The female corps
de ballet, garbed in white, mirror
the crescendo of Tchaikovsky's
music; their swirling group patterns
build to a flurry of movement,
meant to represent a winter
blizzard, which gradually subsides
into angelic harmony.

The second act, set in the
Kingdom of Sweets, is made up of
a string of divertissements
including exotic dances from
Arabia, China and Spain, a waltz of
flowers and a climactic pas de
deux for the Sugar Plum Fairy and
her cavalier.

The less than satisfactory story,
so schizophrenically split, has been
played with in a variety of ways,
including **Rudolf Nureyev**'s
Freudian staging for the Royal
Swedish Ballet and **Mikhail
Baryshnikov**'s version for
American Ballet Theatre, which is
both more unified and more
serious than most other renditions.
In 1984 Peter Wright, working in
tandem with musicologist Roland

John Wiley, staged a Royal Ballet
production that strives to return as
closely as possible to what we still
know of Ivanov's choreography.
The **Peter Schaufuss** version for
London Festival Ballet tries, with
some difficulties and a certain
amount of viewer confusion, to turn
the first act in particular into an
imagined Tchaikovsky biography.

Lineage

Walt Disney's *Fantasia* used
several sections of Tchaikovsky's
score to create clever,
anthropomorphic and highly
entertaining music visualisations;
as such it is a perfect entrée to the
magical world of *The Nutcracker*,
a ballet invariably chosen as a first
one for children. **Coppélia** is
another introductory ballet, while
works such as **Frederick Ashton**'s
Cinderella, Harald Lander's
plotless *Etudes*, David Lichine's
comedy *Graduation Ball* (1940) and
David Bintley's darker fairy tale
The Snow Queen make perfect
next steps for those who express
enthusiasm with *The Nutcracker*.

Follow-up

Nutcracker films include

Pacific Northwest Ballet's, with imaginative and fanciful designs by noted children's book illustrator Maurice Sendak (1983); Peter Wright's Royal Ballet version, complete with Julia Trevelyan Oman's evocative design (1985); and the American Ballet Theatre staging in a 1977 video, with Baryshnikov himself as the Nutcracker and a radiant Gelsey Kirkland as Clara.

The most useful books are Jack Anderson's *The Nutcracker Ballet* (1979) and Barbara Neuman's copiously illustrated survey of the work (1984). Roland John Wiley's *Tchaikovsky's Ballets* (1985) contains a detailed musical analysis as well as some of the original choreographic floor patterns drawn by Ivanov for the Waltz of the Snowflakes.

Stagings

1 **George Balanchine**/New York City Ballet/1954
2 **Yuri Grigorovich**/Bolshoi Ballet/1966
3 **Rudolf Nureyev**/Royal Swedish Ballet/1967
4 **John Neumeier**/Frankfurt Ballet/1971
5 **Kent Stowell**/Pacific Northwest Ballet/1975
6 **Mikhail Baryshnikov**/American Ballet Theatre/1976
7 **Roland Petit**/Ballet de Marseille/1976
8 **Peter Wright**/Royal Ballet/1984
9 **Peter Schaufuss**/London Festival Ballet/1986

Swan Lake

Four acts
Choreography: Lev Ivanov and Marius Petipa
Libretto: Vladimir Begichev and Vasily Geltser
Music: Pyotr Ilyich Tchaikovsky
Premiere: 27th January 1895/ Maryinsky Theatre, St Petersburg

The origins of the world's best-loved ballet are now a matter of speculation. Many of the details of

Fiona Chadwick as the Black Swan in Anthony Dowell's Royal Ballet staging of *Swan Lake*

the first Bolshoi production in 1877 have long been lost. The one thing which seems certain is that *Swan Lake* was an ambitious bid by a group of Moscow intellectuals to create a work of art which could equal the output of the more cosmopolitan St Petersburg company.

Exactly how Tchaikovsky was lured into his first ballet project is no longer known. What we do know is that his music was initially derided by both performers and critics as too symphonic and undanceable (a typical ballet score of the time consisted of oom-pah-pah tunes with a strong, clean rhythmic beat). Today we would say the score was ahead of its time, but at the premiere the moody and vulnerable composer felt only the bitterness of failure. This is probably why writers have had a tendency to portray that first production as a complete flop. Julius Reisinger, the original choreographer, was really only a hack, and the Moscow production was undoubtedly provincial; yet the Bolshoi never completely gave up on it. During Tchaikovsky's lifetime there were at least two other choreographic attempts to make *Swan Lake* work.

The version we now know came about as part of an 1894 St Petersburg memorial programme commemorating the composer's death the year before, when Marius Petipa had his assistant, Lev Ivanov, stage the second act. This proved so successful that the full ballet was presented the following season, with the two men splitting the choreographic assignment. Ivanov created the mythic side of the story (the lakeside 'White Acts'), while Petipa staged the spectacular showpieces of Acts One and Three.

Odette is a spellbound princess who has been transformed into a white swan by the magician Von Rothbart. Her sole hope of salvation is through a pledge of true love. When Prince Siegfried vows his devotion to her, the magician contrives a deception, by disguising his daughter Odile as a black swan. Thinking she is really Odette, Siegfried again swears his love, thus dooming Odette forever. In despair both the White Swan and the Prince drown themselves in the lake. Their double suicide succeeds in breaking the magician's power, and in a final apotheosis Odette and Siegfried are united in death.

Both plot and choreography alternately embrace the other-worldly aura of Romanticism and the formulaic spectacle of classical ballet. Petipa found all the enamelled sparkle of the Black Swan, while Ivanov delved into the emotional heart of the White Swan. When combined (as is traditional), these two characters become one of the most tantalising roles ever devised for a ballerina. Not only does she have to express the graceful poetic tragedy of Odette, she must also flash with the glittery bravura and speedy technical dexterity of Odile.

Ivanov's 'White Acts' are a prime example of nineteenth-century balletic metaphor. The dances for Odette and her sister swans poetically transform the natural movements of birds into their dance equivalents. When Odette first sees Siegfried, she darts to the other side of the stage, where she hovers in trembling fear and hides her head as if under a wing, and the corps de ballet's first entrance recalls migrating flocks coming to rest for the night.

The original star of the Ivanov/Petipa version was Pierina Legnani: a brilliant technician, she became a legend through her ability to perform the Black Swan's astonishing thirty-two fouettés. These fast, whipping turns were beyond the skills of any other dancer of the day (and have proved beyond the powers of some twentieth-century greats, including **Margot Fonteyn**). They have become the sacrosanct signature steps of *Swan Lake*, but Legnani originally startled the Russians with this gimmick in a now lost 1893 Petipa version of *Cinderella*. Ivanov's second act so perfectly encapsulates an ideal that it has often been performed separately. This is how *Swan Lake* was first seen in London when it was performed twice a day during a variety show at the Hippodrome in 1910. **George Balanchine**'s 1951 version of the second act for New York City Ballet remains the most powerful and viable modern version of Ivanov's original.

Lineage

Tchaikovsky's first ballet score became one of the earliest to achieve an independent life. Without his music, the ballet would never have outlived its first production in Moscow. His own **The Nutcracker**, and Igor Stravinsky's **The Firebird** and **Le Sacre du printemps** are other scores which have overriden their initial choreography.

Ivanov's ability to wed story and steps into an indivisible whole reflects the earlier choreography in the second act of **Giselle** and the 'Kingdom of the Shades' scene from **La Bayadère** (although neither has the emotional support of music as symphonically complex as Tchaikovsky's). In the twentieth century, **Antony Tudor** and **Kenneth MacMillan** are both outstanding exponents of the art of storytelling through movement.

Follow-up

Two film versions of Rudolf Nureyev's production feature the Vienna State Opera Ballet (with Nureyev and Margot Fonteyn, 1966) and a Royal Ballet cast headed by Natalia Makarova and Anthony Dowell (1980). C. W. Beaumont's *The Ballet Called Swan Lake* (1952) and Ann Nugent's *Swan Lake* (1985) both provide historical overviews, and there is lengthy musical analysis in Roland John Wiley's *Tchaikovsky's Ballets* (1985).

Stagings

1 **Rudolf Nureyev**/Vienna Ballet/1964
2 **Erik Bruhn**/National Ballet of Canada/1966
3 **Yuri Grigorovich**/Bolshoi Ballet/1969
4 **John Neumeier**/Hamburg Ballet/1976
5 **Peter Darrell**/Scottish Ballet/1977
6 **Anthony Dowell**/Royal Ballet/1987
7 **Natalia Makarova**/London Festival Ballet/1988
8 **Helgi Tomasson**/San Francisco Ballet/1988

Marius Petipa

Born: 11th March 1818/Marseille
Died: 14th July 1910/Gurzuf, Crimea

An autocratic genius who ruled over the world of Russian Imperial ballet for close on half a century, Marius Petipa came from a celebrated dancing family (his elder brother Lucien was one of the most noted male performers of the Romantic age). Marius made his debut in Brussels at the age of thirteen and toured with his itinerant family around Europe and even to North America. He emigrated to St Petersburg in 1847,

where he performed as a leading dancer and served a lengthy choreographic apprenticeship under **Jules Perrot**. Finally appointed ballet master in 1862, he began to consolidate his own choreographic style. This was the time when dance in Paris and London was languishing in the post-Romantic doldrums (where the new craze was for opera) and when **August Bournonville**'s repertory was quietly sequestered in Copenhagen. In this climate of European neglect, Petipa not only kept ballet alive, but gave birth to the grand Russian classical style which still means 'ballet' to most of the world.

Petipa's creativity evolved into a cast-iron formula that proved almost foolproof in terms of pleasing the aristocratic audience at which it was aimed (the Russian Imperial Theatres were a part of the Tsar's household; all pupils and performers were directly supported by the crown and less than a third of the seats for performances were available outside court circles). Petipa both pandered to the tastes of his time and led them on to new heights. He created lavish evening-length productions marked by exotic costumes and settings. This glamorous combination of dance and spectacle told its (often very thin) stories through formulaic mime sequences in tandem with the choreography.

Petipa's manipulation of the corps de ballet in mass formations of continually permuting patterns was offset by suites of dances (or divertissements) where the narrative came to a halt and the celebratory dancing took over. Each of his ballets was centred around the grand pas de deux for the ballerina and her partner. Pushing technique to new peaks of virtuosity, these star turns are like the climactic arias in an opera, the jewel in the crown, the surprise in the centre of a Fabergé egg. The divertissements also included national dances – Spanish, Hungarian, Italian or Polish – which brought a splash of colour to the Russian capitals. This formula reached its zenith with **The Sleeping Beauty**.

An extensive career ended poorly. By the time Petipa was an old man he was viewed as something of a dinosaur by the younger generation. Rebellious budding choreographers like **Michel Fokine** found Petipa's storytelling hollow, stilted and old-fashioned. In 1903 he was forcibly retired, but remained on full salary until his death seven years later.

Lineage

Petipa has influenced virtually every succeeding ballet choreographer. Something of the absolute authority he enjoyed as head of the Imperial Ballet can be seen in **Serge Diaghilev**'s control of the Ballets Russes and **George Balanchine**'s domination of **New York City Ballet**. Diaghilev paid homage to Petipa's choreographic genius with a full-length production of **The Sleeping Beauty** in 1921, while many of Balanchine's creations are direct and loving tributes to the Russian Imperial style. **Ninette de Valois** founded her dream of a national British ballet on a bedrock of Petipa classics and **Frederick Ashton** modelled *A Birthday Offering* on his grand manner.

Even Petipa's predecessors owe him a debt. Without his adaptations of works such as **Giselle** and **Coppélia**, they would have disappeared through neglect.

Follow-up

Petipa's memoirs, *Russian Ballet Master*, were edited by Lillian Moore in 1958.

Don Quixote

Four acts
Choreography: Marius Petipa
Music: Ludwig Minkus
Premiere: 26th December 1869/
Bolshoi Theatre, Moscow

Comedy, fantasy and a robust Spanish atmosphere combine in *Don Quixote* to produce a bustling but inconsequential potpourri of entertainment. Petipa uses the central theme of Cervantes' great novel – the mad Don's starry-eyed quest for his dream love Dulcinea – but this is really only an excuse, a subplot to set off a trifling tale of gipsies and a pair of young lovers (a barber and an innkeeper's daughter) who plot to circumvent her father's opposition to their marriage. The fantasy emerges in a set piece that occurs when the Don, stunned by his encounter with the windmill, dreams of Dulcinea. She appears in a vision with attendant nymphs, to dance an ensemble of limpid classical purity.

No amount of twentieth-century reworking can disguise the weakness of the plot. The two halves of the story do not fit well together and even much of the choreography now seems alarmingly predictable. What keeps *Don Quixote* on the world stage is its grand pas de deux, the crowning moment of the young couple's wedding celebrations. In an example of Petipa's first major choreography, this duet uses flirtatious glances, a fan and Spanish posturings. The steps themselves (including spectacular one-armed overhead lifts) build to a climax of vivid and flashy abandon which makes this classical duet such a showstopper.

Lineage

The vision scene, where the plot stops while the hero has a tantalising glimpse of his ideal love, became a stock Petipa device. The two major examples of this occur in **La Bayadère** and **The Sleeping Beauty**, and, of course, the whole second half of **The Nutcracker** is a vision. Spanish settings to give added zip and colour to classical ballet were used by Petipa in *Paquita* (1847), by **Léonide Massine** and Pablo Picasso in *The Three-Cornered Hat* (1919) and in **Roland Petit**'s **Carmen**. This somewhat stereotypical approach is balanced by a more serious view of the Spanish character in **Kenneth**

MacMillan's 1963 *Las Hermanas*, a one-act ballet based on Federico García Lorca's tragedy *La casa de Bernarda Alba*.

The **George Balanchine** version of *Don Quixote*, staged in 1965 for New York City Ballet with a score by modern composer Nicolas Nabokov, differs totally from Petipa's – Balanchine rejects the comedy element to create a serious dance drama.

Follow-up

Rudolph Nureyev plays the young lover (with Robert Helpmann as the Don) in a 1972 film created with the Australian Ballet; Mikhail Baryshnikov features in an 1983 American Ballet Theatre version.

Stagings

1 **George Balanchine**/New York City Ballet/1965
2 **Rudolf Nureyev**/Vienna Ballet/1966
3 **Mikhail Baryshnikov**/American Ballet Theatre/1978

La Bayadère

Four acts
Choreography: Marius Petipa
Libretto: Sergei Khudekov and Marius Petipa, based on Kalidasa's Sakuntala and The Card of Clay
Music: Ludwig Minkus
Premiere: 4th February 1877/ Maryinsky Theatre, St Petersburg

The story, set in a fantastical India of lush splendour, revolves around Nikiya, one of the sacred temple dancers known as *bayadères*. She is loved by Solor, but he in turn is pledged to the Rajah's daughter. Nikiya is forced to dance at a celebration for the engaged couple. Her jealous royal rival presents her with a basket of flowers, and a snake, concealed in their midst, kills her. The next scene, the famous 'Kingdom of the Shades', is now often performed on its own: here Solor, in a haze of opium-induced remorse, has a vision of Nikiya eternally dancing

with her sister *bayadères*. In the final act, as the royal wedding is taking place, the vengeful gods destroy the temple. Everyone is killed, but the shades of Solor and Nikiya are reunited.

'The Kingdom of the Shades' is both timeless and the most modern of all nineteenth-century choreography. Seen on its own, this act becomes the world's first abstract ballet, a dance about dancing. It is composed of a smooth, symphonically orchestrated stream of variations for the corps de ballet, a trio of female soloists, a ballerina (Nikiya) and her partner (Solor). In their famous entrance, the thirty-two female corps members appear on stage one by one. Each dancer repeats the same arabesque, step forward, arabesque pattern again and again. This slow, sweeping repetitive chain of movements becomes a swelling white river of dance gradually filling the stage. A self-contained universe, 'The Kingdom of the Shades' celebrates ballet as a supreme poetic expression of the eternal.

Lev Ivanov danced the first Solor, and in 1903 Petipa revived the ballet for **Anna Pavlova**. The work was revised in the 1940s in a Kirov version that now ends with 'The Kingdom of the Shades' and was unknown outside Russia until

The Royal Ballet corps de ballet performing
'The Kingdom of the Shades' sequence from
La Bayadère

the Kirov brought the 'Shades' act
to the West in 1961. Kirov
defectors **Rudolf Nureyev** and
Natalia Makarova each staged their
own versions of that act, and in
1980 Makarova re-staged the
ballet in its entirety, even restoring
the final act no longer seen in
Russia.

Lineage

The magnificently inventive use of
the corps de ballet in *La Bayadère*
is unrivalled. The 'Shades' are
echoed in **Lev Ivanov**'s
choreography for **Swan Lake** and
later plotless ballets such as
Michel Fokine's **Les Sylphides** and
George Balanchine's **Serenade**
also use the female corps to create
the same sort of emotional
resonance.

Some post-modern choreo-
graphy, though totally different in
appearance, is based on the same
additive repetitions that open 'The
Kingdom of the Shades'. **Trisha
Brown**, **Lucinda Childs** and
Molissa Fenley have all used
choreographic repetition as a way
of transforming real time into a
seemingly endless stream of
movement.

Stagings

1 **Vakhtang Chabukiany**/Kirov
   Ballet/1940
2 **Rudolf Nureyev**/Royal
   Ballet/1963 (Shades act only)
3 **Natalia Makarova**/American
   Ballet Theatre/1974 (Shades act
   only, restaged for London
   Festival Ballet)
4 **Natalia Makarova**/American
   Ballet Theatre/1980 (full-length)

The Sleeping Beauty

Three acts
Choreography: Marius Petipa
Libretto: Ivan Vsevolojsky and
Marius Petipa, based on Perrault
Music: Pyotr Ilyich Tchaikovsky
Premiere: 15th January 1890/
Maryinsky Theatre, St Petersburg

The lavish spectacle, sweeping
score and mastery of movement in
The Sleeping Beauty represent the
culmination of the Russian Imperial
style. No other Petipa ballet is such
a clear, rational and ultimately
poetic distillation of his
choreographic ideals.

The ballet (first produced under
its French title *La Belle au bois
dormant*) opens with the
christening of the Princess Aurora,
which is attended by magical
fairies. Each bestows a gift such as
grace, charm and beauty, and
their solos, all short and
scintillating, encapsulate the
virtuoso innovations at the heart of
Petipa's style, with a challenging
mix of dexterity, precision and
musical phrasing. They are
interrupted by the forgotten fairy
Carabosse, who revengefully
presents Aurora with the gift of
death. Aurora's guardian, the Lilac
Fairy, is unable to undo this evil
curse but does possess the power
to transform the spell into a
hundred years of sleep.

In the next act, Aurora, now a
young woman, is celebrating her
birthday, courted by a quartet of

princely suitors, who present her with flowers. This – the Rose Adagio – is one of the most famous moments in all ballet. For generations its intricate choreography, filled with complex balances and promenades, has served as a testing ground for the ballerina. As the celebrations continue, an old woman (the wicked fairy in disguise) gives the Princess a spindle. She pricks her finger on its sharp point and the castle is plunged into sleep.

One hundred years later, the Lilac Fairy appears to a young Prince. She conjures up a vision of Aurora surrounded by nymphs, and he immediately falls in love. Satisfied by the Prince's innocence and purity of devotion, the Lilac Fairy guides him to the castle where he awakens the spellbound Aurora with a kiss. The last act is filled with typical Petipa festivities performed by a whole gallery of fairy-tale characters. The fleet Blue Bird pas de deux is the most fully-formed and technically demanding role that Petipa ever choreo-graphed for a man – watch for the elevation and the deft use of speed in two sequences of twenty-four *brisés volés*. It is followed by a grand pas de deux for Aurora and the Prince. Finally, the benevolent Lilac Fairy appears to bless the newly married royal couple.

Time and again, the symphonic harmonies of Tchaikovsky's music (probably the finest ballet score ever written) and the framework of a royal court (modelled on the Versailles of Louis XIV) are transformed by Petipa into subliminal metaphors that depict the hierarchy of classical ballet, where the ballerina is poised at the pinnacle of her own society in the same way that an absolute monarch rules at the centre of his court. This balance and harmony, mirrored in the fairy-tale triumph of good over evil, is one of the deepest, most enduring symbols of *The Sleeping Beauty*. Petipa underscored this parallel by integrating both children and young dancers from the ballet school into his production, notably in the Garland Waltz at the birthday celebrations. Not until **George Balanchine**'s version of *The Nutcracker* in 1958 were children used so effectively. In turn, the Garland Waltz was one of the final works staged by Balanchine just before his death.

Petipa's lengthy dictatorship of the Imperial Ballet led, inevitably, to a turn-of-the-century reaction by young artists anxious to express new ideas. However, *The Sleeping Beauty* continued to be upheld as his supreme creation. It is important to note that **Serge Diaghilev**, that 'tsar of the new', staged the first Western production of this ballet (calling it *The Sleeping Princess*) at the Alhambra Theatre, London in 1921. Eighteen years later, **Ninette de Valois** had the ballet staged for her Vic-Wells (now Royal) Ballet. Since that first performance featuring **Margot Fonteyn** and **Robert Helpmann** as Aurora and her Prince, *The Sleeping Beauty* has remained a cornerstone of the English repertory.

Lineage

No other Petipa ballet has had such a lasting influence on the twentieth century. Continually in repertory in Russia since its premiere, it is the most complete and authentic example of the Russian Imperial style to have survived the changing tastes of succeeding adaptations. Modern versions, such as those staged by **Rudolf Nureyev**, expand the role of the Prince, but remain basically faithful to Petipa's choreography. The most idiosyncratic version is probably the **John Neumeier** staging (Hamburg Ballet, 1978) in which he pushes the time scale forward so that the Prince is a modern denim-jacketed hero dreaming of a Victorian princess.

Follow-up

Film versions include two Kirov productions, from 1965 with Alla Sizova and from 1983 with Irina Kolpakova (ranked with Margot Fonteyn as one of the greatest Auroras). Nureyev's version is performed by the National Ballet of

Canada with Nureyev himself as the Prince and Veronica Tennant as Aurora (1972). *Tchaikovsky's Ballets* by Roland John Wiley (1985) contains the complete text created by Petipa for Tchaikovsky, and George Balanchine's *Festival of Ballet* (1954) includes a lengthy personal appreciation of the work.

Stagings

1 **Rudolf Nureyev**/La Scala, Milan/1966 (and subsequently National Ballet of Canada and London Festival Ballet)
2 **Peter Wright**/Royal Ballet/1968 (with additional later choreography by Frederick Ashton, Kenneth MacMillan and Ninette de Valois)
3 **Robert Helpmann**/Australian Ballet/1973
4 **Yuri Grigorovich**/Bolshoi Ballet/1973
5 **John Neumeier**/Hamburg Ballet/1978
6 **Maina Gielgud**/Australian Ballet/1984
7 **Kenneth MacMillan**/American Ballet Theatre/1986

Raymonda

Three acts
Choreography: Marius Petipa
Libretto: Lydia Pashkova and Marius Petipa
Music: Alexander Glazunov
Premiere: 19th January 1898/ Maryinsky Theatre, St Petersburg

It will come as no surprise to anyone who has seen a full production of *Raymonda* that **George Balanchine** dubbed its plot 'nonsense'. The story takes place against a medieval Hungarian setting. Raymonda is engaged to a knight off on a Holy Crusade, but is secretly drawn to his Saracen rival, Abderakhman, who tries to abduct her. If treated seriously – **Rudolf Nureyev** has staged five different versions since 1964 – as an exploration of repressed sexuality, the ideas, with their

unwanted Freudian overtones, become too weighty for the slight plot. However, when presented as an unadorned fairy tale, as in **Yuri Grigorovich**'s 1984 reworking for the Bolshoi, it seems, in turn, too thin for a three hour plus extravaganza. This tale, like so many others of the classical era, is a formulaic excuse for spectacle intended to please an aristocratic audience.

The 'truth' of *Raymonda* lies in its superb score and magnificent finale where, typically, a wedding celebration gives the choreographer a pretext for the dancing. This minor-keyed suite of solos and ensemble work glows with autumnal splendour, redolent with sultry Hungarian overtones. Here the ballerina is able to dance like a full-blooded adult, with lush, expansive choreography. In the ballet world the heroine is usually coltishly nubile, too rarely grown-up.

Lineage

Petipa's last major work (he was eighty at the time) is, like his *Paquita* and **La Bayadère**, most palatable to late twentieth-century audiences when performed in shortened versions that concentrate on the art and minimalise the plot. Only a year after **Rudolf Nureyev**'s first full-length version for the Royal Ballet, the company had truncated it to the Act Three celebrations; his 1975 version for American Ballet Theatre also failed to last. In 1980 **Mikhail Baryshnikov** devised his own dance-oriented one-act version, while **George Balanchine** used the *Raymonda* music for three different plotless creations: *Pas de dix* (1955) is the closest to the literal Petipa steps, but both *Raymonda Variations* (1963) and *Cortège Hongrois* (1973) are equally true to the Petipa spirit.

Stagings

1 **Rudolf Nureyev**/Royal Ballet/1964 (and subsequently for Australian Ballet, Zurich Opera Ballet, American Ballet Theatre and Paris Opéra)
2 **Yuri Grigorovich**/Bolshoi Ballet/1984

THE
BALLETS
RUSSES

19th May 1909. The exotic elegance of Serge Diaghilev and his
Ballets Russes took Paris by storm. Powerful, sensual and com-
pellingly new, the company struck the West with the heady
perfume of night-blooming orchids. They swept into Europe with
fresh styles, fresh ideas and a bracing approach to ballet that
craftily melded the avant-garde and the chic. Their work
dominated the world of ballet for the next two decades and
changed the face of the art forever.

The Ballets Russes was composed
of young, mostly disaffected
Russians with ideas and ideals too
revolutionary for the stuffy
St Petersburg establishment. They
arrived in Paris at a time when
ballet in Europe was in decline. In
London, dance was relegated to
the music hall. In Paris, the Opéra
had become a questionable
establishment where dandies
ogled pretty ballerinas before
taking them out to supper. The
Ballets Russes brought dancing
back to a central spot in the
theatre.

Diaghilev himself was neither
choreographer, dancer nor
composer. He was a great
entrepreneur who instinctively
chose his collaborators with a
finesse which remains unequalled.
He commissioned all three of
Stravinsky's first, and still major,

ballet scores, *The Firebird*, *Petrushka* and the landmark *Le Sacre du printemps*. Other Ballets Russes composers included Debussy, Prokofiev, Ravel, Satie and Poulenc. To complement the scores, Diaghilev turned to contemporary designers and artists like Picasso, Bakst, Rouault, Matisse, even Coco Chanel.

Both Vaslav Nijinsky and Anna Pavlova danced with Diaghilev in that first 1909 season. Pavlova soon left to begin her travels round the globe with her own company. Nijinsky stayed. As favoured star and budding choreographer, he was encouraged in his experimentation by Diaghilev.

In 1913, with *Le Sacre du printemps*, Nijinsky and Stravinsky dragged their audience, kicking and screaming, into the twentieth century. The pagan ritual of ancient Russia caused an opening-night riot in the Théâtre des Champs-Elysées. The disruptive boos and catcalls, cheers and fist-

fights were so intense that the dancers onstage could hardly hear the loud thrashing notes of Stravinsky's score. Legend has it that Nijinsky stood on a chair in the wings shouting out musical counts to the beleaguered dancers. Stravinsky, some claim, escaped into an alley through the tiny window of the men's toilet.

Diaghilev, who recognised good publicity when he saw it, thrived on this sort of scandal. Throughout his twenty years as tsar of the ballet, he introduced cubism and surrealism to the ballet, and sponsored some of this century's finest choreographers: Michel Fokine (creator of *Les Sylphides*, the first plotless ballet), Nijinsky, his sister Bronislava Nijinska and Léonide Massine, as well as the first ballets from a young Russian called George Balanchine, the last and greatest of the Ballets Russes discoveries.

Left: Vaslav Nijinsky performing the title role in a London production of his *L'Après-midi d'un faune*
Above: A Jean Cocteau sketch of Serge Diaghilev

George Balanchine

Born: 22nd January 1904/St Petersburg
Died: 30th April 1983/New York City

The man who was to become the most radical manipulator of the Russian Imperial heritage originally wanted to be a composer like his father – and, indeed, throughout his lengthy career he was noted for his acute musical sensibilities. Born Georgi Melitonovich Balanchivadze, he became a student at the Imperial Ballet School in St Petersburg by accident, having accompanied his mother and older sister to an audition. His sister, who hoped to be a dancer, was rejected, but the boy (to everyone's surprise and his own initial dismay) was accepted. He entered the company (now the **Kirov Ballet**) in 1921 and began to choreograph student works immediately. In 1924 he obtained permission to take a small troupe (himself and three other dancers) on a brief European tour. They never went back to the Soviet Union. The tour was a flop, the promoters who had booked them were charlatans, and the foursome were virtually starving in Paris when they received a telegram from **Serge Diaghilev** summoning them to Monte Carlo. He hired them on the spot and immediately set Balanchine to work choreographing opera-ballets. Always swift at devising movement, he met the challenge and was soon the last of Diaghilev's five resident choreographers. The ten ballets he created for the Ballets Russes included **Apollo**, his first collaboration with Igor Stravinsky, and **The Prodigal Son**.

Following Diaghilev's death, the ever busy Balanchine served as guest ballet master with the Royal Danish Ballet, worked for a brief time at the Paris Opéra and staged several theatrical shows in London. In 1933 he became artistic director of the short-lived company Les Ballets 1933, and in that same year accepted an invitation from a wealthy American, Lincoln Kirstein, to go to the USA. The two men immediately set about founding the organisation which would evolve into **New York City Ballet**, the most adventurous classical company of the twentieth century. (For Balanchine's American years, see entry in Modern Ballet, page 93.)

Lineage

Despite his experimental approach, Balanchine never lost his respect and love for the heritage left by **Marius Petipa**. In his own eyes he was simply updating the classical vocabulary for contemporary times and, unlike **Michel Fokine** and **Léonide Massine**, he never abandoned his faith in classical technique. His work with Stravinsky during the Ballets Russes years laid the groundwork for a prolific collaboration that included a string of masterworks in Balanchine's later speedy, pared-to-the-bone style of American neo-classicism. **Agon** (1957), *Stravinsky Violin Concerto* and *Symphony in Three Movements* (both part of the 1972 Stravinsky Festival) are amongst the finest. Balanchine's last creation, his 425th, was a 1982 solo for **Suzanne Farrell** to Stravinsky's *Variations for Orchestra*.

Follow-up

Balanchine books abound, and many of the Diaghilev dancers wrote their own biographies and memoirs of the company, but the definitive biography is *Balanchine* by Bernard Taper (1984). The first of Balanchine's ballerina wives, Tamara Geva, was a member of the four-person troupe that left Russia in 1924: she recalls those years in her colourful auto-biography *Split Seconds* (1972). Ballerina Alexandra Danilova (also in the quartet, and who became the next romance in Balanchine's life) covered the Diaghilev years in *Choura* (1987).

Apollo

Serge Lifar as the title role in the original production of George Balanchine's *Apollo*

One act
Choreography: George Balanchine
Music: Igor Stravinsky (Apollon Musagète, 1927)
Design: André Bauchant
Premiere: 12th June 1928/Théâtre Sarah Bernhardt, Paris

The earliest Balanchine ballet to become part of the international repertory, *Apollo* is the work which first illustrated his flair for revitalising nineteenth-century classicism with a sharp, bare-boned brilliance distinctly his own. Striking a balance between modernity and tradition, Balanchine's experimentation, now labelled neo-classicism, is regarded as one of the most significant styles of the twentieth century.

Unlike **Michel Fokine**, who had concentrated on exotic theatricality, or **Léonide Massine** with his comedic storylines, Balanchine went directly to music for inspiration and guidance. Like Stravinsky, he mined his own classical heritage in an attempt to extract the best of the old as a base for the new. In the process he devised a style of acid-edged syncopations and angular, unexpected accents which still quiver with a vivid freshness.

41

The story, suggested by the music, shows the young god Apollo with three of the Muses (poetry, mime and dance). The god infuses each in turn with his divine spark of creativity before leaving the earth to take his place in the pantheon on Mount Parnassus. This series of solos, duets, trios and quartets (there is no corps de ballet) couples the crisp linear edges of Art Deco with a timeless elegance. The influence of the Jazz Age can be seen in the thrusting hips and stabbing legs of the women, but every exaggerated, pepped-up pose is firmly grounded in the rules of classical technique.

Balanchine himself referred to *Apollo* as the turning point in his career, the moment when he realised that his forward-looking inventiveness must also honour the heritage of the great ballet traditions. Throughout his life, Ballanchine re-worked *Apollo*: it was a mother lode rich in possible permutations and new insights. Each version became cleaner, increasingly honed to essentials. Some objected to Balanchine's latest revisions, but, as a compact affirmation of his credo, no single ballet (excepting his 1957 **Agon**) so succinctly delineates his masterful ability to interweave the innovative with the classic.

Lineage

Balanchine's neo-classicism has since influenced nearly all other ballet choreographers. His fusion of past and present – of experimentation within classical rules – can be seen in choreographers as disparate as **Twyla Tharp** and **Jirí Kylián**, **David Bintley** and **Richard Alston**, and is notable in the works of Balanchine's New York City Ballet colleagues **Jerome Robbins** and **Peter Martins**.

Follow-up

The two major video versions of *Apollo* both feature Peter Martins (Canadian Broadcasting Corporation, 1969, and *Balanchine and Stravinsky – Genius has a*

Birthday, 1982). Arlene Croce's book *Going to the Dance* (1982) includes a superb analysis of the work under the heading 'News from the Muses'.

Stagings

1 **George Balanchine**/American Ballet, later New York City Ballet/1937 (and subsequently Royal Ballet)
2 **Patricia Neary**/London Festival Ballet/1988

The Prodigal Son

One act
Choreography: George Balanchine
Libretto: Boris Kochno
Music: Sergei Prokofiev
Design: Georges Rouault
Premiere: 21st May 1929/Théâtre Sarah Bernhardt, Paris

The Prodigal Son is based on the New Testament parable (Luke 15:11–24) and was the last work to be produced by the original Ballets Russes company, with a premiere only three months before **Serge Diaghilev**'s death. This is one of the few Balanchine ballets to have a male central character and, like **Apollo** a year earlier, it starred Serge Lifar.

The opening scene shows the young man straining to break away from the restraints of his family, and the central scene 'In a Far Country' encapsulates his misadventures, graphically depicting the revels in which he is seduced and abandoned by a statuesque woman known only as the Siren. Her cohorts are a troop of grotesque men who often move in a squat-legged unison line; their crouching waddle, rocking from side to side, makes them look like a human centipede out of a German Expressionist film of the period. The Siren is the sole ballerina role in the work: in her stunning first entrance, she not only parades *en pointe* but is crowned by Rouault's towering headdress, giving her a truly monumental stature. She is a blatantly sexual temptress who manipulates her long red cape with a hot erotic suggestiveness that engulfs the naive young man. Once he has been robbed of all his father's goods, and had his clothes stripped from his back, the battered Prodigal is abandoned. The departure of his attackers is a simple, but highly effective, theatrical metaphor: they overturn the banquet table and climb aboard it as though it were a ship. The revellers' arms become the oars and the Siren poses like a figurehead on a prow as her cape is held out to form a sail. In the final scene, the Prodigal returns to his father's house. Prostrating himself before his father, he slowly climbs up the Patriarch's body to nestle like a baby in his arms.

This is the most linear, straightforward story ballet Balanchine ever choreographed; from this point on his focus would be on dance as metaphor rather than narrative. His occasional use of stories during the **New York City Ballet** years was always connected with a homage to the past and his early years in Russia. Works such as *Harlequinade* (from 1965) and **The Nutcracker** are loving recollections of the **Marius Petipa** heritage into which he was born.

The Prodigal Son has remained one of the most cherished male roles in ballet. In 1950, when Balanchine revived the ballet, **Jerome Robbins** became the first American Prodigal; the role passed in the next decade to Edward Villella, a man who did much to debunk prejudices against male dancers. **Rudolf Nureyev** danced the role with the Royal Ballet in 1972, **Patrick Dupond** with the Paris Opéra Ballet in 1978, and **Mikhail Baryshnikov** was outstanding in the role during his brief residence with New York City Ballet.

Lineage

Many choreographers have used religious music (from Bach and Mozart to Poulenc and Fauré) as inspiration, but the Bible has been a more frequent source for Hollywood than for ballet. *The Legend of Joseph*, choreographed in 1914 by **Michel Fokine** to a Richard Strauss score, was re-choreographed by Balanchine for the Royal Danish Ballet in 1931, and by **John Neumeier** for Vienna State Opera in 1977 (unfortunately, this costume drama is all but laughable in its pretensions). **Ninette de Valois** had one of her major successes with *Job* (1931), starring **Anton Dolin**, and later **Robert Helpmann**, as Satan. Among the modern danceworks based on the Bible, the most exuberant and sardonic is **Paul Taylor**'s *American Genesis* (1974). This evening-length work recasts the stories as part of the New World tradition, from the Creation (the Pilgrim Fathers landing on Plymouth Rock) to the Flood (Noah is an evangelistic bigot, his ark a riverboat paddle-steamer).

Follow-up

A Dance in America video (1978) features Mikhail Baryshnikov; the same programme, 'Choreography by Balanchine – Part III', also includes the magnificent *Chaconne* danced by Suzanne Farrell and Peter Martins.

Stagings

1 **George Balanchine**/New York City Ballet/1950 (later revived for Sadler's Wells Royal Ballet and Paris Opéra)

Serge Diaghilev

Born: 31st March 1872/Near Novgorod, Russia
Died: 19th August 1929/Venice

Of all the major personalities in dance history, Serge Diaghilev is genuinely unique. Neither dancer, choreographer, designer nor composer, his principal talent was an ability to mix volatile artistic ingredients into the headiest of cocktails, the natural skill of a born impresario. He was an autocrat who juggled a glamorous public image with the continuous reality of near bankruptcy, and who turned his Ballets Russes into probably the most popular dance company of all time.

Born into the provincial aristocracy, his isolated early life was in marked contrast to his later cosmopolitan success. At eighteen, he was sent to St Petersburg to study law; he had wanted to become a composer, but was thwarted by a lack of creative talent in that direction. In St Petersburg he got involved with a group of young writers and artists whose radical views would sow the seeds of the Ballets Russes aesthetic. Diaghilev became the editor of the group's periodical *Mir Iskosstva* (The World of Art) from 1898 to 1904, and organised exhibitions of modern Russian paintings. He took one of these to Paris in 1906 and followed it up the next year with a series of concerts of Russian music.

In 1908, he introduced Mussorgsky's *Boris Godunov* to the West: the opera was such a success that a second major French season was planned. Almost by accident, this 1909 tour spotlighted ballet. The exotic visual impact of the presentation, with the revelation of the quality of Russian male dancing (particularly by **Vaslav Nijinsky**), excited a tumultuous response. Diaghilev's mission in life was now defined. The phenomenal success of this season, intended as a one-off summer tour, fuelled plans for a second engagement the next spring. In 1911 (the year of the company's London debut), Nijinsky and some of his fellow dancers left the Imperial Ballet, and Les Ballets Russes de Serge Diaghilev became a permanent organisation.

An important factor in Diaghilev's continued involvement in ballet was his personal love for Nijinsky. He saw himself as a mentor, father figure and lover, educating the younger man and urging him to try his hand at choreography. This set a pattern for relationships throughout his life. Diaghilev's partiality to Nijinsky led **Michel Fokine**, who had choreographed all the works in the earlier seasons, to resign in 1912. When Nijinsky married Romola de Pulszky in 1913, Diaghilev felt so betrayed that he fired him on the spot – both Nijinsky and Fokine later returned to the fold, but only briefly.

The First World War and the Russian Revolution cut the company off from its homeland forever. Diaghilev, fascinated by young talent and new ideas, turned for inspiration to the French avant-garde to help create a new, chic metropolitan image. With his next protégé, **Léonide Massine**, he began to work with the French equivalents of his old *Mir Iskosstva* colleagues: Cocteau, Satie, Poulenc, Picasso, even Coco Chanel (who was, anonymously, one of the company's main backers).

In 1921, Diaghilev decided to introduce **Marius Petipa**'s classic ballet, **The Sleeping Beauty**, to the West. The production, lavish in the extreme, premiered in London, but was not the triumph that Diaghilev had expected. The company, broke and on the verge of disbanding, was saved from extinction when Diaghilev was invited to take up residence in Monte Carlo: the principality became the only permanent base the company ever had. There Nijinsky's sister **Bronislava Nijinska** and **George Balanchine** became his last choreographers. Massine, who, like Nijinsky, had married, was replaced in Diaghilev's affections by his final male star, the teenaged **Serge Lifar**. Suffering from diabetes, Diaghilev died during his summer holidays in Venice. He is buried, as Stravinsky was some forty years later, in the island cemetery of San Michele.

Lineage

At the time the Ballets Russes arrived in Paris, few cultivated people would have deigned to consider ballet a serious art form. By the time of his death, Diaghilev had managed to turn that attitude completely around. It is no exaggeration to say that twentieth-century ballet is his creation. Wherever you look, today's major international ballet companies have links going back to the Ballets Russes. **George Balanchine**, **Léonide Massine**, **Michel Fokine** and many of the original dancers settled in America and played key roles in the growth of ballet there. **Ninette de Valois**, **Marie Rambert**, **Anton Dolin** and **Alicia Markova** all served under Diaghilev and emerged to form the companies which constitute the current British dance aristocracy, while **Serge Lifar** became the director of the Paris Opéra Ballet.

Follow-up

Diaghilev (1979), an exhaustive 600-page biography by Richard Buckle, is the most authoritative of dozens of books on the man, his company and his influences. John Percival's *The World of Diaghilev* (1971) is a fine general introduction, while Boris Kochno, his last personal assistant (who purportedly had a fistfight with Lifar over Diaghilev's corpse moments after he died), compiled a beautiful picture book, *Diaghilev and the Ballets Russes* (1970).

Michel Fokine

Born: 5th May 1880/St Petersburg
Died: 22nd August 1942/New York City

The first and in many ways the bravest of **Serge Diaghilev**'s choreographers, Michel Fokine ranks as one of the most important innovators of the early twentieth century. Much against his father's wishes, Fokine entered the Imperial Ballet School at the age of nine. He graduated into the Maryinsky (now Kirov) company in 1898, and by 1902 was teaching and choreographing his first dances for student recitals. His early works include *The Dying Swan* (1907), a short solo for **Anna Pavlova**, dashed off in one afternoon yet destined to become her signature piece for the next quarter of a century.

From the outset, Fokine sought to introduce fresh ideas into what he (and many young Russians) viewed as the stale, outmoded formulas left over from the lengthy regime of **Marius Petipa**. Fokine believed that dance had lost its soul by sacrificing veracity for virtuosity. He wanted each of his ballets to mirror its chosen subject as closely as possible, with both movement and design as authentic reflections of the chosen time and place.

This logical idea was met with contempt from the conservative Maryinsky authorities. They had grown so entrenched in the Imperial format of full-length spectacle that they thought of Fokine as naive, even immoral. When he staged his Greek-themed *Eunice* in 1907, he asked that the dancers perform barefoot. The shocked management finally compromised with his vision of artistic truth: the dancers could appear without shoes, but had to don tights with painted-on kneecaps and toenails. In his other major ballets, such as **Petrushka** and **The Firebird**, only the leading ballerinas would wear point shoes and tutus; other characters were dressed in more appropriate and realistic costumes.

Yet Fokine never abandoned his faith in the tenets of ballet. His *Chopiniana* (premiered on the same night as *Eunice*) shows both his love and respect for the disciplines of classical training. He saw himself as a reformer rather than a radical revolutionary à la **Isadora Duncan**. He did not wish to wipe out the never-never-land magic of ballet so much as to transform it into a series of discrete worlds, each unique to its story and setting.

It was only after joining forces with Diaghilev in 1909 that Fokine's reforms were given free rein. The outcome electrified Paris and made both men's careers. However, the authenticity Fokine was striving for was often as phoney as the fantasy he wanted to replace. In the 1910 *Schéhérazade*, the sultan's harem with its optically turbulent designs, orgy and mass slaughter turned the ballet into a titillating shocker. At the time it seemed violently authentic; today it looks more like vintage Hollywood than ancient Persia, a pageant devoid of much inherent dance value.

Other Fokine works, notably **Les Sylphides** (the revised Diaghilev title for *Chopiniana*) and *Le Spectre de la rose* (1911) are essentially mood pieces meant to be dreamy evocations of their scores. Fokine's most successful meld of time and place, dance and theatrical veracity is *Petrushka*, which remains, with **Bronislava Nijinska**'s **Les Noces** and **George Balanchine**'s **Apollo**, one of the masterpieces of the era.

For the first four seasons of the Ballets Russes, Fokine was the sole choreographer, but when Diaghilev began to push forward his protégé **Vaslav Nijinsky**, Fokine returned to Russia. During the Revolution he went to Scandinavia and eventually settled in the USA. He continued to teach and choreograph, but his later ballets failed to equal the vitality of his Diaghilev creations. His final years were mostly spent re-staging his ground-breaking Parisian triumphs.

Lineage

Fokine's influential ideas have touched virtually all subsequent dancemakers. The questions of authenticity which he raised at the beginning of the century have become the bedrock of much modern art. His quest for artistic unity led him to condense his creations into shorter one-act formats, a concept which has become the norm for almost every Western dance company. It is only in recent years that avant-garde choreographers have started to swing back to evening-length events.

Follow-up

Fokine: Memoirs of a Ballet Master (1961); Cyril Beaumont's *Michel Fokine and his Ballets* (1935); Dawn Lille Horwitz's *Michel Fokine* (1985).

Les Sylphides

One act
Choreography: Michel Fokine
Music: Frédéric Chopin
Design: Alexandre Benois
Premiere: 2nd June 1909/Théâtre du Châtelet, Paris (final form)

Fokine originally titled this ballet *Chopiniana*, but it was re-christened *Les Sylphides* for the Paris debut of the Ballets Russes in homage to **La Sylphide**, the first of the great Romantic ballets. Both titles are equally apt. Chopin's music creates the mood, while the dancing itself is a loving evocation of the Romantic era. Together, they form the atmospheric essence of this ballet.

Set in a lakeside glen drenched in moonlight, *Les Sylphides* has a cast consisting of one man (often billed as The Poet), three ballerinas and a female corps de ballet. The women wear the ankle-length flowing tulle skirts of the Romantic period and, in most productions, even have tiny Sylph-like gossamer wings. There is no story to be told. Music – a nocturne, waltzes and mazurkas – leads to dancing. The choreography is marked by a soft lambent beauty and fluid delicacy.

These days *Les Sylphides* can seem overly sweet, even clichéd, but its impact on the history of dance has been enormous. It is the first successful illustration of Fokine's reforms: the first plotless ballet; the first ballet which dared to be about nothing but dancing.

A triumph from the first performances, *Les Sylphides* became the most ubiquitous ballet of its era and is still performed by companies throughout the world. It first captured the imagination of Western audiences at a time when *La Sylphide* and **Giselle** had all but been forgotten, and before the major Russians classics like **Swan Lake** had been introduced. Put in that context, it is easy to see how *Les Sylphides* became an ideal for a whole generation of ballet-goers.

Lineage

The daring notion of dance for its own sake has had an all-encompassing influence. Fokine saw **Isadora Duncan** dancing to Chopin during her 1904 Russian tour, and subsequently Chopin's music was used by **Anna Pavlova** for her 1918 *Autumn Leaves* and by **Bronislava Nijinska** for *Chopin Concerto* (1937). **Jerome Robbins** has employed the composer's music for several ballets, chief among them **Dances at a Gathering**, also a suite of plotless dances and directly linked to the ideas of *Les Sylphides* even though it bears no physical resemblance. Chopin scores have served for several narrative ballets, notably **Frederick Ashton**'s **A Month in the Country** and **John Neumeier**'s full-length *Lady of the Camellias* (1978).

Follow-up

Film excerpts are featured in *An Evening with The Royal Ballet* (Margot Fonteyn and Rudolf Nureyev, 1964) and *American Ballet Theatre at the Met* (Mikhail Baryshnikov, 1984).

Stagings

The standard rendition is in the repertory of virtually all major companies. A unique staging was: **Alexandra Danilova**/New York City Ballet/1972 (in practice dress with piano accompaniment)

The Firebird

One act
Choreography: Michel Fokine
Music: Igor Stravinsky
Design: Alexander Golovin and Léon Bakst
Premiere: 25th June 1910/Théâtre National de l'Opéra, Paris

This Russian fairy tale swirls around a glittering title character who darts through the story with sharp staccato speed. She is the only character in the ballet *en pointe* and her steps are filled with fleet, flying jumps that flash like a bird on the wing. The story, set in an enchanted garden, begins when a wandering Prince ensnares the Firebird in his arms. After struggling vainly to escape from his grasp, she offers him one of her magical feathers in exchange for freedom. After she flies away, the Prince has a vision of a Princess and her handmaidens frolicking in the garden. Their gently lilting dance, a simple game of catch played with golden apples, is derived from Russian folkloric themes.

The Prince falls in love, but, unknown to him, these maidens are under the spell of the sorceror Kastchei. When the evil magician and his scuttling, insect-like minions surge onto the stage to attack the invading Prince, he whips out his magic feather. The Firebird darts to his rescue, subdues the monsters, who fall into a hypnotised sleep, and then reveals to the Prince that Kastchei's soul (and power) is centred inside an egg. The Prince shatters it and the stage is plunged into darkness. To a thrilling brass anthem, the stage gradually fills with a golden light that reveals a towered city where a stately, all but static, procession depicts the wedding and coronation of the Prince and Princess.

The Firebird is heavily dominated by mime, but is buoyed up by its exotic designs and magnificent score (Stravinsky's first ballet). It was one of **Serge Diaghilev**'s first resounding successes, but modern audiences have come to expect more actual dancing than this work contains. The original production (using designs created by Natalia Goncharova in 1926) is currently in the Royal Ballet repertory. It is now more a historical curiosity than a satisfying ballet.

Several choreographers have attempted to redefine Stravinsky's compelling score. **George Balanchine**, using designs by Marc Chagall, retained the story's framework for his 1949 New York City Ballet production (revised 1970), but attempted to infuse more dancing into the spectacle.

Maurice Béjart jettisoned the story for a modern interpretation that recasts the Firebird as a Phoenix. Now a male role, he has become the leader of a gang of revolutionary partisans; destroyed in combat, he is re-born in the finale as a blood-red symbol of freedom.

Dance Theatre of Harlem has had a resounding popular success with a version choreographed by John Taras: here the traditional story is enlivened by vibrant tropical jungle settings and costumes by Geoffrey Holder.

Lineage

Devotees of *The Firebird* should enjoy all of Fokine's ballets, particularly **Petrushka** and *Schéhérazade*. Other opulent dance pageants include **Frederick Ashton**'s opium dream *Apparitions* (1936) and **George Balanchine**'s mysterious 1946 *La Sonnambula* (also known as *Night Shadow*), which includes a bizarre pas de deux for a Byronic poet and a beautiful, never-waking sleepwalker. Both men also choreographed the sweeping ballroom passions of Ravel's *La Valse* (Balanchine in 1951, Ashton in 1958). The culmination of this genre is Balanchine's luxurious *Vienna Waltzes* (1977): by this point dancing has completely replaced the mime of *The Firebird*. The last of its five scenes, an apotheosis of the benevolent magic of dance, ends with twenty-five couples, the men in tails, the women in flowing white satin, spinning into the infinite spaces of Rouben Ter-Arutunian's mirrored ballroom.

Follow-up

A 1982 film, *Stravinsky's Firebird by Dance Theatre of Harlem*, shows the company rehearsing Taras' version and Geoffrey Holder discussing his designs.

Stagings

1 **George Balanchine**/New York City Ballet/1949, revised 1970
2 **Adolphe Bolm**/American Ballet Theatre/1945
3 **Maurice Béjart**/Paris Opéra Ballet/1970

The Ballerina from *Petrushka*, as portrayed in 1911 by Tamara Karsavina

4 **John Neumeier**/Frankfurt Ballet/1970 (science fiction treatment)
5 **John Taras**/Dance Theatre of Harlem/1982

Petrushka

One act
Choreography: Michel Fokine
Libretto: Alexandre Benois and Igor Stravinsky
Music: Igor Stravinsky
Design: Alexandre Benois
Premiere: 13th June 1911/Théâtre du Châtelet, Paris

In *Petrushka*, Fokine achieved his goal of a new, more believable form of theatrical dancing. It is his most substantial ballet, and one that continues to exert an aura of mysterious power. Fokine's carefully integrated mix of mime, folk themes and classical ballet forms a dramatic synthesis in which atmospherics, character, music and steps become indivisible.

The scene is a public square in St Petersburg during the Butterweek Fair (the Russian equivalent of Mardi Gras) in the 1830s. A bustling crowd of fairgoers, with distinct personalities and quirks, gathers round a booth where an aged Showman animates his trio of life-sized puppets: the Ballerina, the Blackamoor and Petrushka himself. A traditional Russian combination of Punch and Puck, Petrushka jealously (and ineptly) attacks the Moor in a vain bid for the Ballerina's affections. The scene shifts backstage to Petrushka's room. His despondency and loneliness is expressed with a sad clown's floppy jerkiness. The Showman brings the Ballerina to him, but the inarticulate Petrushka is incapable of expressing his longings and she leaves in a huff. In contrast, the Moor's dancing is as silken and self-satisfied as Petrushka's is stuttery, knock-kneed and disjointed. The Ballerina reappears and flirts with the Moor; Petrushka barges in and the Moor drives him away.

Back at the Fair, the merrymaking is interrupted by a terrible commotion from inside the puppet booth. Petrushka breaks out of the booth and is chased through the crowd by the Moor, who strikes him down with a scimitar. Taken aback, the crowd demands that the police be summoned, but the old Showman (in a tricky *coup de théâtre*) shows them that Petrushka's body is nothing but straw-filled rags and the stunned crowd departs. In the gathering darkness, as the Showman is left alone with the remains of his puppet, he is startled to see the spirit of Petrushka rising from the roof of the puppet booth to taunt and haunt him.

The plaintive central character has become a major challenge to a long line of dramatic dancers. **Vaslav Nijinsky** originated the role; both **Rudolf Nureyev** and **David** **Bintley** have given memorable performances. In 1977 **Maurice Béjart** revised the scenario: at a modern carnival, a magician lures a young man into a hall of mirrors where, through a series of transformations, he becomes all three of the central characters. The charismatic Richard Cragun scored a personal triumph in this glittery ambisexual version.

Lineage

Living dolls have been a favourite device throughout ballet history. **Coppélia** and **The Nutcracker** are the most famous examples, but in *Petrushka*, Fokine was able to bring an additional level of psychological depth to the convention.

One delightful *Petrushka* offshoot is the 1937 backstage murder mystery *A Bullet in the Ballet* by Caryl Brahms and S.J. Simon, subsequently turned into a play. In this bitchy comedy, a string of dancers, each playing the title role, is murdered one by one. The *Petrushka* sets and costumes from the play were later donated to **London Festival Ballet** and used for the first British production of Fokine's ballet in 1950.

Follow-up

Geoffrey Ashton reviews the history and the development of the ballet in *Petrushka* (1985). The Joffrey Ballet appeared on Broadway with Rudolf Nureyev in a 1979 all-Nijinsky evening based around scrupulously accurate stagings of *Petrushka, Le Spectre de la rose* and *L'Après-midi d'un faune* (broadcast in 1981); an Italian video of the same three ballets features Paolo Bortoluzzi and Carla Fracci.

Stagings

1 **Léonide Massine**/American Ballet Theatre/1942
2 **Léonide Massine**/Joffrey Ballet/1970
3 **Heinz Spoerli**/Basel Ballet/1974
4 **Maurice Béjart**/Ballet of the 20th Century/1977
5 **John Auld**/Sadler's Wells Royal Ballet/1984

Léonide Massine

Born: 8th August 1895/Moscow
Died: 15th March 1979/Weseke
bei Borken, near Cologne

Léonide Massine's talents perfectly fit the injunction of Dominique Ingres to his students as they passed by the work of Delacroix: 'Remove your hats, gentlemen, but there's no need to stop'. Massine's choreographic ideas have been so absorbed into the fabric of ballet that his inventions now seem old-fashioned, at times even quaint. The radical **Parade** continues to stimulate more from Picasso's cubist designs and Satie's lively score than from the choreography.

Still a doe-eyed teenager when **Serge Diaghilev** plucked him from the Bolshoi, Massine immediately scored a personal triumph dancing the title role in **Michel Fokine**'s 1914 Biblical extravaganza *The Legend of Joseph*. Diaghilev, still smarting over **Vaslav Nijinsky**'s marriage, decided to groom Massine as both on- and off-stage successor. A quick learner, Massine was soon producing made-to-order ballets; of these, the best-remembered (and occasionally revived) are *La Boutique fantasque*, a tale of charmed toys which come to life, and *The Three-Cornered Hat*, filled with authentic Spanish dances scored by Manuel de Falla and designed by Picasso. Massine walked out on Diaghilev in 1921, but returned in 1925, only to leave again three years later. He went to New York where he staged his own version of **Le Sacre du printemps** in 1930 with a young **Martha Graham** as the Chosen Maiden.

Diaghilev's death in 1929 left his company in disarray, and factions quickly arose. In 1932, Massine joined the party run by Colonel de Basil; this led to a bitter copyright dispute when, in 1938, he switched allegiance to René Blum's rival troupe Les Ballets Russes de Monte Carlo.

Massine's first production for Blum was one of his most enduring, the boulevardier genre comedy *Gaîté Parisienne* (1938). He also continued to create his full-scale symphonic ballets. These elaborate choric stagings of major musical scores had begun in 1933 with *Les Présages* (to Tchaikovsky's Fifth) and *Choréartium* (Brahms' Fourth). They were followed by the Berlioz *Symphonie fantastique* (1936), Beethoven's *Seventh Symphony* (1938) and *Rouge et Noir* (Shostakovich's First, 1939). These grandiose works were seen by many as the ultimate high art of the day. Others found Massine's pretensions demeaning to great music.

Fifty years on, they are all essentially lost, but contemporary descriptions, even when laudatory, evoke images which would undoubtedly strike many of today's audiences as over-produced, old-fashioned and too heavily per-fumed. In 1987, **London Festival Ballet** revived **Frederick Ashton**'s one-act *Apparitions*. This 1936 work, also inspired by the libretto for *Symphonie fantastique*, but performed to a variety of short pieces by Liszt, illustrates what Massine's symphonic ballets probably looked like. It also shows how far public tastes have changed.

Lauded in the 1930s as the greatest of European choreographers, Massine's reputation has gone into eclipse; yet he will live forever on celluloid as the mad maker of **The Red Shoes** (in the 1948 film), in which it is possible to get a glimmer of the febrile intensity of his personality.

Lineage

Today few would question a choreographer's right to use whatever music seems most appropriate. Still, despite Massine's pioneering efforts in this realm, few modern dancemakers have taken on the symphonies of Beethoven. Because of their

Léonide Massine, in his late seventies, rehearsing dancers of London Festival Ballet for a 1974 revival of *Parade*

overpowering completeness as discrete works of art, major symphonies have proved hard to handle in ballet terms. **Maurice Béjart** devised an ostentatious *Ninth Symphony* in 1964 (for sports arena performance) and **John Neumeier** is gradually working his way through the mammoth symphonies of Mahler, but most choreographers tend to steer clear of music of such magnitude. **George Balanchine**'s plotless celebration of Bizet's youthful *Symphony in C* (1947) is the prime example of symphonic choreography. Part of its success is due, no doubt, to the fact that Bizet was only seventeen when he wrote this charmingly uncomplicated and unpretentious score.

Follow-up
Massine's autobiography, *My Life in Ballet* (1960), often plays fast and loose with the facts.

Parade

One act
Choreography: Léonide Massine
Libretto: Jean Cocteau
Music: Erik Satie
Design: Pablo Picasso
Premiere: 18th May 1917/Théâtre du Châtelet, Paris

The staging of *Parade* marked the beginning of **Serge Diaghilev**'s collaboration with the artists and composers of the French avant-garde and was a precursor of the experimental ballets which came into vogue during the 1920s. Cocteau's initial concept – radical at the time – was for a comedy of modern movement which would directly mirror the world of its audience. Satie's jaunty music is brimming with popular idioms, jazz syncopations and contemporary sounds (a real typewriter, a siren and pistol shots).

A *parade* is a come-on, a live 'preview of coming attractions'. Here, three *parades* are performed on a suburban Paris street in an attempt to lure passers-by into an itinerant theatre. The first features a Chinese conjuror (originally danced by Massine himself) performing middling magic tricks. Then a spunky young woman called Little American Girl skips through a tongue-in-cheek homage to the cinema: she mimics Chaplin, has a six-shooter showdown with some bad guys and goes through a range of heroine-in-danger histrionics. She is followed by a pair of acrobats who dance a duet which includes a perilous walk on a non-existent tightrope. Finally, in a last vain attempt to attract an audience, they all join in a ragtime number.

Each of these acts is introduced by a different Manager, which allowed Picasso to bring Cubism into the theatre. The costumes for two of the Managers are towering constructions of dizzying perspectives (the American Manager has a tilting skyscraper growing out of his back) and the third Manager is a two-man pantomime horse. Although the over-sized costumes curtailed much dancing, they added stunning visual impact.

Frothy, lightweight – and just plain silly – *Parade* proved a major hit with Paris audiences and prompted poet Guillaume Apollinaire to coin a neologism: *sur-réalisme*. The work disappeared from the repertory after 1926 until the Brussels-based Ballet of the 20th Century revived it in 1964 (without the Picasso designs); the whole package was restored nine years later by the **Joffrey Ballet**.

Lineage

Creating work which strives to capture the spirit of the moment is now standard practice for both ballet and modern dance choreographers. *Parade*'s success produced a string of contemporary works by the Ballets Russes such as **Bronislava Nijinska**'s two 1924 works, **Les Biches** and *Le Train bleu* (the latter a 1920s frolic in chic Chanel bathing costumes). Later highlights of the genre include **Jerome Robbins**' **Fancy Free** and the work *Trinity*, created by Gerald Arpino for the **Joffrey Ballet** in 1969 to celebrate the flower-child generation.

Picasso's first contribution to the ballet is one of the main reasons for the continuing success of *Parade* revivals. Other painters and sculptors have gone beyond the bounds of 'normal' costumes. Robert Rauschenberg has devised a plethora of unorthodox garments for the **Merce Cunningham** company (one of the funniest a rattling harness of tin cans worn in *Travelogue*, 1977). Larger-than-life creatures are a regular feature of **Robert Wilson**'s evening-length creations. In his epic *The CIVIL WarS* (1984) a gigantic Mrs Abraham Lincoln (operated by hydraulics) is so huge that Abe, played by a midget, can sit in the palm of her hand.

Follow-up

The first programme in the Dance in America series featured the Joffrey Ballet in segments of *Parade* and Kurt Jooss's *The Green Table*; this 1976 video includes interviews with both choreographers. Erik Aschengreen's *Jean Cocteau and the Dance* (1986), on the artist's work with the Ballets Russes, has a chapter on *Parade*.

Stagings

1 **Maurice Béjart**/Ballet of the 20th Century/1964
2 **Léonide Massine**/Joffrey Ballet/1973
3 **Léonide Massine**/London Festival Ballet/1974
4 **Gray Veredon**/Metropolitan Opera/1981

Bronislava Nijinska

Born: 8th January 1891/Minsk
Died: 22nd February 1972/Los
Angeles, California

The only woman to choreograph
for **Serge Diaghilev**, the younger
sister of **Vaslav Nijinsky** created
eight very diverse works for the
company. The architectonic **Les
Noces** is not only her personal
masterpiece, but a milestone of
twentieth-century art. At the other
end of the scale, works like **Les
Biches** and *Le Train bleu* celebrate
the frivolous, fashionable mode of
the Ballets Russes.

Trained as a dancer in St
Petersburg, Nijinska was one of the
original members of Diaghilev's
company. When her brother,
whom she idolised, was fired, she
quit the company in sympathy and
returned to Russia to form her own
school. Nevertheless, she returned
to the West in 1921 and served as
the major Ballets Russes
choreographer for four years.

Never a beauty, Nijinska's stage
presence relied on strength and
intelligence rather than delicacy.
In later years she took to wearing
a tuxedo, and even danced the
title role in her own 1934 version of
Hamlet. Throughout her long life,
she continued to teach and
choreograph in the UK, the USA
and Europe. In 1935 she staged the
dances in Max Reinhardt's
Hollywood version of *A
Midsummer Night's Dream* for
James Cagney and Mickey
Rooney, and her 1960 production
of **The Sleeping Beauty** has been
re-staged several times by
ballerina Rosella Hightower
(Marseille 1968, Stuttgart 1977 and
Paris Opéra 1982). However, her
lasting importance rests with her
major Diaghilev ballets.

Lineage
Despite the occasional contribution
from a ballerina like Marie
Taglioni, Nijinska is regarded as
the first major female choreographer. Modern dance, especially in
its formative years, was to be a
matriarchal society, but even today
classical ballet is still dominated
by men. **Ninette de Valois** was
active as a choreographer in the
1930s and 40s, **Birgit Cullberg**'s
Miss Julie (1950) has become a
repertory standard and **Twyla
Tharp** has brought a new vitality to
classicism with her works for
American Ballet Theatre, the
Joffrey Ballet and even New York
City Ballet. Each of them owes a
debt to Nijinska's bold, decisive
manner.

Nijinska's choreographic identity
is closely linked to her brother's
revolutionary ideals. She was in
the original production of **L'Après-
midi d'un faune** and had been
scheduled to dance the Sacrificial
Maiden in **Le Sacre du printemps**
(pregnant, she had to withdraw;
Nijinsky flew into a rage and
accused her of sabotage). His
mental breakdown served as a
catalyst for her own talent: she
admitted that she began making
dances in an attempt to further his
ideas.

Follow-up
Nijinska's final contribution to
dance came with the posthumous
publication of *Bronislava Nijinska:
Early Memoirs* (1981). Edited by
her daughter, Irina, this is a
detailed and intimate portrait of
herself, her brother and the
hothouse world in which they both
lived.

Les Noces

One act
Choreography: Bronislava Nijinska
Music: Igor Stravinsky
Design: Natalia Goncharova
Premiere: 13th June 1923/Théâtre
de la Gaîté-Lyrique, Paris

Les Noces is a compelling ritual
which grows directly out of a
throbbing score on Slavic themes
for choir, four solo singers, four

53

pianos and a large battery of percussion. It depicts a single peasant wedding but, through Nijinska's elemental approach to movement, transcends the specific to become a universal celebration of the sacrament of marriage. The ballet is in four scenes: the blessing of the bride; the blessing of the groom; the departure of the bride from her mother's house; the final wedding celebration.

Nijinska's choreographic vocabulary grows out of her brother **Vaslav Nijinsky**'s radical inventions, particularly those in his **Le Sacre du printemps**. The kinetic energy and excitement of her movement is built on choric ensembles that use dancers as large, massed blocks of movement. There is a stark, even blunt, architectural sensibility in her structure that is balanced against the growing frenzy of the climactic wedding feast. Here, Nijinska has all the individual characters (the bride, the groom and their parents) simply sit watching the orgiastic village celebrations. They are like the still centre of a storm, the sacred versus the profane.

Frederick Ashton, whose personal lyric approach to dance could hardly be more different than Nijinska's, rescued this ballet from oblivion when he asked her to stage it for the Royal Ballet in 1966 (subsequently revived for the Stuttgart Ballet and the Paris Opéra Ballet). No other choreographer has been able to elicit the same depth of feeling from the score. **Jerome Robbins** produced *Les Noces* for American Ballet Theatre in 1965, in a version more closely connected to his own Broadway musical *Fiddler on the Roof* than to Nijinska. Robbins later said that if he had known what a masterpiece the original was he would never have attempted his own re-working.

Lineage
Like **George Balanchine** after her, Nijinska was more interested in evolving the classical vocabulary into the neo-classical than abandoning it as **Michel Fokine** had done in his theatrical dance

dramas. Unlike Fokine (in works such as **Petrushka**), Nijinska uses the crowds in *Les Noces* in a collectivist, non-realistic manner. Her architectural approach came back into style in the utterly different guise of the 1960s American minimalists like **Lucinda Childs** and **Trisha Brown**.

Stagings
1 **Maurice Béjart**/Ballet of the 20th Century/1962
2 **Jerome Robbins**/American Ballet Theatre/1965
3 **Bronislava Nijinska**/Royal Ballet/1966
4 **Lar Lubovitch**/Lubovitch Dance Company/1972
5 **Irina Nijinska**/Oakland Ballet/1981

Les Biches

One act
Choreography: Bronislava Nijinska
Music: Francis Poulenc
Design: Marie Laurencin
Premiere: 6th January 1924/ Théâtre de Monte Carlo

The title *Les Biches* refers to young does and was undoubtedly meant to conjure up images of nubile femininity. The ballet depicts a stylish house party for bright young things on the Riviera (the work is sometimes called *House Party*). Poulenc's slinky, seductive score is complemented by Laurencin's clever sets and costumes in pastel, poisoned-candy colours, and the dancing revolves around games, narcissistic displays and attempted seductions. The whole piece is kept on edge by a sometimes funny, sometimes unsettling, sexual ambiguity. One character, the Page, is danced by a woman but seems meant to be a boy. Wearing an abbreviated blue velvet jacket, tights and toe shoes, the Page moves with a Sphinx-like serenity at odds with the ebullient energies of the other guests. Her measured perambulations *en pointe* are as spiky and delicate as a wading

A performance of *Les Noces* from London Weekend Television's *Stravinsky: A South Bank Show Special*

Vaslav Nijinsky

Born: 12th March 1888(?)/Kiev
Died: 8th April 1950/London

bird's. An enthusiastic athlete, in bathing costume, becomes fascinated by this androgynous creature: the resulting duet teeters between humour and eroticism.

Nijinska herself created the role of the blasé Hostess, a woman of a certain age who brandishes a long cigarette holder and swings an even longer rope of pearls as she indulges in a flirtatious 'Rag Mazurka' with two male guests. As Poulenc said of *Les Biches*, 'This is a ballet in which you may see nothing at all or into which you may read the worst'. The exact amount of sexuality and satire is in the mind of the beholder.

Lineage

Nijinska's use of humour to satirise the sexual mores of the day is a device used by **Frederick Ashton** in **Façade**. **Paul Taylor** often depicts depravity with a shiny social smile, and **Twyla Tharp**'s 1982 *Nine Sinatra Songs* has the same mix of exuberance and irony.

Stagings

1 **Bronislava Nijinska**/Royal Ballet/1964
2 **Irina Nijinska**/Dance Theatre of Harlem/1983

Possessed with phenomenal star power and animal magnetism, Vaslav Nijinsky had a brief and meteoric career, cut short by mental illness, which became the stuff of legend. Withdrawn and shy off the stage, he was a shortish man with thick muscles and a broad-featured Asiatic face. Thanks to an instinctive sense of theatre and a transformational talent with make-up (his parents were Polish circus performers), Nijinsky was able to create a whole gallery of stage portraits: the Romantic Poet of **Les Sylphides**, the sinuously exotic Golden Slave in *Schéhérazade*, the ethereal *Le Spectre de la rose* and the barely human title character in his own ballet **L'Après-midi d'un faune**.

A controversial personality in Russia, where he had begun training at the Imperial Ballet School as a child, Nijinsky was regarded as an undeniably talented misfit. Seeking new freedom, he threw in his lot with **Serge Diaghilev**, and made a

55

sensational impact during the first Ballets Russes seasons in Paris and London. Diaghilev, who loved Nijinsky and treated him as a special protégé, pushed him towards choreography. The Greek-influenced *Faune* was quickly followed by *Jeux* and the barbaric **Le Sacre du printemps**, both from 1913.

Along with the 1916 *Tyl Eulenspiegel*, each of these works presented a new aesthetic. Radical and unorthodox, they turned their backs on the classical heritage and have since garnered the accolade of being ballet's first 'modern' choreography. Each, in its own specific way, was a shock. *Jeux*, the simplest of his works, used everyday movement; this trio for Nijinsky and two women was set on a tennis court with the game mirroring an emotionally tangled eternal triangle (and Nijinsky's own sexual ambivalence).

In 1913 the Ballets Russes went on a South American tour. The superstitious Diaghilev, who had been warned by a gipsy that he would die on water, remained behind. On his own for the first time, Nijinsky took a drastic and unexpected step, by marrying a well-to-do minor Hungarian dancer, Romola de Pulszky. Their shipboard romance must have been bizarre: at the time of the wedding neither could speak the other's language. Diaghilev was furious, and in a fit of jealousy, fired them both.

At the outbreak of the First World War, Nijinsky (still a Russian citizen) was interned in Budapest, but American intervention freed him for appearances in the USA. There he worked on *Tyl Eulenspiegel*, but, traumatised by the preceding years, he tipped over into schizophrenia. During a stay in a Swiss sanatorium he wrote his eccentric and tormented *Diary*, and after a final performance for an invited audience in 1919, the remainder of his life was spent in a sequence of institutions. Romola moved him to England in 1947, and he died there three years later (although he is buried in the cemetery at Montmartre).

Lineage

Dubbed 'The God of the Dance', Nijinsky was modern ballet's first male superstar. If the nineteenth century was the era of the ballerina, then the twentieth has been the domain of Nijinsky and his successors. His feral dance style with its powerful, soaring leaps and his intense acting both captured and liberated audiences. His physical strength allowed him to perform feats beyond the reach of his contemporaries, and he set a whole new standard of dancing, in much the same way as the later Russians **Rudolf Nureyev** and **Mikhail Baryshnikov** have done for contemporary ballet dancers.

Follow-up

Of the dozens of books on Nijinsky, Richard Buckle's 1971 study is the most thorough; Romola de Pulszky's 1933 biography of her husband is filled with prejudices. Some of Nijinsky's special qualities can be gleaned from the excellent photographic collection *Nijinsky Dancing* (1975) with commentary by Lincoln Kirstein. Nijinsky served as the subject of an unsuccessful 1980 Hollywood bio-pic and a 1975 BBC documentary *Nijinsky – God of the Dance*. Maurice Béjart choreographed an evening-length spectacle called *Nijinsky, Clown de Dieu* in 1976, based on quotations from Nijinsky's diary.

L'Après-midi d'un faune

One act
Choreography: Vaslav Nijinsky
Music: Claude Debussy
Design: Léon Bakst
Premiere: 29th May 1912/Théâtre du Châtelet, Paris

The only one of Nijinsky's ballets to survive intact, *L'Après-midi d'un faune* is an essay in stylised eroticism. A faun (Nijinsky) lazes on a rock. Greek maidens enter; the faun startles them; they run away. In their hurried flight, one of the nymphs drops her scarf, which the faun picks up before returning to his rocky perch. He spreads out the scarf and lowers himself on top of it. The final thrust of his hips into the silken scarf sent scandalised shock waves through the first-night audience.

This final moment of blatant sexuality gave the ballet instant notoriety, but its lasting significance arises from Nijinsky's idiosyncratic movement motifs. Culled from Greek friezes, the choreography breaks every rule of classical ballet training. The dancers, in sandals, move in two-dimensional planes back and forth across the stage, as though compressed between two plates of glass. Arms and feet kept parallel to the audience, their sharply angled poses are an attempt to reproduce the flatness of vase paintings and wall carvings. One of the most difficult and innovative aspects of this work is its relationship to Debussy's score. Instead of exploiting distinct rhythms, Nijinsky used the lush tone poem simply as atmospheric accompaniment. As in his other ballets, Nijinsky devised complex methods for counting out the individual movements of each dancer. These had to be learned by rote rather than felt intuitively through the music's rhythmic tempos.

The creation of Nijinsky's first ballet was an arduous task. He began work on it as early as 1910, and though the ballet is brief – barely twelve minutes – Nijinsky demanded at least one hundred and twenty rehearsals before he deemed it ready for performance. His overwhelming mania for perfection was already making itself visible.

Lineage

The archaic style of *Faune* was too specific to be translated into other ballets, even to Nijinsky's other works. However, his sense of music as a blanket of sound rather than a strict rhythmic accompaniment is an early precursor of the **Merce Cunningham**/John Cage collaborations which present music and dance as separate but equal creative entities that simply share the same time and space. Several choreographers have reworked Debussy's score. The best known of these is **Jerome Robbins**' *Afternoon of a Faun*, a tentative love duet for a pair of ballet dancers who encounter one another in a rehearsal studio. They relate to each other only by watching themselves in the (invisible) mirror which makes up the audience's 'wall' of the setting. The final moment is transformed into a gentle kiss when the young man looks directly at the girl for the first and only time.

Follow-up

In 1912, the photographer Baron Adolf de Meyer took a series of studio photographs of the original production; these were published in 1983, with an essay by Jennifer Dunning, as *L'Après-midi d'un faune, Vaslav Nijinsky, 1912*.

Staging

1 **Elisabeth Schooling**/Joffrey Ballet/1979 (and later London Festival Ballet)

Le Sacre du printemps

One act
Choreography: Vaslav Nijinsky
Libretto: Igor Stravinsky and Nicholas Roerich
Music: Igor Stravinsky
Design: Nicholas Roerich
Premiere: 29th May 1913/Théâtre des Champs-Elysées, Paris

No single ballet has achieved such mythic proportions as *Le Sacre du printemps* (The Rite of Spring). The premiere, with its near riot between disputing factions of the audience, is the most notorious night in dance history.

The work's subtitle is 'Pictures from Pagan Russia in Two Parts'. The primal story is simple: a prehistoric Russian tribe celebrates the arrival of spring with a propitiatory virgin sacrifice. In the second scene, the Chosen Maiden dances herself to death. Both score and choreography were so unexpected and avant-garde that the first audience was either shocked or insulted. Nijinsky inverted the basic poses of classical ballet in an effort to find a brutal, primitive style that would suit the surging pulse of Stravinsky's score. He converted the first position of ballet technique (heels together, legs turned out, toes pointing in opposite directions) into its mirror image, so that *Sacre*'s major pose is a pigeon-toed stance with toes almost touching and heels spread apart.

Similarly, where ballet dancers traditionally try to convey an expansive, easy sense of flight in their buoyant leaps, Nijinsky devised heavy, compressed jumps whose weight seems to be driving into the ground rather than bounding off it. Another non-balletic notion is the way in which Nijinsky focussed on group movements. Although they are dancing on stage at the same time, each group of performers is driven by a different set of rhythmic pulses. The combination of these counterpoint rhythms (rather than flashy balletic technique) forms the heart of Nijinsky's rite.

The original version was abandoned after only seven performances and was not to be seen again for seventy-five years. **Marie Rambert** had been hired by **Serge Diaghilev** to help Nijinsky with the score's intricacies, and in 1955 Robert Joffrey went to her with the idea of trying to revive the work. However, it was not until 1987 that the **Joffrey Ballet** presented a new vision of the original. This was the joint creation of dance historian Millicent Hodson and artist Kenneth Archer (who recreated the sets and costumes),

a project which took Hodson twelve years to piece together. There is no way of gauging its accuracy, but it looks and feels authentic. Perhaps the most impressive thing about this version is the way in which the movement is able to hold its own against the titanic score, something other versions have singularly failed to do.

Lineage

Stravinsky's score has been a siren to a host of ballet and modern dance choreographers. Among the plethora of versions are productions by **Léonide Massine** (a pallid 1920 re-working), **Kenneth MacMillan**, **Maurice Béjart** (overtly erotic), **Glen Tetley**, Hans van Manen, **Pina Bausch** and **Martha Graham** (who herself danced the Chosen Maiden in a 1930 revival of the Massine version). **Paul Taylor**'s rendition (to Stravinsky's two-piano reduction) is the most unorthodox, and thus most successful, since Nijinsky's. Taylor jettisons the scenario and replaces it with an American cartoon-style version about a kidnapped baby, Chinatown hoods, corrupt cops, stolen jewels and a mild-mannered Clark Kent look-alike hero. The black comedy ends in a pile-up of dead bodies, and the final dance is performed by the baby's grief-stricken mother, the sole survivor of the carnage.

Follow-up

Richard Buckle's *Nijinsky* (1971) includes one of the most complete explanations of *Sacre*.

Stagings

1 **Kenneth MacMillan**/Royal Ballet/1962
2 **Maurice Béjart**/Ballet of the 20th Century/1959
3 **Glen Tetley**/Munich Ballet/1974 (subsequently staged by Stuttgart Ballet and American Ballet Theatre)
4 **Hans van Manen**/Dutch National Ballet/1974
5 **Pina Bausch**/Wuppertal Dance Theatre/1975
6 **Paul Taylor**/Paul Taylor Dance Company/1980

7 **Richard Alston**/Ballet Rambert/1981
8 **Jean-Pierre Bonnefous**/ Metropolitan Opera/1981
9 **Martha Graham**/Martha Graham Dance Company/1984
10 **Millicent Hodson**/Joffrey Ballet/1987

Anna Pavlova

Born: 12th February 1881/St Petersburg
Died: 23rd January 1931/ S'Gravenhage

Hailed as the supreme lyricist of her generation, Anna Pavlova was already a young star when **Serge Diaghilev** engaged her for the debut season of the Ballets Russes. She and **Vaslav Nijinsky** had been acclaimed in Russia for their atmospheric **Giselle**, and in 1907, **Michel Fokine** had devised *The Dying Swan* for her, a slight but plaintive solo to Saint-Saëns' music which was to become Pavlova's signature dance.

Her conservative outlook clashed with Diaghilev's thirst for modernity. She refused the title role in **The Firebird** because she found Stravinsky's score ugly. After leaving the Diaghilev company she assembled her own troupe and spent some twenty years almost permanently on the road. Gentle and genteel in performance, Pavlova's strict and essentially reactionary concepts led her to proclaim that the modern reforms of the Ballets Russes were more suited to the circus than the ballet stage. She favoured roles like Giselle and inconsequential (but effective) little vignettes with titles such as *The Dragonfly* or *The California Poppy*, lightweight musical visualisations that became her stock-in-trade. Her death from pneumonia just before her fiftieth birthday was sudden and unexpected.

Lineage

Pavlova's poetic image remains the

A studio portrait of Anna Pavlova in her celebrated role as *The Dying Swan*

fantasy ideal of a ballerina: soft, ethereal and delicately shimmering in moonlight. Her role as an indefatigable ambassador of the dance is her greatest legacy. Her lengthy tours, often composed of demanding one-night stands, introduced ballet to new audiences in Australia, India, Japan and the Americas. An example of her far-flung influence occurred during a 1919 South American tour. In Lima, an overwhelmed youngster called **Frederick Ashton** decided on the spot to devote his life to ballet.

Follow-up

Pavlova's home base, Ivy House in Golders Green, London, is now a part of Middlesex Polytechnic; a room of Pavloviana is preserved as a museum. The first Pavlova Festival was organised there in April 1988. Keith Money's *Anna Pavlova* (1982) is the most complete and exhaustively illustrated of many books available. Shortly after her death, Pavlova's husband and manager, Victor Dandré, assembled forty minutes of film footage called *The Immortal Swan*; an Anglo-Russian documentary (*Pavlova, A Woman For All Time*) was produced in 1984.

THE BIRTH OF MODERN DANCE

16th March 1900. Isadora Duncan's first European performance took place in London. By the time she died in a freak accident in 1927 (strangled by her scarf when it caught in the spokes of a car wheel), Isadora had become an international celebrity and her radical notion of a dance form that replaced academic strictures with intuitive inspiration was set to become a central theme of twentieth-century dance.

Duncan had crossed the Atlantic – on a cattle boat with her mother, sister and brother in tow — in search of an artistic climate which might prove more conducive to her aims than that of her native America. In a remarkably short space of time, she became a cult figure. Performing barefoot and in a loose-flowing tunic, she gave her audiences a highly individual and subjective vision of dance. Some thought that Isadora was a goddess, others merely saw her as a crackpot. History confirms her as a mixture of the two; legend reveals her distinctive quality as charisma. This was coupled with an unshakeable belief in her own genius. Both qualities were part of the legacy she passed on to her fellow dance pioneers. Martha Graham, Mary Wigman and Doris Humphrey were all larger-than-life stage presences who could mesmerise audiences even when they had little comprehension of what the dancers were trying to accomplish.

Isadora Duncan made two lasting contributions to dance. She liberated herself and those who succeeded her from the con-stricting paraphenalia of corsets, petticoats, long sleeves, high collars and heavy skirts worn by the women of her day. Her second, equally important innovation, was to insist that her art merited concomitantly great music. She danced to Gluck, Wagner and Bach, and even Beethoven's Seventh Symphony. The music critics were almost as scandalised by her temerity as the ballet aficionados were by her bare feet.

Western theatrical dance was at one of its lowest ebbs when Isadora first appeared in Europe. Tightrope walkers and contort-ionists shared the music hall stages with 'toe dancers', Vaslav Nijinsky was still an unknown student and neither Frederick Ashton nor George Balanchine had been born. Another American expatriot, Loie Fuller, was a star attraction at the 1900 World Fair in Paris, but her performances were more illusionist gimmickry than dancing. Fuller, one of the first dancers to use electricity creatively, achieved her stage effects by manipulating gigantic veils of silk into fluid patterns enhanced by changing coloured lights to lose window.

Fuller's exoticism would flower into the pageantry of the Denishawn school, but by the time of the Great Depression, all frivolity had been sternly quarantined. Martha Graham and Doris Humphrey in America, and Mary Wigman in Germany were deadly serious about the new dance forms they were creating and felt that the only way they could make their audiences realise this was to choreograph no-nonsense dances. Among other things, this 'high art' stance was an attempt to stave off the inevitable jeers of uncomprehending ridicule. Having heard Isadora's clarion call of individualism, the dance pioneers of the 1930s answered with their own strong voices. Contemporary dance rebels are still doing the same.

Lucy Burge in Frederick Ashton's *Five Brahms Waltzes in the Manner of Isadora Duncan*

Fred Astaire

Born: 10th May 1899/Omaha, Nebraska
Died: 22nd June 1987/Los Angeles, California

Without a doubt the greatest popular dancer of his time, Fred Astaire made dancing look easier than walking, more natural than breathing. Dance, as he executed it, was the seemingly effortless expression of an ingratiating, suave yet basically ordinary fellow who just happened to circulate in a showbiz or high society milieu.

The son of an emigrant Austrian brewery employee, Astaire (born Frederick Austerlitz) made his professional debut at the age of five accompanying his older sister Adele on the vaudeville circuit. They worked steadily for more than a decade, eventually achieving stardom on the musical stages of Broadway and London. After Adele's premature retirement, Fred's career continued to flourish. Blessed with consummate musicality, he sang and danced to the best show music of the day: Cole Porter, Jerome Kern and the Gershwins. Astaire's understated mastery of a sophisticated mélange of jazz, tap and ballroom styles worked well in the cinema. Basing himself in Hollywood in the early 1930s, his impeccable technique as a dancer and his ceaseless choreographic invention set new and still unsurpassed standards in the art of onscreen dance.

Slender, long-legged, with a thinning hairline and a reedy (though charming) singing voice, Astaire epitomised happy-go-lucky, man-about-town elegance. His debonair nonchalance, wit and sheer grace effectively masked any difficulties caused by the rhythmic intricacies of his dancing. He was both a superlative soloist and a dream partner for a parade of leading ladies. Regardless of the extent of their talent – and a few

were ballet-trained – dancing with Astaire usually made them look their best. His most famous pairing, and rightly so, was with Ginger Rogers; even today, their dancing in films like *Top Hat*, *Swing Time* and *Shall We Dance* carries some of the charge of live performance. They made dancing seem carefree and rapturously romantic.

Astaire devised all his own choreography, more often than not assisted by dance director Hermes Pan. It was common for Astaire's dances to advance the plots of his films or to reveal character, anticipating both the Broadway work of **George Balanchine** (*On Your Toes*, 1936) and **Agnes de Mille** (*Oklahoma!*, 1943), and later movie musicals starring Gene Kelly and directed by Stanley Donen, Vincente Minnelli (both of whom worked with Astaire) and others.

Clearly, within his own somewhat narrow dynamic range, Astaire was a genius. A meticulous craftsman, he had little tolerance for high art pretensions. He continually tried to extend himself, whether that meant dancing on the ceiling, while playing golf or conducting an orchestra, or in tandem with a lithe and lovely woman. The presentation of his dances was direct, uncluttered, frequently intimate and always, in his own words, 'rehearsed down to the last flick of the wrist'.

Lineage

Astaire was the heir of Vernon and Irene Castle, the Anglo-American couple who turned ballroom dancing into a theatrical form in the 1910s, and he was also influenced by black tapper John Bubbles. Although he studied with **Anton Dolin** in the twenties, he rarely ventured into ballet movement, unlike Gene Kelly, his only serious cinematic rival. Yet Astaire's influence in that sphere has been considerable: **Mikhail Baryshnikov**, **George Balanchine** (*Who Cares?*, 1970), **Jerome Robbins** (*I'm Old-Fashioned*, 1983) and **Twyla Tharp** (*Nine Sinatra Songs*) are just a few of the choreographers who have paid tribute to Astaire verbally or onstage. American Ballroom Theatre (a company specialising in the re-creation of popular dance forms) likewise owe a debt to him. **Rudolf Nureyev**, who credits Astaire with much of the attention given to male dancers in this century, says he drew on Astaire-style partnering for a pas de deux in his 1977 **Romeo and Juliet**.

Follow-up

Astaire made thirty-one musical films over four decades, and a handful of television specials. The value of his autobiography *Steps in Time* (1959) is outweighed by Arlene Croce's *The Fred Astaire and Ginger Rogers Book* (1972) and John Mueller's exhaustive *Astaire Dancing: The Musical Films* (1985).

Denishawn

Ruth St Denis
Born: 20th January 1879/
Somerville, New Jersey
Died: 21st July 1968/Hollywood,
California

Ted Shawn
Born: 21st October 1891/Kansas
City, Missouri
Died: 9th January 1972/Orlando,
Florida

Ruth St Denis and Ted Shawn were the most charismatic, complicated and influential couple in modern dance history to date. Beneath the pseudo-oriental glamour they exuded there was something that was essentially American: a sense of showmanship, business savvy and total dedication to their individual and joint artistic pursuits. They were the most important and best paid variety performers of their era.

As a teenager, St Denis appeared in Broadway musicals and was a protégé of music-hall producer David Belasco. Inspired by an advertisement for Egyptian Deities cigarettes, she subsequently based the bulk of her long career on seductive, highly decorative interpretations of dances from India, Egypt and Asia. The titles of her dances – *Cobras*, *Incense* and *Radha*, all created in 1906 – give some indication of their exotic, perfumed atmosphere, a brand of sincere kitsch-spirituality which caught on first in Europe, where she appeared as a recitalist. Having returned to America to form a touring company, she met Ted Shawn in New York in 1914; they married the same year.

Shawn was a former theology student who had turned to dance to strengthen his legs after a bout of diphtheria. Neither he nor St Denis were particularly inventive choreographers or technically expert dancers, but both were beautifully proportioned, riveting performers. Shawn was blessed with a he-man physique, while the slim-figured St Denis, whose hair began to turn a magisterial white before she was thirty, made exquisite use of gesture, sinuous body language and the manipulation of draperies and veils.

In 1916, St Denis choreographed the Babylonian dances in the most striking section of D. W. Griffith's silent epic *Intolerance*. No wonder Hollywood studios sent their stars to Denishawn, the friendly, luxurious school she and Shawn had founded in Los Angeles in 1915. Designed to bolster body, mind and soul, the institution sprouted branches throughout America and its wildly eclectic curriculum embraced everything from ballet to all manner of Eurasian dances. Touring extensively, the company was probably the first taste of dance some provincial Americans ever had.

Denishawn lasted until 1931, as long as the couple's tumultuous marriage. After their separation, Shawn, a champion of dance as a masculine activity, purchased a farm in the Berkshire Mountains of Massachusetts and founded a community of male dancers. This group, Ted Shawn and his Men

Dancers, toured during the 1930s, presenting a variety of Shawn's dances using native American, aboriginal and folk material. 1941 – the year after the group disbanded – saw the start of Jacob's Pillow, an annual summer school/festival devoted to all forms of dance (it took its name from a large boulder on Shawn's property). Shawn served as artistic director and continued to perform and write until his death.

St Denis remained equally active into her eighties, mining the same vein of divine dance on which her fame had rested, and exploring her theory of 'music visualisation' (derived from **Isadora Duncan** and Emile Jaques-Dalcroze), in which each dancer's movements corresponded note for note to a particular instrumental part in a score.

Lineage

By extension, the work of every modern choreographer this century can be traced back to Denishawn. Nicknamed Miss Ruth and Papa Ted, they were the artistic parents of a whole brood of dancers, dancemakers and teachers. From the cradle of their school emerged **Martha Graham**, **Doris Humphrey** and Charles Weidman, the major American choreographers of the next generation. The myth and mysticism of Denishawn was filtered down through Graham to **Erick Hawkins**, **Glen Tetley**, **Anna Sokolow** and **Meredith Monk** among others, while their emphasis

Dancers from the Denishawn company performing al fresco on Laguna Beach, south of Los Angeles, circa 1926

on spectacle is present in the work of Lester Horton, Katherine Dunham and **Alvin Ailey** (whose company has performed Shawn's 1935 *Kinetic Molpai*).

Like **Isadora Duncan**, St Denis received a miscellaneous training, modified the ballet language to suit her own needs, and was celebrated on the Continent. Unlike Duncan (or that other American dance pioneer adored by Europe, Loie Fuller), St Denis triumphed on home turf too. Shawn, meanwhile, was instrumental in combatting the secondary status male dancers had been given on nineteenth-century stages, paving the way for **José Limón**, **Maurice Béjart**, **Rudolf Nureyev**, Edward Villella and others to continue the struggle.

Follow-up

Books by or about Denishawn are plentiful. St Denis published her autobiography, *An Unfinished Life* in 1939; Shawn produced a two-volume biography of his wife, subtitled *Pioneer and Prophet*, as early as 1920, and later wrote his own autobiography *One Thousand and One Night Stands* (1960) with Gray Poole. Jane Sherman's *Soaring: The Diary and Letters of a Denishawn Dancer in the Far East, 1925–26* (1976) provides an insider's view, while Suzanne Shelton's 1981 *Divine Dancer* is a deservedly award-winning life of St Denis.

Films and tapes of Denishawn are retained in the Dance Collection of New York's Library and Museum of Performing Arts, including a 1941 version of *Radha*, St Denis's breakthrough Hindu temple dance from 1906, and several short documentaries, all of which feature performance footage.

Isadora Duncan

Born: 26th May 1877/San Francisco, California
Died: 14th September 1927/Nice

Isadora, the artist freed of all restraints and expressing her inner soul to the fullest, has become an emblem of euphoric self-expression. In her own eyes a Greek goddess liberating the sophisticated capitals of the world, Duncan first came to prominence in Europe, where she had dragged her complete (fatherless) family in 1903. Driven on by her own notions of ancient Greece, she threw off her shoes, tossed out her corsets and, in defiant bare feet and loose flowing draperies, set herself up as a serious soloist performing personal interpretations of music. Her use of pieces by Beethoven, Schubert and Chopin – and the underlying belief that great dance required great music – represented a radical departure.

Isadora Duncan was first and foremost a soloist, whose dancing was based on her own intuitive feelings. Time and again her attempts to form academies ended in failure; her style, which she was unable to codify into a technique, inspired disciples rather than pupils.

In performance, Duncan aimed at creating an image of free-spirited spontaneity. She was so successful at this that her dancing often appeared to be totally improvised. The evocative way in which she stripped dance down to essentials of running, hopping and skipping may have been highly controversial, but it was also hugely successful: after settling in Paris in 1908, she toured repeatedly in Europe. However, America remained unwelcoming, partly for political reasons (sympathetic to the young Soviet Union, she set up a school in Moscow and married the poet Sergei Esenin) and partly because of moral disapproval of her very public private life.

Her liaisons with artists and millionaires, the tragedy of her two illegitimate children (drowned in a freak car accident in 1913) and her own bizarre death, strangled by her scarf when it caught in the wheel of a sportscar: the facts provided the basis for the myth. In her lifetime, she propagated her own legend in much the same way as Sarah Bernhardt had done, with a scandalous flouting of the rules. Had she been born twenty-five years later, she could have been one of the original Hollywood stars.

Despite her attempts to prove otherwise, Duncan was an instinctive artist whose personal excesses made headlines, and who, along the way, helped to popularise her radical vision of dancing as an elevated art worthy of high esteem.

Lineage

No single dance name represents so much while providing so little. Isadora Duncan *was* daring, particularly in her use of major classical scores, but her importance is now symbolic rather than demonstrable. American dancer Annabelle Gamson based a brave 1970s career on re-creations of the most famous Duncan solos, but coming after a real modern dance revolution of ideas, these programmes were at best touchingly naive. Duncan's life and art served as the subject for ballets by **José Limón** (1972), **Maurice Béjart** (1976) and **Kenneth MacMillan** (1981), but none managed to tap the essence of her personal power. The finest (simplest) tribute to her is *Five Brahms Waltzes in the Manner of Isadora Duncan*, choreographed for **Lynn Seymour** by **Frederick Ashton** in 1975 and revived for Lucy Burge by **Ballet Rambert** in 1976.

Follow-up

Duncan's gushing autobiography, *My Life*, appeared in 1927; a more reasoned work, *The Art of the Dance*, came out in 1928. Highlights of an extensive Duncan bibliography are Francis Steegmuller's *Your Isadora* (1974) and Fredrika Blair's scholarly *Isadora* (1986). Nothing puts Duncan into context better than Elizabeth Kendall's 1979 *Where She Danced*. Ken Russell's 1966 film for the BBC starring Vivien Pickles was followed by Karel Reisz's Hollywood epic (*Isadora*, 1968, with Vanessa Redgrave). *Trailblazers of Modern Dance* (1977), a Dance in America video on the American dance pioneers, includes Lynn Seymour dancing Ashton's *Waltzes*, as well as what is thought to be the only (brief) film footage of Isadora herself, dancing at a Parisian garden party.

Martha Graham

Born: 11th May 1894/Allegheny, Pennsylvania

The doyenne of modern dance, Martha Graham is a tenth-generation American who created a unique, highly personalised movement vocabulary for her own body, and codified this into a technique which is now taught the world over. Its basic motor principle focusses on the centre of the body as source of both energy and emotion. Where classical ballet stretches out in long clean lines away from an erect spine, Graham technique draws everything into the solar plexus. Her now famous 'contraction' is a sharp, quick tightening of the stomach muscles that shoves back against the spine. This impulse, curving the upper back and

drawing the body in around itself, is countered by the 'release': a burst of outward-flowing energy. Taking this to its logical extension, the dancer's body tips vertiginously off its axis or jumps in curved-over positions with the head almost touching the uplifted knees.

Graham, who grew up in California, studied and performed with **Denishawn** between 1916 and 1923 before striking out on her own. Her very early works were tinged with that school's distinctive exoticism. However, the major body of her choreography (from 1930 to 1960) seems antithetical to the decorativeness of Denishawn. *Lamentation* (1930) is a study in grief for a seated dancer encased in a hooded shroud of dark jersey. She stretches and jabs her body into angular contortions visually heightened by the strain and pull of the fabric. Graham's first major group work, *Primitive Mysteries* (1931), devised for herself and a chorus of twelve women, is a trio of ritualistic scenes as harsh as the Southwestern desert sun which inspired its creation.

The first phase of Graham's career concentrated on American themes. The most notable works are the solo *Frontier* (1935); *El Penitente* and *Letter to the World* (both 1940); and **Appalachian Spring**. *El Penitente* featured **Merce Cunningham** and **Erick Hawkins**, the first men to dance with Graham's company.

Another work from the same period is *Deaths and Entrances* (1943), nominally based on the life of the Brontë sisters, although insiders have called it an autobiography of Graham and her own sisters. In this piece, her experimentation with time sequences began to come into play. She repeatedly used this episodic format in the next phase of her career. Graham's mythic Greek dances, from *Dark Meadow* (1946) to *Clytemnestra* (1958) and beyond, all feature female protagonists gazing back over past events, reliving the significant incidents of their stories in film-like flashback. Men are invariably subordinate. They are often little more than adversarial phallic symbols who torment, goad or seduce the heroine.

Over the years, the Graham technique has become more pliant. Some of the rigid jaggedness of its origins has been smoothed down to suit the times. When Graham formulated her style it was loudly anti-ballet, but by the mid-1970s (she herself retired as a performer in 1969), a more lyric version had come to the fore. In 1975, she symbolically ended the war against ballet by creating *Lucifer* for **Rudolf Nureyev** and **Margot Fonteyn**. Subsequently, Nureyev often appeared as a guest with her company and in 1983 arranged for the Graham company to be the first outside troupe ever to dance on the stage of the Paris Opéra. This late Graham style strikes some as a deluxe, degenerate parody of her earlier principles. Where she used to work with the sculptor Isamu Noguchi, she now collaborates with fashion designer Halston; he has dressed all of her works since 1975.

Graham's contribution to the development of dance has been recognised by a number of major awards, including the Medal of Freedom (America's highest civilian honour) and the French Légion d'honneur. No less than Stravinsky in music or Picasso in painting, Graham became a forceful figurehead for modernity, and her sense of epic theatre and her exceptional abilities as a dancing actress did much to promote and popularise the art of modern dance.

Lineage

Unlike her fellow modern pioneers **Doris Humphrey**, **Hanya Holm** and **Anna Sokolow**, Graham always centred her creations around a leading soloist (usually herself). While the others stressed the communal, democratic nature of new movement, Graham never did displace the stellar hierarchy inherent in ballet.

In 1967, **Robert Cohan**, who had danced with Graham since 1946,

was invited to England to set up the **London Contemporary Dance Theatre** and School. Both his own choreography and the London training programme have direct links to the Graham technique. In addition to **Erick Hawkins** and **Merce Cunningham**, other major choreographers who danced with the Graham company and went on to develop styles of their own include Sokolow, **Glen Tetley**, **Paul Taylor** and **Dan Wagoner**.

Follow-up

The major Graham biography is Don McDonagh's 1974 *Martha Graham*. An exceptional pair of photographic records are by Barbara Morgan (1941) and Leroy Leatherman (1961), while Paul Taylor's autobiography *Private Domain* (1987) includes a lively, loving, though not always complimentary portrait of Graham. *A Dancer's World*, the 1957 half-hour film documentary in which Graham talks about her art, is illustrated with scenes from a technique class. A 1976 Dance in America video, *The Martha Graham Dance Company*, includes five works (three of them solos); the high point is a lyrically ebullient *Diversion of Angels*, a plotless work from 1948.

Appalachian Spring

One act
Choreography: Martha Graham
Music: Aaron Copland
Design: Isamu Noguchi
Premiere: 30th December 1944/ Library of Congress, Washington DC

The culmination of Graham's Americana phase, *Appalachian Spring* is one of her most hopeful and straightforward works. Buoyed up by Copland's Pulitzer Prize-winning score, it is an ideal introduction to Graham's personal notions of movement theatre.

The early nineteenth-century setting depicts the yard of a farmhouse on the edge of the frontier. The dance opens with a processional entrance (a typical Graham device) which both introduces the characters and sets the scene. A young couple, who wed and take possession of their new house, share the story with a revivalist preacher, his flock of four doting female followers, and a staunch Pioneer Woman who seems to sum up all the stoic self-reliance of the early American settlers. The events of the dance have a celebratory tone of con-secration.

The main characters each perform solos which reveal their inner feelings. During these monologues, the other characters, deep in their own thoughts, are a passive, but resonant background. The husband is a confident extrovert asserting control over his new domain. The young bride, one of the softest roles Graham ever created for herself, is excited by the new vistas opening up for her, but lacks her husband's bounding self-assurance. The Revivalist who marries them in a short, simple ceremony has the most striking solo; he 'preaches' a wedding sermon filled with hard, angular, body-thumping hellfire and brimstone. His dark visions are soothed (though not negated) by the Pioneer Woman's benediction. The dance closes with another procession as the bride and groom are left alone. She sits in a rocking chair while he stands beside her, hand on her shoulder. Posed like a typical period portrait, they gaze out at the horizon and their future life together.

During the 1930s and 40s, American themes acted as a clarion call for the first generation of modern dance choreographers. This was a genuine and logical outcome of a desire to deal with their own lives and roots, and was meant to signal a break from the shackles of the European past. Graham repeatedly drew on American subject matter: the solos

Frontier (1935) and *Salem Shore* (1943) are juxtaposed by a pair of major group works, *American Document* (1938) and *Letter to the World* (1940), which incorporate spoken texts. The latter, based on the life of poet Emily Dickinson, is one of her finest works. Graham was also inspired by the American Southwest, then still a vast, empty and virtually unknown wilderness. Both her breakthrough piece *Primitive Mysteries* and the trio *El Penitente* were influenced by the rites of Mexican Catholicism.

The original cast of *Appalachian Spring* featured both **Erick Hawkins** (whom Graham had married earlier that year) and **Merce Cunningham**. Rudolf Nureyev made several guest appearances with the Graham company in the 1970s: the Revivalist is the most notable of his Graham roles.

Lineage

Doris Humphrey created both *The Shakers* (1930) and **Day on Earth** as paeans to the American spirit. Her protégé, **José Limón**, used his Mexican-American heritage repeatedly. Both ballet and Broadway choreographers have also turned to Americana. **Eugene Loring**'s **Billy the Kid** and **Agnes de Mille**'s **Rodeo** have both become staples of the American Ballet Theatre and Joffrey Ballet repertories – de Mille also choreographed the musicals *Oklahoma!* (1943) and *Paint Your Wagon* (1951). **George Balanchine** invigorated classical technique with Americana in *Western Symphony* (1954), and in *Square Dance*, three years later, mixed the patterns of American folk dance with music by Vivaldi and Corelli, pepped up with an authentic square dance caller on stage.

Follow-up

There are two film versions of *Appalachian Spring*: Graham herself features in the 1959 film; a second version performed by members of her company was included in *The Martha Graham Dance Company* (1976).

Night Journey

One act
Choreography: Martha Graham
Music: William Schuman
Design: Isamu Noguchi
Premiere: 3rd May 1947/
Cambridge, Massachusetts

Like all of Martha Graham's Greek cycle (which ran from the mid-1940s to the early 60s), *Night Journey* is emotionally charged dance-theatre depicted through strong, percussive movement and heated by a frank, tormented sexuality. The incestuous Oedipus myth, recounted from the viewpoint of Jocasta, begins at the drama's climax – the moment before Jocasta's suicide – and then travels back in time to explore the events which have led up to this point.

Graham's manipulation of time adds bitter irony to the tragic moment of revelation. The rope which Jocasta is about to use as her noose becomes a web that ensnares husband and wife, and is simultaneously an umbilical cord tying mother to son. This is echoed in movement where (from the audience's point of view) ecstasy takes on maternal overtones. Oedipus's swaggering seduction of the older woman is akin to a boastful son showing off for his watching mother, while the couple's later lovemaking is laced with movements that replicate a mother's cradling of her child. Graham's use of movement as double-edged metaphor is at its most acute in this primal horror story.

The strength and sexual vulnerability of the feminine psyche provide the terrain of Graham's great dramas. Her characters are caught at a moment of crisis which both signals their downfall and awards them their mythic stature. Other major works in the series include *Dark Meadow* and an essay on Medea, *Cave of the Heart* (both 1946), *Errand into the Maze* (a 1947 duet for Ariadne and the Minotaur) and *Clytemnestra*, Graham's only full-evening work (1958). Like her Biblical works, the Greek dances are skilful fusions of dance and acting with design.

The set of *Night Journey* is dominated by Isamu Noguchi's raised and tilted platform supporting a bone-like structure. Suggestively pelvic, it functions as bed, throne and bier in turn. From 1944 onwards, Noguchi collaborated with Graham on some twenty works. His bold, sculptural designs form a major element in Graham's dramatic vision. He also worked with **George Balanchine** on the ballet *Orpheus*, Balanchine's 1948 version of that Greek myth.

Lineage

Graham's psychological probings have an affinity with the ballets of **Antony Tudor**, and there is a dark strand in **Paul Taylor**'s choreography that mirrors the spiritual dis-ease of society, though never with the pinpoint focus of Graham's doomed individuals. **Twyla Tharp** produced a pair of dance dramas, *When We Were Very Young* (1980) and *The Catherine Wheel* (1981), which are radically different in intent, yet directly connected to Graham's sense of theatre and her kaleidoscopic manipulation of time.

Follow-up

A 1960 film version of *Night Journey* features Graham (Jocasta), Bertram Ross (Oedipus) and Paul Taylor (the blind soothsayer Tiresias). Marcia B. Siegel analyses the work in 'The Epic Graham', a chapter from her book *The Shapes of Change* (1979).

Seraphic Dialogue

One act
Choreography: Martha Graham
Music: Norman Dello Joio
Design: Isamu Noguchi
Premiere: 8th May 1955/ANTA Theater, New York City

The lone heroine in conflict with the world around her is a favourite Graham theme: here her chosen subject is Joan of Arc at the moment of beatification. The piece opens with Joan kneeling in front of an altar window. This huge, but exquisitely delicate Noguchi sculpture is a brass-rod tracery, framing Joan's 'beloved voices', St Michael, St Catherine and St Margaret. Then three women, wearing voluminous velvet cloaks, enter in procession. They represent Joan herself as Maid, Warrior and Martyr. The Maid has a frolicsome, light-hearted solo that ends abruptly when she first hears the Voices; her fear is converted to exultation as she whips off her headscarf and waves it in the air like a banner. Then the saints present The Warrior with a sword (part of the tracery structure). St Michael descends from his perch to lead her into battle; urged on by his exhortations, she rides on his back as though he were her charger. The Martyr is in turn presented with a tracery cross. Her agony turns the cross into a crutch which she uses to drag herself across the stage. Finally, Joan, now dressed in gold, ascends the altar and steps into the sculpture (into heaven) with St Michael standing protectively over her.

Martha Graham used the dramatic device of fracturing one woman into different characters as early as her 1940 *Letter to the World*, in which the reclusive and eccentric poet Emily Dickinson is portrayed by two women: One Who Dances and One Who Speaks. Towards the end of her exceptionally long performance career (she continued to appear in her own works until the age of seventy-five), physical necessity forced Graham to explore the concept of an older woman who reflects on her life passing across the stage like a remembered dream. *Seraphic Dialogue*, a work in which Graham herself never appeared, is perhaps the fullest and most radiant example of this technique.

Lineage

Maurice Béjart, the most theatrical of modern European choreographers, uses the split-personality device in his sprawling work *Nijinsky – Clown de Dieu*, based on the life of **Vaslav Nijinsky**, in which the hero is played by no less than five different dancers. In a more abstract manner, some of the later **Merce Cunningham** pieces allude to this technique. This is particularly notable in *Quartet* (1982), where Cunningham hovers in the background as four dancers perform steps that seem to be thoughts issuing directly from the choreographer's brain.

Follow-up

A 1969 US film version of *Seraphic Dialogue* features the Martha Graham Dance Company.

Erick Hawkins

Born: May 1909/Trinidad, Colorado

Erick Hawkins is the maverick medicine man of modern dance, a cult artist and teacher whose calm, carefully thought-out dances are as likely to elicit boos as bravos. He was one of the first ballet-trained dancers to switch exclusively to the modern style.

After majoring in Greek at Harvard, Hawkins studied with **Mary Wigman**'s pupil Harald Kreutzberg and at the School of American Ballet, where **George Balanchine** considered him to be a promising neophyte choreographer. In the mid to late 1930s, he danced with American Ballet and Lincoln Kirstein's Ballet Caravan, both forerunners of **New York City Ballet**. He was the first male to dance with **Martha Graham** (from 1938 to 1951), originating roles in her *Letter to the World*, **Appalachian Spring** and **Night Journey** among others. He was also, for two years, Graham's husband. The dissolution of their marriage marked the formation of his own, radically different troupe in conjunction with composer Lucia Dlugoszewski and designer Ralph Dorazio. As Hawkins' continuous collaborator, Dlugoszewski frequently performs her music on stage (using her own delicate handmade instruments). Hawkins boasts of never having performed without live music.

As a dancer, Hawkins has been noted for his tender, virile virtuosity. The fluid dances he creates may be inspired by nature (clouds, constellations, butterflies, leopards) but they retain a quality of ceremonial abstraction. The Hawkins style, in pieces like the 1957 *Here and Now with Watchers*, is a subtle blend of weight displacement, balance, imbalance and stasis. His work features cushioned leaps, big melting jumps and a curiously innocent eroticism which arises from the dancers' occasional near-nakedness (in, for example, *Angels of the Inmost Heaven*, 1971). Sometimes, however, they don strange, surreal masks and costumes. Designed with an almost oriental minimalism – although Hawkins is actually of American Indian descent – his dances are as economic and polished as haiku. Some find them exquisite, others call them precious. Hawkins' followers claim that the best way to view his work is to shed preconceptions and stop looking for what is not there.

Lineage

Hawkins' ascetic aesthetic is a sincere attempt to transcend both the geometric dogmas of ballet and the heavy drama of the first generation of American dancemakers. Whereas **Martha Graham** uses the pelvis as a central, sexual source of tension and conflict, Hawkins is a passive ritualist for whom limbs and spine extend like free-flowing weights from the pelvic fulcrum (**Merce Cunningham** also broke away from the strictures of her kind of dance). Neither Hawkins' dancers nor the members of **Pilobolus Dance Theatre** have qualms about appearing nearly nude on stage; but whereas Pilobolus literally turns the body beautiful on its head, Hawkins simultaneously ignores and, by implication, celebrates it in an asexual way. Although **Dana Reitz** has a less contrived approach than Hawkins, her work has engendered a similar cult following.

Follow-up

Hawkins writes about his art in one chapter of *Modern Dance: Seven Statements of Belief*, edited by Selma Jeanne Cohen (1966).

Hanya Holm

Born: 3rd March 1893/Worms, Germany

Hanya Holm's career as a dancer was eclipsed by her skill as a choreographer, particularly for the musical comedy stage. She is best known as a brilliant teacher, who managed to graft a distinctly American energy onto her own European modern dance background.

Born Johanna Eckert, she was first a pupil of the music and movement theoretician Emile Jaques-Dalcroze. Throughout the 1920s, she worked as both teacher and dancer with the great German innovator **Mary Wigman**, becoming Head of Faculty in Wigman's Dresden Central School, and emigrating to America in 1931 to establish a branch of the school in New York. The offshoot flourished, and so did Holm, to a degree that made it necessary for her to open her own studio in 1936. There, as teacher and choreographer, she adapted the disciplines of Wigman's approach, with its emphasis on space as an integral part of movement, to the freer rhythms and speed of American dance. Grounded in sound general principles, Holm's teaching favoured creative exploration over rigid formulas.

The pinnacle of Holm's concert-hall choreography was *Trend*, an epic 1937 depiction of a society caught in a cataclysmic struggle with its own false values. This ambitious, rarely performed dance, with music by Wallingford Riegger and Edgard Varèse, featured a collective protagonist: nearly three dozen women occupying a three-dimensional stage space of platforms connected by steps and ramps. Structurally the piece consisted of five episodes centring around, but never dominated by, a soloist. Its action came in an unbroken state of continuous flux. There were bold entrances and exits as individuals or contrapuntal masses of bodies hurled themselves in long, sustained sweeps across the performing area. Frequent fluid changes of weight, direction and dimension were intended to give an element of rhythmic expression to the conflicting social forces on view.

However, dance for Holm was more than a tool for dramatic social criticism. Her work could equally be lyrical, humorous and eminently popular, as she demonstrated in her award-winning choreography for hit Broadway musicals like *Kiss Me, Kate* (1948), *My Fair Lady* (1956) and *Camelot* (1960).

Lineage

Holm aligned the sense of musicianship she had acquired from her studies with Dalcroze to an instinctive, yet almost scientific, understanding of form gleaned from her long association with **Mary Wigman**. Like Wigman, **Isadora Duncan**, **Ruth St Denis**, **Martha Graham** and **Doris Humphrey**, Holm both taught and made dance: her own pupils, in turn, included **Alwin Nikolais** and **Glen Tetley**. She was also one of the first proponents of the Dance Notation Bureau, a service organisation promoting the kinetic recording systems of **Rudolf von Laban**. The late Lee Theodore's American Dance Machine (dedicated to the preservation of the dances of the American musical) includes a segment of Holm's *My Fair Lady* choreography in its repertory.

Follow-up

Walter Sorell produced a life of Holm (*The Biography of an Artist*) in 1969, while Sali Ann Kriegsman's vast, exhaustive *Modern Dance in America: The Bennington Years* (1981) contains numerous references to Holm, including lengthy descriptions of *Trend* and other works. There is a 25-minute film of her surrealistically designed dance about alchemy, *The Golden Fleece*, in which Holm plays the element mercury.

Doris Humphrey

Born: 17th October 1895/Oak Park, Illinois
Died: 29th December 1958/New York City

Doris Humphrey, as a choreographer, performer and one of the major pedagogues of American modern dance, was the person most responsible for codifying the radical ideas of the 1920s and 30s into a recognisable and usable vocabulary of movement. While her contemporary **Martha Graham** was making the art form popular to a wider public, Humphrey was conscientiously laying the foundations which would sustain modern dance as a legitimate style.

Unlike Graham, Humphrey did not evolve her technique as a showcase built around her own performing talents. Instead, she focussed on group movement as the ideal format for expressing her concepts. These theories are dominated by a belief in the ability of dance to function in a contemporary and independent way. She pared away all the trimmings (even devising several dances to be performed without the aid of music) and although her structures often involve complex contrapuntal patterns, they are always presented in a clear and logical fashion.

Humphrey's movement technique is based on what she called 'the arc between two deaths'. These 'deaths' are both positions of stasis: standing up straight, or lying flat on the ground. Every movement, each shift of weight, was seen as a fall towards, or a recovery from, these two absolute positions. The drama of her movement style (felt by the dancer, sensed by the viewer) is found in the displacement of weight as the body either gives in to or strives to resist the pull of gravity.

Her theories and her movement technique are demonstrated in works ranging from the choric abstraction of *Water Study* (1928), *The Shakers* (1931) and *New Dance* (1935), to the dramatic intensity of *Lament for Ignacio Sánchez Mejías* (1946) and the universal humanism of **Day on Earth**.

After teaching dance in Chicago as a teenager, Humphrey went to California for a 1917 summer course at **Denishawn**, but ended up spending the next decade performing, choreographing and teaching for them. During this time she worked closely with Ruth St Denis (Martha Graham, who terminated her Denishawn connections in 1923, was more closely linked with Ted Shawn). After years of touring, including an arduous eighteen-month stint in the Far East, Humphrey and her colleague Charles Weidman broke away from Denishawn to form their own school and company in New York. Known as Humphrey-Weidman, the group gave its first concerts in 1928 and continued into the early 1940s with Weidman's comic pieces acting as a leavening agent for Humphrey's more serious-minded works.

From 1934, Humphrey, Weidman, Graham and **Hanya Holm** all taught pioneering summer sessions at Bennington College in Vermont, the first time modern dance had been systematically included in a university curriculum. In addition, Humphrey acted as the major teacher at the American Dance Festival at Connecticut College. Both these programmes mixed student classes with premieres by the professional companies of the instructors, and Humphrey created some of her most significant works during these summer schools, including the 1936 *With My Red Fires*.

Suffering from arthritis of the hip, Humphrey was forced to stop dancing in 1944, but continued to choreograph. When her protégé **José Limón** established his own company two years later, he appointed her artistic director, a position which allowed her to go on developing her ideas and which she held until her death.

Lineage

Humphrey's impact has been prodigious. She taught two generations of American modern dancers and her book on theory (*The Art of Making Dances*) is still regarded as one of the most lucid documents on choreography. **José Limón** continued and expanded her ideas, and several Humphrey works remain in that company's repertory. Her formal ideas on composition and her use of group dynamics have been so thoroughly integrated into contemporary dance that many young choreographers and modern audiences no longer recognise or even know their original source.

Follow-up

The Art of Making Dances was first published in 1959; an unfinished autobiography served as the opening sections of Selma Jeanne Cohen's *Doris Humphrey: An Artist First* (1972). Marcia B. Siegel's *Days on Earth* (1987) is an informed survey of Humphrey's career and creations, and seven of her dances are discussed at length in Siegel's 1979 *The Shapes of Change*.
The largest collection of Humphrey works on film resides in the Dance Collection at the New York Public Library.

Day on Earth

One act
Choreography: Doris Humphrey
Music: Aaron Copland (Piano Sonata, 1941)
Premiere: 10th May 1947/Beaver County Day School, Brookline, Massachusetts

Simple and monumental, this cyclical saga of the common man is one of Humphrey's most concise statements. *Day on Earth* is devoid of mimed story-telling, and is presented without any sort of descriptive setting. Performed by a man, two women and a child, it evokes images of work, love, marriage, family, death and generational rebirth. The only piece of scenery is a cube which the dancers sit on when resting. The sole prop is a large piece of fabric. Its clear, bold movement is so apt that Humphrey's pure dance steps crystallise into narrative.

The man opens the dance, moving from the cube to cross the stage on a diagonal line. His bold, thrusting arm gestures suggest planting, sowing, harvesting.

A sprightly young woman, whose steps are filled with skips and light leaps, momentarily distracts the man from his work, but, although they have fun playing together, the man is drawn back to his tasks. Another woman, weightier and more substantial, then joins him: their duet is a true wedding of similar movement qualities. Walking to the cube, they lift the fabric from the floor to reveal a child. The 'new parents' dance happily with her, and then return to their duties. When the child leaves the stage, the adults are plunged into grief. After consoling the woman, the man returns to his work with a new ferocity. The woman slowly, tenderly folds up the cloth.

Finally, the three female dancers line up behind the working man and form a processional back to the cube. The dance concludes with a simple inversion of its opening image: the child sits alone on the cube as the adults lie down and pull the cloth over their bodies.

The elegant economy of gesture in *Day on Earth* allows the audience to create the story. The dancers neither point to their ring finger nor clasp their hands to their heart (as characters traditionally do in story ballets). No one mimes the agonies of dying: the little girl exits, that is all. It is the quality of movement performed by the man and the woman left behind which imparts a sense of sadness and 'tells' us what has happened. Few other dance creations are so finely poised between abstraction and reality.

Lineage

José Limón, who danced the role of the man in the original production (premiered by his eponymous dance company), sought to expand Humphrey's technique in several dances such as **The Moor's Pavane**. Many choreographers, from **Anna Sokolow** to **Paul Taylor** and **Twyla Tharp**, have also created works that strive to convey dramatic atmosphere without directly relating a story. Meaning through movement without recourse to pantomime is one of the basic tenets of modern dance and contemporary ballet. In *Ivesiana* (1954), **George Balanchine** uses the dissonant music of Charles Ives to convey the darker sides of urban life. **Frederick Ashton**'s 1968 *Enigma Variations*, to Elgar's gallery of musical portraits, depicts the complex relations of a group of Edwardian intellectuals, again with no 'story'. The **Kenneth MacMillan** works **Song of the Earth**, *Requiem* (1977) and *Gloria* (1980), to music by Mahler, Fauré and Poulenc, also belong to this emotionally suggestive genre.

Follow-up

Three film versions of *Day on Earth* date from 1959, 1972 and 1975; the work is described in detail in Marcia B. Siegel's *The Shapes of Change* (1979).

Kurt Jooss

Born: 12th January 1901/ Wasseralfingen, near Stuttgart
Died: 22nd May 1979/Heilbronn, near Stuttgart

In his work as a choreographer and teacher, Kurt Jooss strove to develop a socially-conscious form of dance drama which streamlined the excesses of ballet technique, but did not abandon its essential logic or rigorous discipline. After studying at the Stuttgart Academy of Music, Jooss worked with **Rudolf von Laban**, and quickly became his star pupil. In 1924, Jooss started to work as a ballet master in Münster before moving to Essen three years later to found the Folkwang School and form a company, the Folkwang Tanzbühne, which won a major prize with **The Green Table** at a 1932 choreographic competition in Paris.

Another of his strongest works, *The Big City*, received its premiere four months later. The ballet is a perfect distillation of Jooss's principles. Although the dancers often move in large group patterns, their individual characters have visible links to the common man of the day. Their seemingly natural movement (the Jooss ballerinas never danced on point, for example) efficiently conveys a story of how the honest people are corrupted and defeated by immoral urban opportunists.

Jooss always insisted on calling himself a ballet choreographer. The choice of words was deliberate: even though his works now feel very much part of 1930s *art moderne*, it is still clear that his reforms were aimed at the decadent and dated mannerisms of ballet, rather than ballet itself.

Along with his company, Jooss was forced out of Germany by the Nazis and settled in England in 1934, establishing a base first at Dartington Hall in Devon, and subsequently in Cambridge; during the war years Ballets Jooss toured under the auspices of the ENSA cultural programme. In 1949, Jooss returned to his Essen school, where he worked until his retirement in 1968.

Lineage

Jooss's notion of reforming ballet, rather than wanting to jettison it completely in favour of modern dance, echoes the stance taken by **Michel Fokine** during his years with the Ballets Russes. One of the most important aspects of Jooss's works is that they are not simply prosaic pageants using everyday movements, but are first and foremost creations which express their ideas in recognisable dance terms. Unlike the American modern dance pioneers, who remade dance from the ground up and to suit their own idiosyncratic styles, Jooss never chose to move all the way to abstraction. The psychological ballets of **Antony Tudor** are the closest that Anglo-American art ever came to his philosophy. One of the last Jooss pupils was **Pina Bausch**: she has

dropped his focus on ballet, but continues to express his ideal of dance as a voice for the common man.

Follow-up

The Joffrey Ballet's 1976 Dance in America video featuring *The Green Table* also includes documentary footage and commentary by Jooss's daughter Anna Markard. The major book is *The New Ballet: Kurt Jooss and His Work* (1946) by A. V. Coton; it includes 64 pages of production photos with many costume sketches and drawings.

The Green Table

One act
Choreography: Kurt Jooss
Music: Fritz Cohen
Design: Hein Heckroth
Premiere: 3rd July 1932/Théâtre des Champs-Elysées, Paris

An Expressionist dance of death, *The Green Table* (original title *Der Grüne Tisch*) exposes the horrors of war in a compelling narrative told with the utmost simplicity. The dance pits the oily machinations of bureaucrats and racketeers against the folk-like monumentality of the people.

The work opens with bald-pated, rubber-masked diplomats arguing across a foreshortened green baize table. These greedy manipulators are made twice as unctuous by the infectious tinkly piano tune to which they bicker and bargain.

In a blackout, the diplomats are replaced by the looming figure of Death (helmeted and dressed in a skeleton costume). His stomping, clench-fisted march becomes a recurring motif as, in scene after scene, he reappears to claim his victims: a soldier, a standard-bearer, an old woman, a female

Kurt Jooss in front of the central props from
The Green Table

partisan. At one point, Death
becomes a benevolent angel when
he takes a young girl from a
soldiers' brothel. The piece
culminates in 'The Aftermath', a
parody of the medieval dance of
death, in which the spectre leads
his victims across the stage in a
snaking line. The ballet ends back
where it began, with the diplomats.
They continue their treacherous
negotiations as if nothing has been
changed, nothing settled.

Lineage

The humanist aspirations
expressed in *The Green Table* are
a common theme to many
twentieth-century artworks, even
when the horrors of war are not the
direct subject. Anti-war ideals are
present in **Antony Tudor**'s 1963
Echoing of Trumpets, **Kenneth
MacMillan**'s First World War dirge

Gloria, and **Jirí Kylián**'s all-male
Soldiers' Mass (1980), while the
partisan version of **The Firebird** by
Maurice Béjart turns totalitarian
resistance into a modern myth. In
addition, American modern dance
choreographers such as **Anna
Sokolow** (in *Dreams*, 1961) and **José
Limón** (*Missa Brevis*, 1958)
repeatedly asked audiences to
examine their own consciences in
relation to the dehumanising
effects of war.

Follow-up

The Joffrey Ballet performs *The
Green Table* in a 1976 Dance in
America video.

Stagings

1 **Kurt Jooss**/Dutch National
  Ballet/1965
2 **Anna Markard**/Joffrey Ballet/1967
  (also Northern Dance Theatre,
  now Northern Ballet, 1973 and
  Lyon Opéra Ballet, 1983)

Rudolf von Laban

Born: 15th December 1879/
Pozsony, now Bratislava
Died: 1st July 1958/Weybridge,
Surrey

The best known of today's dance notation systems is the one developed by Rudolf von Laban, often acknowledged as the father of modern dance theory. In his youth, he studied painting, acting and ballet in Paris and came into contact with a variety of ethnic dance forms as well as the studies of movement theoretician François Delsarte. From 1910 he was the founder or director of various schools, theatres and institutions in several major German cities.
In addition to his development of a highly popular and influential amateur organisation called Bewegungschöre (movement choirs), he created dances for the 1936 Berlin Olympic Games. Shortly afterwards, he emigrated to England to concentrate on modern educational dance and the use of movement in industrial settings. This research was formalised through the creation in 1946 of the Art of Movement Studio (with his close collaborator Lisa Ullmann). The centre's courses were later incorporated into the curriculum of Goldsmith's College, University of London.
  Von Laban's theories vastly outweigh his significance as a dancer or choreographer. His inquiring, analytical mind sought a way of ordering the principles of human movement into a consistent philosophy. From his studies he evolved such systems as choreutics (the relationship of the body to the space around it) and eukinetics (a formulation of all possible types and directions of bodily movement) and an understanding of the connection between psychology and motion.

His accurate, detailed system of Labanotation, first published in the 1920s, is written from a dancer's point of view. This uses a set of graphic symbols arranged on a vertical staff which represents the human body and allows for a continuous indication of movement. The timing of a given move is denoted by the length of the symbols. Labanotation is commonly recognised as a means of both copyright protection and reconstruction of choreography; its use is cultivated by the Dance Notation Bureau (founded in New York in 1940 by, among others, **Hanya Holm**), the Laban Centre, London, and the Kinetographic Institute in Essen.

Lineage

The history of recording movement through symbols on paper stretches back several centuries: Pierre Beauchamps (who taught dancing to Louis XIV), **Arthur Saint-Léon** and Margaret Morris (author of *My Life in Movement*, 1969) are just some of the many dancers, choreographers and teachers who devised codification systems. In the mid-1950s Rudolf and Joan Benesh, the latter a dancer with the Royal Ballet, developed a system called choreology, using a horizontal five-line musical staff. Adopted by the Royal Ballet, it is now employed by ballet companies the world over. Noa Eshkol and Abraham Wachmann are responsible for an alternative, mathematical system named after Eshkol and based on the circular nature of all anatomical movement.
  Although not responsible for notation systems themselves, the French-born François Delsarte, the Swiss Emile Jaques-Dalcroze and the German **Oskar Schlemmer** likewise propounded scientific approaches to movement. **Ted Shawn** was a advocate of Delsarte's theories, while **Mary Wigman** and **Kurt Jooss** were pupils of both von Laban and Dalcroze. Through them and Dalcroze pupil **Marie Rambert**, this principle of aligning sound with rhythmic movement had an

influence on thousands of dancers, actors and musicians.

Follow-up

One of the best Labanotation books is von Laban's own *A Life for Dance*, issued in an English-language version forty years after its 1935 publication. Ann Hutchinson Guest's *Your Move: A New Approach to the Study of Movement and Dance* (1983) is also useful.

José Limón

Born: 12th January 1908/Culiacán, Mexico
Died: 2nd December 1972/ Flemington, New Jersey

Few choreographers have had such an immediate and broad-based impact as José Limón. During the 1950s and 60s in particular, his company was an unparalleled standard-bearer for American modern dance.
A powerful and striking man of Mexican-American lineage, Limón (like **Paul Taylor**, **David Gordon** and **Richard Alston**) originally intended to be a painter. After moving from Los Angeles to New York, he was so impressed with a performance by German modernist Harald Kreutzberg that he decided to become a dancer. In 1930, he began studying at the **Doris Humphrey**–Charles Weidman studio, where he became personally involved with Weidman but eventually married the company's designer Pauline Lawrence.
Limón danced with Humphrey-Weidman throughout the thirties. Deeply affected by the philosophy of Doris Humphrey, he began making his own dances as early as 1931, but it was only in 1946, after a Second World War stint in the US Navy, that he formed his own performance ensemble. By this time, his mentor Humphrey had retired as a dancer. Limón asked her to become the artistic director of his company. This was an unprecedented step in the highly individualised world of American modern dance, but his respect for Humphrey's talents benefited both of them. He learned from her superior sense of craftsmanship, while Humphrey was presented with a company which could continue to express her ideas.
In 1950, Limón was invited by Ruth Page to share a Paris bill with her own Chicago-based ballet company; Limón's dancers performed **The Moor's Pavane** and *La Malinche*. The season was a misunderstood débâcle, but is noteworthy as the first European appearance by a major American modern dance company. This breaching of the European opera-house mentality would bear fruit in succeeding tours by **Martha Graham**, Paul Taylor and **Merce Cunningham**, and in 1957 the Limón company crossed the Atlantic again for a four-month, nine-country tour opening in London (where Graham had made her European debut in 1954). In addition, the Limón troupe made several highly successful tours of Mexico and South America.
As a choreographer, Limón is the great humanist of the modern movement. His classic work, *The Moor's Pavane*, is typical of his approach; other major pieces include *The Traitor* (1954, based on Judas's betrayal of Christ), *Missa Brevis* (1958, on the survival of faith in post-war Eastern Europe), *There is a Time* (1956, based on the passage from Ecclesiastes), *The Unsung* (a 1970 all-male work danced in silence, honouring eight great American Indian warriors) and *La Malinche* (1949), a dramatic trio based on the true story of the Indian woman who served as translator for Cortez during his conquests in Mexico.
The José Limón Dance Company became the first American dance troupe to survive the death of its founder. Prior to this, it had been taken for granted that a modern choreographer's work was dependent on his or her own physical presence. The fact that

Limón's company outlived him was an important step in establishing the idea of American modern dance as a legitimate art form rather than merely the idiosyncratic vision of individual artists.

Lineage

Limón's choreographic style stems from the influence of **Doris Humphrey**. It is filled with big, fluid movements that use a natural sense of weight as its central dramatic drive. Throughout his life, he continued to deal with large passions, and during the radical 1960s ran the danger of seeming out of step, but he refused to acknowledge the viability of the new abstract experimentation of the post-modern generation. Both Louis Falco and Jennifer Muller danced with Limón in the 1960s and went on to form companies that achieved great international popularity.

Follow-up

The two Doris Humphrey biographies by Marcia B. Siegel and Selma Jeanne Cohen (see page 74) contain biographical information on Limón; Daniel Lewis has written *The Illustrated Dance Technique of José Limón* (1984).

The Moor's Pavane

One act
Choreography: José Limón
Music: Henry Purcell, arranged by Simon Sadoff
Design: Pauline Lawrence
Premiere: 17th August 1949/ Connecticut College, New London, Connecticut

The poetic dramas of Shakespeare and the formal restraints of the courtly pavane are not attitudes normally associated with the raw energy and individualism at the centre of the American modern dance movement, but José Limón wedded these two elements into one of the most successful and enduring works of the genre. In his version of *Othello*, Limón stripped the story to its essentials and then set it within the structure and the strictures of an Elizabethan dance form.

There are only four characters – The Moor, His Wife, His Friend and His Friend's Wife – and the entire plot is contained within the attitudes of the characters in relation to each other. The fundamental themes of jealousy and betrayal are seen and felt but never explicitly explained. Desdemona's handkerchief remains the crux of the piece, but without prior knowledge of Shakespeare's play, a member of the audience would find it difficult to extract the storyline of *Othello* from Limón's dance. That same person, however, could easily identify what makes these characters tick.

The Moor's dignity, with its undertones of self-importance; Iago's manipulative deviousness; Desdemona's fatally naïve and helpless innocence; Emilia's none-too-pure complicity in the theft of the handkerchief: all are depicted through movement. The Moor has a proud, manly gait, while the spidery shiftiness of His Friend is evil incarnate. When he whispers his insidious secrets, he all but perches on the Moor's shoulders like some malevolent omen of doom.

The formal dance music adds its own tension as the rhythms of the pavane keep calling the quartet back into its ritualistic patterns. This contrast – between the public manners of the dance and the internal emotions of the characters – is an inspired choreographic device. It both reveals the interior sufferings of the characters and shows us their vain attempts to hide private feelings within the public framework.

The whole approach is summed up in the final moment of the work, when the Moor, having strangled his wife, commits suicide. The

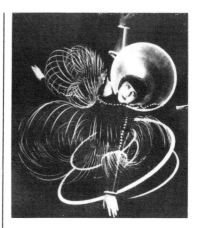

A double exposure of the Spiral Costume and the Wire Figure from the Bauhaus production of Oskar Schlemmer's *Triadic Ballet*

Friend and his wife veil this private tragedy from the public eyes of the audience with a gracious bow, during which they spread out Emilia's voluminous velvet skirt like a theatre curtain, to mask the dead.

The Moor's Pavane became one of the first modern dances to make a successful transition to the ballet repertory. Great interpreters who have danced the role of the Moor (originally taken by Limón) include **Erik Bruhn** and **Rudolf Nureyev**.

Lineage

Shakespeare has long been a source of choreographic inspiration. Prokofiev's score for **Romeo and Juliet** (some of the most splendid dance music of the twentieth century) has led to a multitude of stagings. There are also full-length versions of *A Midsummer Night's Dream* (**George Balanchine** 1962, **Heinz Spoerli** 1975, **John Neumeier** 1977), *The Taming of the Shrew* (**John Cranko**, 1969) and **The Tempest** (**Glen Tetley**).

Condensing Shakespeare plots down to one-act dance works is less often done. Of these, the most successful are **Frederick Ashton**'s **The Dream** and the **Robert Helpmann** version of *Hamlet* (1942). **Antony Tudor** also choreographed a one-act version of *Romeo and Juliet* in 1943.

Follow-up

The Limón company features in a 1950 film version; other television renditions date from 1953 (US), 1957 (UK) and 1973 (Sweden).

Stagings

1 **José Limón**/American Ballet Theatre/1970
2 **José Limón with Daniel Lewis and Edward De Soto**/National Ballet of Canada/1972
3 **José Limón with Daniel Lewis and Jennifer Scanlon**/Royal Swedish Ballet/1972

Oskar Schlemmer

Born: 4th September 1888/Stuttgart
Died: 13th April 1943/Baden-Baden

Oskar Schlemmer encompassed many roles, as painter, sculptor, teacher, theatre theorist, designer, dancer and dancemaker. He was one of the leading lights of the Bauhaus, the German school of design, architecture and crafts in the 1920s. As 'Master of Form', he headed up the sculpture studio, which developed into a theatre workshop. His explorations of form, light, geometry, colour and motion resulted in a series of 'archi-tectonic dances' that brilliantly illustrated the relationship between the human figure and abstract space.

As their titles – *Space Dance*, *Hoop Dance*, *Gesture Dance* – suggest, the dances (all created between 1926 and 1929) are simple, yet their scope is wide. Sometimes the effect is stunning: in *Pole Dance* a black-clad dancer, against a black backdrop, manipulates a battery of white sticks attached to his or her own limbs. In *Block Play*, the emphasis is on play, with an amusing, satirical edge. Three of Schlemmer's standard puppet-style figures, encased in helmet-like masks and padded, primary-coloured costuming to unify their appearance, manipulate large, soft building blocks. Schlemmer never felt that such strange garb dehumanised the dancers into mere mechanical robots. For him, the use of these costumes was a liberating force, since it magnified the dancers' movements and underlined their essential humanity.

Triadic Ballet, Schlemmer's best known work, is his most sustained experiment in the application of kinetic, geometric strategies to the human figure, or Abstrakter Tanz. The original Bauhaus production, staged in Stuttgart in 1922, but prefigured by earlier versions in 1911 and 1916, consisted of twelve dances, eighteen costumes and three performers (two male, one female) divided into three colour-coordinated sections: lemon yellow, pink and black, respectively corresponding to what has been called 'a gay burlesque, a solemn ceremony and a mystical fantasy'.

The result was far more a designer's than a choreographer's dream. The piece's simple, repetitive movements – later set to Paul Hindemith's mechanical organ music – were less memorable than the costumes, some of which appear to have been based on the silhouette of a ballerina's tutu (about as close to classical dance as Schlemmer wanted to get). Made up of spirals, triangles, cones and ovoids, they suggest a gathering of weird kitchen utensils and malevolent nursery toys inside a futuristic pinball machine.

Since 1982, New York dancer and movement therapist Debra McCall and colleagues have meticulously recreated Schlemmer's Bauhaus Dances for museum and concert-stage performances throughout America and Europe. In their preparation, they were closely counselled by Andreas Weininger, a former student and performer in Schlemmer's theatre course. The dances represent curious and fascinating footnotes to modern dance history.

Lineage

Léonide Massine's attempt in **Parade** to translate the principles of Cubist art into theatrical terms echoes Schlemmer's endeavours. Even earlier, **Michel Fokine** had used mechanical figures in a more overtly anthropomorphic and certainly more narrative sense in **Petrushka**. Schlemmer cited as influences theatrical designer Gordon Craig, a great believer in the use of masks and inanimate figures onstage, and E. T. A. Hoffman, one of whose stories was the basis for **Coppélia**. The influence of Schlemmer's ideas is evident in the work of many modern dance/theatre experimentalists who are interested in examining the relationship between movement dynamics, spatial concepts, props and the visual arts, particularly **Alwin Nikolais**, **Meredith Monk** and **Robert Wilson**.

Follow-up

Lincoln Kirstein's 1970 *Movement and Metaphor* contains costume sketches for *Triadic Ballet* and an informative essay about Schlemmer's work. Walter Gropius, director of the Bauhaus, edited *The Theatre of the Bauhaus* (1925). Schlemmer's widow Tut served as artistic advisor for a 1967 film reconstruction of *Triadic Ballet*.

Anna Sokolow

Born: 9th February 1915/Hartford, Connecticut

Uncompromising about her role as an artist with a social conscience, Anna Sokolow is a soapbox choreographer who, in her hope for a better world, slaps us in the face with man's inhumanity to man.

Her concerns range from the Spanish Civil War to the Holocaust and the increasing depersonalisation of contemporary urban life.

Her parents were immigrant Polish Jews; she grew up on the Lower East Side of New York City and left home at fifteen to become one of the original **Martha Graham** dancers. She began to make her own work as early as 1934, but it was in 1939, when she was invited to teach in Mexico City, that she found her own voice. For the next decade she spent half of each year in Mexico, where she formed that country's first modern dance company, La Paloma Azul. Her own troupe, the Lyric Theatre Company, was formed in New York in 1962, but was later disbanded. Since the sixties, Sokolow has been a freelance teacher and choreographer (she stopped performing in 1954), travelling around the world and working in the Dance Department of the Juilliard School of Music in New York.

Sokolow's major works include **Rooms**, *Lyric Suite* (1953), set to Alban Berg's twelve-tone score of the same name, and *Dreams* (1961). These dreams are really nightmares loaded with imagery stemming from Nazi oppression. Dancers, trapped in the prisons of their own souls, are caught in stark scenes of horror and death and scrutinised by blind, indifferent 'angels', who calmly step on the dying without seeming to feel the squirming bodies twitching beneath their feet.

Lineage

Sokolow's commitment and scathing honesty have left her something of an outsider, and the bleak brutality of her works does not always appeal to audiences (it is perhaps significant that she worked for a while with Samuel Beckett). During the 1960s and 70s, whenever a choreographer made a dour, deeply felt work, he or she was liable to be accused of 'pulling an Anna Sokolow'. Her notions of alienation and confrontation are linked to such post-modern choreographers as **Pina Bausch**,

William Forsythe and Lloyd Newson, director of London's **DV8 Physical Theatre**. They all owe a debt to her unflinching exploration of modern man as a victim of his own society. This confrontational mode has also served such diverse artists as **Jerome Robbins** and 'angry' black choreographers from **Alvin Ailey** to **Bill T. Jones**. Another of Sokolow's most lasting contributions has been her pioneering work with progressive jazz composers, notably Teo Macero.

Follow-up

Sokolow's succinct 1966 summation of modern art, 'The Rebel and the Bourgeois', was re-published in *The Vision of Modern Dance*, edited by Jean Morrison Brown (1979). A black and white film from 1966, *Anna Sokolow Directs 'Odes'*, shows both rehearsal and performance of a work set to the music of Edgard Varèse.

Rooms

One act
Choreography: Anna Sokolow
Music: Kenyon Hopkins
Premiere: 24th February 1955/ 92nd Street YM-YWHA, New York City

This classic of alienation is hard to watch. Its naked emotions and structural simplicity carry the force of body blows delivered by a prize fighter. The driving screech of Hopkins' jazz score increases the urban tension.

The eight dancers are totally isolated from the outside world, either incapable of coping with it or too frightened to try. When the lights come up, each is sitting on a chair which becomes his or her lifeline. These chairs represent the separate rooms confining them as efficiently as though they were in prison cells. The tense anxiety and fierce intensity of feeling is produced through blunt, angular movement: arms reach out, heads flop to the side, bodies rock back and forth in tight frustration. Each of these neurotics is caught on a treadmill of his or her own making. They dance a set of traps exposed to the audience through a series of individual moments. The sections cover a diversity of desperation: 'Alone', 'Dream' (a nightmare), 'Escape' (a woman tries to fantasise a sexual encounter by conjuring a lover out of a second empty chair), 'Going' (a ferociously active man is locked in a single place), 'Desire' (three unconnected couples duplicate a need to touch, but are unable to see their partners), 'Panic', 'Daydream' (three women preen and pose), 'The End' (suicide) and a final return to the full group in a reprise of 'Alone'. The dance ends with the performers frozen in their chairs as the music crashes to a close.

Lineage

The dangerous, disaffected jitters of these urban misfits resurface in two of the most powerful works of the 1980s: **Twyla Tharp**'s *Bad Smells* (1982) and **Paul Taylor**'s *Last Look* (1985). Tharp turns Sokolow's lonely vision into a quasi-militaristic society grotesquely distorted by a cameraman who weaves amongst the dancers: his close-up view is projected on a large screen behind the dancers. Taylor's work is even bleaker. He builds isolation to a horrific, orgiastic conclusion that is made doubly monstrous by the fact that the dancers only relate to their mirrored selves, rather than to the bodies beside, and sometimes even on top of, them. Lloyd Newson's *My Body, Your Body* (1987) for **DV8 Physical Theatre** allows eight men and eight women to make contact but to no avail.

Follow-up

There is a lengthy analysis of *Rooms* in Marcia B. Siegel's 1979 *The Shapes of Change*, and a 1966 film version of the work.

Staging

1 Joffrey Ballet/1967

Mary Wigman

Born: 13th November 1886/ Hanover
Died: 18th September 1973/ West Berlin

Germany's most famous dancer was also the greatest influence on modern dance in Europe for half a century. Early in her career she studied eurhythmics with Emile Jaques-Dalcroze, and during the First World War she was **Rudolf von Laban**'s assistant in Switzerland, but as a choreographer and teacher she had her own ideas about dance.

Wigman widened the range of possibilities for dance expression as well as advancing its underlying theories. She championed a new movement form called 'absolute dance', a style of dance which had no great reliance on exterior elements such as music or plot. Although she was capable of executing light, joyous dances, her best known choreography consists of sombre, often macabre studies of man's darker nature and gloomy fate.

She made her public debut in 1914 in the earliest version of her famous solo *Witch Dance*. Sheathed in a brocade wrap and wearing a stark, gaunt mask, Wigman performed the dance (partially from a sitting position) in a kind of demonic trance, her hands clawing the air as if in a futile attempt to exorcise some pervasive evil. It is by no means a pretty dance. The piece's disturbing mood, emphasised by Wigman's distorted body shapes, was a clear indication of the close connection between her work and German Expressionist art.

Many of her early compositions were choreographed and performed in silence, counter to her sound-and-motion studies with Dalcroze. In this way, Wigman asserted dance's independence as an art form. Many modern choreographers, ranging from **Doris Humphrey** to **Trisha Brown**,

Mary Wigman in Dresden in 1928, the year of her London debut

Dana Reitz and Twyla Tharp, have experimented with dances performed in silence. Even ballet choreographers occasionally create works without music: Serge Lifar tried this, and Jerome Robbins achieved a lasting success with *Moves* (1959). Once Wigman had solved this problem for herself, her dances were able to coexist with the accompaniment of a simple melodic line supported by percussive rhythms.

Wigman's solo recitals were a hit in Zurich and Hamburg during 1919. The Dresden Central School, which she opened the following year, became a mecca of modern dance, developing branches throughout Germany, and, thanks to Wigman's star pupil and dance company member Hanya Holm, in the United States. As a dancer, Wigman made her London debut in 1928 and later appeared several times in America, where her gutsy emotionalism and use of space as an almost tangible presence caused quite a stir. The Nazis closed her school, and during the Second World War her activities were severely limited. She retired from dancing in 1942, but after the war opened another school based in Leipzig and then West Berlin; it closed in the 1960s because of Wigman's declining health.

Lineage

As John Martin notes in his concise yet comprehensive *Book of the Dance* (1963), Wigman and others of her generation took Isadora Duncan as a model for their own creative expression. But if Duncan discovered the soul of dance, Wigman gave it a body. She added a strong emotive element to Rudolf von Laban's rather clinical studies and used space architecturally, relating the figure to its surroundings in a manner similar to the work of Oskar Schlemmer.

Follow-up

Wigman's book *The Language of the Dance* was translated into English in 1966. *The Mary Wigman Book*, edited by Walter Sorell, appeared in 1973, and *Mary Wigmans Choreographisches Skizzenbuch 30–61*, an extensive and expensive 1987 volume, includes her dance sketches and working drawings.

MODERN
BALLET

17th October 1933. The day George Balanchine arrived in New York City marks the start of the experimentation which would evolve into Balanchine's American neo-classicism. His modernist re-shaping of the nineteenth-century classical style made his company, the New York City Ballet, one of the most stimulating in the world.

'The art of progress is to preserve order amid change and to preserve change amid order'. This statement by the mathematician and philosopher Alfred North Whitehead is a perfect distillation of Balanchine's contribution to ballet. He bent, but never abandoned, the rules. The classical ballet vocabulary which had accrued since the time of Louis XIV was Balanchine's bedrock, Marius Petipa his fountainhead.

The death of Serge Diaghilev in 1929 had thrown the ballet world into chaos. He had so completely dominated ballet for the two previous decades that no one quite knew where to turn. Various individuals made attempts to keep the Ballets Russes together. These offshoots were quickly reduced to factions who bickered over billing, copyright and personal allegiances. For decades the general public continued to believe that the only great dancers were Russian, and even after Diaghilev (through less frequently), performers changed their names to something which sounded Russian, or at least exotic.

It was in England that a pair of

percipient women, who had both performed with the Ballets Russes, realised that the way forward was to be found by building on Diaghilev's legacy rather than attempting to ape his past successes. Marie Rambert and Ninette de Valois lured Alicia Markova back to London and then were content to let the Continental upheavals pass them by. This was less a case of insularity than a determinedly single-minded policy aimed at creating a British ballet that would be second to none. Fate brought them Frederick Ashton, Margot Fonteyn, Antony Tudor – and Nicholas Sergeyev, the former general director of the Maryinkey (now Kirov) Theatre. When he fled the October Revolution, he had packed his cases with the notations from the nineteenth-century classics. With these enduring works, rather than the more transient ballets of the Diaghilev repertory, young British dancers and choreographers were presented with an ideal barometer for their own creations.

Across the Atlantic, Balanchine was not the only choreographer with a vision of an American ballet. In the 1940s, there was an upsurge in Americana themes: the first of these, Agnes de Mille's *Rodeo*, was (ironically) premiered by the Ballet Russe de Monte Carlo, which had emigrated to America to avoid the Second World War. The 1940 debut of Ballet Theatre (later American Ballet Theatre) was on a grand scale, meant to reflect a broad-based melting pot of the classic and the new, from *Giselle* to the riotously popular *Fancy Free*, staged with modern flash by Jerome Robbins in 1944.

Meanwhile, Balanchine kept beavering away, refining and polishing, and above all nurturing the first generation of dancers trained to dance his way. The opening of an academy, the School of American Ballet, had been his priority on arriving in New York. By 1946, when he and his associate Lincoln Kirstein unveiled their Ballet Society, the raw talent of 1933 had been shaped into the speedy, articulate and musically sensitive ensemble that Balanchine had come to America to create.

Not all modern ballet was allowed to look forward. In the USSR, staunch conservatism kept new ideas at bay. Politically restrained from experimentation with content, the Russians turned to context: the ballet dancer's body. Moving almost as far from Petipa as Balanchine (though in the opposite direction), the Soviets began to develop the superdancer, an athlete capable of virtually anything. Their teaching systems sometimes seemed to be stressing acrobatic displays of physicality for its own sake, but there was no doubt about the excitement generated by the virtuosity of such daredevils as Maya Plisetskaya, Vladimir Vasiliev, Maris Liepa and eventually Rudolf Nureyev, the man who brought Russian bravado to the West.

A New York City Ballet performance of the George Balanchine ballet *The Four Temperaments*

American Ballet Theatre

Formed: 1940, as Ballet Theatre

Conceived both as a rival to the European opera house ballets and as a platform for indigenous choreography, American Ballet Theatre (ABT) was founded around members of the Mordkin Ballet, a floundering Ballets Russes offshoot. The company made its debut with a full ensemble of eighty-five dancers and a repertory which included **Giselle** and six world premieres. Originally called simply Ballet Theatre ('American' was added in 1957), its financial survival was principally due to the personal wealth of dancer Lucia Chase, who, with stage designer Oliver Smith, ran the company from 1945 to 1980. Founding choreographers **Agnes de Mille** and **Antony Tudor** – as well as **Michel Fokine** and **Léonide Massine** – contributed new works and restaged past hits, as would **George Balanchine** with the Tchaikovsky *Theme and Variations* in 1947.

Throughout its existence, ABT has been devoted to a glamorous image of ballet, promoting its own stars and spotlighting more guest artists than any other troupe in the world. **Alicia Markova** was the company's first leading ballerina (as she had been for the Vic-Wells Ballet), Alicia Alonso emerged from the corps, and Nora Kaye exemplified the dramatic intensity needed to put across Tudor's **Pillar of Fire** and de Mille's *Fall River Legend* (1948). These, with **Jerome Robbins'** *Fancy Free*, were the most original of ABT's early creations. After Robbins left in 1950, the company went through a lean choreographic period and switched its focus to the classics.

ABT's contemporary choreography has rarely reached the heights of its early days, although dancer **Eliot Feld** choreographed his first works for the company, and **Glen Tetley** produced several pieces in the 1970s. The only hit to match the rapturous reception of *Fancy Free* has been *Push Comes to Shove*, created by **Twyla Tharp** for **Mikhail Baryshnikov** in 1976. In recent years the company has experimented with works by non-ballet names like **Paul Taylor** and even **Merce Cunningham**, plus new-wave choreographers such as **David Gordon**, **Mark Morris** and **Karole Armitage**.

During the seventies, Chase openly catered to the Russian defectors: **Rudolf Nureyev**, Alexander Godunov and **Natalia Makarova** have all had close associations with ABT, while Baryshnikov – after a brief period with **New York City Ballet** – returned to take over the reins from Chase in 1980. **Kenneth MacMillan**, who joined ABT four years later as an artistic associate, has staged his versions of **Romeo and Juliet** and **The Sleeping Beauty**. In the autumn of 1988, Twyla Tharp was also appointed artistic associate. ABT has produced major stars of its own including Fernando Bujones, Cynthia Gregory and Martine van Hamel, while the guest roster is a *Who's Who* of world ballet (including **Erik Bruhn**, Toni Lander, **Gelsey Kirkland**, Carla Fracci, Marcia Haydée and **Anthony Dowell**).

Lineage

With an annual spring season at the Metropolitan Opera House in New York, American Ballet Theatre is the only US company of substance to tour annually across the whole country. In both size and scope, it ranks with **New York City Ballet**, the **Royal Ballet**, **Paris Opéra Ballet**, the **Kirov Ballet** and the **Bolshoi Ballet** as one of the world's leading companies.

Follow-up

The Turning Point (1977) is thinly disguised *cinéma à clef*: the movie's director Herbert Ross was married to Nora Kaye; the juvenile ballerina lead Leslie Browne was

their godchild; and many ABT
dancers and teachers feature in
the film. ABT films and videos
include a 1970 *Giselle*, with Fracci,
Bruhn and Lander; *American Ballet
Theatre: A Close-Up in Time* (1973,
including a magnificent *Pillar of
Fire*) and Baryshnikov's *Don
Quixote* and *The Nutcracker*. A
company history by Charles
Payne, *American Ballet Theatre*
(1978), includes personal essays by
Alonso, Bruhn, Chase and Kaye,
while Clive Barnes' *Inside
American Ballet Theatre* (1977) is a
fine tourist's guide to the company.

Frederick Ashton

Born: 17th September 1904/
Guayaquil, Ecuador
Died: 18th August 1988/Eye,
Suffolk

The graciously lyrical ballets of
Frederick Ashton are the
quintessence of the soft, pliant
British style of dancing which he
defined, refined and polished to
perfection. Ashton grew up in
Peru, where, in 1917, he saw and
was forever smitten by **Anna
Pavlova**. Sent to school in England,
he was working in an office in 1921
when he finally began taking ballet
classes. Finances were tight, but
one of his elder brothers agreed to
pay for lessons on condition that
Ashton would never become a
chorus boy.

Marie Rambert was convinced
of his talent, but was also aware
that he had started too late to fulfil
his desire to be 'the greatest
dancer in the world'. Cleverly, she
manoeuvred him towards
choreography: his first ballet,
A Tragedy of Fashion (part of a
1926 revue at London's Lyric Hammersmith), told the story of a
couturier (Ashton) and his cigar-
smoking partner (Rambert). When
he ruins a gown, the mortified
dressmaker stabs himself with his
scarlet scissors. The work proved
to be a big hit, and over the next

decade Ashton made nearly
twenty ballets for Rambert,
including *Capriol Suite* (1930, to a
Peter Warlock score based on
sixteenth-century dance forms) and
his first unqualified triumph,
Façade. During the 1928–29 season,
dancing in Paris with Ida
Rubinstein's vanity company, he
encountered **Bronislava Nijinska**,
who, like Pavlova, became one of
his idols.

Ashton was lured away from
Ballet Rambert in 1935 by **Ninette
de Valois**. Her Vic-Wells (now
Royal) Ballet offered him the
prospect of a larger stage and
company of dancers to work with.
Early treats for the Vic-Wells
include two works from 1937, his
skating-party romp *Les Patineurs*
and the eccentrically captivating
A Wedding Bouquet, devised to a
text by Gertrude Stein. This was
his second encounter with the
author: he had travelled to New
York in 1934 to stage the Virgil
Thomson/Stein opera *Four Saints in
Three Acts*.

Following war service, Ashton
returned to the Vic-Wells for its
transfer to the Royal Opera House
in 1946. His first work there was
the great **Symphonic Variations**,
and in 1948 he created the first full-
length English ballet **Cinderella**
(his only full-length work to an
original score came ten years later
with *Ondine*, composed by Hans
Werner Henze).

Throughout his career, Ashton
usually turned down offers to
create works for other companies,
stating that he preferred familiar
surroundings and dancers, but in
1950 he staged *Illuminations*
(Britten's song cycle to Rimbaud's
poems) for **New York City Ballet**,
and in 1955 went to the Royal
Danish Ballet to stage the first
Western production of Prokofiev's
Romeo and Juliet. Back at Covent
Garden, he followed this with two
of his most charming and distinctly
English works, **La Fille mal gardée**
and *The Two Pigeons* (1960 and
1961 respectively), both two-act
works, rather than the traditional
three-act format which Ashton
claimed to find uncomfortable.

In 1962 he was knighted and

made Chevalier of the Légion d'honneur; a year later he succeeded de Valois as artistic director of the Royal Ballet (see second Ashton entry in The Ballet Boom, page 136).

Lineage

In contrast to **George Balanchine**, who defined the tone and the energy of the twentieth century with his unique, angular streamlining of classical ballet, Ashton's movement is more atmospheric and pinpoints individual characters, situations and storylines. This specificity was perhaps his greatest gift. It arose, like Balanchine's talent, from an innate musicality, but whereas Balanchine strove to reinterpret and customise the rules of **Marius Petipa**, Ashton seems to have seen himself as merely one step along a gradually evolving path.

Follow-up

David Vaughan's detailed *Frederick Ashton and His Ballets* (1977) is the major printed source on the choreographer. There is no biography, but Ashton was reportedly working on an autobiography not for publication until after his death.

Façade

One act
Choreography: Frederick Ashton
Music: William Walton
Design: John Armstrong
Premiere: 26th April 1931/ Cambridge Theatre, London

This light-hearted comedy is composed of divertissements inspired by music hall and popular dancing. Filled with parody, puns and sometimes juvenile humour, the whole ensemble is tossed together with an insouciant sparkle. The original 1922 *Façade* was a staged reading of Edith Sitwell poems accompanied by a score

from William Walton. Later, Ashton asked Walton to devise a suite from the music. He retained Sitwell's title, but otherwise the action bears no link to the poems.

The ballet opens with a pas de trois, a Highland fling with kilts: the man seems so delighted at having two partners that he scoops the girls up simultaneously and bounces them off one another like a pair of cymbals. A milkmaid enters, pursued by a trio of lederhosen-clad swains, who clown and flirt with her and impersonate a cow, complete with a splay-fingered udder for milking. Then a polka is danced by a woman who rips off her skirt to perform in ruffled bloomers: this solo includes the most classically demanding steps of the ballet. She is followed

Karen Donovan dancing the Polka from *Façade* in a 1984 Sadler's Wells Royal Ballet production

onstage by a pair of flappers (who do the charleston with their bespectacled beaux); four waltzing girls; and then the deadpan comedy of 'Popular Song', a close unison number for two gents in blazers and boaters.

The comedy culminates in a tango for a louche gigolo and a dim-witted socialite. He runs his fingers up and down her spine as if she were a keyboard; she wriggles in response as though he were a creepy-crawly. In the middle of their mock-torrid duet (and much to her surprise), he turns her head over heels in a cartwheel. All the characters come together for a razzle-dazzle, jazz-baby finale.

Still a novice choreographer when he created the piece, Ashton received a £5 fee from the Camargo Society, a private group which sponsored occasional West End ballet evenings in an attempt to fill the vacuum left by the demise of the Ballets Russes.

Lineage

Façade confirmed Ashton's budding reputation as *the* young British choreographer of the era; as the decade progressed, he repeatedly used the convenient and fruitful divertissement format, particularly in *Les Rendezvous* (1933), a garden party for dallying debs, and *Les Patineurs* (1937), where all the dancers pretend they are skaters on a frozen pond. Ashton's parody of social dancing and manners owes a debt to the late Ballets Russes style exemplified by **Bronislava Nijinska**'s **Les Biches**. Other works springing from a popular dance base include **George Balanchine**'s *Who Cares?* (a 1970 suite of Gershwin tunes) and **Kenneth MacMillan**'s *Elite Syncopations* (a 1974 romp to the rags of Scott Joplin).

Stagings

1 **Ballet Rambert**/1931
2 **Vic-Wells (now Royal) Ballet**/1935
3 **Joffrey Ballet**/1970
4 **Australian Ballet**/1972

Symphonic Variations

One act
Choreography: Frederick Ashton
Music: César Franck
Design: Sophie Fedorovitch
Premiere: 24th April 1946/Royal Opera House, London

The culmination of Frederick Ashton's early career and, simultaneously, the beginning of his mature style, *Symphonic Variations* was the first work he created in the Vic-Wells Ballet's new home at Covent Garden. Reserved exclusively for the **Royal Ballet**, it is a distillation of the classical heritage of **Marius Petipa**, softened by Ashton's poetic English gentility.

Populated by just six dancers and lasting a mere eighteen minutes, the ballet is named after the 1885 Franck score and is devoid of any story. Three men and three women, all in white, perform a series of serene trios, quartets, solos and duets, elegantly supported by Sophie Fedorovitch's simple cyclorama of spring-bud green covered with its curving calligraphy of flowing black lines.

Whenever the dancers are not moving, they adopt a signature pose in which one leg is casually crossed in front of the other (the foot nonchalantly resting on its toes). There are no entrances or exits, a rare occurrence in classical ballet, where performers often require a dash into the wings to regain their composure and gulp for breath after impressing the audience with feats of expertise. But then there is little need for that in this demanding, but distinctly unemphatic creation.

Among the most beautiful moments in *Symphonic Variations* is a sequence of delicate and gentle lifts performed by the central couple as they travel round the stage in a circle. The man lifts the ballerina only a few inches off the floor, yet these skimming arcs, an Ashton signature, convey a sense of floating ease often missing from the more exaggerated and attention-grabbing overhead lifts of other modern ballet choreographers.

Lineage

Ashton created plotless ballets less frequently than **George Balanchine**, for whom the format was an almost constant modus operandi. Other Ashton ballets with no direct storyline include the brief pair of trios set to Erik Satie and collectively known as *Monotones* (1965 and 1966), the grand Russian-Imperial *Birthday Offering* (1956) and *Rhapsody* (1980), an eightieth birthday gift to Ashton's longtime friend HRH Queen Elizabeth, the Queen Mother. His 1948 *Scènes de ballet*, to an eponymous Stravinsky score, is organised in a sculptural, balanced harmony. Ashton believed the piece could be viewed from any one of its four sides with an equal amount of satisfaction, an idea which **Merce Cunningham** brought to the fore when he began staging dances in museums and other unorthodox spaces. However, unlike Ashton, whose carefully worked out geometries exist within the traditional hierarchies of ballet, Cunningham gives each dancer democratic equality and leaves the focal point up to the individual viewer.

Cinderella

Three acts
Choreography: Frederick Ashton
Music: Sergei Prokofiev
Design: Jean-Denis Malclès
(revised by David Walker)
Premiere: 23rd December 1948/
Royal Opera House, London

If Igor Stravinsky was the ideal composer for the new plotless ballets of the twentieth century, then Sergei Prokofiev was the man who did the most to keep the grand evening-length story ballets alive. His two major scores in this format – **Romeo and Juliet** and *Cinderella* – were both composed in the Tchaikovsky manner, with each section of the music describing the action both through sound and via a written scenario. The two scores have led to dozens of productions, in the vast majority of which the action has remained firmly dictated by Prokofiev.

Frederick Ashton was the first Western choreographer to use these scores. His *Cinderella* (the first evening-length work produced for the **Royal Ballet**, and now the standard against which other versions are gauged) is perhaps the softest and most light-hearted of all. He makes fine use of the English traditions of Victorian pantomime: the Ugly Sisters, originally danced by **Robert Helpmann** and Ashton, are a comic pair of panto dames. They may be self-centred and spoilt, but they are never the bullies who appear in several other versions (Ashton completely dropped the true villainess of the piece, the Stepmother). These sisters pose no real threat to Cinderella's eventual happiness, and Ashton clings firmly to the notion of an out-and-out fairy tale.

This is a much-loved ballet, yet it is not a total success. The lack of a grand pas de deux for Cinderella and the Prince to round off the evening can leave dance fans feeling somewhat cheated. The ballet in fact ends with a lustrous tableau in which the couple are surrounded by fairies; as the curtain comes down, the Prince lifts Cinderella above his head and slowly turns her in circles. It is as if she is being transformed into a moon around which all the magic is now revolving. This is a gorgeous moment, but the story has been wrapped up too abruptly. Unlike the royal couple at the end of **The Sleeping Beauty**, Cinderella and her Prince are not allowed a final love duet.

Ashton also left out one of the most jaunty sections of Prokofiev's score, the Prince's journey round the globe in search of his lady of the glass slipper. Prokofiev, taking a cue from the second act of **The Nutcracker**, had composed a series of exotic ethnic melodies ideal for the character dancing of various women longing to fit into the slipper. This omission seriously truncates the last act and seems to produce a rush to the finale.

   Cinderella was originally staged by Rostislav Zakharov for the Bolshoi in 1945. Among the many subsequent versions, two of the cleverest come from France. **Rudolf Nureyev** boldly turned his Paris Opéra Ballet production into a modern fairy tale: the Prince becomes a Hollywood film star while the Fairy Godmother, now a Godfather, is a cigar-chomping producer (played by Nureyev). Cinderella makes her processional entrance to the ball (a nightclub party) surrounded by twinkling lights, the flashbulbs of a horde of paparazzi trailing in the wake of this unknown starlet. **Maguy Marin**'s version, conceived for the Lyon Opéra Ballet, is even more exotic, recast as if the dancers were children. The action takes place in a doll's house which fills the stage, and the characters wear masks that make them look like bulbous-faced china dolls. Here the ball is a birthday party for the Prince. He later searches for Cinderella on a rocking-horse, in front of an unrolling panorama of exotic locales (the same device used in the original production of *The Sleeping Beauty* when the Lilac Fairy ferries the Princes across the lake).

Lineage

The story of *Cinderella* is much easier to follow than **The Nutcracker**, and the Ugly Sisters can be very entertaining. Consequently, this should be an ideal ballet for children, and yet it has neither the otherworldly wonder of *The Nutcracker* nor the lightness and charm of **Coppélia**. Much of this is due to Prokofiev's music, which, even at its happiest, lacks the joyous optimism of the Tchaikovsky and Delibes scores.

Follow-up

Film versions include a garish 1961 Bolshoi rendition and a 1987 BBC film which features the Paris Opéra Ballet, with Nureyev and rising star Sylvie Guillem. The Maguy Marin interpretation is scheduled for release by Channel 4 in 1989.

Stagings

1 **Rostislav Zakharov**/Bolshoi Ballet/1945
2 **Konstantin Sergeyev**/Kirov Ballet/1946, revised 1964
3 **Ben Stevenson**/Washington National Ballet/1970 (and subsequently London Festival Ballet)
4 **Mikhail Baryshnikov and Peter Anastos**/American Ballet Theatre/1984
5 **Maguy Marin**/Lyon Opéra Ballet/1985
6 **Rudolf Nureyev**/Paris Opéra/1986

George Balanchine

Born: 22nd January 1904/St Petersburg
Died: 30th April 1983/New York City

The foundation of the School of American Ballet, which opened on New Year's Day 1934, was George Balanchine's immediate priority when he arrived in New York. Wealthy intellectual Lincoln Kirstein had brought him to America in the hope of fulfilling his dream of a major company to rival those in Europe and Russia. Today's **New York City Ballet** (NYCB) is focussed round Balanchine's unprecedented stream of plotless ballets, performed in practice clothes to modern scores; but no company can be created overnight, even if Balanchine did choreograph **Serenade** for his students only six months after the School opened.

The profile of NYCB is not exclusively modernist, however. Balanchine continually paid homage to his Russian heritage in such joyous creations as *A Midsummer Night's Dream* and **The Nutcracker** (NYCB has now given over a thousand performances of this work, more than any other single production in ballet history). He also devised many plotless celebrations of dancing choreographed to the lush music of Tchaikovsky and other nineteenth-century masters. In 1967, Balanchine judiciously mixed these modes into a three-act plotless ballet called *Jewels*. 'Emeralds' (to music by Fauré) has the dreamy elegance of Paris circa 1840; 'Rubies' (to Stravinsky) is jazzy, syncopated and witty; 'Diamonds' (to Tchaikovsky) is Russian Imperial classicism.

In the time between his arrival in America and the founding of NYCB, Balanchine had worked consistently on Broadway. His eighteen musicals included the 1935 edition of The Ziegfeld Follies and *On Your Toes*, with its famous 'Slaughter on Tenth Avenue' finale. He also devised dances for five Hollywood films, and in 1942 called on Stravinsky to write *Circus Polka*, which Balanchine then staged with fifty women atop fifty elephants for the Ringling Brothers and Barnum & Bailey Circus.

More orthodox commissions were for the Ballets Russes de Monte Carlo, where his former lover Alexandra Danilova was prima ballerina; American Ballet Theatre (*Theme and Variations*, 1947); and the Paris Opéra (*Le Palais de cristal*, also 1947, now rechristened *Symphony in C*). During this time, the School was progressing and training a new crop of American dancers for Balanchine. In 1946, he and Kirstein founded Ballet Society which, two years later, became New York City Ballet (see NYCB entry, page 117).

Balanchine married three times during his American years. All three were his ballerinas: Vera Zorina, Maria Tallchief and the gamine Tanaquil Le Clercq, one of the first stars to be entirely trained

from childhood at the School of American Ballet, but tragically cripped by polio at the height of her career in 1956. Balanchine, like **Martha Graham**, received both the Presidential Medal of Freedom and the Légion d'honneur. (For Lineage, see Balanchine entry in The Ballet Russes, page 40).

Follow-up

Balanchine's Hollywood films are *Dark Red Roses* (1929), *The Goldwyn Follies* (1938), *On Your Toes* (1939), *I Was an Adventuress* (1940) and *Star-Spangled Rhythm* (1942). Bernard Taper's *Balanchine* (revised in 1984) is the standard biography, but Richard Buckle's *George Balanchine*, *Ballet Master* (1988), although uneven, is particularly informative on the interim years 1933 to 1946.

Serenade

One act
Choreography: George Balanchine
Music: Pyotr Ilyich Tchaikovsky (Serenade in C Major for String Orchestra, 1880)
Premiere: 10th June 1934/ Woodlands, the estate of Felix M. Warburg, White Plains, NY

Serenade opens in moonlight: a tableau of women each with one arm raised towards the moon. In unison their arms curve in, curl around their heads and glide down to resting. Then, suddenly, their feet shoot out into first position. This movement has the effect of an electric shock. In that one simple gesture (the primal principle on which all ballet is based) a world is born. The stage switches from waiting to being, from passive to active. The first link in the chain has been forged, a corps de ballet created.

The dancing that follows is light and elegant, youthful and frolicking. Balanchine orchestrates the entire stage with sweeping cascades of unaffected lyricism.

Quintessential Balanchine: Peter Martins and Suzanne Farrell performing the pas de deux from *Agon* for the New York City Ballet

Then, unexpectedly, the dancers are back in their opening position. Another woman enters and wanders through this garden of statues. She finds, takes, accepts her place and, looking over her shoulder to make certain she has the correct stance, raises her arm. She too is a dancer.

As the rest of the corps leaves the stage, a man enters. Walking up behind the single remaining woman, he touches her gently on the shoulder and they begin to waltz. Another transformation is taking place: the woman who became a dancer is now turning into a ballerina. When the corps re-enters to join the waltz, this storybook romance melts of its own accord.

Another metamorphosis is needed to complete the cycle. When the other dancers rush away again, the woman collapses onto the floor. Behind her, a different man is brought on, guided by a woman who walks behind with one of her hands covering his eyes.

She leads him forward, and as he takes the fallen woman's hands, rises into an arabesque. Slowly she spins over their heads -
a goddess, a muse, a fate,
a guardian angel.

The three dance together, but the mood darkens. The guide, her arms like swooping black wings, recaptures the man and leads him away. The ballerina is left behind in solitary anguish. The final change has been accomplished. She is once again a woman, but now with a fuller, deeper experience of life. Members of the corps return and the woman is lifted above their heads; as the curtain falls, she is being carried off, as if in a cortège. The cycle is now complete. She has been transformed into a goddess, a Balanchine ballerina.

This interpretation is, of course, subjective. Balanchine was not intent on telling stories; instead he saw himself as an illustrator of music, a conduit between composer and audience. Yet, throughout his long career, he returned again and again to the theme of the glorification of woman as ballerina.

The creation of *Serenade* reveals Balanchine's practical attitude towards the job of choreography. The ballet was made with whichever dancers happened to turn up each day at his new School of American Ballet (whose students gave the first performance). His quick sensitivity to music was such that he even incorporated their mistakes into the finished piece. The initial entrance of the solitary woman, for instance, was derived from the fact that the dancer actually arrived late at rehearsal. Similarly, her collapse stems from an accidental slip which Balanchine then transformed into art.

Lineage

Serenade was the first ballet George Balanchine created after arriving in America. It remains his most lyrical work, undoubtedly because his new students were not yet capable of performing the more demanding classical style he had learned in Russia and which he had used in his Ballets Russes works like **Apollo**. Time and again, he would return to Tchaikovsky, whose music led to some of Balanchine's most enduring works: *Ballet Imperial* (1941, now called *Tchaikovsky Piano Concerto No. 2*), *Theme and Variations* (1947), *Allegro Brillante* (1956), 'Diamonds' (the third act of his plotless *Jewels*, 1967), and his version of **The Nutcracker**. The final New York City Ballet festival during Balanchine's lifetime was devoted to Tchaikovsky and included his last dancework of genius, *Mozartiana* (1981).

Follow-up

A 1957 New York City Ballet production was filmed by the Canadian Broadcasting Corporation: a 1973 German television version (performed by NYCB) is marred by overactive camerawork and editing.

Stagings

The most popular of all Balanchine ballets, *Serenade* is in the repertory of virtually every major Western ballet company.

The Four Temperaments

One act
Choreography: George Balanchine
Music: Paul Hindemith
Premiere: 20th November 1946/ **Central High School of Needle Trades, New York City**

This ballet created and defined the idiom which we still call 'modern' ballet. That *The Four Temperaments* continues to look as if it could be premiered tomorrow is a measure of its perfection. Nothing in this ballet is gratuitous or tossed in simply for effect. It is a spare, yet enormously rich universe, a swirling, ever-expanding exploration of human geometry.

The ballet opens with three short pas de deux. They succinctly state the themes which form the framework for the variations in the four main sections. These are loosely based on the human temperaments of medieval philosophy – melancholic, sanguine, phlegmatic and choleric – but references to these temperaments in the dancing are implicit rather than overt.

For all its angular modernity, the ballet is grounded in politeness, in a courtly and courting sense of male-female relationships. The hands extended to other hands or the angular reverences of the piece may not be instantly recognisable as lovers holding hands or courtiers bowing, but that is what they represent.

Balanchine's conquests of space are like chivalric battles. At one point, a trio forms itself into a straight line and faces four dancers who form the corners of a square. These two forces confront one another on an invisible, but palpable diagonal line that shoots across the stage. Immediately you know that they are destined to clash, that each of the two groups wants to claim the stage space as its sovereign territory. Yet, just before battle commences, the trio executes an abstracted bow to their opponents. The move is as sharp as an acute angle, but as civilised as a throne room curtsy.

Within Balanchine's aesthetic cleanliness there is a sense of lushness that reaches a climax in the finale, where the ballerinas are repeatedly lifted in scooping arcs that travel along the horizontal lines of the corps de ballet, like rockets surging into the air, starburst clusters erupting in radiant human fireworks.

Balanchine's work in Hollywood had left him, at least temporarily, a wealthy man. In 1937 he contacted Paul Hindemith's agent to find out the price of a new score from the composer. The answer was $500. Seven years passed before the work was staged – for Ballet Society, a forerunner of New York City Ballet – but it is typical of Balanchine that he should use his movie-musical gains to further his view of art by commissioning a score from the then controversial Hindemith.

Lineage

Balanchine's explorations of movement for movement's sake and his use of dancers as a sketch-book for ideas began in this ballet and extended through a long series of works that include *Ivesiana* (1954), **Agon** (1957), *Episodes* (1959), *Movements for Piano and Orchestra* (1963), *Symphony in Three Movements* and *Violin Concerto* (both part of the 1972 Stravinsky Festival) and another work to Hindemith, *Kammermusik No. 2* (1978).

Follow-up

The 1979 Dance in America film *Choreography by Balanchine: Part I* includes a New York City Ballet performance of *The Four Temperaments*.

Stagings

Like Balanchine's *Serenade*, this ballet is performed by most major companies including New York City Ballet (from its inception) and the Royal Ballet (from 1973).

Agon

One act
Choreography: George Balanchine
Music: Igor Stravinsky
Premiere: 27th November 1957/
City Center, New York City

Agon is the Greek word for 'contest'. That is the only clue you need when watching this ultimate Balanchine ballet. Together, both choreographer and composer manipulate classic forms: Stravinsky based his music on sixteenth and seventeenth-century courtly dances such as the sarabande and the galliarde; Balanchine based his movement on the academic vocabulary of classical ballet. The two men toy, push and play with these forms in such a way that the contest of the title turns into a challenge to the audience, who are asked to see and hear classical material in a contemporary guise.

The dancers' uniforms are simple black and white practice clothes. The sharp, angular attack of each movement, the sense of competitive playfulness and the speed radiating out from one brief encounter to the next are all perfect counterparts to the score. Balanchine's often quoted summary is: '*Agon* contains twelve pieces of music. It is a ballet for twelve dancers. It is all precise, like a machine, but a machine that thinks'.

The ballet, featuring eight women and four men, is composed of brief, compressed quartets and trios which culminate in an astonishing modernist inversion of the pas de deux. Here, the male dancer manipulates the ballerina as though she were as flexible as rubber, yet as tensile as steel. The most famous moment in the work is when she strikes a classically academic arabesque and her partner, according to tradition, promenades her in a rotation that displays the ballerina's perfect form. The twist is that the man does this while he is lying on his back and scuttling around the ballerina like a crab. The audience does not know whether to be amused or amazed, or both.

Just as Stravinsky daringly turns courtly dances into twelve-tone sound structures, so Balanchine relentlessly strips opulent classicism down to the bare bones of contemporary sculpture. In *Agon* he has wittily redefined the heritage of **Marius Petipa**. Rather than despairing over our frenetic, urban age, Balanchine glorifies it. He seeks what is beautiful in jet-propelled power, discovers what is personal within the anonymity of skyscrapered cities. The choreographer himself pointed out that 'agon' is the root of both 'protagonist' and 'agony', two definitions which add further resonance to the essentially abstract movement.

The quick sharpness and compact pressure of *Agon* will, admittedly, not be to everyone's tastes. There is very little display dancing and the steps, intricate though they are, are rarely what one could call spectacular. But for those who are able to hear the dancing and see the music (as Balanchine and Stravinsky once described their collaboration), this ballet is a rich, never diminishing source of magnificence.

Lineage

Agon was to complete the Greek trilogy which the two men began with **Apollo** and continued in *Orpheus* (1948). The notion of a third mythological ballet was quicky abandoned, but *Agon* is still thought of as the finale of this trio. Other major works in the same genre (which had started with the Hindemith ballet **The Four Temperaments**), include Stravinsky's *Movements for Piano and Orchestra*, *Symphony in Three Movements* and *Violin Concerto*. The latter two, in particular, are both freer and less formal than *Agon*. Several other choreographers have attempted to use the *Agon* score, including **Kenneth MacMillan** (1958), but these versions pale beside the original.

Follow-up

Dance Writings is a 1986 collection of the work of major American critic Edwin Denby. Approximately a quarter of its 600 pages are devoted to Balanchine, including the thought-provoking 'Three Sides of *Agon*'. Lincoln Kirstein, who commissioned the score from Stravinsky, writes about the ballet in *Movement and Metaphor* (1970), and Marcia B. Siegel analyses *Agon* in the 'Balanchine's America' chapter of *The Shapes of Change* (1979). Performances have been filmed by the Canadian Broadcasting Corporation (1960) and for the 1983 Dance in America segment *Balanchine Celebrates Stravinsky*.

Stagings

1 Stuttgart Ballet/1970
2 Dance Theatre of Harlem/1971
3 Royal Ballet/1973
4 Paris Opéra Ballet/1974
5 Basel Ballet/1987

Ballet Rambert

Formed: 1935, from Ballet Club

Marie Rambert
Born: 20th February 1888/Warsaw
Died: 12th June 1982/London

As a teenager, Marie Rambert (born Cyvia Rambam) was sent to France to study medicine, but quickly gravitated towards Parisian artistic life. Soon she was giving private recitals in the style of **Isadora Duncan**, whom she had seen in Warsaw. In 1910, Rambert went on a two-week summer course in Germany with Emile Jaques-Dalcroze and ended up staying for three years as one of his chief assistants. Dalcroze's system of eurythmics directly correlated a musical score to body movements and, in 1913, **Serge Diaghilev** hired Rambert to guide **Vaslav Nijinsky** through the rhythmic complexities of Stravinsky's **Le Sacre du**

printemps. However, her Dalcroze classes for the Ballets Russes proved unpopular and were soon abandoned. Although as scornful of classical ballet as the dancers were of eurythmics, she was drafted into the corps de ballet for the company's 1913 South American tour. In mid-ocean, Rambert was suddenly and forever bitten by the ballet bug. When her contract was not renewed at the end of the tour, Rambert moved to London, where she met and married playwright Ashley Dukes.

In her early London years, Rambert taught and organised performances wherever she could. Her first major success came in 1926 with a revue at the Lyric Hammersmith, when she had **Frederick Ashton** stage his first ballet, a comedy called *A Tragedy of Fashion*. By 1930, she and Dukes had begun to convert an old

Marie Rambert in the mid–1920s, just before her first major success with Frederick Ashton's *A Tragedy of Fashion*

church in Notting Hill into the Mercury Theatre. The stage was only eighteen feet wide with a staircase across half of its back wall, and the capacity was a mere one hundred and fifty, yet during the ensuing years it became a theatre of remarkable vitality. Dukes produced plays while Rambert formed her Ballet Club, which had evolved by 1935 into Ballet Rambert. The small troupe began touring Britain as early as 1931, and even made a number of television experiments in the thirties. The repertory fostered new works, but always included the classics. **Michel Fokine**'s **Les Sylphides** became Ballet Rambert's signature piece alongside **Giselle**, **Coppélia**, **L'Après-midi d'un faune** and, in 1960, the first English production of **La Sylphide**. One of the company's greatest triumphs was a 67-week tour of Australia and New Zealand in 1948/49; it was also the first British ballet company to tour China, in 1957.

Known as Mim, Rambert (made Dame Marie in 1962) was a small, vivacious, even volatile woman who continued to turn cartwheels (her party piece) until her seventieth birthday. She was a talent spotter, a mothering force who guided others towards fulfilling their potential and who repeatedly saw her artists move on. Rambert philosophically kept going, training new dancers, encouraging new choreographers, even though Ballet Rambert, always short of money, came close to disbanding on a number of occasions. In 1966, with her latest choreographic discovery Norman Morrice, Rambert took the bold step of switching from classical ballet to contemporary dance (see Rambert Dance Company entry in The Dance Explosion, page 217).

Lineage

In tandem with **Ninette de Valois**, Marie Rambert is the most important personality in the birth of British ballet. Her major finds were **Frederick Ashton** and **Antony Tudor**; other choreographic alumni included Andrée Howard, Walter Gore and Frank Staff. Among the Rambert dancers were Celia Franca, founder of the **National Ballet of Canada**, and Peggy van Praagh, the first artistic director of the **Australian Ballet**. Norman Morrice became artistic director of the **Royal Ballet** and **Christopher Bruce** is now the resident choreographer of **London Festival Ballet**.

Follow-up

Rambert's autobiography *Quicksilver* was published in 1972. Mary Clarke's *Dancers of Mercury* (1962) chronicles the first thirty years of the company, and *Ballet Rambert: 50 Years and On* is a liberally illustrated company history that first appeared in 1976 (revised 1981). From the earliest days, Rambert was keenly interested in filming her ballets: an anthology of her recordings – *Ballet Rambert and the Ballet Club* – is in the archives of the National Film Theatre, London.

Bolshoi Ballet

Formed: 1776, by Michael Maddox and Prince Urusov

With 300 dancers and over 400 backstage staff, the sheer size of the Bolshoi Ballet justifies its name (the word 'bolshoi' is simply Russian for 'big'). The classics, and new works by current artistic director **Yuri Grigorovich**, are conceived and executed on a grand scale. The dancers, meanwhile, are trained to exhibit a dramatically vivid, technically full-out amplitude of movement that marks them as champions of their art. They are the products of an eight-year course at the Moscow Choreographic Institute, which takes on eighty new pupils annually from the Soviet bloc countries. Only the cream of the crop join the Bolshoi on graduation.

The Bolshoi was formed by Michael Maddox, an English entrepreneur, and Prince Urusov, a patron of the arts, who received a government licence to promote ballet in Tsarist Russia. Its first dancers were principally recruited from the Moscow Orphanage. Classes were conducted from 1773 by the Italian dancing master Filippo Beccari, who was given three years to whip this raw material into performance-level shape.

The company has been dancing on the site of its present theatre since 1780. In its first decades the repertory consisted of ballets and divertissements employing pantomime, mythology and folkloric or patriotic themes. Initially, the Bolshoi was overshadowed by its glittering Imperial cousin – now the **Kirov Ballet** – in the country's cultural centre (and then capital) St Petersburg, where the performing style was cooler and more purist. In contrast, dance in Moscow tended to be earthier, more contemporary in theme and emotional in approach, and was regarded (sometimes legitimately) as inferior.

Substantial artistic progress came with **Marius Petipa**'s 1869 production of **Don Quixote** and the first staging of **Swan Lake** in 1877. The arrival of the St Petersburg-trained dancer Alexander Gorsky at the turn of the century proved even more crucial to Moscow's balletic development. A highly cultured man, Gorsky was a dedicated follower of both **Isadora Duncan** and Konstantin Stanislavski's Art Theatre, where the ultimate goal was extreme honesty and realism in performance. He revitalised the Bolshoi's somewhat hidebound repertory by revising the Petipa oeuvre (including an 1898 production of **The Sleeping Beauty** staged in just three weeks). In his own ballets, he utilised innovative stage designs, introduced dramatic action into dance and adapted symphonic music to the ballet vocabulary. Gorsky remained company director until his death in 1942, seeing the Bolshoi through the 1917 Revolution that shifted the nation's political clout to Moscow and opened the theatre's doors to a new mass audience.

The Bolshoi continued to be fuelled by the classical tradition, both before and after the Second World War. Yet, with the exception of major works like the overtly political *The Red Poppy* in 1927, the most important new Soviet ballets were still created in Leningrad. The creative emphasis only shifted to Moscow when **Leonid Lavrovsky** transferred as artistic director from the Kirov to the Bolshoi in 1944, accompanied by **Galina Ulanova**, the lyrical heroine of Soviet ballet par excellence. Ulanova and **Maya Plisetskaya** ranked high amongst the company's stars when the Bolshoi began touring in the West after Stalin's death in the mid-fifties.

When Yuri Grigorovich assumed company leadership in the sixties, he added a fresh shot of adrenalin to the Bolshoi's artistic blood-stream, which had once again grown sluggish. His reworkings of the classics stressed dancing, rather than mime, without any loss of theatrical power, while his own ballets (including **Spartacus** and **The Golden Age**) have raised the Bolshoi style to new, spectacularly heroic heights with stars like Natalia Bessmertnova (Grigorovich's wife), Andris Liepa and Irek Mukhamedov.

Lineage

The Bolshoi has evolved from ballet's earliest Franco-Italian roots, as well as absorbing the popular heritage of Russian folk dance. As with the **Kirov Ballet**, the bedrock of the company's repertory is the choreography of **Marius Petipa**. **Yuri Grigorovich**'s ballets, with their emphasis on psychological portraiture expressed in bold movement, can be aligned with the work of **John Cranko**, **Kenneth MacMillan** and **John Neumeier**. From 1977, former Bolshoi stars Vladimir Vasiliov and Natalia Kasatkina directed Moscow Classical Ballet; in 1988 they co-produced the first-ever Anglo-Soviet version of **Swan Lake**.

Follow-up

Iris Morley's *Soviet Ballet* (1945) contains insights into company styles and productions. *The Bolshoi Ballet* (1981, English version 1984) is a mainly pictorial volume. Natalia Roslavleva's *Era of the Russian Ballet* (1966) offers a Soviet view of ballet past and present, while Mary Grace Swift's 1968 *The Art of the Dance in the USSR* analyses both political and artistic aspects. The centrepiece of Paul Czinner's 1956 film *The Bolshoi Ballet* is Galina Ulanova's *Giselle*. *The Bolshoi Ballet Tours America* (1959) follows the company visiting sites like Disneyland, and gaping at rehearsals of Balanchine's *Agon*. Of the various videos available, *The Magic of the Bolshoi Ballet* (1987) is a compilation of rehearsals, class and performance clips spanning fifty years. Video versions of artistic director Yuri Grigorovich's ballets *Spartacus* and *Ivan the Terrible* have been released (1975 and 1977 respectively), and a BBC video of *The Golden Age* was filmed by the BBC in 1987 with Bessmertnova and Mukhamedov.

Birgit Cullberg

Born: 3rd August 1908/Nyköping, Sweden

Birgit Cullberg has made Sweden's most important contribution to the development of dance, with a choreographic language that embraces a classical as well as modern vocabulary. After studying literature at Stockholm University she turned to dance, training with **Kurt Jooss** in England and **Martha Graham** in New York, before touring the Continent in the late 1940s with the Svenska Dansteatern, an avant-garde company which she had co-founded with Ivo Cramér. Her first big success – and the ballet for which she is still best known – was a 1950 adaptation of *Miss Julie*, Strindberg's play of lust and humiliation between an aristocratic young seductress and her butler. Both in its themes and the portrayal of eroticism through classical technique, the work shared much in common with **Roland Petit**'s **Carmen**, which had premiered the previous year, and which Cullberg had seen. Other notable Cullberg ballets include adaptations of *Medea* (1950), a Lapp folk tale called *Moon Reindeer* (1957) and Ibsen's *Lady From the Sea* (1960). During the fifties, Cullberg was both resident choreographer of the Royal Swedish Ballet and a busy international freelancer until she founded the state-supported Cullberg Ballet in 1967.

Lineage

Like **Antony Tudor**, Cullberg tends to use dance as a means of psychological study. The title role in *Miss Julie* is a plum part for dramatic ballerinas, while male dancers must try to equal or sur-pass the acclaim **Erik Bruhn** received for his interpretation of the butler. Cullberg's sons Niklas and Mats Ek have also danced in her company, the latter emerging as a choreographer in his own

right, although he shares with his mother a penchant for using folk legend and stage dramas as an inspirational source. Together, mother and son formed the Mats Ek/Cullberg Ballet; one of the troupe's most successful productions is Ek's radical **Swan Lake**.

Follow-up

Cullberg, who won a 1961 Prix d'Italia for the TV ballet film *The Evil Queen* (a retelling of *Snow White*), wrote about televised dance in the second edition of Walter Sorell's *The Dance Has Many Faces* (1966). A 1964 film, *Sweden: Fire and Ice*, contains a performance of *Miss Julie* in the Drottningholm Court Theatre; a 1981 video of the same ballet features Galina Panova in the title role. Eva Evdokimova is a featured dancer in the 1985 video of Cullberg's *Family Portrait*.

Agnes de Mille

Born: 18th September 1909/New York City

One of the great purveyors of a specifically American style of dance, Agnes de Mille is best known for introducing popular dance idioms into academic ballet. She was born into a rich, smart Hollywood family (her uncle was movie magnate Cecil B. De Mille) and after graduation from the University of California, studied and gave solo recitals in Europe. In London, she appeared in musical comedies, and danced with **Marie Rambert**'s company in the original production of **Antony Tudor**'s 1937 *Dark Elegies*. Back in America, she followed her first important choreography – the 1941 morality burlesque *Three Virgins and a Devil* – with her break-through piece **Rodeo** the next year. This ballet, along with *Fall River Legend*, is her most popular work. Created for Nora Kaye, but danced on opening night by Alicia Alonso, *Fall River Legend* (1948) is a highly dramatic ballet based on the infamous Lizzie Borden murder case, which offers a particularly meaty role for the ballerina. This was one of the original **American Ballet Theatre** hits; forty years later, de Mille made a choreographic comeback at ABT with *The Informer*, a 1988 ballet set to Celtic tunes.

To some extent, de Mille's work falls through the cracks between ballet and modern dance. She carved a large, important niche for herself in show business. On Broadway she choreographed *Oklahoma!* (1943), the show that revolutionised the American musical-comedy form in its integration of storyline, song and dance, and followed this with *Carousel (1945), Brigadoon* (1947), *Gentlemen Prefer Blondes* (1949) and *Paint Your Wagon* (1951).

Lineage

De Mille's Americana corresponds to **Antony Tudor**'s very English, psychologically-based story ballets. Her cinematic sensibility and her interest in translating popular culture and folk myths into narrative dance are reflected in **George Balanchine**'s 'Slaughter on Tenth Avenue' from the musical comedy *On Your Toes*, **Eugene Loring**'s **Billy the Kid**, and **Jerome Robbins**' **Fancy Free**. Dances from *Brigadoon* and *Carousel* are in the repertory of the late Lee Theodore's American Dance Machine.

Follow-up

De Mille adapted her original choreography for the 1955 film version of *Oklahoma!*, while the 'dream dance' from *Carousel* was faithfully retained by the 1956 film's choreographer Rod Alexander. A skilled speaker, lecturer and dance consultant, de Mille is also a talented author, who has written widely on dance, including the autobiographical *Dance to the Piper* (1951) and two personal histories, *The Book of the Dance* (1963) and *America Dances* (1980).

Rodeo

One act
Choreography: Agnes de Mille
Music: Aaron Copland
Design: Oliver Smith and Kermit Love
Premiere: 16th October 1942/ Metropolitan Opera House, New York City

Both forthright and frothy, *Rodeo* (subtitled *The Courting at Burnt Ranch*) is a folksy embodiment of some of America's most cherished clichés. A tomboy, trying to win her beau by competing with him – unsuccessfully – on his own terms, finally succeeds by donning a skirt and going girlish.

The comic Cinderella of *Rodeo* is the Cowgirl, danced by de Mille herself in the original production for the touring Ballet Russe de Monte Carlo. She is head over heels in love with the Head Wrangler of a Texas ranch, but he only has eyes for the ranch owner's daughter. The Cowgirl tries to focus attention on her own abilities by breaking into the men's rodeo, where she attempts to tame a bucking bronco, but ends up being thrown and made a laughing-stock. All the tussles with horses, steers and flying lassoes are, of course, depicted through mime.

The scene shifts to a Saturday night square dance that includes a tap dance by the Champion Roper, who is a cajolingly tolerant big brother figure for the Cowgirl. Everyone lines up for a Virginia reel, but the Cowgirl is left without a partner. Humiliated, she dashes from the scene, only to reappear moments later in a loud red dress. The transformation may only have been from ugly duckling to gawky goose, but immediately both the Champion Roper and the Head Wrangler want to dance with her. The Roper wins out, claims the Cowgirl, and the ballet ends with everyone dancing in exuberant celebration.

Lineage

The implicit sexism of *Rodeo* will rankle modern audiences, but if you can swallow the period-piece Cinderella philosophy, it remains a ballet full of homespun energy. De Mille's seamless integration of folk, tap and social dances was to serve her well from this point on, particularly in the Broadway musical *Oklahoma!* a year later. **John Cranko**'s **Pineapple Poll** rings Royal Navy variations on the same theme. **Antony Tudor** also explored the role of the outsider, but with serious, even tragic overtones: **Pillar of Fire** and *Undertow* (1945) both depict the devastating consequences of a need to conform.

Follow-up

The first section of *Rodeo* is included in the compilation film *American Ballet Theatre: A Close-Up in Time* (1973). De Mille writes about the creation of *Rodeo* in *Dance to the Piper* (1952), and *Inside American Ballet Theatre* (1978) features a long interview with de Mille by critic Clive Barnes. Marcia B. Siegel's *The Shapes of Change* (1979) perceptively questions the clichés and stereotypes that occur in this work.

Stagings

1 **American Ballet Theatre**/1950, latest revival 1987
2 **Joffrey Ballet**/1976

Ninette de Valois

Born: 6th June 1898/Baltiboys, County Wicklow, Ireland

Known to one and all simply as 'Madam', the architect of the **Royal Ballet** was born Edris Stannus. Her family moved to England when she was seven, and despite suffering a mild case of polio (not fully diagnosed until she was in her mid-twenties), she took avidly to dancing and received her first taste of celebrity as one of Lila Field's Wonder Children in 1913. After appearing in a variety of theatricals, she danced in the 1919 opera season at Covent Garden and spent a season with a short-lived English company organised by **Léonide Massine** during one of his breaks from the Ballets Russes.

De Valois' future mission in life crystallised during the seasons she danced in Europe with the Ballets Russes (from 1923 to 1925). The vitality of the dancers, and the subsidised theatres on the Continent, convinced her that England needed a national ballet of its own. After opening her own studio, the London Academy of Choreographic Art, she boldly approached Lilian Baylis with her plans. The formidable Baylis, who had already turned the Old Vic into a venue for popular opera and theatre, must have recognised a kindred spirit in de Valois. She agreed to add ballet to the roster if de Valois would also stage the dances needed for the Old Vic productions.

When the renovated Sadler's Wells Theatre, the second of the Baylis flagships, opened its doors in 1931, de Valois closed her studio and moved her students and new company there. Since they were going to be performing in both theatres, the company's first name was the Vic-Wells Ballet. In retrospect, it is astonishing how rapidly de Valois turned dreams into reality. Her determination and sound judgment, her early programming of the great nineteenth-century classics, and the advent of **Frederick Ashton** as resident choreographer created the foundation on which the Royal Ballet is built.

As soon as she had trained others to replace her, de Valois stopped dancing. Her own choreography also took a back seat in her drive towards a British ballet worthy of international recognition. Her best remembered ballets, all featuring contemporary English scores, date from the 1930s, when the repertory was still in need of new works. *Job* (Subtitled *A*

Masque for Dancing) was inspired by the art of William Blake and created in 1931 to a score by Ralph Vaughan Williams. *The Rake's Progress* (1935) mirrors the famed series of Hogarth etchings and is danced to music by Gavin Gordon. Her most enduring ballet, *Checkmate* (1937), has a score by Arthur Bliss. The characters are warring chess pieces: the Black Queen seduces and then murders the Red Knight, and her victory becomes absolute when her minions, the pawns, corner the enfeebled Red King (one of **Robert Helpmann**'s finest roles).

By the outbreak of the Second World War, the company had already defined a distinctly lyrical British style exemplified by the Ashton ballets performed by **Margot Fonteyn**. During the war years, the company gained a broad-based audience hungry for entertainment. In 1946, the company finally moved to the Royal Opera House in Covent Garden where it received its Royal Charter a decade later. Hundreds of artists, teachers and administrators had all played their parts, but de Valois both charted the course and steered the helm.

She turned the directorship of

June Brae and Harold Turner in the original production of Ninette de Valois' *Checkmate*

105

the Royal Ballet over to Ashton in 1963, when she switched her main focus to the two Royal Ballet Schools, working there full time until 1971 and even in her eighties continuing to offer special classes and coaching to individual dancers. She became Dame Ninette in 1951, received the Légion d'honneur in 1959 and was the first woman ever to receive the Dutch Erasmus Prize.

Lineage

As methodically determined as a great general, there was something Churchillian about the way de Valois ran her company. She had learned her trade (both what and what not to do) from **Serge Diaghilev**. Unlike Diaghilev, de Valois had to start virtually from scratch, as **George Balanchine** had to do when he emigrated to America in 1933. Lucia Chase, one of the founding directors of **American Ballet Theatre**, was another dancer who essentially forfeited her own performing career for the sake of a company.

Follow-up

De Valois, who claims she would have been a writer but for ballet, has published three volumes of memoirs: *Invitation to the Ballet* (1937), *Come Dance With Me* (1957) and *Step to Step* (1977). Kathrine Sorley Walker's *Ninette de Valois: Idealist Without Illusions* (1987) is a thoroughly researched overview of her career augmented by several short de Valois essays.

Anton Dolin

Born: 27th July 1904/Slinfold, Sussex
Died: 25th November 1983/Paris

Anton Dolin, of Anglo-Irish descent (he was born Sydney Healey-Kay), was the first British male dancer to earn an international reputation. This fame rested less on brilliant technique than on a commanding presence, a sense of showmanship and impeccable partnering. Besides helping to lay the foundations for what later became the **Royal Ballet** and **American Ballet Theatre**, he brought some of the zest and panache of variety theatre to classical ballet.

While still a child actor in straight plays and musical comedy, Dolin studied with **Bronislava Nijinska** and Serafina Astafieva, both associated with the Ballets Russes. Allegedly he liked to dance on point so much that he learned many ballerina parts, a feat that would serve him well as a partner. Billed as Patrikieff, he appeared in the corps de ballet of **Serge Diaghilev**'s 1921 London production of **The Sleeping Beauty**. Two years later he settled on the name Dolin, and joined the company as a soloist, creating roles in Nijinska's *Le Train bleu* (1924) and **George Balanchine**'s **The Prodigal Son** and *Le Bal* (both 1929).

After Diaghilev's death, Dolin helped found the Camargo Society, a ballet production club (in 1930) and created the role of Satan in **Ninette de Valois**' *Job*. He was a soloist with the Vic-Wells Ballet until 1935, when he and **Alicia Markova** formed the first of their own companies. In 1940, he became ballet master, choreographer and *premier danseur* of the newly established Ballet Theatre in New York. There he mounted his version of **Pas de quatre** (1941) and in the same year danced the comic lead in one of **Michel Fokine**'s last ballets, *Bluebeard*. From another troupe, newly formed with Markova, there emerged **London Festival Ballet** in 1950: Dolin was artistic director and first soloist until the early sixties. His choreographic output included a tour de force male equivalent of *Pas de quatre* called *Variations for Four* (1957), which is now in the repertory of the **Central Ballet of China**. Dolin spent the last two decades of his life producing and staging ballets, miming roles, teaching and writing. He was knighted in 1981.

The charm, high spirits and gymnastic abilities Dolin had displayed with the Ballets Russes helped make him a star overnight, but he is best remembered for his later achievements. He incorporated acrobatics into the classics – for instance, in **Giselle**, rolling down stairs to her tomb. A master of period dance styles, he also knew how to fill long musical phrases with meaningful movement and characterisation. And he was a dream partner, always gallant, attentive and dependable. He danced with many major ballerinas from Alexandra Danilova to Carla Fracci, but his most famous pairing was with Markova.

Lineage

Although not as renowned a choreographer as other protégés of **Serge Diaghilev** such as **Michel Fokine**, **Léonide Massine** or **Serge Lifar**, Dolin learned from Diaghilev how to assemble talent, build a repertory and mould successors. He had a knack for discovering and nurturing novices (Frederic Franklin and Vera Zorina among them) into stars, and like **Robert Helpmann**, he was a man of multiple talents. The harmony and timing Dolin shared with **Alicia Markova** make their partnership a precursor to the later, celebrated teamings of **Margot Fonteyn** and **Rudolf Nureyev** or **Gelsey Kirkland** and **Mikhail Baryshnikov**, while the athleticism he brought to ballet was only surpassed by members of the **Bolshoi Ballet**.

Follow-up

Dolin, who appears as Enrico Cecchetti in the 1980 film *Nijinsky*, wrote several volumes of memoirs including *Divertissement* (1931), *Ballet Go Round* (1938), *Autobiography* (1960) and *Last Words* (1985). He also wrote *Pas de Deux: the Art of Partnering* (1949), and two biographies, *Alicia Markova* (1953) and *The Sleeping Ballerina* (1966, on Olga Spessivtseva). He features in his close friend John Gilpin's *A Dance With Life* (1982). Andrew Wheatcroft compiled the pictorial biography *Dolin: Friends and Memories* (1982).

Margot Fonteyn

Born: 18th May 1919/Reigate, Surrey

Peggy Hookham, the child who was to become the supreme example of the poised, graceful British ballet style, began studying in England and continued her lessons in Shanghai. In 1934, at the end of a six-month visit to London with her mother, she auditioned at Sadler's Wells and received a postcard telling her to report for rehearsals as one of the snow-flakes in **The Nutcracker**.

Fonteyn modelled her early dancing on the Vic-Wells ballerina **Alicia Markova**, who left the company in 1935. Both artistic director **Ninette de Valois** and choreographer **Frederick Ashton** quickly realised Fonteyn's potential and pushed her into the leading classical roles: **Swan Lake**, **Giselle** and, in particular, **The Sleeping Beauty**.

From *Le Baiser de la Fée* (1935) to *Marguerite and Armand* (1963), Fonteyn served as Ashton's ideal muse. He created many of his most impressive roles for her, ranging from plotless works such as **Symphonic Variations**, *Scènes de ballet* and *Birthday Offering*, to dramatic ballets like *Apparitions*, **Cinderella** (although Moira Shearer danced the premiere due to a Fonteyn injury) and *Ondine*. This paean to Fonteyn's gracious style is the tale of a water sprite who, like **La Sylphide**, falls disastrously in love with a mortal. In her opening solo, after emerging from a waterfall, Ondine sees her shadow for the first time: initially frightened, she is soon toying with it in the way a kitten plays with a ball of yarn. Ashton based this sprightly number on an idea used by **Jules Perrot** in his own *Ondine* of 1843.

At the age of forty, Fonteyn relinquished her place as a regular member of the Royal (a compulsory step for ballerinas at the Paris Opéra) and took on guest star status. She would probably have retired if **Rudolf Nureyev** had not arrived on the scene. The Russian defector's fiery enthusiasm, mingling with and melting Fonteyn's pristine reserve, led to the most legendary of all ballet partnerships. Together they became such a box office draw that the Royal Ballet instigated a special ticket category for their performances.

After *Marguerite and Armand*, and intermingled with the classics, came **Kenneth MacMillan**'s **Romeo and Juliet**. The pair appeared around the world and made head-lines wherever they went: in 1969 they hit the front pages when they spent five hours behind bars as the result of a drugs bust at a San Francisco party they were attending.

Fonteyn will always be coupled with Ashton and Nureyev, but she also created Ophelia in **Robert Helpmann**'s 1942 *Hamlet*, performed in a modernist version of *Paradise Lost* by **Roland Petit** (1967), in *Poème de l'extase* by **John Cranko** (1970) and the title role of *The Merry Widow* by Ronald Hynd for the Australian Ballet in 1975. Earlier that year, minus her toe-shoes, she gamely backed up Nureyev in **Martha Graham**'s *Lucifer*.

She became Dame Margot in 1956, and in 1979 was canonised by the Royal Ballet with that rarest of all honorary titles, *prima ballerina assoluta*.

Lineage

Margot Fonteyn, the first major ballerina of this century not to have had direct contact with **Serge Diaghilev**, shares with **Anna Pavlova** the distinction of being the most popular ballerina of all time. Neither was ever a flashy dancer and both expressed distrust in technical gimmickry, preferring to build their stage personae around delicate and expressive musicality.

Follow-up

The major Fonteyn films are *Ondine* (1958), *Romeo and Juliet*

(1966) and *Marguerite and Armand* (included in Nureyev's 1973 *I Am a Dancer*). In 1979, Fonteyn devised and narrated *The Magic of Dance*, a six-part BBC series; this personal history of the art form was sub-sequently published as a book. *Margot Fonteyn: An Autobiography* appeared in 1975, and Keith Money has produced a pair of lavish photo books.

Robert Helpmann

Born: 9th April 1909/Mount Gambier, South Australia
Died: 28th September 1986/Sydney

Helpmann was a chameleon par excellence, a clown who could play Hamlet (and did, both in a ballet of his own creation and as an actor). His remarkably successful career as dancer, choreographer, actor, director and producer earned him the tag 'enigma of the English theatre' from **Royal Ballet** founder **Ninette de Valois**. His most notable achievements occurred during more than thirty years in England, but his life and his life's work began and ended in his native country.

The son of a prosperous sheep farmer and a frustrated actress, Helpmann performed profession-ally from childhood. His first ambition, one he never shook, was to be an actor, but **Anna Pavlova** converted him to ballet at the age of fourteen, taking him into her company as a student member during an Australian tour. After nine years in musical comedy, he came to London in 1933, and soon found a place in the Vic-Wells (now Royal) Ballet corps. A quick learner with a striking presence – slightly built, but with a full mouth, flaring nostrils and protruding eyes – he was dancing within a year roles originated by company principal **Anton Dolin** and

Robert Helpmann and Frederick Ashton as the Ugly Sisters in Ashton's *Cinderella*

partnering **Alicia Markova** in *Giselle*; two years later he danced opposite **Margot Fonteyn** in her first performance of the same ballet. Their pairing lasted until Helpmann left the company in 1950 to concentrate on acting and play production.

Helpmann's versatility was indispensable to wartime British ballet, when there was a shortage of good male dancers. His long line and imposing manner served him well in lieu of virtuoso technique in the classical repertory. His forte was characterisation; he is perhaps best remembered for applying his brilliant gift for mime and mastery of make-up effects to such comic roles as the bossy Ugly Sister in **Frederick Ashton**'s **Cinderella**, the bridegroom in Ashton's *A Wedding Bouquet* and Doctor Coppelius in **Coppélia**, but he was as much at home in dramatic parts like the Red King in de Valois' *Checkmate*. Of his own choreography, only a flashback, Freudian version of *Hamlet* (1942), and *Miracle in the Gorbals* (1944), a modern-day Christ allegory set in the Glasgow slums, merit attention today. As it is, they are rarely revived.

While Helpmann continued to function as guest artist and choreographer for the Royal Ballet in the 1960s, his professional base was the **Australian Ballet**, where he was the company's artistic director with Peggy van Praagh from 1965 to 1976.

Lineage

Like **Serge Lifar** and **Anton Dolin**, Helpmann gained acclaim despite a late start as a serious dancer. A mark of his performing range was his ability to play either the evil witch Carabosse or the heroic Prince Florimund in **The Sleeping Beauty**. The versatility Helpmann exemplified can be found in other actor-dancers such as **Fred Astaire**, **Mikhail Baryshnikov** and **Rudolf Nureyev**.

Follow-up

Helpmann danced in and choreographed the title ballet of the milestone British film *The Red Shoes* (1948). He also co-directed and played the title role in the 1973 film of Rudolf Nureyev's *Don Quixote*. Elizabeth Salter's *Helpmann – the Authorized Biography* appeared in 1982.

The Red Shoes

Direction: Michael Powell and Emeric Pressburger
Choreography: Robert Helpmann (with Léonide Massine)
Music: Brian Easdale
Production design: Hein Heckroth
Release: 1948

One of the most famous British films of its era, *The Red Shoes* was the first film to portray serious dance onscreen as something more than isolated filler material intended simply to impress audiences. The script, about the Cinderella-like career and conflicting love life of a young ballerina (played by the exquisite Moira Shearer), reeks of the heady perfume of the backstage ballet world. Take this classic exchange: 'Why do you want to dance?', Shearer is asked by her autocratic mentor, a Svengali figure superbly played by Anton Walbrook. Her answer: 'Why do you want to live?'

In this film, dance is indisputably a matter of life and death. The film's centrepiece, a fourteen-minute ballet mostly choreographed by Robert Helpmann, is based on a Hans Christian Andersen fable about a young girl sold a pair of enchanted slippers. Initially she is delighted, until (shades of **Giselle**) the shoes refuse to let her stop dancing and she dies.

The parallel between Shearer's on- and off-stage selves is made obvious, paving the way for a preposterous trumped-up tragedy à la *Anna Karenina*. The net effect is of unforgettable kitsch of a high order. Besides Helpmann, the cast features **Léonide Massine**, who devised his own role as the ballet's evil shoemaker, and Ludmila Tcherina as temperamental dance stars. Three years later the same team – Powell, Pressburger, Shearer, Helpmann, Massine and Tcherina, augmented by **Frederick Ashton** – failed with a follow-up dance film entitled *The Tales of Hoffman*.

Lineage

This film, like the 1961 screen version of *West Side Story* (choreographed by **Jerome Robbins**) and the 1975 Broadway musical *A Chorus Line* (by Michael Bennett), influenced a generation of young people to study dance. Dutch choreographer Rudi van Dantzig claims to have seen it forty-eight times. Numerous later ballet or dance-orientated films owe a debt to *The Red Shoes*, including *An American in Paris* (1951, with Gene Kelly), *The Tales of Beatrix Potter* (1971, choreography by **Frederick Ashton**) and *Dancers* (1987), starring **Mikhail Baryshnikov** and Alessandra Ferri.

Leonid Lavrovsky

Born: 18th June 1905/St Petersburg
Died: 26th November 1967/Paris

The principal claim to fame of Leonid Lavrovsky is his creation of the greatest Soviet dramatic ballet from the first half of this century. A good classical dancer and partner, he appeared with **George Balanchine** in Fyodor Lopokov's controversial *Dance Symphony* (1923); with its mix of academics and acrobatics, this was a precursor of the plotless ballets that were later to become commonplace, although at the time it was panned by the critics. Lavrovsky himself was an exponent of narrative ballets which fused emotional realism and kinetic poetry. After an early start at both teaching and choreography, including the Pushkin-inspired *Prisoner of the Caucasus* (1938), he produced his major work, **Romeo and Juliet**, for the **Kirov Ballet** in 1940, moving on to the **Bolshoi Ballet** for the definitive production in 1946. This was the ballet with which the Bolshoi conquered London a decade later. A measure of Lavrovsky's importance to Soviet Ballet is the fact that he headed the Kirov from 1938 to 1944 before becoming chief choreographer and artistic director of the Bolshoi from 1944 to 1956, and again from 1960 to 1964.

Lineage

The West identifies **Yuri Grigorovich** as the inheritor of Lavrovsky's mantle as the prime creator of twentieth-century Soviet dramatic ballet. Lavrovsky's son Mikhail became one of the Bolshoi's leading principal dancers, and a frequent partner of Natalia Bessmertnova.

Follow-up

Natalia Roslavleva's *Era of the Russian Ballet* (1966) and Mary Grace Swift's *The Art of the Dance in the USSR* (1968) both discuss Lavrovsky's contribution to Soviet dance. Lavrovsky himself wrote about Sergei Prokofiev in the latter's 1956 *Autobiography, Articles, Reminiscences.*

Romeo and Juliet

Three acts
Choreography: Leonid Lavrovsky
Music: Sergei Prokofiev
Premiere: 11th January 1940/Kirov Theatre, Leningrad

Pride of place among full-length twentieth-century ballets belongs to *Romeo and Juliet*. Prokofiev's popular score, which has inspired dozens of versions, faithfully follows the story and structure of the Shakespeare play and is so specific that no choreographer can achieve genuine success without adhering to its programmatic scenario. When **Yuri Grigorovich** created an abstracted reworking in 1978, the result was met with critical derision and audience incomprehension.

The story is ideal for dancing. The rebellious passion of the two young lovers allows for lush, romantic pas de deux, set against vivid full-company set pieces, ranging from the Capulets' ball, where Romeo and Juliet first meet, to the brawling scenes for the young men in the town square.

Unfortunately, some two-thirds of the way through, the story becomes temporarily unhinged. It is virtually impossible for Friar Laurence to explain to Juliet (and the audience) how the mock suicide sleeping potion will save her, nor how he plans to arrange her reunion with the now banished Romeo. Mime cannot convincingly convey these actions and their repercussions. This scene is invariably a hiccup where a choreographer must rely on programme notes and the audience's prior knowledge of Shakespeare's narrative.

One of the most dramatic and telling moments is in the **Kenneth MacMillan** version for the Royal Ballet, at the point when Juliet, alone in her room, must decide if she is going to swallow the potion. The music builds to a dynamic crescendo which the choreographer reinforces by having Juliet sit in frozen stillness. Her immobility points up both her childlike vulnerability and her desperate situation. From the awakening physical passion of the balcony pas de deux to her final suicide, Juliet remains the ballet's central character. Her love and Romeo's impetuous actions are the catalyst for her new-found maturity.

Lineage

Romeo and Juliet ballets date back as far as 1811, and before Lavrovsky staged his Kirov version, the Prokofiev score had first been used in a now lost 1938 Czechoslovak production. The most significant alternative to the Prokofiev score is a one-act version by **Antony Tudor** (for American Ballet Theatre, 1943), danced to music by Delius. **Jerome Robbins**, in collaboration with Leonard Bernstein, turned Romeo and Juliet into *West Side Story*, one of the most important of all Broadway dance musicals. In 1969, Igor Tchernichov used selections from the eponymous Berlioz score to create a four-character ballet which was immediately banned in the Soviet Union. Juliet was to have been **Natalia Makarova**, with **Mikhail Baryshnikov** as Mercutio and Valeri Panov as Tybalt.

Follow-up

The Lavrovsky version was filmed in 1954 with Galina Ulanova. A popular 1966 film stars Fonteyn and Nureyev in the Kenneth MacMillan staging for the Royal Ballet, while a second film of the same version features Alessandra Ferri and Wayne Eagling.

Stagings

1 **Antony Tudor**/American Ballet Theatre/1943 (one act version)
2 **Frederick Ashton**/Royal Danish Ballet/1955 (and London Festival Ballet, 1985)
3 **John Cranko**/La Scala, Milan/1958 (Stuttgart Ballet, 1962)
4 **Kenneth MacMillan**/Royal Ballet/1965 (and American Ballet Theatre, 1985)
5 **Michael Smuin**/San Francisco Ballet/1976
6 **Heinz Spoerli**/Basel Ballet/1977
7 **Rudolf Nureyev**/London Festival Ballet/1977

Serge Lifar

Born: 2nd April 1905/Kiev
Died: 15th December 1986/Lausanne

While most of the many ballets choreographed by Serge Lifar have now fallen out of favour, he remains significant both as a dancer in the last phase of the Ballets Russes and as director and star of the **Paris Opéra Ballet** for three decades. His career was a classic example of making the maximum use of good fortune.

Serge Lifar in *The Freaks*, a ballet number from C. B. Cochran's 1930 revue at the London Pavilion

Lifar was introduced to ballet unexpectedly at the age of fifteen, when a friend brought him to one of **Bronislava Nijinska**'s free classes at her Kiev studios. Nijinska left to work for **Serge Diaghilev** again, but three years later, when she cabled for a handful of her best pupils to join the corps of the Ballets Russes, Lifar substituted for someone who could not be traced. His rudimentary technique was bolstered by sensational good looks (he later had his nose flattened to accentuate his exoticism) and a burning ambition to better himself. Diaghilev noticed: Lifar became the last of the great impresario's male dance protégés, exposed to a panoply of art forms, as well as receiving special training from Nicolai Legat and Enrico Cecchetti, who had both taught **Vaslav Nijinsky** and **Michel Fokine**.

Within two years, Lifar had replaced **Anton Dolin** as Diaghilev's *premier danseur* in ballets by Nijinska and **Léonide Massine**. George Balanchine created two outstanding roles for him in the late twenties: **Apollo** and **The Prodigal Son**. After Diaghilev's death in 1929, Lifar took over a production at the Paris Opéra from Balanchine, who was indisposed. Shortly afterwards, Lifar became artistic director, completely revitalising the company and exerting tremendous influence on the then rather desiccated French dance tradition. The only hitch in Lifar's long reign occurred during the 1940s – accused of collaboration with the Germans, Lifar left the Opéra for a few seasons. He returned fully exonerated. His ballets, usually vehicles for his own brilliant dancing, dominated the Opéra repertory long after he left the company in 1959. The Opéra had experienced serious decline after the Romantic era: Lifar brought it back to life. A tireless self-promoter and ballet champion, he continued to lecture and write until his death. One of the few Lifar ballets to survive its creator is *Suite en blanc* (1943), which is now in the repertory of **London Festival Ballet** and the **Australian Ballet**.

Lineage

Lifar, another **Serge Diaghilev** discovery, followed in the footsteps of **Vaslav Nijinsky**, **Léonide Massine** and **Anton Dolin**. Like **Rudolf Nureyev** (one of his successors at Paris Opéra), Lifar stressed the importance of the male dancer, even altering the staging of **Giselle** to enlarge his role. His 1935 work *Icare* is notable for its choreography without music (a percussive score was added later); this predates the direction taken by **Merce Cunningham** and John Cage, who treat sound and movement as separate entities.

Follow-up

Lifar published more than two dozen books, including a memoir, *Serge et Diaghilev* (1939) and the autobiography *Ma Vie* (1965). Richard Buckle's painstakingly researched *Diaghilev* (1979) covers Lifar's relations with his mentor in detail.

London Festival Ballet

Formed: 1950, as Festival Ballet

Chief among Britain's 'other' major ballet companies, the nucleus of London Festival Ballet was formed from dancers recruited to support **Alicia Markova** and **Anton Dolin** during a regional tour. But what began as an ad hoc concert group soon became an established company under the management of Polish impresario Julian Braunsweg. Dolin was the first artistic director, a post he held for a decade, while Markova (who dropped out in 1952) supplied the company's name, basing it on the designation of 1951 as the year of the Festival of Britain.

The new company attracted appreciative audiences and press from the start, with a repertory consisting of the classics, popular one-act works (like Harald Lander's *Etudes*) and revivals, including several of **Michel Fokine**'s Ballets Russes works. This broad-based formula still works today. The international outlook assumed by the involvement of Dolin and Markova was reinforced by the interest of foreign promoters who offered the company extensive overseas tours throughout the 1950s. Festival Ballet thus became an important cultural ambassador, despite the fact that until the early 1960s it was virtually unsubsidised.

The company stood on financially shaky ground into its second decade, even enduring voluntary liquidation in 1962. By the time former Royal Ballet ballerina Beryl Grey took over artistic directorship in 1968, however, 'the world's most travelled ballet company' was back on course. One of Grey's first and most significant achievements was to secure the London Coliseum as the company's second regular home venue (seasons are now divided between the Coliseum and the company's long-time venue, the Royal Festival Hall). In addition, Grey continued the policy of staging the classics and reviving the Ballets Russes repertory, paying scrupulous attention to reconstruction of the designs. She persuaded **Léonide Massine** to re-stage a clutch of his ballets and encouraged the choreographic services of former Royal colleague Ronald Hynd. Meanwhile, a contemporary dance element was introduced into the company via choreographers Barry Moreland and **Glen Tetley**.

London Festival has frequently played host to guest stars: the most glamorous such acquisition during Grey's term was **Rudolf Nureyev**, who mounted spectacular, highly acclaimed productions of **The Sleeping Beauty** in 1975 and **Romeo and Juliet** in 1977, the latter created especially for the company. **Natalia Makarova** has staged her version of 'The Kingdom of the Shades' from **La Bayadère** and a streamlined but still intense **Swan Lake**.

Peter Schaufuss began his association with the Festival Ballet in 1970, and in 1979 was responsible for an award-winning production of **La Sylphide**. Five years later he replaced John Field as artistic director. One of his early actions was the launch of LFB, a small group of fifteen to twenty dancers drawn from (and interchangeable with) the parent company, to present new or existing works, generally in small or mid-sized venues. The troupe's repertory ranges from a restaged **Napoli** to **Michael Clark**'s *Drop Your Pearls and Hog it, Girl* (1986) and a major revival of **Christopher Bruce** and **Lindsay Kemp**'s 1977 *Cruel Garden*. Schaufuss also spearheaded a 1985 resurrection of **Frederick Ashton**'s *Romeo and Juliet*.

Lineage

In terms of size, function and accomplishment, London Festival Ballet falls somewhere between the **Royal Ballet** and its offshoot Sadler's Wells Royal Ballet. In the United States, it bears comparison to the **Joffrey Ballet** and **San Francisco Ballet**.

Follow-up

Company co-founder Julian Braunsweg wrote about his career in *Braunsweg's Ballet Scandals* (1973), while John Gilpin (an early star dancer and later artistic director) features the company in his memoirs *A Dance With Life* (1982). The company appears as the Ballets Russes in Herbert Ross's misguided 1980 film *Nijinsky*.

Eugene Loring

Born: 1914/Milwaukee, Wisconsin
Died: 30th August 1982/Kingston, NY

Eugene Loring's reputation as a choreographer now rests almost entirely on the Americana ballet **Billy the Kid**, which he created in 1938 for Lincoln Kirstein's Ballet Caravan. He had been dancing professionally for two years when he joined Kirstein's company in 1936. Four years later, Loring was one of the original members of Ballet Theatre, now **American**

Ballet Theatre. For the inaugural performance, he collaborated with author William Saroyan on *The Great American Goof*, a 'ballet-play' with dialogue. Before moving to Los Angeles in the mid-1940s, he formed his own small, short-lived company Dance Players. Once in California, he opened the American School of Dance and worked in films before his appointment as chairman of the dance department at the University of California, Irvine.

Lineage

In the 1930s and 40s, a groundswell of American choreographers sought ways to express their own folklore in terms which could stand side by side with the Russian-European heritage. Important ballets in this vein were **Agnes de Mille**'s **Rodeo** and *Fall River Legend*. Modern urban settings also served as ballet material: Ruth Page's *Frankie and Johnny* is the best known, along with Lew Christensen's *The Filling Station* (both 1938). The use of vernacular movement reached its peak with **Jerome Robbins**' **Fancy Free**.

Follow-up

Loring's most successful Hollywood choreography was for Fred Astaire in *Funny Face* (1956) and *Silk Stockings* (1957).

Billy the Kid

One act
Choreography: Eugene Loring
Libretto: Lincoln Kirstein
Music: Aaron Copland
Design: Jared French
Premiere: 16th October 1938/Chicago Opera House

Based on the true tale of a young outlaw, William H. Bonney, who killed twenty-one men before he himself was gunned down by his former partner turned sheriff, Pat Garrett, this ballet is every small child's Wild West fantasy transformed into a vigorous dance format. Throughout, Loring inventively employs the mime of childhood games to suggest everything from six-shooters to men on horseback. He also daringly uses the childhood trick logic of 'If I can't see you, you can't see me'. Whenever a character holds his flat hand in front of his face, he is meant to be hidden from the others on stage (by night-time darkness or behind non-existent rocks and ridges).

A 1942 Ballet Caravan staging of *Billy the Kid* with Eugene Loring (striped trousers) as Billy

The story sweeps along in a series of fast scenes that have the flow and scope of a film. The personal tragedy of Billy, the outsider (performed by Loring in the original Ballet Caravan production), is bracketed by scenes of frontier expansion. The ballet opens and closes with an endless 'Westward Ho!' processional of pioneers crossing the stage. Scenes of local New Mexico colour include saloon girls and gamblers as well as earnest pioneer folk.

The murderous career of Billy the Kid starts at the age of twelve, when he stabs the man who has accidentally shot his mother during a brawl. Billy, now beyond the pale, is next seen as a hardened killer, an outlaw who will be hunted down and shot in ambush. Just before his death, Billy dreams of (and dances with) his Mexican sweetheart. She is the only dancer on point in the entire ballet and, in an Oedipal twist, is performed by the same woman who plays his mother. Another of Loring's psychological tricks is to have all Billy's victims played by a single male dancer, a nemesis called Alias.

Lineage

The dream device used to provide Billy with a brief moment of happiness went on to become a cliché through its repeated use in ballets, Broadway shows and movies. It was an **Agnes de Mille** trademark in works like *Oklahoma!* and *Brigadoon*. *Billy the Kid* was the first of Aaron Copland's Americana scores for native choreographers: he followed this with **Rodeo** for de Mille, and **Appalachian Spring** for **Martha Graham**.

Follow-up

Billy the Kid forms half of a 1976 Dance in America video performed by American Ballet Theatre (coupled with Frederick Ashton's *Les Patineurs*).

Stagings

1 **American Ballet Theatre**/1941
2 **Dance Theatre of Harlem**/1988

Alicia Markova

Born: 1st December 1910/London

Alicia Markova (born Lillian Alicia Marks) was one of the first British dancers to gain worldwide acclaim as a Russian-trained ballerina. The eldest, but smallest, of four sisters, she initially took dance lessons to strengthen what were thought to be weak limbs. **Serge Diaghilev** spotted her in ballet class at the age of ten; charmed by her gossamer grace, he hired her for the Ballets Russes four years later, and Russianised her name.

While other girls her age were in school, she was touring Europe working with the likes of **George Balanchine** (she created the title nightingale role in his 1925 revival of the Stravinsky ballet *Le Chant du rossignol*) and was probably the last great ballerina to receive training from the distinguished teacher Enrico Cecchetti. After Diaghilev's death, she turned as a creative refuge to the various clubs and societies formed during British ballet's pioneering days. At **Ballet Rambert** and the Vic-Wells Ballet, she danced in the first English productions of **Giselle** and **Swan Lake**, and created roles in the early **Frederick Ashton** ballets **Façade** and *Les Rendezvous*.

Markova was partnered by most of the top male dancers of her era (including **Serge Lifar**, Frederick Franklin, **Erik Bruhn**, **Léonide Massine** and Robert Helpmann), but her most famous partner was **Anton Dolin**, with whom she formed several companies from 1935 onwards. One of these evolved into **London Festival Ballet**, where Markova acted as prima ballerina between 1950 and 1952. She also triumphed in America with the Ballet Theatre. Magnificent in sylph parts, she danced Giselle with special sympathy. Rather than springing from the ground, she seemed to float or soar softly completely without effort. This was her favourite role, followed by the female lead in **Antony Tudor**'s 1943 **Romeo and Juliet**. Markova retired from the stage in 1962, after a decade as guest artist for companies around the world. In the 1960s she was ballet director at the Metropolitan Opera House, New York and has since lectured, taught and promoted ballet on both sides of the Atlantic.

Lineage

In the purity and delicacy of her technique, Markova was one of the closest successors to **Anna Pavlova**, and was an ideal interpreter of the Marie Taglioni role in **Pas de quatre**. She was virtually the only British ballerina capable of dancing the great nineteenth-century classics in the 1930s. Her departure for America led to **Margot Fonteyn**'s accession as the prima ballerina of the Royal.

Follow-up

Anton Dolin wrote the biography *Alicia Markova: Her Life and Art* (1953); Markova herself authored *Giselle and I* (1960) and *Markova Remembers* (1986).

New York City Ballet

Formed: 1948, from Ballet Society

When Ballet Society was invited to become a component of the New York City Center for Music and Drama, **George Balanchine** and his partner Lincoln Kirstein had finally found a home for the company they first envisioned back in 1933. The first performance under the name New York City Ballet took place on 11th October 1948.

The route to that inaugural night included a number of false starts. The two men had begun by creating American Ballet, which became the dance wing of the Metropolitan Opera from 1935 to 1938. Balanchine choreographed twenty-three operas there, notably an innovative 1936 production of Gluck's *Orfeo ed Euridice*, with singers in the pit and dancers enacting the story on stage. Although in the following year the company was given an evening of its own devoted to Stravinsky (including **Apollo** and the premiere of *The Card Game*), the management refused to allow regular all-ballet programmes in the European tradition.

At the same time, Kirstein and the Christensen brothers (see **San Francisco Ballet**) had organised a touring group called Ballet Caravan. Their repertory included **Billy the Kid** and two major Balanchine works: *Concerto Barocco* and *Ballet Imperial*, the latter now known as *Tchaikovsky Piano Concerto No. 2* (both 1948). During this time the first generation of dancers was emerging from the School of American Ballet which Balanchine had helped to found, and in 1946 he and Kirstein created Ballet Society. Like **Marie Rambert**'s Ballet Club in the early thirties, admission was exclusively by subscription. Two years later, the company was invited to join the opera and theatre troupes at City Center, marking the official beginning of New York City Ballet (NYCB).

In 1949, **Jerome Robbins** joined for a decade as an associate ballet master (he returned for a second stint in 1969). Balanchine, who also called himself a ballet master, always refused the title of artistic director. A variety of other choreographers briefly visited NYCB, including **Frederick Ashton** and **Antony Tudor**, and former company dancers such as Todd Bolender and John Taras choreographed several works. Nonetheless, it was Balanchine who dominated the repertory.

Balanchine was always intrigued by experimentation. One of the most important examples occurred in 1959, when he and **Martha Graham** shared an evening to the music of Anton Webern. The event, called *Episodes*, began with a Graham dance about Mary, Queen of Scots. In contrast to this pageant, Balanchine created one of his most startlingly terse modernist works, including a spidery solo for **Paul Taylor**, then a Graham company dancer.

In 1964, the company moved to the much larger New York State Theater at Lincoln Center. The stage and orchestra pit were constructed to Balanchine's specifications and the floor, also designed by him, was a revolutionary basket weave of crisscrossed slats of wood forming a honeycomb of air. Much copied, it is known as a 'Balanchine' or 'sprung' floor. NYCB performs here for half of each year in an annual pair of winter and spring seasons. Like European opera ballets, the company shares its home with New York City Opera, but, contrary to European practice, the two troupes perform in rotation rather than intermingling the two repertories.

A particular NYCB trademark has been a series of festivals focussing on specific composers – Stravinsky (1972), Ravel (1975), Tchaikovsky (1981) – all blending existing ballets with an unprecedented number of new works. The Stravinsky Centennial Celebration in 1982 marked the culmination of the unique and fruitful collaboration between Balanchine and the composer.

Jerome Robbins' ongoing contribution to the NYCB repertory has been substantial, and since 1978, dancer **Peter Martins** has also regularly choreographed. On Balanchine's death the two were appointed dual ballet masters in chief. The company shows no sign of degenerating into a Balanchine museum, but its legacy continues to be the cornerstone of the NYCB repertory.

Lineage

No other ballet company has ever been such an obvious laboratory for its choreographer's personal vision. **Maurice Béjart**, **John Neumeier** and **John Cranko** all dominated their respective companies, but none could equal Balanchine's sheer productivity.

New York City Ballet's size (it now has over one hundred dancers) is rivalled in the West only by **Paris Opéra Ballet** and the slightly smaller **American Ballet Theatre**. NYCB's training ground, the School of American Ballet, is second to none.

Follow-up

Thanks in particular to the Public Broadcasting System, New York City Ballet's repertory is the best documented in existence. The Dance in America series includes no less than twenty-six Balanchine ballets, while eighteen works have been recorded by the French Network of the Canadian Broadcasting Corporation. Nancy Reynolds' *Repertory in Review* details every NYCB ballet from 1934 to 1976; *New York City Ballet* (1973) is one of the most handsome dance books ever; and Nancy Goldner's *The Stravinsky Festival* captures the energy and excitement of the event through a day-by-day chronology.

Roland Petit

Born: 13th January 1924/ Villemomble, France

For more than forty years, Roland Petit has moved comfortably between the worlds of ballet and musical comedy: he is synonymous with French dance entertainment. As a child, he studied at the Paris Opéra with **Serge Lifar** and joined the company in 1940, but although this was the foundation of his career, Lifar's domination and the classical atmosphere cramped his style and restless energy. He left the Opéra establishment at twenty to work with a group of artists (including Jean Cocteau) in forming Les Ballets des Champs-Elysées; Petit's father, the proprietor of a Paris bistro, helped finance their first ballets.

Four years later, Petit founded the Ballets de Paris, and was again the star dancer and chief choreographer. Two of his most famous ballets date from this period: *Le Jeune Homme et la Mort* (1946), an archetypal piece of post-war existentialism about a suicidal, lovelorn artist (a role originated by the bravura dancer Jean Babilée) and the 1949 **Carmen**. The latter paired Petit with dancer Renée Jeanmaire, whom he later married and with whom he shares a reputation for glittering professionalism.

Since 1972, he has been head of Ballet de Marseille, the second most important company in France, after the Opéra. He has choreographed an extensive range of short and full-length works there and for other companies, as well as innovative revivals of classics like **Coppélia** and **The Nutcracker**. Several of his ballets revolve around the pet theme of a humiliated or physically deformed hero hopelessly in love: from Cyrano de Bergerac and the Hunchback of Notre Dame to the Phantom of the Opera and the lycanthropic protagonist of *Le Loup* (1953).

Twenty years later, he choreographed *La Rose malade* for the Bolshoi star **Maya Plisetskaya**, and in 1985 devised *The Blue Angel* for **Natalia Makarova** (Petit himself appeared as the besotted professor).

Petit's brand of theatrical chic has enabled him to make regular forays into the cinema and music hall. Regardless of the medium, his work is noted for its sensuality, wit and vivid decorative sense.

Lineage

Some of **Serge Lifar**'s neo-classicism seeped into Petit during his training. In turn, Petit's own bold, blunt dramatic verve has been absorbed by **Maurice Béjart** and **Kenneth MacMillan**, whose *Manon* (1974) certainly owes a debt to **Carmen**. Petit's work imparts something of the flavour of the last decade of the Ballets Russes, particularly in his collaboration with leading designers and artists, including Christian Dior, Max Ernst and Erté.

Follow-up

Petit's extensive film work includes *Hans Christian Andersen* (1952), *The Glass Slipper* (1954), *Daddy Longlegs* (1955) and *Anything Goes* (1956). He and Jeanmaire appear in *Black Tights* (1962), a filmed record of several Petit pieces. Rudolf Nureyev and Jeanmaire performed a revised version of *Le Jeune Homme et la Mort* in a 1973 film; Mikhail Baryshnikov can be seen dancing this role at the start of the 1985 film *White Nights*.

Carmen

One act
Choreography: Roland Petit
Music: Georges Bizet
Design: Antoni Clavé
Premiere: 21st February 1949/ Prince's Theatre, London

At the time of its premiere, *Carmen* was the last word in chic. Now, after surviving twenty-five years of being démodé, it is once again back in fashion, and seems as much an emblem of its time as Christian Dior's New Look. Carmen herself (danced originally by Petit's future wife Renée 'Zizi' Jeanmaire) is a tough but gamine anti-heroine. *Carmen* follows the downward spiral of Merimée's novel and Bizet's opera, but here she embraces her fate with an existential largesse. In the finale, she dashes at Don José from across the stage and virtually impales herself on his knife. All of the characters are spiky, edgy, modern malcontents, and like the designs, the choreography merely hints at period Spanish authenticity. Don José, the only person on stage who lacks streetwise savvy, is constantly taunted for displaying honest emotions.

There is a belligerent edge to all of the movement, bristling with challenge and full of steamy stances (for both sexes) that loudly threaten 'I dare you'. Dancers rub up against each other like salt in a

Roland Petit as Don José and Renée Jeanmaire as the title role in the bedroom scene from the original production of Petit's *Carmen*

wound or cats on heat, and the central love duet for Carmen and José must be among the most sexually explicit couplings ever put on a ballet stage. José's rival, the Toreador, does not appear until the final scene outside the bullring. His movement is so rigidly stylised, so struttingly cock-of-the-walk, that he becomes a parody of sexual potency.

The **Antonio Gades** version of *Carmen* (1983), set in a modern Flamenco dance studio, restores the story to its original tragic dimension in a way that Petit's sultry chic does not begin to fathom. Alberto Alonso's 1967 condensation for the Bolshoi Ballet set the whole ballet inside the bullring and called it *Carmen Suite* (with **Maya Plisetskaya** as the heroine).

Lineage

Petit has long been a strong voice for sexual explicitness in ballet, but this trend reached its peak in the erotic pas de deux in **Kenneth MacMillan**'s **Mayerling**. In the work of Hans van Manen, **Glen Tetley** and **Maurice Béjart**, the approach to sexuality is inevitably a battle. A more contemporary and even more disturbing focus surfaces in the work of **Pina Bausch, William Forsythe** and DV8 Physical Theatre.

Follow-up

Carmen is part of the 1962 film *Black Tights*, while a later version features Mikhail Baryshnikov as Don José – both star Renée Jeanmaire.

Stagings

1 **Royal Danish Ballet**/1960
2 **Ballet de Marseille**/1972
3 **London Festival Ballet**/1986

Maya Plisetskaya

Born: 20th November 1925/ Moscow

Maya Plisetskaya is the quintessential Soviet ballerina, steely yet incredibly supple, with long, aristocratic limbs, curving back and a zesty temperament. Her mother was a silent screen actress (Plisetskaya has also taken straight cinematic roles) and most of her family were involved in ballet or the theatre. She entered the Bolshoi school in 1934, dancing solos even before her graduation in 1943. Bypassing the corps de ballet altogether, Plisetskaya soon became a principal in whose movement vocabulary the word 'impossible' apparently did not exist. She combined regal power and a challenging spirit with the pure, sculpted lines of her body and a flawless, expansive technique.

Plisetskaya is noted for her fast spins, scissor-like leaps and heel-to-head backwards kicks, the latter feat best exploited in her portrayal of Kitri in **Don Quixote** (her other most noted classical role is Odette/Odile in **Swan Lake**). Even in her sixties she was assigned top female parts. A painstaking artist (who repeatedly studied **Romeo and Juliet** for five years before dancing it) and something of a maverick, she has more freedom than many Soviet artists, probably due as much to her offstage character as to her international stature onstage. The Cuban choreographer Alberto Alonso created *Carmen Suite* for her in 1967; this remains one of the roles with which she is most identified. Plisetskaya has also danced with **Roland Petit**'s company in the premiere of his duo *La Rose malade* (1973), and appeared with **Maurice Béjart**'s Ballet of the 20th Century as his Leda and Isadora.

Her own choreographic efforts include adaptations of *Anna Karenina* (1972) and *The Seagull* (1980).

Lineage
Plisetskaya's flamboyant exuberance is in contrast to the more subtle poetry of **Galina Ulanova**. She originated the role of Mistress of the Copper Mountain in **Leonid Lavrovsky**'s *The Stone Flower*, in which Ulanova also starred in 1954.

Follow-up
Natalia Roslavleva wrote *Maya Plisetskaya* (English edition, 1956). The 70-minute documentary *Plisetskaya Dances* (1964) is a feast of excerpts from the Bolshoi classics; she also features in full-length versions of *Swan Lake* (1959) and *The Humpbacked Horse* (1961). *The Magic of the Bolshoi Ballet* is a 1987 compilation with Plisetskaya being coached in *Swan Lake* and dancing Kitri's variations in *Don Quixote*. For an under-standing of her personality and politics, read George Feifer's *Our Motherland* (1973), with its description of her reactions while watching herself on film.

Jerome Robbins

Born: 11th October 1918/New York City

The career of Jerome Robbins, America's pre-eminent native-born choreographer, falls into a number of distinct, though often over-lapping phases. His first ballet, the 1944 **Fancy Free**, was the sort of debut that all artists dream of: an instant popular and critical success. At that point he had already danced in several Broadway musicals and been a member of **American Ballet Theatre** for four years (where **Petrushka** was one of his roles).

In 1949 Robbins joined **New York City Ballet**. During his first (ten-year) stint with the company, he devised nine ballets including *Afternoon of a Faun*, **The Concert** and the insect-inspired allegory of *The Cage* (1951). In this period he also danced the title role in **George Balanchine**'s **The Prodigal Son**. At the same time, Robbins continued to work on Broadway (*The King and I*, 1951 and *Peter Pan*, 1954) before creating the landmark *West Side Story* (1957); in this urban New York version of *Romeo and Juliet*, commercial theatre and the art of dance were perfectly geared to capture the emerging American teen culture.

To allow himself the freedom to explore new trends, Robbins formed his own small company, Ballets: USA, for which he created *N.Y. Export: Op. Jazz* (a hep 1958 ballet in the *West Side Story* mould) and *Moves* (1959, performed in silence). This troupe had two successful summer seasons in Europe, but failed to catch on in America and disbanded. More Broadway shows such as *Gypsy* (1959) and *Fiddler on the Roof* (1964) were followed by a 1965 version of **Les Noces** for American Ballet Theatre. Robbins then spent some years in an experimental workshop, but this never led to public performance.

In 1969 he made a triumphal return to New York City Ballet with **Dances at a Gathering** and a large-scale staging of Bach's *The Goldberg Variations* (1971). Since then, he has remained with NYCB and produced a string of hits that include the controversial, Eastern-inspired *Watermill* (1972), Ravel's *Piano Concerto in G* (1975) and *Opus 19/The Dreamer* (1979, to Prokofiev's Violin Concerto No.1). Robbins also co-opted the post-modern composer Philip Glass for his *Glass Pieces* (1983) and has worked in collaboration with the versatile **Twyla Tharp** on *Brahms/Handel* (1984). Following the death of Balanchine in 1983, Robbins, with **Peter Martins**, was appointed joint ballet master of the company.

The Robbins style is a mix of social dance (both ethnic folk styles and more contemporary movement) with the classical ballet vocabulary. This often gives his works a likeable and immediate sense of fraternal easiness and marks him out as the most accessible of modern ballet choreographers.

Lineage

Broadway in its heyday could boast **George Balanchine**, **Agnes de Mille** and **Hanya Holm** among its choreographers, but no one moved back and forth so easily between the worlds of art and commerce as Robbins. Both **Bob Fosse** and Michael Bennett shied away from Robert Joffrey's invitations to create works for the **Joffrey Ballet**. Reversing the process, **Twyla Tharp**, the only other American choreographer truly at home with classical ballet, had commercial success with the film version of *Hair*, but bombed with her Broadway adaptation of *Singin' in the Rain*.

Follow-up

Robbins won two Oscars for the 1961 Hollywood version of *West Side Story*, and also recreated his 'Small House of Uncle Thomas' ballet for the film *The King and I* (1956). *An Evening of Jerome Robbins Ballets* (recorded by US television in 1980), features *Afternoon of a Faun* and *The Cage*.

Fancy Free

One act
Choreography: Jerome Robbins
Music: Leonard Bernstein
Design: Oliver Smith and Kermit Love
Premiere: 18th April 1944/ Metropolitan Opera House, New York City

This *cherchez la femme* comedy is the story of a trio of sailors let loose on weekend leave in New York City during the Second World War. Brimming with vernacular movement, the ballet is built around an 'odd man out' ploy which two of the guys use to con the third into paying for the beers. The game turns serious when, later in the evening, they only manage to track down two girls. The result is a dance competition in which each sailor struts his stuff to see who will win a date.

The first show-off solo is full of acrobatic hep-cat flash. The second sailor's solo is the exact opposite – smooth, boyish, even ingenuous – while the last (danced by Robbins in the original production for Ballet Theatre) has the swivel-hipped, come-hither allure of the rhumba. Unfortunately, the girls are unable to make up their minds. This provokes a brawl which gets so hectic that the women stomp out. Realising they have been deserted, the buddies shake hands and down another beer before dashing off after yet another potential conquest.

A milestone of American dance, *Fancy Free* was the first ballet by Jerome Robbins, the first dance score by Leonard Bernstein. It was an overnight sensation, soon expanded into a Broadway show and a Hollywood movie (*On the Town*). At the time, it was the last word in up-to-the-minute realism, but these sailors are actually no more dangerous than overgrown puppies let off the leash. An indication of just how far sexual and social attitudes have changed can be seen in the clowning incident where the threesome 'steal' the first girl's purse and gleefully taunt her by tossing it back and forth just out of her reach. In a 1980s ballet by **Pina Bausch** or **William Forsythe** this would lead to a mugging or worse; in a work by **Michael Clark** the outcome would undoubtedly be some rude transvestite joke.

Lineage
Lew Christensen's modern American fable *Filling Station* and Ruth Page's visualisation of the popular song *Frankie and Johnny* both pre-dated *Fancy Free*, but Robbins was the ballet choreographer who most genuinely tapped into the contemporary American conscience. *Sunset* (1983) is a disturbingly beautiful and bucolic 'on leave' work by **Paul Taylor**, but here both the soldiers and the women they encounter are as knowing as they are loving.

Follow-up
The movie version of *Fancy Free* (called *On the Town*) appeared in 1949, starring Frank Sinatra, Gene Kelly and Jules Munshin.

Stagings
1 New York City Ballet/1979
2 Dance Theatre of Harlem/1986

The Concert

One act
Choreography: Jerome Robbins
Music: Frédéric Chopin
Design: Irene Sharaff
Premiere: 6th March 1956/City Center, New York

This comedy, created for **New York City Ballet**, remains one of those rare ballets guaranteed to make you laugh out loud every time you see it. Despite what seems today like too much blatant sexist stereotyping, *The Concert* succeeds because so many of its jokes stem directly from Robbins' comic vision of the music. The recital of the title is an onstage concert by a pretentious pianist. His listeners are a collection of instantly recognisable cliché characters lifted directly from a stock farce: a hen-pecked, cigar-chomping husband and his domineering wife; a dithery curvaceous blond; a belligerent female student; a wimpy young man in glasses; and a pair of chattering young women who noisily disturb the concert with their cellophane-wrapped sweets. As the music takes possession of their imaginations, they dance out their fantasies. These range from a riotous out-of-sync sextet of inept ballerinas to a take-off of Russian folk dances where the husband (now garbed in butterfly wings) defends his would-be mate (the blond, also impersonating a butterfly) from an invading horde of heel-stomping male moths. He wins the battle – only to be swatted dead by his shrewish wife.

Lineage

In *The Concert*, Robbins pokes fun at the very music which was to inspire some of his finest works, particularly *Dance at a Gathering*. Jirí Kylián created an atypical comedy in *Symphony in D* (1976), and all of the works of **David Gordon** contain moments of movement satire, but genuine humour in dance is a very rare occurrence. **Twyla Tharp**'s *Deuce Coupe* (1973, to the Beach Boys) and *Sue's Leg* (1975, to Fats Wallcr) derive much of their ebullience from a sly combination of contemporary and period attitudes. **Frederick Ashton**'s *Façade* also uses its William Walton score as a source of humour. Less successful are **Kenneth MacMillan**'s blatant 1974 *Elite Syncopations* (to Scott Joplin) and **Antony Tudor**'s 1955 *Offenbach in the Underworld*.

Staging

1 Royal Ballet/1975

The Royal Ballet version of *The Concert* by Jerome Robbins, with Michael Coleman and Vergie Derman

Dances at a Gathering

One act
Choreography: Jerome Robbins
Music: Frédéric Chopin
Premiere: 8th May 1969/State Theater, New York City

In *Dances at a Gathering*, ambience is all. Jerome Robbins, back with **New York City Ballet** after a decade working on Broadway and with a variety of other dance groups, resolutely turned his back on plot and any sort of direct storytelling. This ballet focusses on dancing, on movement growing out of a response to the music – eighteen piano pieces by Chopin. The dance, which lasts almost an hour, and the dancers (five men, five women) inhabit a bare stage backed by a blue cyclorama with clouds moving across it. The women wear simple, flowing dresses; the men have soft leather boots. The gathering of the title is never spelt out, but the mazurkas and waltzes of the music, and the spontaneous way in which the performers flow in and out of the piece all conjure up a summer meadow, even an abstracted harvest festival.

The relationship between the dancers is one of comradeship, of community. There are intricate ballet steps combined with some spectacular lifts, as well as the kind of heel-toe-heel, arms-akimbo moves that recall folk dancing, and some traditional waltzing. The ballet is a series of ever-changing moments. These incidents include several tender duets, a friendly jock-like competition for two men, and a lyrical solo for a woman who tries to interest three different men in dancing with her. One of the group dances finishes with three women being passed from man to man in a series of ever-higher lifts.

Near the end of the ballet, one

man kneels down to touch the floor, and then all ten dancers watch something (invisible to the audience) pass by above their heads. The moment has led to much speculation about its significance: a storm cloud, an airplane, intimations of mortality, even suggestions of war. This plethora of interpretations irked Robbins and prompted him to send the following letter to *Ballet Review* in 1972: 'For the record, would you please print in large, emphatic and capital letters the following: THERE ARE NO STORIES TO ANY OF THE DANCES IN *DANCES AT A GATHERING*. THERE ARE NO PLOTS AND NO ROLES. THE DANCERS ARE THEMSELVES DANCING WITH EACH OTHER TO THAT MUSIC IN THAT SPACE.' While this is undoubtedly the truth from the choreographer's perspective, viewers are still moved to interpret these dances and colour the situations with their own emotional responses.

Lineage

Dances at a Gathering is a descendant of **Michel Fokine**'s **Les Sylphides** (also set to Chopin and also without a direct storyline). Robbins' next ballet was *In the Night* (1970), a trio of duets to Chopin nocturnes. This is a more formal response to the music and seems to be set in a ballroom rather than out of doors. In 1976, he devised *Other Dances* (a direct extension of *Gathering*) for **Natalia Makarova** and **Mikhail Baryshnikov**. This work includes four Chopin mazurkas and the waltz Fokine used for the first solo in *Les Sylphides*. Robbins' incessant use of Chopin led to **Les Ballets Trockadero de Monte Carlo**'s deft parody of *Dances at a Gathering* entitled *Yes, Virginia, Another Piano Ballet* (1977).

Follow-up

One of the few published Robbins interviews deals with *Dances at a Gathering*. This conversation is published in *Balanchine's Complete Stories of the Great Ballets* (1977).

Staging

1 Royal Ballet/1970

The Royal Ballet

The Royal Ballet
Formed: 1931, as the Vic-Wells Ballet

Sadler's Wells Royal Ballet
Formed: 1946, as Sadler's Wells Opera Ballet

Britain's two-tiered national ballet started out modestly as an offshoot of Lilian Baylis's Old Vic Theatre. Baylis had brought drama and opera to a mass audience at low prices and, in doing so, laid the foundations for Britain's national theatre and opera companies. In 1926, she agreed to sponsor **Ninette de Valois'** visionary plans for a ballet, provided de Valois also staged dances for Old Vic productions. Baylis kept her part of the bargain, installing de Valois' school and company in the rebuilt Sadler's Wells Theatre in 1931.

Initially de Valois choreographed curtain-raisers at both theatres, hence the original name of the Vic-Wells Ballet. **Anton Dolin** guested at the company's first all-dance evening on 5th May 1931 at the Old Vic (the first Wells presentation followed ten days later). During its formative years, the company developed a following largely through the charismatic power of **Alicia Markova**. When she and Dolin left to form their own troupe in 1935, the public transferred affections to the young **Robert Helpmann** and the teenaged **Margot Fonteyn**. Yet the Vic-Wells' early success was as much due to de Valois' organisational determination and shrewd artistic policy as it was to any celebrity prowess.

Frederick Ashton became company choreographer in 1935. His and de Valois' own ballets dominated the modern repertory and were systematically supplemented by the classics: **Swan Lake, Coppélia, The Nutcracker** and **The Sleeping Beauty** (a company signature piece). All of these were first staged by Nicholas Sergeyev from notation he had spirited out of St Petersburg at the time of the Revolution, and provided exactly the sort of traditional artistic soil in which de Valois knew her company would flourish.

In best chin-up fashion, the company carried on throughout the Second World War, after narrowly escaping capture on tour in the Netherlands at the outset of the 1940 German invasion. Back in London, audiences were eager to be entertained even when conditions were unsatisfactory and risky. In the absence of a live orchestra, the company would dance to gramophone records, and to offset the lack of male dancers, boys from the school were pressed into stage service prior to military recruitment.

During its second decade, the company changed both its name – to Sadler's Wells Ballet – and, ironically, its home base, shifting from the Wells to the Royal Opera House, Covent Garden, in 1946. That year also saw the foundation of a second, smaller company of thirty dancers originally known as Sadler's Wells Opera Ballet (later Theatre Ballet).

Founded in part to appear in operas there, the second troupe was meant to be an alternative to, not a lesser substitution for, its big sister at Covent Garden. This touring troupe functioned as a valuable, secure training ground for young dancers and budding choreographers, designers and composers (**John Cranko, Kenneth MacMillan** and **David Bintley** all started there). Despite the sometimes bewildering inconsistency of its size and direction, and inevitable overshadowing by the original company, this offshoot has persevered.

In 1956 came the highest of accolades, a Royal Charter, and the company's most significant and ideal name change. At this juncture, the second company, expanded to sixty dancers, became known as the Royal Ballet's Touring Section. Several

non-British works were incorporated into the repertory, notably from **Léonide Massine** and **George Balanchine**, but de Valois continued to focus on English choreography and the classics. In 1963, she passed directorship of the Royal to Ashton, who saw out the decade. He was responsible for revivals of **Bronislava Nijinska**'s **Les Biches** and **Les Noces**, as well as creating ballets such as *Marguerite and Armand*, tailored to the phenomenal talents of de Valois' first discovery (Fonteyn) and her last acquisition (**Rudolf Nureyev** as guest artist), a teaming which brought the Royal to a pinnacle of global popularity.

After Ashton's retirement in 1970, Kenneth MacMillan directed the company for seven years. Apart from developing his speciality, the full-length dance drama, MacMillan strengthened both companies' modern classical styles with imports from **Jerome Robbins**, **Glen Tetley** and Hans van Manen. The second company, redubbed the New Group, shrank into a vehicle for twenty-one soloists (minus corps de ballet) to present short, experimental dances. Its repertory and size eventually returned to more familiar territory with audience favourites like Ashton's **La Fille mal gardée**, **Giselle** and established modern classics such as Balanchine's **The Prodigal Son**. This identity, plus the name Sadler's Wells Royal Ballet (SWRB), settled on in 1976, seems to have stuck.

Norman Morrice, **Marie Rambert**'s partner during her company's radical switch from classical to modern repertory, bridged the gap between the MacMillan years and star dancer **Anthony Dowell**'s appointment as director in 1986. Morrice reinforced company morale by cutting back on guest stars and invited **Richard Alston** to make his first ballet for the Royal with *Midsummer* (1983). The company's regular in-house workshops, known as the Choreographic Group, have given dancers like **Ashley Page**, Wayne Eagling and Michael Corder the opportunity to stage ballets; from the SWRB, Graham Lustig, Jennifer Jackson and Susan Crow went on to become founding members of the chamber-sized classical company **Dance Advance**.

Dowell's regime began with a declared policy of rejuvenating the classics. His production of *Swan Lake* strove to capture as closely as possible the choreography of the 1885 version: it joins Peter Wright's recent production of *Giselle* (1985) and the long-absent *The Nutcracker* (1984) as handsomely refurbished examples of the company's nineteenth-century heritage. In 1988, Dowell persuaded Ashton to permit his full-length *Ondine* to be restored to the repertory after an absence of twenty-two years. He has also commissioned new full-length works: MacMillan's version of Benjamin Britten's *The Prince of the Pagodas* for 1989, and a new three-act ballet for 1990 from David Bintley, the Royal's resident choreographer.

Lineage

The triumph of **Ninette de Valois** and her contemporaries was to show that the British could create their own ballets and develop them into a whole performance style, adapting what they needed from the Russian (or French or Danish) heritage. Both she and **Marie Rambert** had links with **Serge Diaghilev**. Their parallel activities – supported by the Camargo Society, a private group dedicated to sponsoring new British ballet – helped fill the gap left by Diaghilev's death in 1929. The Royal Ballet represents the result of de Valois' ability to substitute stability and tradition for the roving, rarefied Diaghilev manner.

Follow-up

The company's first television broadcast was in 1936; the 1964 documentary *Ballet Class* is one of the best of many later telefilms. Feature films include Paul Czinner's *The Royal Ballet* (1960) with Fonteyn in *Ondine*, *The Firebird* and *Swan Lake*, and Fonteyn and Nureyev in the same

director's version of MacMillan's *Romeo and Juliet* (1966). David Vaughan's book *The Royal Ballet at Covent Garden* (1975) picks up where Mary Clarke's excellent *The Sadler's Wells Ballet: A History and an Appreciation* (1955) leaves off. Kathrine Sorley Walker and Sarah C. Woodcock's *The Royal Ballet: A Pictorial History* and Alexander Bland's *The Royal Ballet: The First Fifty Years* (both 1981) continue the saga.

San Francisco Ballet

Formed: 1933, as San Francisco Opera Ballet

America's oldest ballet company is renowned for a string of artistic firsts early in its history, and for half a century's directorship by the brothers Christensen: William, Harold and Lew. These pioneers of twentieth-century American ballet were born in Utah to a family of music and dance teachers of Danish-Mormon descent. While still youngsters, they toured the vaudeville circuit as hoofers and classical dancers.

The company was actually founded as a rib of the San Francisco Opera by Adolph Bolm, a Russian emigré, who had toured with the Ballets Russes and **Anna Pavlova**. Company appearances in opera productions were supplemented by occasional all-dance evenings. In 1938, William, the eldest Christensen – then aged thirty-six – took over the reins and within a few years had turned the troupe into an independent institution; brother Harold was appointed director of the ballet school in 1942. By then, San Francisco Ballet (SFB) had entered the history books via William's stagings of the first full-length American productions of **Coppélia** and **Swan Lake**. In 1944, he launched a celebrated holiday tradition by mounting America's first complete **Nutcracker** (opulently restaged in 1986). William left the company in 1951 to establish the first dance department at an American university – this later became Ballet West, based in Salt Lake City, Utah.

Brother Lew, William's replacement in San Francisco, brought with him a reputation as America's first *premier danseur* and a strong link to **George Balanchine** or **New York City Ballet** (he was Balanchine's original American **Apollo**). Under Lew's guidance, SFB proved that dance could thrive far from the competitive, conformist pressures of Manhattan. His eclectic, sometimes eccentric, but always well-crafted choreography featured strongly in the repertory for more than three decades, though he is best known for *The Filling Station*, a lively piece of cartoon Americana commissioned by Lincoln Kirstein for a South American tour of his short-lived Ballet Caravan, one of the precursors of NYCB.

In 1974, the company suffered – and survived – a major financial crisis. As part of the subsequent massive reorganisation, former company member Michael Smuin left **American Ballet Theatre** (where he had been hailed as America's best young character dancer) and assumed co-directorship with Lew. It was a sound choice: Smuin had worked in television, nightclubs and stage musicals, and shared with the Christensens a dual interest in academic dance and popular entertainment. His vulgar show-biz classicism expanded SFB's audience, particularly with ballets like *A Song for Dead Warriors* (1979), a knockout multi-media elegy for the American Indian. He also staged his own version of **Romeo and Juliet** (1976) and a glittery full-length rendition of **The Tempest** (1980).

After Lew Christensen's death in 1984, Smuin passed control of one of America's largest ballet companies to former NYCB dancer Helgi Tomasson, thus perpetuating the Balanchine connection. An Icelander who was a protégé of **Erik Bruhn** before joining NYCB, Tomasson's choreography bears the same hallmarks of pristine clarity and good taste as his dancing. Since 1985, his tack as artistic director has been a consolidation of SFB's status as a ballet company of national, rather than regional, interest. He is also raising its international profile by adding dances from Frankfurt-based expatriate **William Forsythe** (*New Sleep*, a 1987 commission), the Canadian James Kudelka (artistic director of Les Grands Ballets Canadiens) and Britain's **David Bintley** (whose 1985 *Sons of Horus* received its US premiere at SFB).

Lineage

The Christensen brothers were in the tradition of such earlier, equally prolific dance clans as the Vestris, Petipa and Taglioni families. Under their guidance San Francisco Ballet came to occupy a place on the American dance scene comparable to **London Festival Ballet** or **National Ballet of Canada**, companies that provide a broad audience with first-rate entertainment from a wide repertory. The Christensens' influence extends further through Kent Stowell, once a dancer with both SFB and NYCB; he and his wife Francia Russell have been co-directors of the Seattle-based Pacific Northwest Ballet since 1973.

Follow-up

There is a film of SFB in Lew Christensen's 1966 ballet *Beauty and the Beast*. Dance in America filmed Smuin's *Romeo and Juliet* and *A Song for Dead Warriors*. Lew appears as an armour-wearing prince in George Balanchine's seven-minute fantasy-parody of *Swan Lake* in the 1940 Hollywood film *I Was an Adventuress*, proving that Balanchine had a healthy regard for popular entertainment, even kitsch.

Antony Tudor

Born: 4th April 1908/London
Died: 19th April 1987/New York City

The monumental reputation and pervasive influence of Antony Tudor is based on a surprisingly small choreographic output. Less than half a dozen Tudor ballets can be classed as major, yet each of these is of such high calibre that their effect on twentieth-century ballet is crucial. Each Tudor work conveys its world with an absolute authority; no single gesture is out of place, and each of those gestures, no matter how small or even mundane its origin, is a vitally revealing part of the psychological landscape.

Born William Cook, Tudor was working as a clerk in the meat market at Smithfield when he first began studying with **Marie Rambert** in 1928. Two years later, in order to allow him to quit his job, she promoted him to stage manager and secretary to her Ballet Club. He created his first work in 1931, a short piece inspired by *Twelfth Night* called *Cross Garter'd*. Two of his most important ballets come from the Rambert days: **Lilac Garden** and the sombre ritual of *Dark Elegies* (1937), danced to Mahler's *Kinder-totenlieder*. In the same year, Tudor created a work for the new medium of television: *Fugue for Four Cameras* was a solo for Maude Lloyd, the original Caroline in *Lilac Garden*. (Together with her husband Nigel Gosling, she was later known to London readers as the *Observer* dance critic Alexander Bland.)

Tudor, his friend Harold Laing and several other Rambert performers broke away in 1937 to form their own company, known first as Dance Theatre and then London Ballet (1938 to 1940). When **Agnes de Mille**, who had made her only Rambert appearance in one of the *Dark Elegies* solos, returned to the States, she urged that Tudor be invited to join the inaugural season of the Ballet Theatre (now **American Ballet Theatre**). He and Laing left for New York, and for the next decade Tudor was a staff choreographer for the company. There he restaged his English works and added to his triumphs with **Pillar of Fire** and a highly personalised one-act meditation on **Romeo and Juliet**.

In 1949 (and again in 1963), Tudor served as guest choreographer for the Royal Swedish Ballet, while in New York he was appointed director of the Metropolitan Opera Ballet School and taught at the Juilliard School of Music from 1952. Both Tudor and Laing were aligned with **New York City Ballet** during the 1951–52 season, but Tudor concentrated on teaching during the middle years of his life.

His long choreographic silence was broken with *Echoing of Trumpets* (1963) for the Swedes, and *Shadowplay* (1967) for the Royal Ballet. These works, along with the earlier pieces such as *Dim Lustre* (1943) and *Undertow* (1945), have quirky flashes of his genius, but lack the stature of his rare masterworks.

By the time Tudor returned to American Ballet Theatre as an associate director, he was nearly seventy and a confirmed Zen Buddhist; during this period he produced two more works, both featuring **Gelsey Kirkland**. His delicate, even lyrical, suite of dances to Dvořák, *The Leaves are Fading* (1975), is one of his finest, but the moderately horrific, folk-inspired *The Tiller in the Fields* (1978, and also to music by Dvořák) quickly disappeared from the repertory.

Introspective and painstaking as a creator, Tudor was a demanding taskmaster to his dancers. His search for the precise gesture which would illuminate his characters' states of mind led him to an exactitude which some dancers found difficult to cope with. Of himself, Tudor told writer John Gruen: 'I am the most cold-blooded son-of-a-bitch that ever happened, but my characters aren't'.

Lineage

Tudor's interest in expanding the ballet vocabulary to reveal the psychological complexity of his characters is an advanced outgrowth of the reforms begun by **Michel Fokine** at the beginning of the century. The nineteenth-century choreographers told their stories through conventionalised gesture, but for Tudor the mime *was* the dancing, the dancing was the mime. There is also a kinship, especially in the bluntness of *Dark Elegies*, with the style of **Kurt Jooss**. Between them, Tudor and Jooss (in New York and Essen, respectively) exerted a strong influence on a German student named **Pina Bausch**. Any dramatic choreographer working today owes a debt to Tudor. His style of ballet went into eclipse in America where the neo classical abstractions of **George Balanchine** set the prevailing tone for ballet, but modern choreographers such as **Meredith Monk** continue to devise new ways in which movement can reveal inner feelings to an audience.

Follow-up

A biography of Tudor has yet to be written, but in 1983 American historian Selma Jeanne Cohen and London critic John Percival co-authored a monograph for the now defunct quarterly *Dance Perspectives*. A 1960 film, *Modern Ballet*, includes Tudor talking about his works and features duets from *Pillar of Fire*, *Romeo and Juliet* and other ballets danced by Hugh Laing and Nora Kaye.

Lilac Garden

One act
Choreography: Antony Tudor
Music: Ernest Chausson (Poème, 1896)
Design: Hugh Stevenson
Premiere: 26th January 1936/ Mercury Theatre, London

This ballet is a quiet, small-scaled tragedy conveyed in physical nuances as delicate and probing as the innuendos in a Henry James novel. Originally titled *Jardin aux lilas*, it takes place during an Edwardian garden party celebrating the engagement of Caroline and The Man She Must Marry. The two other major characters are Her Lover (Caroline's true heart-throb) and the Woman In His Past (the Man's former mistress). The four of them slip and slide through a series of interrupted intimate moments filled with furtive gestures. Caroline craves a last meeting with Her Lover; the Woman In His Past tries to challenge the fiancé, who now rebuffs her. It all comes to nothing, except a stifling acceptance of society's rules and necessities. True feelings are blocked, stoppered, even erased by the sense of social obligation.

The dramatic climax comes when Caroline, threatened with exposure, swoons into her future husband's arms. The entire stage freezes and Caroline, rising from her faint, has a momentary respite from reality. While the other characters remain locked in position, she briefly wanders among them, then, tragically, returns to her swooning position in her fiancé's arms. She has given up, she is no longer willing to fight for her own happiness. This relinquishment of personal ecstasy in exchange for the niceties of social approval is one of the most heartrending moments in contemporary ballet.

The Man She Must Marry takes Caroline from the party before she has the chance to say her final goodbye to the man she really loves. Just before they leave, Caroline's lover thrusts a spray of the garden's lilacs into her hand. The ending is so enigmatic that you are left wondering whether she will cherish this memento forever or toss the flowers into the gutter as she leaves youthful frivolity behind her.

Lineage

This is the work where ballet grew

up. The psychological probing of character and motivation are developments of **Michel Fokine**'s concept that each character in every ballet should move and react with a unique individualism. Tudor's refinements are both more Chekhovian and Freudian than anything Fokine ever did, and are the balletic equivalent of the tragic danceworks created by **Martha Graham**.

He has had an equally universal influence on subsequent choreographers, though (as with Graham) few have managed to achieve the same finely honed insights. Tudor's ballets demand exactitude in every detail; placed next to the grand (even grandiose) dramas of choreographers like **Maurice Béjart** and **Kenneth MacMillan**, *Lilac Garden* seems to have the subtlety of chamber music or the intricate precision of cloisonné enamels.

Stagings
1 **American Ballet Theatre**/1940
2 **New York City Ballet**/1951
3 **National Ballet of Canada**/1954
4 **Royal Ballet**/1968
5 **Royal Danish Ballet**/1970
6 **Les Grands Ballets Canadiens**/1981

Pillar of Fire

One act
Choreography: Antony Tudor
Music: Arnold Schönberg (Verklärte Nacht, 1899)
Design: Jo Mielziner
Premiere: 8th April 1942/ Metropolitan Opera House, New York

If **Lilac Garden** is Antony Tudor's English masterpiece, then *Pillar of Fire* merits the same accolade for his American output. The ballet, created for Ballet Theatre, goes even deeper than *Lilac Garden* in its exploration of sexual frustration and despair. Set in a small town at the turn of the century, the story centres on Hagar, a pent-up young woman who is both dominated by her rigid elder sister and jealous of her prettier younger sister.

Hagar, 'a plain girl', is distraught when the man she loves (The Friend) seems to fall under the spell of her flirtatious younger sister. In desperation, and rebelling against the fear of future spinsterhood, Hagar gives herself to a debauched character called The Young Man from the House Opposite. Their duet is one of conflicting sexual hungers: the Man's open, yet casual appetite and Hagar's yearning indecisions. At the point of capitulation, Hagar leaps at the Man who catches her in mid-flight. She freezes in this pose as if she has been trapped in the cage of his arms. Then she follows him into his house.

When Hagar emerges alone, it is obvious what has happened to her and how unfulfilling an experience it has turned out to be. Now plunged into guilt, she finds her open 'secret' turns everyone against her. The prim citizens stare straight through her, shunning her as though she were not there. The Friend returns and demands her attention. Her shame makes her try to resist, but he forces his honest love on her and the ballet ends as the two of them walk away from the restrictions of their claustrophobic small-town past.

Lineage
Pillar of Fire is the most renowned setting of Schönberg's *Verklärte Nacht* (Transfigured Night). The music has frequently been used by choreographers, notably **Jiří Kylián** (Netherlands Dance Theatre, 1975), and **Roland Petit** (Paris Opéra Ballet, 1976). **Kenneth MacMillan**'s ballets (such as **The Invitation** and the incestuous *My Brother, My Sisters*, 1978) carry the exploration of sexuality even further than Tudor's works. In **Birgit Cullberg**'s *Miss Julie*, most of Petit's ballets and several **Glen Tetley** works, such as his version of Arthur Schnitzler's *fin de siècle* play *La Ronde* (1987), the sexuality is up front but lacks the inner complexity of Tudor's characters.

Follow-up

Nora Kaye (the original Hagar) and Hugh Laing dance the seduction scene as part of the half-hour film *Modern Ballet* (1960). Many distinguished ballerinas, including Natalia Makarova, have had success with this role, but none have equalled Sallie Wilson, a close Tudor associate and as great a dramatic actress as Kaye herself.

Antony Tudor and Nora Kaye in a 1946 production of Tudor's *Pillar of Fire*

Wilson can be seen in a superbly filmed version of the complete ballet in the 1973 *American Ballet Theatre: A Close-up in Time.*

Stagings

1 Royal Swedish Ballet/1962
2 Vienna State Opera Ballet/1969

Galina Ulanova

Born: 8th January 1910/St Petersburg

A potent symbol of the aesthetics and philosophy of the Soviet ballet, Ulanova was born to dance. Her parents, members of the Maryinsky Theatre (later the **Kirov Ballet**) had danced with **Anna Pavlova** in England and Germany. Her father was the company régisseur, her mother one of young Galina's teachers in the school she entered just after the Revolution and from which she graduated in the late 1920s. Ulanova's other teacher was Agrippina Vaganova, a former dancer who later became director of the Kirov. Vaganova was responsible for a generation of Russian ballerinas whose artistry and spirit extended classical dance beyond a narrow, merely academic sphere.

Although Ulanova was no obvious virtuoso, this small, pale young woman radiated a particularly human genius onstage. As the embodiment of the ideal Soviet heroine, her dancing evinced an extraordinarily eloquent simplicity and sincerity of feeling. She knew how to efface technique in the passionate service of her art, her underlying purpose to create poetry by making music visible through movement.

Ulanova was the leading Russian ballerina in the 1930s and 1940s, when ballet in that country was re-establishing itself. She performed the classics, while at the same time functioning as muse for a host of Soviet choreographers, creating roles in many new ballets. Her turning point was Rostislav Zakharov's *The Fountain of Bakhchisaray* (1934); cast as an aristocratic Polish girl who dies in a harem, Ulanova's performance was a touching blend of exquisite dance and mime, in which her whole body registered every nuance of the characterisation. She was equally unforgettable in **Leonid Lavrovsky**'s **Romeo and Juliet** in productions for the Kirov and the **Bolshoi Ballet**.

She made her Western debut in the mid-1940s, and was in her own late forties at the time of a sensational New York debut. She went into semi-retirement that same year (1959), followed by full retirement in 1962, but continued to teach and act as an ambassasdor for Soviet ballet.

Lineage

The legend that has built up around Ulanova (the **Margot Fonteyn** of Soviet ballet) is as compelling as that of **Anna Pavlova**, though based on fewer performances. Because of her soaring lightness, enchanting tenderness and pale fragility, particularly in **Giselle**, Ulanova was said to have resembled that role's first interpreter, Marie Taglioni (although no one actually knows what Taglioni looked like). Ulanova's application of Stanislavski's acting methods to dance brings to mind the approaches of later ballerinas like **Natalia Makarova** and **Gelsey Kirkland**.

Follow-up

Marie Rambert's translation of M. Sizova's *Ulanova, Her Childhood and Schooldays* appeared in 1962. Ulanova herself writes about 'The Making of a Ballerina' in *The Bolshoi Ballet Story* (1959). Film of Ulanova is plentiful: a 1954 colour version of *Romeo and Juliet*, a 1956 Bolshoi *Giselle*, and a 1964 documentary bearing her name, which features a string of performance excerpts. In *The Magic of the Bolshoi Ballet*, a 1987 compilation video, Ulanova dances segments from Lavrovsky's restaging of the 1927 revolutionary ballet *The Red Poppy*.

THE BALLET BOOM

17th June 1961. At Le Bourget airport outside Paris, Rudolf Nureyev, who was being sent back to Russia in the middle of a Kirov Ballet tour, suddenly threw himself at a pair of startled gendarmes and begged for asylum. The incident was front page news, and Nureyev was an instant celebrity about to jolt Western ballet into the contemporary world.

Nureyev turned out to be the sort of phenomenon not seen in the West since Vaslav Nijinsky. His dazzling technique and fierce commitment to every role instigated a revolution in the standard of male dancing.

The West was not without its share of talented performers – and Nureyev claimed his desire to work with and learn from the Danish star Erik Bruhn as a motivating factor behind his defection — but few had the daring and fervent intensity which burned in Nureyev.

His excesses were a shock to those hidebound traditionalists who preferred politely mannered civility to animal magnetism, but Nureyev wanted to be a star, not just the man supporting a ballerina. His redefinition of acceptable male behaviour on the stage became the crux of his style and the spark plug for the ballet boom. By the end of the decade, men were dancing with a new and open boldness and exerting as much claim on audience popularity as the ballerinas. It was the first time since Marie Taglioni had wafted through the moonlight in *La Sylphide* that men were once again legitimate ballet stars.

Choreographers were quick to exploit the audiences' new thirst for dynamism. As the 1960s progressed, the Joffrey Ballet openly catered to the youth market with contemporary ballets danced to rock music (such as the flower-powered *Trinity*). Stuttgart director John Cranko opted for theatrical intensity rather than purity of style and was rewarded with a huge audience who cheered the onstage passions of Brazilian ballerina Marcia Haydée and her power-house American partner Richard Cragun. When the Stuttgart Ballet appeared in New York for the first time in 1969, the company was hailed as 'a miracle' and their season at the Metropolitan Opera House led to lines around the block. Even five years earlier, only Nureyev and Fonteyn could have produced the same response.

By the time that Nureyev and the Joffrey had joined forces for a Nijinsky tribute, the ballet boom was in full swing. Kenneth MacMillan's *Romeo* and *Juliet* had been a popular feature film, Arthur Mitchell was breaking new ground with the Dance Theatre of Harlem, and young choreographers such as Eliot Feld, Jirí Kylián and Twyla Tharp were pumping fresh blood into ballet. The arrival of another brilliant Russian, Mikhail Baryshnikov, pushed public interest even higher. Between 1965 and 1975, the American dance audience grew from an annual one million to over fifteen million.

The negative effect was that the ballet boom turned dance into a spectator sport. The new mass audience's desire for invigorating Technicolor entertainment was met by a brand of choreography which was flashy, happy, fun to watch and, like much else in the pop culture, thoroughly disposable. Some would say that, along the way, the subtlety and the nuances of great ballet (which should be savoured, not gobbled up and tossed away) had been lost.

Rudolf Nureyev in the title role of George Balanchine's *The Prodigal Son*

134

Frederick Ashton

Born: 17th September 1904/
Guayaquil, Ecuador
Died: 18th August 1988/Eye,
Suffolk

When **Ninette de Valois** ended her thirty-year career as artistic director of the **Royal Ballet**, the only logical successor was Frederick Ashton. His appointment in 1963 fortuitously coincided with the arrival of **Rudolf Nureyev**, who had made his first guest appearance with the company in February 1962. Ashton teamed the tempestuous young Russian with **Margot Fonteyn**, his particular and long-standing muse, in *Marguerite and Armand* (1963), based on the Dumas novel *La Dame aux camélias*. It was an instant box office success. Fonteyn and Nureyev are the only two dancers Ashton ever allowed to perform the ballet (fortunately it was filmed as a part of the Nureyev omnibus *I Am a Dancer*). A one-act dramatic work, *Marguerite and Armand* is the bridge between Ashton's full-length ballets and his later, condensed masterpieces **The Dream**, *Enigma Variations* and **A Month in the Country**.

Even more succinct are the two trios called *Monotones*. Both are danced on a bare stage and, like **Symphonic Variations**, focus on the dancers' sublime mastery of their craft. The first *Monotones*, choreographed in 1965, is set to Erik Satie's *Trois Gymnopédies*, and is danced by two men and a woman. A year later, Ashton used Satie's *Trois Gnossiennes* for a second pas de trois, this time for two women and one man. Each of the adagio trios is stripped to essentials that expose a limpid purity of line and a musicality as profound as the late Beethoven string quartets.

In 1970, Ashton passed the reins of the Royal to **Kenneth MacMillan**, but continued to choreograph when the spirit moved him. His next project, among the most charming of his entire career, was a ballet film, *The Tales of Beatrix Potter* (1971). The cast are all Royal dancers, and Ashton himself appears as the hedgehog washerwoman Mrs Tiggy-Winkle. In addition to *A Month in the Country*, Ashton's late works include the dances for Benjamin Britten's final opera *Death in Venice* (1973) and the lovely, almost adorational *Five Brahms Waltzes in the Manner of Isadora Duncan*, created for **Lynn Seymour** in 1976. *Rhapsody*, Ashton's last work (1980), featured guest artist **Mikhail Baryshnikov** and Royal ballerina Lesley Collier.

Much of Ashton's early work is now lost, yet the ballets which have remained in the repertory are essentially the backbone of the Royal Ballet. In recent years, serious attempts have been made to retrieve some of the older ballets. Sadler's Wells Royal Ballet rescued the 1947 chamber work *Valses nobles et sentimentales* from obscurity in 1987, and the following year the Covent Garden company staged *Ondine* for the first time in over twenty years. This successful revival revealed some of Ashton's most intricate and sustained choreography for a large corps de ballet. There is a deliberately old-fashioned air to the mimed second act set aboard a floating ship which sinks in a violent storm. **London Festival Ballet** strove to breathe new life into *Apparitions*, a 1936 work for Fonteyn, remounted in 1987 for **Natalia Makarova**, but this really only worked on a historical level. (For Lineage, see the Ashton entry in Modern Ballet, page 89).

Follow-up

Of Ashton's later works, there are video versions of *Enigma Variations* (1970); *Marguerite and Armand* (in *I Am a Dancer*, 1973); and *La Fille mal gardée* (1981) with Lesley Collier and Michael Coleman. A half-hour black and white film, *Behind the Scenes with the Royal Ballet* (1967), includes a sequence of Ashton rehearsing *Monotones II*.

La Fille mal gardée

Two acts
Choreography: Frederick Ashton
Music: Ferdinand Hérold,
arranged by John Lanchbery
Design: Osbert Lancaster
Premiere: 28th January 1960/Royal
Opera House, London

The locale, background, story and music all stem from pre-Revolutionary France, but Frederick Ashton's bucolic comedy, *La Fille mal gardée* (The Unchaperoned Daughter), is the most English of all ballets. The simple story is delightfully told through a series of frolicking group numbers that include clogging, ribbon dances, a maypole and even morris dancing, while the main pair of lovers express themselves in good-natured duets as light and delicate as a pastoral watercolour.

Lise, the daughter of the Widow Simone, loves Colas, one of the local farm lads, but the Widow is determined to marry her off into the local gentry, even if the candidate, Alain, is something of a booby. The Widow is so intent on keeping Lise and Colas apart that she locks her daughter in the house while she herself sees to the chores. Unknown to either mother or daughter, Colas has hidden himself beneath the stack of harvest sheaves that have just been delivered. He and Lise are in the middle of a joyous duet when Mama returns unexpectedly. In a panic, Lise hides Colas in her upstairs bedroom. Then the unsuspecting Widow sends Lise to her room to get dressed for her wedding. To be on the safe side, she even locks her in.

Alain, his proud father and the whole village arrive to witness the signing of the wedding contract; the Widow ceremoniously hands him the keys to Lise's room. When poor Alain opens the door, Lise and Colas are standing there in an embrace. Alain's father tears up the contract and they leave in a huff. The young lovers beg for the Widow's blessing, which she of course gives, and the ballet ends with a luminous love duet.

Throughout the action, Ashton rings every possible advantage out of ribbons. The lovers use them as talisman, and in a clever first-act duet make a cat's cradle out of them. Both Colas and Alain play at being horses with ribbons as bridles and bits, and a second-act duet for Lise and Colas (leading on to the Maypole Dance) features a backdrop of eight corps de ballet girls who manipulate ribbons in a variety of ingenious patterns.

La Fille mal gardée was first performed in July 1789, just two weeks before the outbreak of the French Revolution (see page 11). The original choreography has long since been lost. Throughout the past two hundred years, a string of choreographers have adapted the ballet, but Ashton's version is by far the best known. Another popular rendition, created for the Paris Opéra Ballet by **Heinz Spoerli**, retains much of the charm, but is populated by characters who seem to live and work on large country estates rather than small family farms.

Lineage

Ashton's treatment of comic characters, both here and in other ballets such as **Cinderella**, is the gentlest, most loving and humane since the days of **August Bournonville**. Ashton has a special knack for being able to make character jokes that are never harsh, cruel or mocking. The pretentious Widow Simone (played in drag by a man) and the weak-minded, inept Alain are prime examples of this.

Follow-up

There is a charming Royal Ballet video (1981) which features Lesley Collier and Michael Coleman as the young lovers and Brian Shaw as the clog-dancing Widow Simone.

Stagings

1 **Jean Dauberval**/Grand Théâtre de Bordeaux/1789
2 **Marius Petipa and Lev Ivanov**/ St Petersburg/1885
3 **Bronislava Nijinska**/American Ballet Theatre/1940
4 **Frederick Ashton**/Royal Danish Ballet/1964 (and later Australian Ballet, Joffrey Ballet and National Ballet of Canada)
5 **Heinz Spoerli**/Paris Opéra/1981 (and later Basel Ballet)

The Dream

One act
Choreography: Frederick Ashton
Music: Felix Mendelssohn, arranged by John Lanchbery
Design: Henry Bardon and David Walker
Premiere: 2nd April 1964/Royal Opera House, London

Frederick Ashton's distillation of Shakespeare's *A Midsummer Night's Dream* is like watching a Pollock's Toy Theatre burst into life. The ballet is set entirely in the woodland realm of the warring Oberon and Titania, the king and queen of the fairy world. The amorous mix-ups among the four human lovers and Bottom's transformation into an ass (all magicked by Oberon and his henchman Puck) are included, but the other strands of the Bard's plot have been dropped.

The humans are costumed to reflect the era of Mendelssohn's 1843 score. This, in turn, ideally suits the corps de ballet of female fairies and helps to evoke allusions to the ethereal sylphs of Romantic ballet. Another clever costume touch is the transformation of Bottom, who gets not just an ass's head but also hooves (in the guise of black point shoes). He paws and prances *en pointe* and in the comic duet with the fairy queen friskily matches Titania point for point. After nudging her off balance with his nuzzling nose, he bends down

Bruce Sansom as Oberon in a Royal Ballet production of Frederick Ashton's *The Dream*

so that she can ride side-saddle as he canters round in a circle.

This mismatched duet is in marvellous contrast to the finale when Oberon and Titania are finally reconciled. The climax of the ballet, it is Ashton's most rapturous pas de deux. Titania acquiesces to Oberon with an abandoned and joyous enthusiasm that shows she is doing so by choice and out of true love. She is like Stravinsky's *Le Rossignol*, happy to stay and sing for her emperor as long as she is not caged. Ashton's evocation of mutual love, with the two dancers often mirroring each other's choreography in ideal harmony, is one of the most lush (and truly liberated) duets in all of classical ballet.

Lineage

Commissioned by the **Royal Ballet** to celebrate Shakespeare's 400th anniversary, *The Dream* marked the birth of the perfect partnership between **Antoinette Sibley** and **Anthony Dowell**. There is an ideal English charm to Ashton's delicate version that is missing from all other dance renditions of the play. No one else comes so close to capturing the Bard's all-embracing humanity and moonstruck magic. The Mendelssohn score has been used repeatedly: now lost versions go back as far as **Marius Petipa** (1877) and **Michel Fokine** (1902). The two best known full-evening versions are by **George Balanchine** and **John Neumeier**. Balanchine tells the story in about the same time as Ashton (fifty minutes) and then uses the second half of the evening for a celebratory grand divertissement. Neumeier purposefully fractures rather than weds the different spheres of the story. His human lovers dance to Mendelssohn; Bottom and his friends to a barrel organ; and the gymnastic, space-age fairies to an electronic score.

Follow-up

There is a BBC studio recording of Ashton's version (1967). Space is tight, but it does capture Sibley and Dowell near the beginning of their partnership.

Stagings

1 **Australian Ballet**/1969
2 **Joffrey Ballet**/1973
3 **Royal Swedish Ballet**/1975
4 **National Ballet of Canada**/1978

A Month in the Country

One act
Choreography: Frederick Ashton
Music: Frédéric Chopin, arranged by John Lanchbery
Design: Julia Trevelyan Oman
Premiere: 12th February 1976/ Royal Opera House, London

If **The Dream** is Frederick Ashton's ideal one-act comedy, then

A Month in the Country is his supreme drama, a bittersweet tangle of lover's knots played out with an ironic and at times even comical indulgence towards the foibles of the human heart.

Based on Ivan Turgenev's play, it is set in the 1850s on the summer estate of Yslaev and his wife Natalia. The family circle includes Natalia's young son Kolia, her teenaged ward Vera, and Rakitin, the then stock character of the accepted 'lover'. In this case he is more a trusted confidant than any sort of passionate partner for Natalia.

Introduced into this world is Beliaev, an attractive young man hired for the summer to be the boy's tutor. His arrival sets off a round-robin eruption of emotions. The boy dotes on him, the maid flirts with him, but it is his relationship with Natalia and Vera which forms the core of the action.

Vera's schoolgirl crush is not taken seriously by Beliaev, but at the end of a duet during which she tries to confess her love, Natalia walks in on them and, in instinctive anger, slaps Vera's face. Immediately contrite, she tries to apologise, but Vera dashes away. Natalia's shock (actually jealousy) emboldens Beliaev to declare his own affections for Natalia. This leads to a ravishing duet during which she gradually surrenders to the ecstasy of the moment.

Coincidence, as only passionate melodrama can produce, has Vera turn up in time to see their final embrace. Still scorching from Natalia's slap, she rushes between them and, calling the other members of the household, angrily denounces them. Natalia shrugs off the incident and retreats to her bedroom. Rakitin, the 'official' lover, realising the true danger of the situation, insists that both he and Beliaev leave at once. No one is satisfied by this action, but all bow to convention.

Left alone, Natalia stands plunged in thought. Beliaev sneaks back into the room to say a final goodbye, changes his mind and leaves again after tossing at her feet the rose she has given him.

She sees it and, clutching it to her breast, stands in grief as the curtain slowly falls.

As with his **Symphonic Variations**, Ashton restricted performing rights in *A Month in the Country* exclusively to the Royal Ballet. **Lynn Seymour** and **Anthony Dowell** triumphantly created the roles of Natalia and Beliaev. Both **Antoinette Sibley** and guest artist **Natalia Makarova** have had great success in the ballet, and **Mikhail Baryshnikov** brought an earthy Russian peasant quality to the role of the tutor.

Lineage

As in **The Dream**, the audience can all but hear Puck declaiming 'What fools these mortals be!', yet Ashton's wise and generous humanity allows the characters to be fools without ever making them look foolish. No other choreographer could have been so honest and at the same time so gentle. The romantic pains of the characters are real enough, but this is no grand tragedy like **John Cranko**'s **Onegin**, nor the artfully distilled compulsions of love expressed in **George Balanchine**'s *Robert Schumann's 'Davidsbündlertänze'* (1980).

Follow-up

A 1976 BBC video of *A Month in the Country* features the original cast and includes brief comments on the work by the choreographer.

Australian Ballet

Formed: 1962

A successful first European tour in 1965 demonstrated how quickly the Australian Ballet had achieved an international standard, despite being geographically so far removed from most of the world's ballet activity; much of the credit must go to the example and input of ex-**Royal Ballet** dancers, directors and choreographers. Yet the Australian Ballet's antecedents stretch farther back, to the Russian school of classical ballet, via Edouard Borovansky, a former dancer with **Anna Pavlova** and a soloist with the various Ballets Russes troupes founded after the death of **Serge Diaghilev**. Both Borovansky and Helene Kirsova, another Ballets Russes dancer, visited Australia on tour in the 1930s. They settled there – Borovansky in Melbourne, Kirsova in Sydney – and opened schools in their respective cities, from which companies developed. Kirsova's lasted until 1946, when she returned to Europe, but the company headed by Borovansky and his wife Xenia carried on, presenting its first professional season in 1944.

Borovansky's death in 1959 was a blow to the popular, persevering ballet troupe that bore his name. Peggy van Praagh stepped in as artistic director, and did so well that she was asked, in 1962, to take charge of the Australian Ballet, a new company created from the Borovansky's ashes. Van Praagh had had a fruitful tenure from 1941 to 1956 with the Royal and Sadler's Wells Royal Ballets, where her encouragement of the choreographic talents of **John Cranko**, **Kenneth MacMillan** and others had been a tremendous boost to the repertory. In Australia, she expanded Borovansky's classical base to include works by **Michel Fokine**, **George Balanchine**, **Frederick Ashton** and **Antony Tudor**, but, from the outset, was equally keen to promote creativity indigenous to Australia, from dancers and designers to composers and choreographers. Sometimes these categories overlapped, as when company dancers like Garth Welch and John Meehan made ballets (such as, respectively, *Othello*, 1971 and *Night Encounter*, 1975).

Robert Helpmann's *The Display* (1964), drawing an analogy between the behaviour of young people and the mating-dance of the lyre-bird, was the first of several dances he produced for the company using native themes and subjects. The year after its premiere, Helpmann brought his glamour and theatrical savvy to the Australian Ballet on a permanent basis, becoming joint director.

One of van Praagh's most significant accomplishments before her 1974 retirement was the association she fostered between the company and guest stars including **Margot Fonteyn** and particularly **Rudolf Nureyev**. In 1965, Nureyev staged one of his many complete versions of **Raymonda** and, five years later, a **Don Quixote** that cast Helpmann to great effect in the title role. Helpmann's own retirement (in 1976) was preceded by the premiere of the company's first three-act ballet commission, *The Merry Widow*, combining his staging and scenario with Ronald Hynd's choreography.

The long van Praagh/Helpmann reign was succeeded by brief directorial stints from English dancer Anne Woolliams and company dancer Marilyn Jones (who later became artistic director of Sydney City Ballet). Maina Gielgud assumed the post in 1983, having danced for **Maurice Béjart** and **London Festival Ballet**, as well as choreographing and teaching at Sadler's Wells Royal Ballet. Under her guidance, the company has maintained the same extrovert strength and drive that made Australian Ballet's initial reputation.

Lineage

The Australian Ballet has had continuous links to the British ballet scene. Like the **National Ballet of Canada**, it was modelled after the **Royal Ballet** – both Peggy van Praagh and **Robert Helpmann** had played vital roles in the development of the Royal. Ballet master Ray Powell and Margaret Scott, head of the Ballet School, are also ex-Royal. While not officially designated as such, the Australian Ballet is essentially a national company, complemented by the four state companies: two modern troupes, Australian Dance Theatre and **Sydney Dance Company**, the latter directed by Graeme Murphy, a van Praagh alumnus; and a pair of smaller classical groups, the West Australian and Queensland Ballets.

Follow-up

Rudolf Nureyev and Robert Helpmann co-directed and starred in a fine film version of Nureyev's *Don Quixote* (1973). Peggy van Praagh's *Ballet in Australia* was published in 1965; Edward Pask has written two volumes on dance in Australia – *Enter the Colonies Dancing* (1979) and *Ballet in Australia: The Second Act 1940–1980* (1982).

Ballet Gulbenkian

Formed: 1965, by the Calouste Gulbenkian Foundation

This promising Lisbon-based company has never suffered from lack of patronage. It operates in luxurious surroundings from a sound financial base, courtesy of the Armenian magnate who gave the troupe its name. But money is no guarantee of artistic stability, and it is only now, in its third decade, that the company is gaining a distinctive personality. During the Gulbenkian's first half-decade, the dancers received a thorough professional grounding in the traditional classical repertory from Walter Gore, a British dancer-choreographer who was the company's first artistic director. His successor, the Yugoslav Milko Sparemblek, led the company into more contemporary fields of dance. Where Gore had brought in the likes of **Léonide Massine**, **Serge Lifar** and **Anton Dolin** to stage ballets, Sparemblek exposed his dancers to Lar Lubovitch and **Birgit Cullberg**.

Since 1977, with the appointment of Lisbon-born Jorge Salavisa, the repertory has widened even further, as the company moves closer to finding a more defined Portuguese identity. Salavisa, a former principal dancer with **London Festival Ballet** and Scottish Ballet, has trained approximately one third of the company's present thirty-plus dancers in the Gulbenkian's school. Unlike previous company incarnations, when there was a high turnover among the dancers (few of whom were Portuguese), the current crop appear likely to stay longer, and most are native Portuguese. Their attractive, extrovert youthfulness and animal vitality are displayed in a repertory that ranges from the flashy body-beautiful aerobics of the American Louis Falco to the innovative formalism of Hans van Manen. These guest choreographers (**Christopher Bruce** is another) have returned repeatedly to create new works on the company, but Salavisa has been careful to nurture Portuguese talent as well. Dances by resident choreographer Vasco Wellenkamp are supplemented by the less conventional pieces of company dancer Olga Roriz.

Lineage

The Gulbenkian's first artistic director Walter Gore was a leading light of the early **Ballet Rambert**. Just as the Rambert troupe has changed radically over the decades, so has the Gulbenkian, leaving behind the classical repertory promoted in favour of a more forward-looking image. Of the company's most active native choreographers, Vasco Wellenkamp tends to make diluted versions of the earnest ballets of **Glen Tetley** or Jirí Kylián, while Olga Roriz owes a debt to **Pina Bausch** and **William Forsythe** for the impassioned tone and subject matter of some of her work. Ballet Gulbenkian is particularly adept at performing *Ghost Dances*, the **Christopher Bruce** piece first danced by the company in 1981; here the Gulbenkian demonstrates what an earthy, ardent and tight-knit ensemble it can be.

Mikhail Baryshnikov

Born: 27th January 1948/Riga, Latvia

Mikhail Baryshnikov arrived in the West like a fireworks explosion. His 1974 decision to break away from a Soviet tour in Canada was (like **Rudolf Nureyev** and **Natalia Makarova**'s before him) prompted by a search for artistic freedom of expression. No one has fulfilled that urge more, and his career has embraced film and television as well as classical and experimental ballet.

Small and powerful, Baryshnikov provided the same sort of jolt to the dance world as had Nureyev in 1962. In a league by himself, Baryshnikov was capable of aerial feats no other dancer could match. Coupling this amazing physical talent with an onstage sense of humour, he became the most accessible and immediately likeable of classical dancers.

In 1964, he was sent from his home school to the **Kirov Ballet**, where he finished his studies with the great Alexander Pushkin, who also trained Nureyev. The shortest boy in his class, he joined the company in 1967, and although he received raves for his Albrecht in **Giselle**, was kept away from the major classical roles because of his size and little-boy appearance. His flair for comedy led to two new Soviet roles: *Vestris*, a 1969 solo character study inspired by the great eighteenth-century dance master, and the impish Adam in the modern ballet *The Creation of the World* (1971).

His arrival in the West immediately took him to **American Ballet Theatre** and led to a magnificent partnership with **Gelsey Kirkland**. He was soon working with a string of choreographers, particularly **Twyla Tharp**, whose *Push Comes to Shove* (1976) has become his signature piece. A successful venture as producer with **The Nutcracker** (1977) was followed the next year with a staging of **Don Quixote**. Baryshnikov then took the surprising decision to move from ABT to **New York City Ballet** to work with **George Balanchine**. Although the already ailing master never created a major work for him, Baryshnikov danced several Balanchine roles with distinction, particularly **The Prodigal Son** and the syncopated 'Rubies' section of the full-length *Jewels*. **Jerome Robbins**, who had devised *Other Dances* as a gala duet for Baryshnikov and Makarova, created *Opus 19/The Dreamer* for him in 1979. In the following year, **Frederick Ashton** choreographed his last important work, *Rhapsody*, for Baryshnikov, who also brought a subtle and authentic flavour to **A Month in the Country**.

In 1980, he returned to American Ballet Theatre to take over from Lucia Chase as artistic director. There, he added to the full-length ballets with **Cinderella** (1984), commissioned works from a diversity of choreographers, and

asked first **Kenneth MacMillan** (1984) and then Tharp (1988) to join him as artistic associates.

Lineage
Baryshnikov's verve and seemingly off-the-cuff approach is unique. A new generation of dancers such as Irek Mukhamedov (Bolshoi Ballet), Faroukh Ruzimatov (Kirov) and the Argentinian Julio Bocca (now with American Ballet Theatre) can match his power and technical expertise, but none can equal the insouciance Baryshnikov brings to classical dancing.

Follow-up
Baryshnikov's principal film roles are *The Turning Point* (1977), *White Nights* (1985, with choreography by Tharp), and *Dancers* (an unsuccessful 1987 attempt to weld a parallel modern story onto *Giselle*). Television programmes include a performance of *The Prodigal Son*; *Baryshnikov by Tharp* (featuring *Push Comes to Shove*); and *Made in USA*, with choreography by David Gordon. Videos are available of *The Nutcracker* with Gelsey Kirkland and *Don Quixote* with Cynthia Harvey. *Baryshnikov at Work* (1976), his own thought-provoking analysis of all his roles to that point, is handsomely illustrated; *Baryshnikov in Russia* (1984) is a thorough documentation of his early career. A first biography by Gnadi Smakov appeared in 1981.

Mikhail Baryshnikov in his signature piece, *Push Comes to Shove* by Twyla Tharp

Maurice Béjart

Born: 1st January 1927/Marseille

Maurice Béjart is one of the most provocative figures in contemporary ballet, revered by a fanatical mass audience, yet loathed by several leading (British, and especially American) critics. Few choreographers have attained his phenomenal level of popularity, which has allowed him to stage ballets for huge crowds in sports arenas. His 1966 version of **Romeo and Juliet**, for example, was seen by 300,000 people in two years.

Béjart (the son of a philosopher, his real surname is Berger) studied dance in Marseille, Paris and London before making his debut in Vichy in 1945. After seasons with **Roland Petit** and the Royal Swedish Ballet, the first of his own companies was founded in 1953 (with himself as star soloist and artistic director). It scored a hit with a 1959 production of **Le Sacre du printemps**, commissioned by the Théâtre Royal de la Monnaie in Brussels. Full of a propulsive, overt sexuality typical of his later work, the piece was so well received that the theatre invited him to form a new company on the premises. It remained the home of the renamed Ballet of the 20th Century until 1987, when a dispute with the theatre management compelled Béjart and the troupe to relocate in Lausanne.

In an essay entitled 'Dynamic Tradition' in the 1974 book *Ballet and Modern Dance*, Béjart compared choreography to political action, citing the stage as 'the last refuge in our world where a man can discover the exact measure of his own soul'. His programme notes are just as lofty, and considerably vaguer. For Béjart, dance is 'total theatre', not just steps. Mudra, the school he formed in 1970, is named after Hindu hand gestures, but its full title is 'European Centre for Perfection and Research for Artists Taking Part in the Productions'. Choreographically, his works tend to be slick, repetitive and simplistically academic, their power dependent on sexy visual presentation, the physical gifts and personalities of the dancers, and Béjart's uncanny ability to tap into popular consciousness.

An eclectic showman, he concocts great, ceremonial brews of allusions and references. In **The Firebird** (1970), the ballerina of the original fairy-tale libretto becomes the male leader of a band of partisans. In *Notre Faust* (1975), Béjart transforms Goethe's play into a black mass set to Bach and

tangos, casting himself as a microphone-wielding Mephistopheles. He has no qualms about mixing soft slippers, point shoes and bare feet in one dance (*Cantate No. 51*, 1969), or using an onstage warm-up as the holy centrepiece of another (*Choreographic Offering*, 1971). And only a truly gutsy choreographer would dare to have forty-seven avenging samurai commit hara-kiri for a finale, as Béjart did in *Kabuki* (1986).

His cultural grave-robbing extends to tributes to such icons as **Vaslav Nijinsky**, Charles Baudelaire, André Malraux, Greta Garbo and **Isadora Duncan** (created for **Maya Plisetskaya**). Béjart's choreography, however, is generally not very favourable towards women. He lavishes far more attention on displaying the males in his corps de ballet to their best advantage.

Lineage

Béjart's brand of dance-theatre lends an expressionistic intensity to **Roland Petit**-style flash and glitter. His fascination with ersatz Eastern mysticism recalls the **Denishawn** school, while his emphasis on outré theatrical spectacle links him with progressive dancemakers like **Robert Wilson**, **Lindsay Kemp**, **Martha Clarke** and butoh practitioners **Sankai Juku**. Other pop-messiah choreographers such as **Alvin Ailey** and **John Neumeier** are able to elicit a similarly fervent audience response.

Follow-up

A feature-length documentary of the First International Competition of Ballet Artists, held on the Bolshoi stage, contains a couple of Béjart dances, including portions of *Bhakti* (1968), in which Hindu devotional poses are given a neo-hippie treatment. Béjart's company takes turns with the Kirov Ballet dancing outdoors in Leningrad in the 1987 tele-film *White Nights of Dance*. American critic Arlene Croce mounts a brilliant attack on his work, entitled 'Folies Béjart', in her 1977 essays *Afterimages*.

Bolero

One act
Choreography: Maurice Béjart
Music: Maurice Ravel
Premiere: 10th January 1961/
Théâtre Royal de la Monnaie,
Brussels

Ravel's 1928 score, the most blatant piece of 'mood music' ever written by a classical composer, was commissioned by the rich and glamorous Ida Rubinstein (**Michel Fokine**'s Cléopâtre). The original, long since lost choreography was by **Bronislava Nijinska**, with designs by Alexandre Benois, who clothed the exotic Rubinstein à la Goya and à la gitane. This version was set in a Spanish tavern where Rubinstein's gipsy, leaping atop a table, induced a cumulative sense of frenzy among her mesmerised onlookers (who included a somewhat scrawny Englishman called **Frederick Ashton**).

Maurice Béjart's version, similar in intent, is perhaps his simplest, and therefore most compelling, spectacle. There is no set and virtually no costuming – just one person on a huge circular table and forty men sitting on chairs around the edge of the stage. The orgiastic push and pull of the gradually accelerating score turns the central figure into a magnet. She (and in recent years, he) repeats the same simplistic 'come hither' phrase over and over. As the music builds, this dancing sex symbol lures the men into dancing themselves. One by one they rise from their chairs and begin to duplicate the phrase as they move in closer to the table. By the thrashing finale, everyone on the stage has linked arms in Greek folk dance style and is churning round the table in a circle.

Bolero was the first work Béjart choreographed for his newly established Ballet of the 20th Century. It has been called everything from 'cabaret kitsch' to 'pornographic' to 'monumental'.

Whatever level of artistic significance one places on it, it is impossible to deny its effectiveness as a piece of dance-theatre.

Lineage

The great Soviet ballerina **Maya Plisetskaya** danced the central role in an all-Ravel programme with the Paris Opéra Ballet in 1976. Jorge Donn, who became the first man to dance the *Bolero* soloist, is the archetypal Béjart dancer: muscular, golden-maned and usually magnificently overwrought, demonstrating again and again how compelling (or tiresome) crudeness can be when inflated with complete conviction. The build-up and incessant repetition of *Bolero* can be traced as far afield as **Marius Petipa**'s 'Kingdom of the Shades' sequence from **La Bayadère** and the minimalist dances of **Lucinda Childs** and **Molissa Fenley**.

Stagings
1 **Paris Opéra**/1976
2 **London Festival Ballet**/1987

David Bintley

Born: 17th September 1957/
Huddersfield, West Yorkshire

The most diverse and prolific English choreographer of his generation, David Bintley joined Sadler's Wells **Royal Ballet** as a dancer in 1976. He was appointed company choreographer in 1983, and has been the resident choreographer of the Royal Ballet at Covent Garden since 1986, yet he still continues to perform as well. Bintley is an outstanding **Petrushka**, and exhibits a fine flair for comedy, particularly in the works of **Frederick Ashton**: as Bottom in **The Dream**, the clog-dancing Widow in **La Fille mal gardée** and the timid Ugly Sister in **Cinderella**.

His first ballet for SWRB, *The Outsider* (1978), was inspired by

David Bintley rehearsing Leanne Benjamin (Gerda) and Roland Price (Kay) for *The Snow Queen*

Camus. Another dramatic work, *Metamorphosis* (1984), is drawn from Kafka's bleak social satire and depicts the havoc wreaked on a family when one of its members is transformed into a cockroach. This effect is created with the dancer silhouetted in lurid red light. He seems to be hovering in space as his arms and legs flail convulsively. Bintley has produced a pair of three-act fairy-tale ballets (with a third scheduled for 1990). However, despite the drama of *The Swan of Tuonela* (1982) and **The Snow Queen**, stories are not Bintley's central focus. Most of his one-act works are essentially abstract dancing created in felicitous response to his chosen music, and all of them display a lithe and elegant approach to the formal elements of classical ballet.

There is a Scottish atmosphere to the kilted *Flowers of the Forest* (1985), a sense of serene mystery in his evocation of Egyptian gods in *The Sons of Horus* (1985), and a playful eighteenth-century graciousness in *Allegri Diversi* (1987), while *Galanteries* (1986) skims along on melodies from the young Mozart. In 1988, Bintley produced the immensely popular *'Still Life' at the Penguin Café*. This sprightly, lightweight romp sports a cast of exotic characters, all of which are on the endangered species list.

Lineage

Like **John Cranko**, an earlier resident choreographer with Sadler's Wells Royal Ballet, Bintley is at home with a variety of comedic, dramatic and abstract styles. He has also been deeply influenced by the neo-classical style of **George Balanchine**. Both *Young Apollo* (1984) and *The Sons of Horus* pay homage to the master with direct quotes, but more importantly through a contemporary expression of Balanchine's acute musical sensitivity.

Follow-up

An LWT South Bank Show video entitled *David Bintley* features selections from *Choros*,

Metamorphosis and *Consort Lessons*. *Galanteries*, which premiered at the 1986 Vancouver Expo, is the focus of an hour-long BBC video that includes both rehearsal and interview footage plus a complete performance of the ballet.

The Snow Queen

Three acts
Choreography: David Bintley
Music: Bramwell Tovey, adapted from Modest Mussorgsky
Design: Terry Bartlett
Premiere: 28th April 1986/ Birmingham Hippodrome

Inspired by a Hans Christian Andersen tale, the ballet begins with a short prologue in the Snow Queen's arctic kingdom. The evil but glamorous suzerain shatters a magic mirror so that its shards can be used to pierce men's eyes and freeze their hearts.

The first act, reminiscent of **Petrushka**, is set at a Lenten country fair. Here the hero and heroine, Kay and Gerda, are only children. Among the entertainers at the fair are the Queen's lieutenant, the White Dwarf, and a trio of her henchmen, who are white wolves in human disguise. Their attempts to kidnap Kay are thwarted by the villagers, but not before the Queen bewitches him with a kiss.

The next act, set ten years later, begins with a reflective pas de deux for the now grown-up lovers. It is the eve of Kay and Gerda's wedding and there is a boisterous celebration filled with folk dancing competitions among the village lads. The wolves, invisible to all but Kay, arrive to claim him on behalf of their Queen. Manipulating pieces of magic mirror, they dazzle him and turn him into a mesmerised slave. He belligerently drives the villagers away, and as soon as he is alone, the Snow Queen materialises to complete the spell.

The final act begins with the journey to the Queen's frozen kingdom. Unknown to Kay and the Queen, the desperate Gerda is following them in the hope of saving her fiancé. In the icy throne room, there is a divertissement for the wolves and the Snow Queen's female attendants. When Gerda arrives, she is mercilessly mocked by the White Dwarf and remains unrecognised by the bewitched Kay. The ballet ends with Gerda left to die alone. The final vision is of the triumphant Snow Queen with the devoted Kay, once again transformed into a child, at her side.

Lineage

There are close parallels between this story and another Hans Christian Andersen tale, *The Ice Maiden*, which served as the inspiration for Igor Stravinsky's *Le Baiser de la Fée* (The Fairy's Kiss). Musically the Stravinsky is finer, but as with **Le Sacre du printemps**, it has repeatedly defeated choreographers as distinguished as **George Balanchine**, **Frederick Ashton**, **Kenneth MacMillan** and **John Neumeier**. *The Snow Queen* is both dramatically sounder and theatrically more effective, even if none of Bintley's choreography can match the excellence of the plotless *Divertimento from 'Le Baiser de la Fée'* which Balanchine produced for the 1972 Stravinsky Festival.

The Snow Queen (created for Sadler's Wells Royal Ballet) is not Bintley's most inventive choreography, but it may be his most important ballet, in that he has shown an ability to cope with the demanding three-act structure which is the essence of all the great nineteenth-century ballets and still much in demand by audiences. Few modern choreographers create new story ballets from scratch. Bintley's interest in this format links him to the tradition of **Marius Petipa**, Ashton and **John Cranko**, and marks him out as an equal to MacMillan, Neumeier and **Heinz Spoerli**.

Erik Bruhn

Born: 3rd October 1928/
Copenhagen
Died: 1st April 1986/Toronto,
Ontario

His flawless technique, regal
bearing and handsome looks
embodied the essence of the ballet
prince. Erik Bruhn, regarded as
the era's supreme classicist, was a
dancer whose icy reserve was a
direct contrast to the fiery energy
of **Rudolf Nureyev**.

Bruhn entered the Royal Danish
Ballet School at the age of nine and
became a member of the company
ten years later. In 1949, he began
the globehopping phase of his
career. The first of the Danish
dancers to travel the world as a
guest artist, Bruhn set a precedent
for other Danes such as **Peter
Martins**, **Peter Schaufuss** and Ib
Andersen.

Nureyev's defection to the West
(he claimed Bruhn's talents as one
of his motives) led to a close
working friendship. In 1962, the
Royal Ballet invited both men to
Covent Garden. Bruhn appeared
to great acclaim in **The Sleeping
Beauty**, but the public was more
captivated with Nureyev's
revolutionary magnetism than
Bruhn's cool precision. Moving on
to Stuttgart, Bruhn appeared in a
new version of *Daphnis and Chloe*
(1962) choreographed for him by
John Cranko. This was a hit, but
almost immediately after the
premiere Bruhn withdrew due to ill
health. His career was to be
plagued by pain. He was
repeatedly told the cause was
nerves, and it was not until he was
hospitalised in 1972 that the truth
(an ulcer) was finally discovered.

Bruhn was one of the greatest of
all **August Bournonville** dancers.
His James in *La Sylphide* is often
cited as the ultimate interpretation
of the role. In 1964, the **National
Ballet of Canada** invited Bruhn to
stage the first North American
production of the work. Three

years later, he created a
controversial version of **Swan Lake**
for the same company. Bruhn's
reading is laden with Freudian
overtones, which include the
Prince's mother doubling as the
evil force who controls the
bewitched swans. Dramatically it
works, but some of Bruhn's
choreographic alterations are
definitely not improvements on the
original.

Bruhn served as the Royal
Swedish Ballet's director (from
1967 to 1971), but continued
dancing with other companies on a
regular basis. An uncharacteristic
pair of roles from the modern
repertory – Don José in **Roland
Petit**'s **Carmen**, and the repressed,
sadistic butler in **Birgit Cullberg**'s
Miss Julie – brought a new
dramatic intensity to Bruhn's
performance style. His
interpretation of Othello in **The
Moor's Pavane** led to a series of
guest performances with the **José
Limón** Dance Company. In the
mid-1970s, Bruhn began to switch
to character roles such as Madge
(the witch in *La Sylphide*) and the
crazed toymaker Dr Coppelius in
his own 1975 Canadian staging of
Coppélia.

In 1983, he accepted the
directorship of the National Ballet
of Canada. His close concern with
every phase of company activities,
from the school to the most senior
of artists, from the preservation of
the classics to the search for young
Canadian choreographers, helped
raise the company to a prominent
new place in the international
world. Just before his death from
lung cancer he established the
Erik Bruhn Prize for young
dancers.

Lineage
Like his contemporary Henning
Kronstam, Erik Bruhn was an ideal
exponent of the **August
Bournonville** style. Kronstam,
however, chose to remain in
Denmark and was eventually
appointed company director in
1979. The next generation
produced **Peter Martins** (now
director of New York City Ballet)
and **Peter Schaufuss** (head of

London Festival Ballet). The Icelandic dancer Helgi Tomasson, who was a Bruhn protégé in Copenhagen before joining New York City Ballet, is now director of San Francisco Ballet. Clearly, Bournonville training, which (more than any other style) gives equal focus to both sexes, produces not only exceptionally talented, but also intelligent dancers.

Follow-up

Erik Bruhn partners Carla Fracci in a 1978 American Ballet Theatre film of *Giselle*. Bruhn co-authored a manual, *Bournonville and Ballet Technique*, with Lillian Moore in 1961, and contributed an essay called 'Re-staging the Classics' to the splendid and beautifully illustrated *American Ballet Theatre* (1978). A Bruhn biography, *Danseur Noble* by John Gruen, was published in 1979.

Central Ballet of China

Formed: 1959, as the Peking Ballet

The history of this classically-based company is as much about politics as it is about pirouettes and point shoes. Central Ballet began as an outgrowth of the Beijing Dance Academy's Experimental Ballet Society, co-founded by Dai Ailian, who had studied in England with **Anton Dolin**, **Kurt Jooss** and **Rudolf von Laban** during the 1930s. The company's first ballet master was Pyotr Gusev, a former director of both the **Bolshoi** and **Kirov Ballets**. He supervised several productions that are still in the repertory, including his staging of **Swan Lake** and the collectively created Chinese fairy-tale ballet *The Maid of the Sea* (1979), which evolved from choreographic workshops conducted by Gusev in the late 1950s.

The company's famous modern revolutionary ballet *Red Detachment of Women* (1964), set during the civil war of 1927–37, was a stirring, stomping sign of things to come. Two years after its premiere, the Cultural Revolution arrived. All the arts were affected, with institutions deemed elitist, including the Peking Ballet, being farmed out to rural areas. There dancers and administrators discovered firsthand why their countrymen needed staunchly Marxist ballet instead of decadent, bourgeois classics.

After Mao's death, the country's culture was re-invented once more. For the dance world this meant re-opened schools, new choreographers, archival research, a proliferation of folk dance groups and a government policy of non-interfering financial support. At the Peking Ballet (renamed Central Ballet of China in 1980), the traditional ballet repertory from Russia was slowly revived. At the same time, elements of modern dance and ballet were assimilated into the Chinese traditions of folk dance, acrobatics and martial arts. The result is a fusion of Asian and occidental styles that tries to do justice to both. The company is large (more than seventy dancers), young (average age twenty–five) and in the process of finding and refining its own style. The dancers are strong in attack, aiming for a combination of pinpoint perfection and robustness that befits their British and Soviet background, but sometimes lack fluidity.

Shortley before his death, Anton Dolin gave the company his *Variations for Four*, a male equivalent of the bravura dancing in **Pas de quatre**. The company also performs Ben Stevenson's *Three Preludes*, a classroom exercise in lilting romantic formalism. These pieces, along with standards like **Giselle** and **Don Quixote**, allow the dancers to display their springy, supple precision. The company's homegrown ballets, such as *The Maid of the Sea* and artistic director Jiang Zuhui's 1980 *The New Year's Sacrifice*, are large, naive, absurdly plotted entertainments in calendar-art colours; here the dancers' charms come through despite (or perhaps because of) the declamatory style.

Lineage

The Central Ballet of China balances the Soviet influence of the **Bolshoi** and **Kirov Ballets**, as taught by Pyotr Gusev, with an English style imported via **Anton Dolin** and Ben Stevenson (now artistic director of Houston Ballet).

Follow-up

The film version of the opera on which *Red Detachment of Women* was based has been heavily broadcast in the West; script and score were published by Foreign Language Press, Peking in 1972.

John Cranko

Born: 15th August 1927/ Rustenburg, South Africa
Died: 26th June 1973/On an airplane travelling from Philadelphia to Stuttgart

One of the pivotal figures in the ballet boom of the 1960s, John Cranko was only sixteen when he choreographed his first work for the Cape Town Ballet Club. At the end of the Second World War, he came to London to study. Within a year he was a member of Sadler's Wells Theatre Ballet (the then new touring company created when the first company, the **Royal Ballet**, moved to Covent Garden). He immediately began staging works there, was named resident choreographer in 1950, and achieved immense popularity with his comedy **Pineapple Poll**. He staged some thirty dances while in England, including his first full-length ballet *The Prince of the Pagodas* (1957). Although it is structured like a traditional fairy tale, Cranko and composer Benjamin Britten fabricated the story from scratch. It was only a marginal success in England, but

Cranko staged it at La Scala, Milan, five months later, and for the **Stuttgart Ballet** in 1960, where he became artistic director the following season.

Here Cranko created what would be trumpeted as 'The Stuttgart Miracle'. The warm family relationship he fostered built up a tight-knit troupe of dancing actors and provided them with a repertory that played up (rather than smoothed out) their individual idiosyncrasies. These works exuded a dramatic intensity mirrored in a volatile physicality. Cranko had been deeply influenced by the **Bolshoi Ballet**'s first visit to London in 1956 and for the rest of his career capitalised on the athletic energies and excesses of the Soviet style. Cranko's works are never subtle and rarely tender. His full-length narrative ballets are **Romeo and Juliet** (for the young Carla Fracci at La Scala in 1958, re-choreographed for his Stuttgart diva Marcia Haydée in 1962), **Onegin**, *The Taming of the Shrew* (1969) and **Carmen** (1971). A 1963 staging of **Swan Lake** was his most successful adaptation from the classics.

In addition to *Pineapple Poll*, his most popular one-act ballets include the broad, cartoon-like comedy of *Jeu de Cartes* (1965) and the celebratory, plotless *Initials R.B.M.E.* (1972), which showcased his Stuttgart stars Richard Cragun, Birgit Keil, Marcia Haydée and Egon Madsen.

Lineage

If **Rudolf Nureyev** is the dancer most responsible for the ballet boom, then John Cranko was its most celebrated choreographer. The unprecedented success of the Stuttgart Ballet's first season at the Metropolitan Opera House in 1969 became one of the watershed moments in dance history. This season tipped the scales towards a new mass popularity for ballet. Cranko and **Kenneth MacMillan**, along with **Maurice Béjart**, the **Joffrey Ballet**'s Gerald Arpino, and **Glen Tetley** and Hans van Manen of the **Netherlands Dance Theatre**, all fostered a new powerhouse

aesthetic of flashy, vigorous and exciting theatrical entertainment which could appeal to audiences who had never even thought of going to the ballet before. The next generation of choreographers all learned from these men: **Eliot Feld**, **John Neumeier**, **Heinz Spoerli** and **Jiří Kylián** in particular.

Follow-up

John Percival's *Theatre in my Blood: A Biography of John Cranko* appeared in 1983.

Pineapple Poll

One act
Choreography: John Cranko
Libretto: Adapted from W.S. Gilbert's Bab Ballads
Music: Arthur Sullivan, arranged by Charles Mackerras
Design: Osbert Lancaster
Premiere: 13th March 1951/ Sadler's Wells Theatre, London

This jaunty nautical comedy was the first resounding hit for John Cranko after his appointment as resident choreographer for Sadler's Wells Theatre Ballet in 1950. It recounts the story of Poll, a Portsmouth trinket seller, and Jasper, a naive potboy in one of the alehouses on the docks. Jasper dotes on Poll, but she (like every other woman in sight) only has eyes for the dashing Captain

Belaye. This is the sort of comedy where Belaye's mere smile causes women to swoon en masse. He, however, is busy coping with his dithering fiancée Blanche and her officious chaperone Mrs Dimple.

The lovesick Poll disguises herself as one of the lads and sneaks aboard Belaye's ship, HMS Hot Cross Bun. When Jasper finds her normal clothes on the quay, he is convinced that Poll has drowned herself in unrequited love. His little hang-dog solo is one of the few gentle moments in this broad comedy.

The scene switches to the deck of the ship with seasickness and all sorts of behaviour unbecoming to the Royal Navy: when Belaye orders a cannon to salute Blanche's arrival, the cowering tars dash to the other side of the deck. Poll is not the only girl in Portsmouth who has thought of disguise. In fact, Belaye's entire crew is now women. When they drop their whiskers, the shocked Blanche flounces off in a huff. Belaye pursues her into his cabin as the real tars (with Jasper in tow) arrive to castigate their sweethearts. The Captain returns, in Admiral's uniform, passes on his old uniform to Jasper, and all the couples pair up for a happy finale that includes a mock apotheosis with Mrs Dimple as Britannia draped in a Union Jack.

John Cranko used his flair for comedy far less frequently than his dramatic talents. This *HMS Pinafore* on point is richer and more humane than his other two well-known comedies *Jeu de Cartes* and *The Taming of the Shrew*. The former has dancers impersonating three poker hands, including a five-card flush strong-man team and a capering acrobatic Joker. *Shrew*, with its pratfalls and inventively combative duets for the main characters, has proved popular from America (Joffrey Ballet) to the Antipodes (Australian Ballet), but is more uneven and overblown than the all-but-perfect *Poll*.

Lineage

Nautical ballets range from **August Bournonville**'s *Far From Denmark* (1860) to New York City Ballet's *Union Jack* (1976). Bournonville also has a pair of women dancing sailor lads, but in his ballet they are really meant to be boys. This ballet also ends with shipboard celebrations complete with an Indian war dance. **George Balanchine** uses hornpipes in *Union Jack* (as does Cranko); for the finale he has the entire company pick up nautical flags and semaphore 'God Save the Queen' as a stage-wide Union Jack rises triumphantly in the background.

Stagings

1 **National Ballet of Canada**/1959
2 **Joffrey Ballet**/1970

Onegin

Three acts
Choreography: John Cranko
Music: Pyotr Ilyich Tchaikovsky, arranged by Kurt-Heinz Stolze
Design: Jürgen Rose
Premiere: 13th April 1965/ Württemburg State Theatre, Stuttgart

Pushkin's verse novel, used by Tchaikovsky for his opera *Eugene Onegin* in 1879, is also the source for John Cranko's ballet, although not a single note of the dance score is taken from the opera.

Onegin is an emotionally charged tale of love and rejection. The young and provincial Tatiana is captivated by the sophisticated, brooding stranger Onegin. Impetuously, she writes him a letter confessing her love. He rejects her and, to prove his indifference, flirts with her sister Olga. Lensky, Olga's fiancé and Onegin's closest friend, is so offended by this that he challenges Onegin to a duel. Accepting reluctantly, Onegin kills him. The final scenes take place in St Petersburg several years later. Tatiana, now married to a Prince, has become an elegant and worldly woman. When Onegin meets her again, he is stunned by her transformation. In a reversal of roles, he now writes a love letter to her. Though clearly still in love with him, Tatiana sends him away.

The heart of this ballet is a pair of steamy virtuoso duets. In the first, Tatiana (who has fallen asleep while writing her letter) dreams that Onegin steps through her bedroom mirror to dance with her. The second, at the end of the ballet, shows Tatiana struggling to retain her dignity. The ecstasy of both duets is conveyed through elaborately acrobatic partnering. Tatiana is spun, flung, flipped and twirled around the stage, carried high overhead, slid across the floor and entwined in Onegin's arms as the paroxysms of her emotions are translated into movement. The intensity of the ballerina can transcend the choreographer's gymnastics and convey the consuming thirst for love which is the essence of Tatiana's fantasy. The greatest interpreter of this role has been its creator Marcia Haydée. Cranko capitalised on the Brazilian-born ballerina's dramatic instincts and her daredevil willingness to try anything in order to create a dynamic character. Her fiery passion infuses every move and transforms both the choreographic and her own stylistic excesses of style with a unique theatrical frisson. Other ballerinas who have had noted success in the role of Tatiana include **Natalia Makarova** and **Lynn Seymour**.

Lineage

Like **Romeo and Juliet**, *Onegin* is a dramatic spectacle where the main character's emotional traumas are offset by large production numbers for the corps de ballet. The popularity of Cranko's full-length narrative works with the new broad-based audience which emerged during the 1960s set a precedent and provided a format that is still being used today.

John Neumeier spent six years with Cranko in Stuttgart before becoming director of the Hamburg Ballet, where he created several evening-length ballets including *Die Kameliendame* (1981), a King Arthur ballet *Artus-Sage* (1982), and *Peer Gynt* (1987). Soviet epics, such as **Yuri Grigorovich**'s **Spartacus**, are essentially similar in their approach to the story ballet.

Follow-up

The Stuttgart Ballet production was broadcast on German television in 1975; a video of the National Ballet of Canada staging was filmed in 1986.

Stagings

1 **Munich State Opera**/1972
2 **Australian Ballet**/1976
3 **Royal Swedish Ballet**/1976
4 **London Festival Ballet**/1984
5 **National Ballet of Canada**/1984

Dance Advance

Formed: 1984

A sextet of former dancer-choreographers from the **Royal Ballet**'s two companies, Dance Advance have set themselves an admirable task: filling the need for a contemporary, chamber-sized British dance troupe operating from a classical base. The group originally started in 1984, when their intention was to perform only occasionally; this allowed the members an outlet for any creative frustrations caused by working within the confines of large institutionalised companies. They finally established themselves on a permanent basis in 1988.

Dance Advance consists of Michael Batchelor, Susan Crow, Jennifer Jackson, Sheila Styles (all four, along with Graham Lustig, company founders), Russell Maliphant and Stephen Sheriff. Their image is progressive, their pedigree is good, and they are transportable. Not only are they deft dancers, but their policy is to perform to live musical accompaniment provided by the four-person ensemble Quorum. They are in the process of compiling a repertory worthy of their talent and potential, including original work (often created collectively in the manner of **Pilobolus Dance Theatre** alongside ballets by recognised choreographers such as **Kenneth MacMillan** and the late Choo San Goh. Significantly, MacMillan undertook his first small-scale commission for the group, a one-act dance-theatre piece inspired by *Hamlet* and entitled *Sea of Troubles* (1988).

Lineage

Several Dance Advance members have made ballets for Sadler's Wells Royal Ballet, notably Jennifer Jackson (*One by Nine*, 1987) and Graham Lustig (*Paramour*, 1987), while Royal Ballet dancers **Ashley Page** and Jonathan Burrows have choreographed in more experimental contexts. Other individuals and groups have explored the interface between classical and modern dance: **Karole Armitage**, GRCOP (the **Paris Opéra Ballet**'s experimental wing) and **Garth Fagan**. Dance Advance has some way to go before it can boast of so accomplished a juxtaposition of point work and modern moves as **Twyla Tharp**'s *Deuce Coupe* and *Push Comes to Shove*.

Dance Theatre of Harlem

Formed: 1969, official debut 1971

Dance Theatre of Harlem, America's first outstanding classical ballet company of black dancers, started out as a ghetto experiment that quickly reached world-class level. It was the brainchild of Arthur Mitchell, a student of the School of American Ballet. In 1956, he had broken through classical ballet's colour barrier by becoming the first black dancer to join an internationally renowned company, the **New York City Ballet**, where he created a leading role in **George Balanchine**'s **Agon**. Mitchell's beautifully proportioned body and assured technique belied the prejudice that blacks were physically unsuited to classical dance.

He first conceived of a black ballet company in 1968, as a tribute to the principles of Martin Luther King. Although Mitchell had been instrumental in setting up a national ballet company in Brazil in the same year, the impulse to do something for both black America and the dance world nagged at him. The outcome was a school, its first location a disused garage in the heart of Harlem; the doors were kept open to admit air, and anyone who looked in was invited to enrol. The first class of thirty students grew to four hundred by the end of the school's first summer season. Their training embraced modern and ethnic as well as classical dance.

With Karel Shook (a former teacher at the **Dutch National Ballet**) as associate artistic director, and encouragement from Balanchine and his partner Lincoln Kirstein, Dance Theatre of Harlem (DTH) made its official debut at the Guggenheim Museum in January 1971. Most of the initial repertory

came from Mitchell, who supplied his eager dancers with serviceable, audience-pleasing, neo-classical ballets. The company's dancers are known for their warmth and vitality: the women tend to be voluptuously long and refined, in the Balanchine mould, while the men are sleek, muscled and marked by an unaffected strength.

Balanchine's oeuvre is central to the company's identity. DTH is an almost exclusively black company performing the legacy of white seventeenth-century French monarchs as filtered through the Russian school of classical dance via **Serge Diaghilev** and Balanchine. Yet Mitchell consistently tries to foster black choreographic creativity, even when the results are less than enduring. Exceptions include **Garth Fagan**'s 1986 ballet *Footprints Dressed in Red*, and popular jazz-orientated or ethnic pieces such as *Dougla* and *Banda* (1974 and 1982 respectively) by choreographer-designer Geoffrey Holder.

DTH's long list of revivals ranges from the Americana of **Agnes de Mille**, **Eugene Loring** and **Jerome Robbins** (DTH are particularly adept interpreters of **Fancy Free**) to highlights from the Diaghilev era such as **Les Biches** and the ultra-exotic *Schéhérazade*. Productions of *Paquita* and an award-winning **Giselle** (the latter transplanted to the nineteenth-century Creole society of moss-hung, pre-Civil War Louisiana) prove that the company is equally able to handle the classics.

Lineage

Dance Theatre of Harlem is a black alternative to **New York City Ballet**. Pennsylvania Ballet and Pacific Northwest Ballet are prominent among American companies likewise shaped by the movement principles and output of **George Balanchine**. Although **Alvin Ailey**'s American Dance Theatre and **Garth Fagan**'s Bucket Dance Theatre have garnered acclaim comparable to DTH, neither of those two companies have chosen

Dance Theatre of Harlem in their interpretation of Jerome Robbins' *Fancy Free*

to express themselves in the language of classical ballet.

Follow-up

Arthur Mitchell and Suzanne Farrell dance most of the *Agon* pas de deux in the half-hour film *Dance: New York City Ballet* (1965). DTH itself has made several appearances in the Dance in America series, notably an hour-long 1976 film (*Dance Theatre of Harlem*). This includes selections from five works: *Forces of Rhythm* (choreography by Louis Johnson), *Bugaku* (George Balanchine), *Holberg Suite* (Arthur Mitchell), *The Beloved* (Lester Horton) and *Dougla* (Geoffrey Holder); Mitchell and Karel Shook describe the Dance Theatre's growth. The company is profiled in Moira Hodgson's slim but useful *Quintet* (1976).

Anthony Dowell

Born: 16th February 1943/London

From the age of ten, Anthony Dowell has been a part of the **Royal Ballet**, first as a pupil at the school, then as one of the company's most exemplary dancers, now as its director. His elegant, airborne ease and fleet footwork mark him out as the Royal's premier stylist, one of the supreme classicists of the era.

Dowell joined the company in 1961 and first came to notice the following season in a staging of the third-act dances from **Napoli**, mounted by guest artist **Erik Bruhn**. Dowell was chosen by **Frederick Ashton** to create the role of Oberon in **The Dream**. This marked the beginning of one of the most outstanding of contemporary ballet partnerships: **Antoinette Sibley** (Titania) was Dowell's ideal match in lithe precision and attention to detail.

Promoted to principal dancer in 1966, Dowell has performed all the major classical roles and has had a large number of works created for him. These include a pair of plotless ballets: Ashton's cool pas de trois *Monotones* and Hans van Manen's 1975 *Four Schumann Pieces*. When **Antony Tudor** returned to England after more than a quarter of a century in America, he chose Dowell to dance the central role of 'The Boy with Matted Hair' in *Shadowplay* (1967), his quasi-mystical allegory which draws some of its inspiration from Kipling's *Jungle Book*. In 1974, Dowell was Sibley's lover in **Kenneth MacMillan**'s evening-length *Manon*.

Venturing outside the bounds of his home company for the first time, Dowell spent a season as guest artist with **American Ballet Theatre** (1978/79) and guested with the **Joffrey Ballet** as the narrator of Gertrude Stein's text for Ashton's *A Wedding Bouquet*. In 1981, Dowell and **Natalia Makarova**

created the dancing roles of the Fisherman and the Nightingale in the Metropolitan Opera staging of *Le Rossignol*. The choreography was by Ashton, the designs by David Hockney, and the entire evening a celebration of Igor Stravinsky. In the final work of this triple bill, Dowell followed in the footsteps of Jean Cocteau by serving as the narrator for Stravinsky's oratorio *Oedipus Rex*.

Dowell, who has occasionally designed costumes, began working behind the scenes at the Royal Ballet in 1984, when he was appointed assistant to the director. Two years later (though still continuing to perform) he succeeded Norman Morrice as head of the company. His first production, **Swan Lake**, meticulously attempted to return as closely as possible to the **Marius Petipa/Lev Ivanov** version of 1895. The next season, Dowell continued his custodial role by persuading Ashton to allow the first staging of *Ondine* in more than two decades.

Lineage

Anthony Dowell's dancing has always been more refined and less emphatic than **Rudolf Nureyev**'s and is without the impish snap of **Mikhail Baryshnikov**'s performances. **Frederick Ashton**'s final ballet *Rhapsody* (1980) was created for Baryshnikov and later passed on to Dowell, who danced it with a more polished restraint, if not the same impetuosity. The aristocratic demeanour in Dowell's stage presence links him most closely with that ultimate ballet prince **Erik Bruhn**.

Follow-up

At the beginning of Ken Russell's overblown *Valentino* (1977), there is a fascinating and intense little scene where Rudolf Nureyev, as Valentino, teaches the fine points of the tango to Dowell, as Nijinsky. Dowell's Royal Ballet videos include *Swan Lake*, *Manon*, and *The Nutcracker*. In 1976, Nicholas Dromgoole and photographer Leslie Spatt published *Sibley and Dowell*, a record of the partnership.

Patrick Dupond

Born: 14th March 1959/Paris

Brimming with charm and an irrepressible bent towards show-biz dazzle, Patrick Dupond is a latter-day Puck (a role he has portrayed superbly for **John Neumeier**) capable of drawing audiences who would not normally turn up at classical ballet performances. His layering of individual pyrotechnics on top of the French style may make purists cringe, but it also generates healthy box office.

His success started early, with a gold medal at the prestigious international competition at Varna, Bulgaria in 1976. His six solos – including selections from **Giselle** and Harald Lander's *Etudes*, coached by **Anton Dolin** and John Gilpin – left spectators in a frenzy. In addition to securing the top honour, Dupond returned home with a special citation for technical excellence, putting him in the company of **Mikhail Baryshnikov**, Fernando Bujones and Vladimir Vasiliev. He was seventeen at the time.

'Home' was the **Paris Opéra Ballet**, which Dupond had joined in 1974, the youngest dancer ever accepted into the company. One source of his astonishing aptitude for pirouettes was a teacher who let him dance in point shoes; his second teacher and mentor was Max Bozzoni, a pupil of **Serge Lifar**. Dupond advanced through the school and company ranks at speed, gaining the status of *étoile* in 1980. His celebrity reached such proportions that the Opéra granted him a special contract, allowing him great freedom to appear as a guest artist around the world. In 1988, he became artistic director of Ballet de Nancy, with whom he had first danced ten years earlier.

Dupond's style is a blend of decorative technique and an electric emotional charge. At the start of his career in particular, he

Patrick Dupond in mid-flight

was criticised for a lack of control favouring show-off flair over discipline and depth. His physical gifts are obvious: a startlingly high, bold jump, uninhibited energy, enormous flexibility and an extravagantly long line, used to showstopping effect in the pas de deux from *Le Corsaire* and in **Roland Petit**'s *Le Jeune Homme et la Mort*. His flamboyant talents have been exploited in the world premieres of Petit's *Phantom of the Opera* and **Alwin Nikolais**' *Schema* (both 1980), **Heinz Spoerli**'s 1981 version of **La Fille mal gardée** (with Dupond excellent as Alain), and **Alvin Ailey**'s *At the Edge of the Precipice* (1983), a piece of pop hagiography on Jim Morrison. In 1979, **John Neumeier** created a portrait of **Vaslav Nijinsky** (entitled simply *Vaslav*) for Dupond. It remains one of the pieces with which he is most identified.

Lineage

Dupond's vivid stage presence, restless temperament and sheer virtuosity are reminiscent of **Rudolf Nureyev** and **Peter Schaufuss**. He has said his ultimate goal is to be a stage and screen star, in the manner of both Nureyev and **Mikhail Baryshnikov**. To that end, he has released some pop singles in France.

Follow-up

Dupond is one of photographer Pierre Petitjean's *Ten Dancers* (1982), an oversize book with text by Holly Brubach that captures superstar dancers in performance and offstage. He dances the Black Swan pas de deux from *Swan Lake* in the 1985 video *The Paris Opéra Ballet: Six Ballets*. In *Patrick Dupond*, a 1988 video documentary, he can be seen in *Coppélia* and Maurice Béjart's *Salome*.

Dutch National Ballet

Het Nationale Ballet
Formed: 1961

The Dutch National Ballet was the result of a merger between two pre-existing ballet companies: Het Nederlands Ballet, run by Sonia Gaskell, and the Amsterdams Ballet, directed by Mascha ter Weeme. Gaskell, who had worked with **Serge Diaghilev** and could draw on a Russian-Dutch heritage (she was born in Lithuania), eventually took over sole control, setting off on a long, some might say obsessive, course of compiling a large classical repertory, including full-length versions of

Giselle, **Swan Lake**, **The Sleeping Beauty** and **Romeo and Juliet**. Such was the scope of the list that the Ballet was referred to as a 'choreographic supermarket'. Although Gaskell succeeded in establishing a major ballet company in the Netherlands, any kind of distinctive style was slow in coming. Her intention of trying to create a Dutch version of the **Royal Ballet** was well-founded, but the company lacked a native equivalent of the Royal's **Frederick Ashton**.

A change in atmosphere occurred when some of the homegrown choreographic talents she had nurtured emerged to positions of influence in the company. In 1968, Rudi van Dantzig became co-director, and later sole artistic director. Assisted by compatriots Hans van Manen and Toer van Schayk, van Dantzig developed a more selective repertory, supplementing the classics with works by Ashton, **Antony Tudor** and especially **George Balanchine** (the company is one of the largest Balanchine strongholds in Europe). The Dutch triumvirate was also responsible for some strikingly original dances.

Van Manen had been a founding member and major choreographer of the **Netherlands Dance Theatre** (a 1959 breakaway from Gaskell's earlier Nederlands Ballet) before joining the National Ballet in 1973. He has gradually moved away from the jazzier works of his earlier period towards cooler, more formal movement-constructions like *Twilight* (1972), *Adagio Hammerklavier* (to Beethoven, 1973) and *Four Schumann Pieces*, made for **Anthony Dowell** and the Royal Ballet in 1975. Many of van Manen's ballets can be heavy-going, but his popular *5 Tangos* (1977) aims at entertainment. It reworks torrid South American dances with ballet vernacular, spiced by a tinge of low-life slang.

Van Dantzig concentrates more on the problems of humans in contemporary society, often backed by *musique concrète* or electronics. His free use of a classical vocabulary in a modern, personal manner is seen at its best in works like *Monument for a Dead Boy* (1965), a tragic study of the isolated life of a homosexual; *Epitaph* (1969), a meditation on death and the difficulties of communication; and *Ropes of Time*, an allegorical pas de trois created for **Rudolf Nureyev** at the Royal Ballet in 1970.

The lead role in van Dantzig's ballets has often been taken by van Schayk, a fine arts student responsible for many of the company's decors, and a choreographer since the early 1970s – he created the first full-length Dutch ballet, *Landscap*, in 1982.

In 1987, the National Ballet moved into Het Muziektheater, the largest theatre building in the Netherlands. However, the company's artistic future is uncertain: van Dantzig is due to depart in 1991, and van Manen returned in an associate capacity to the Netherlands Dance Theatre in 1988.

Lineage

Although short of a singular style, Dutch National Ballet clearly owes a lot to American choreographers and teachers. Visits to the Netherlands in the 1950s by the companies of **George Balanchine** and **Martha Graham** were a direct stimulus on Sonia Gaskell and all the Dutch choreographers.

Follow-up

The documentary film *Making of a Ballet* follows the rehearsals and staging of van Dantzig's 1971 ecological lament *Painted Birds*. *Monument for a Dead Boy* was filmed for German television in 1967. There are videos of the company dancing van Manen's *Grosse Fuge* (1971), a ritualistic exercise for four couples set to Beethoven's string quartets, and his tri-part *Piano Variations*. The latter includes an interview with van Manen. Van Dantzig writes about the cultural conditions that have promoted and hindered Dutch dance in the 1974 book *Ballet and Modern Dance*.

Suzanne Farrell

Born: 16th August 1945/Cincinnati, Ohio

Suzanne Farrell was barely sixteen when **George Balanchine** brought her into the **New York City Ballet** from his School of American Ballet. Within a year he was challenging her with some of the major roles in his repertory, and by 1963 she was already becoming his principal muse. Long-limbed, high-waisted, with the neck of a swan and the stamina of a racehorse, Farrell is an exceptionally daring dancer with a highly personal and spontaneous sensitivity to music. Exemplifying the Balanchine ideal, she is the ballerina beside whom all others must be measured.

The first phase of their symbiotic relationship reached its apogee in Balanchine's version of **Don Quixote**, with the choreographer himself regularly giving performances as the Don in thrall to Farrell's ideal dream woman, Dulcinea. Then, in 1968, she did the unthinkable (in Balanchine's eyes) by marrying Paul Mejia, a company dancer whom Balanchine was grooming as a potential choreographer. They quickly left NYCB and spent five years in Europe with **Maurice Béjart** (from 1970 to 1974).

Farrell made a triumphant return to NYCB in 1975, and with **Peter Martins** as her regular partner, became the star of the company in roles that ran the gamut from the fiery gipsy in *Tzigane* (from the 1975 Ravel Festival) to the ballerina as goddess in *Mozartiana* (1981 Tchaikovsky Festival). The Farrell/Martins partnership was at its modernist peak in the pas de deux from **Agon**, and most classically pure in the 'Diamonds' act of *Jewels* and the radiant *Chaconne* (from Gluck's *Orfeo ed Euridice*).

Mejia, who did not return to NYCB, went to work for the Chicago City Ballet, where his new boss was Maria Tallchief (Balanchine's third wife from 1946 to 1952). Farrell has appeared with the company as a guest artist in Mejia's versions of **Cinderella** and **Romeo and Juliet**.

A catalogue of Farrell's Balanchine roles would be prodigious, but she also appeared in several **Jerome Robbins** premieres including *In G Major* (1975 Ravel Festival), again with Martins. Following Balanchine's death and Martins' retirement from performing, Robbins created *In Memory of…* (1985). Set to music written by Alban Berg as an elegy to his daughter, it is also the sole major post-Balanchine role choreographed for Farrell, so the title takes on at least a double, if not triple-edged resonance.

In 1987, Farrell underwent a major hip operation, but before a year had passed, she returned to the stage in some of her less strenuous roles.

Lineage

The Pygmalion-like relationship between a choreographer and his muse is a periodic phenomenon in ballet annals. **Margot Fonteyn** inspired much of **Frederick Ashton**'s finest choreography and the image of **Lynn Seymour** is ever present in the ballets of **Kenneth MacMillan**. Marcia Haydée created most of **John Cranko**'s leading roles and Natalia Bessmertnova is the recurrent star in **Yuri Grigorovich**'s strongest ballets. In all these instances the ballerina plays a very real part in the development of the choreography. These are inexplicable relationships of dual creativity where the dancer defines a choreographer's style by helping him to devise it.

Follow-up

Suzanne Farrell's career is well documented. She dances Titania in the 1967 feature film of Balanchine's *A Midsummer Night's Dream*, while *Tzigane*, *Jewels*, *Chaconne*, *Apollo* (all partnered by Peter Martins), *Vienna Waltzes* and *Mozartiana* are all included in the Dance in America Balanchine programmes. The *New Yorker* critic Arlene Croce is a perceptive chronicler of Farrell's art. Her three volumes of collected criticism are peppered with profound insights into the Farrell/Balanchine partnership.

Eliot Feld

Born: 5th July 1942/Brooklyn, NY

As a choreographer and artistic director, Eliot Feld is tenacious, temperamental and (at times) enormously talented. His training, at New York's School of American Ballet, encompassed both modern and classical technique. Still in his teens, he was cast in **Jerome Robbins**' 1957 Broadway staging of *West Side Story*, and appeared in the equally celebrated film version, before joining the corps of **American Ballet Theatre** in 1963. A wiry, bantamweight performer, within two years he became a soloist noted for his sharp interpretations of character roles.

It was Robbins who persuaded ABT's artistic director Lucia Chase to let Feld stage his first ballet, *Harbinger*. When it premiered in 1967, Feld was immediately proclaimed contemporary ballet's great white hope and the company's best bet as a resident choreographer since Robbins' own debut with **Fancy Free**. Feld's next ballets – *At Midnight* (1967), *Meadowlark* (1968) and *Intermezzo* (1969) – confirmed his versatility, musicality and inventiveness. His association with ABT was, however, short-lived. Feld quit the company to pursue a freelance career until he formed the American Ballet Company in 1969. Although well received critically, the small troupe folded after only two years due to a lack of bookings. After another period of freelance work, Feld – with the help of New York Shakespeare Festival producer Joseph Papp – gave birth to a second company (bearing his

name), which has dominated his creative life since.

The Feld Ballet is a classically-based company run along modern lines. Dances are staged on a comparatively intimate, easily tourable scale and there is no hierarchy among the dancers. Feld's choreographic output (over fifty ballets) forms the core of the company's repertory.

At its best, Feld's work extends rather than merely rehashes the established classical vocabulary. The plotless, neo-classical Brahms piano ballet *Intermezzo*, with its resonant emotional atmosphere springing directly from the music, echoes Robbins' **Dances at a Gathering**, made the same year. However, the 1984 *Intermezzo No. 2*, forced, mechanical and overloaded with the showy high lifts for which Feld is famous, is a pale carbon copy of his light, rapturously romantic approach. Perversely, while his dancemaking skill has increased, some of his work has grown impersonal and negligible, as if he were merely skimming the surface of the potential so brilliantly suggested at the start of his career.

This is not to gainsay the importance of Feld's often unconventional achievements. His interest in various kinds of dance styles and subjects is as impressive as his catholic taste in music, which includes Celtic and American folk tunes, ragtime and Elizabethan lute music. Since 1984, he has obsessively devised more than half a dozen ballets propelled by the repetitive permutations of American composer Steve Reich. The ramps and trampolines that feature in such Reich-derived dances as *Grand Canon* (1984) and the bravura solo *Medium: Rare* (1985), enhance Feld's blend of virtuoso gymnastics with the more formal rhythmic patterns he picks up from the music.

In 1978, Feld opened the year-round, non-paying New Ballet School, an organisation aimed at offering inner-city children the chance to become dance professionals. Since 1982, the company has been based at the

Joyce Theatre, a small mid-Manhattan venue purchased and renovated by the company specifically for dance.

Lineage

Both Feld and his mentor, **Jerome Robbins**, developed **Doris Humphrey**'s use of a democratic mix of male and female dancers in an all-dance context. Feld shares with **Jirí Kylián** a facility for storyless romantic ballets full of breathtakingly fast duets, tricky partnering and the incorporation of folk dance steps into a balletic idiom, and like Kylián, he is not above self-plagiarism.

Follow-up

Feld can be seen as Baby-John in the film of *West Side Story*. *American Ballet Company – Eliot Feld, Artistic Director* (1971) is a fascinating record of the formation of Feld's first company from initial auditions to debut performance. The later Feld Ballet features in a 1979 Dance in America programme. This company is profiled in Moira Hodgson's 1976 book *Quintet*; for perceptive essays on Feld's early ballets, read Marcia B. Siegel's *Watching the Dance Go By* (1977) and *The Shapes of Change* (1979).

Yuri Grigorovich

Born: 2nd January 1927/Leningrad

Yuri Grigorovich's status as master of the **Bolshoi Ballet** is matched by his reputation as the leading Soviet choreographer of his generation. He began his career as a capable, though not outstanding, dancer at the **Kirov Ballet**. Grigorovich was best at *demi-caractère* roles, but early on showed an interest in choreography. His breakthrough came with the 1957 *The Stone Flower*. Set to Prokofiev's last ballet score and based on a folk tale from the Ural mountains, it was hailed as a milestone for its clear, uncluttered staging, delineation of character through movement rather than mime, and inspired use of a large ensemble in village and gipsy scenes. It was such a success that Grigorovich restaged it for the Bolshoi two years later. He scored a second hit at the Kirov with *Legend of Love*, a 1961 ballet about the clash between love and duty (also remounted for the Bolshoi). Having risen through the ranks at the Kirov, Grigorovich switched allegiance in 1964 and became the Bolshoi's chief choreographer and artistic director, a position he has held ever since.

Today's Bolshoi is stamped with his particular style, a bravura blend of 'total' theatre that stresses strenuous spectacle as it plays on audience emotion to the hilt. Grigorovich is usually his own librettist, sketching his plots in broad, bold strokes of sweeping dance action, in epic stagings like **Spartacus** (1968) and *Ivan the Terrible* (1975). The fates and psyches of the main characters are explored against a socio-historical canvas, although the drama of individuals is sometimes eclipsed by Grigorovich's manipulation of the Bolshoi's huge corps de ballet. The subject matter dictates the rather rigid ways in which the sexes are choreographed: energetic male prowess, lyrical female suppleness. A leading exponent of Grigorovich's female style is his wife Natalia Bessmertnova, a prima ballerina for more than two decades.

Grigorovich's quarter-century reign at the Bolshoi has not been untroubled. The company survived the defection of a few of its dancers (including Alexander Godunov) in the late 1970s; Grigorovich has since been accused of dominating the repertory by stemming new choreographic blood. Aesthetic and administrative criticisms aside, he is undeniably one of the century's ballet giants. Like **Martha Graham**, **George Balanchine**, **Merce Cunningham**, **Maurice Béjart** and others, he has created an unmistakeable and individual form of dance-theatre.

Lineage

Fyodor Lopokov (1886–1973), artistic director of both the **Bolshoi** and **Kirov Ballets**, set the foundations of neo-classical and modern dance in Russia. He introduced acrobatics into Soviet classical dance, now a Grigorovich hallmark, and his interest in plotless, abstract ballets (paralleled by **Léonide Massine**'s symphonic ballets) was a reaction against the literary realist traditions of the previous century. Grigorovich took up the cause, modifying it to his own needs. Both in his original work and his re-stagings of the classics he has consistently pruned away the mime element in favour of a more purely dance-orientated, grandiose approach. He uses dance to propel the storyline forwards and to express the current of moral idealism that runs through all Russian ballet.

Spartacus

Three acts
Choreography: Yuri Grigorovich
Music: Aram Khachaturian
Design: Simon Virsaladze
Premiere: 9th April 1968/Bolshoi Theatre, Moscow

This archetypal Bolshoi blockbuster is based on the true story of a slave rebellion against the corrupt Roman Empire. On the surface, Grigorovich's ballet (the third, definitive version attempted by the Bolshoi) bulges with attractions, with a staging straight out of the sword, shield and swoon school.

The show-biz, crowd-stirring dramatics afford the dancers,

Yuri Grigorovich's *Spartacus*, interpreted by the Bolshoi Ballet stars Natalia Bessmertnova and Irek Mukhamedov

particularly the men, the opportunity to display maximum impact within an unfortunately narrow dynamic range.

The cinematic narrative alternates mammoth, highly regimented corps de ballet work (goose-stepping soldiers on parade; decadent patrician orgies; downtrodden slaves in mournful subjugation or defiant uprising) with 'monologues' for the four leading characters: Spartacus; his saintly, suffering wife Phrygia; the depraved Roman general Crassus; and the wicked Roman courtesan Aegina.

Lyrical love duets, cued by Khachaturian's sugar-coated blood and thunder score, are punctually inserted. The overall effect is ardent and monumental. Grigorovich's relentless pace and Cecil B. De Mille approach overpower his theme, the indomitability of the human spirit.

Lineage

Grigorovich's elaborate pageant, the essence of the modern Soviet heroic style, and the most successful Russian ballet since **Leonid Lavrovsky**'s **Romeo and Juliet**, is a front-runner in the line of revolutionary-style ballets that can be traced from *The Red Poppy* (1927) through *Red Detachment of Women* (**Central Ballet of China**, 1964) and Grigorovich's own *Ivan the Terrible*. Other later, mainly Eastern European ballets created from the same source material fail to match Grigorovich's bombastic production, due partly to his unique symphonic style and partly to the fact that most other companies could never attempt an epic on this scale.

Follow-up

In the 1975 film version of *Spartacus*, Vladimir Vasiliev is the slave, with Natalia Bessmertnova as Phrygia. Nearly ten years later, Irek Mukhamedov assumed the title role for the filming of a live performance. A typically intense, expansive Bolshoi dancer, he adds a smooth, flowing musicality often lacking in the company's punchy style.

The Golden Age

Three acts
Choreography: Yuri Grigorovich
Libretto: Yuri Grigorovich and Isaac Glikman
Music: Dmitri Shostakovich
Design: Simon Virsaladze
Premiere: 4th November 1982/Bolshoi Theatre, Moscow.

Shostakovich's first ballet score was used for a short-lived 1930 **Kirov Ballet** production, featuring a libretto which had won a competition for new scenarios propounding Soviet ideals. The story centred around a clash between the fascists and a Soviet football team.

The revision seen today is set in 1923 somewhere on the Black Sea coast, where *The Golden Age* is now the name of a decadent nightclub. The story is worthy of Hollywood movies of the period. Its hero, Boris, an upright fisherman, falls in love with Rita, who turns out to be a dancer at the club. He rescues her from the clutches of her partner, the leader of a gang of thugs when he is not doing exhibition dancing. After chases, abductions and some spectacular fights, Boris and Rita, supported by their worker friends, dance a rousing finale.

The plot is really unimportant, just an excuse for boy meeting girl. The story is told as a populist cartoon: the villain wears black and slinks around like a rapacious fox, while the hero, all in white, is a stalwart super-worker. The designs like the story, have the ring of brightly coloured propaganda posters.

The delightful score is full of Hollywood tinges: it croons for the love duets, soars for the chases and builds to laudatory anthems for the masses of hearty, happy workers. Best of all, it includes a slinky set of variations based on *Tea for Two*, danced by the nightclubbers in champagne-soaked high spirits.

Lineage

Both the structure and choreographic style of *The Golden Age* are carbon copies of Grigorovich's **Spartacus** and *Ivan the Terrible*. This interchangeable format – of colossal crowd scenes alternating with intimate duets and solos – is more palatable here because neither characters nor situations are so heavily weighted towards a 'significant message'.

Follow-up

The part of Rita is one of Natalia Bessmertnova's most famous roles. Recently, Boris has become the property of Irek Mukhamedov, the USSR's most obvious heir to the star status of Nureyev and Baryshnikov. A BBC video version of *The Golden Age* was filmed in performance at the Bolshoi in 1987, starring both Bessmertnova and Mukhamedov.

Joffrey Ballet

Formed: 1956

Robert Joffrey
Born: 24th December 1930/Seattle, Washington
Died: 25th March 1988/New York City

Born Abdulla Jaffa Anver Bey Khan, Robert Joffrey began taking ballet classes at the age of nine in an attempt to combat asthma. He claimed he always wanted to have a company of his own, and as early as 1954 formed the Robert Joffrey Ballet Concert. From the beginning, Joffrey, like **Glen Tetley** a few years later, had little patience with the ballet versus modern dance feud that had long split the New York dance world. He also had the foresight to found his own school, American Ballet Center, which, since 1953, has been the major training ground for Joffrey Ballet dancers.

In 1955, **Marie Rambert** invited him to London to work with her company. He set two ballets on her troupe that season, but more importantly, he was fascinated by Rambert's stories of her days with the Ballets Russes. Her tales of **Vaslav Nijinsky** fired Joffrey with a long-term goal of preserving the great works of the **Serge Diaghilev** era for modern audiences.

His Robert Joffrey Ballet, formed in 1956 in America, consisted of six dancers who set off on a cross-country tour in a borrowed station wagon. Among them were Tetley and Gerald Arpino, who would spend the next eight years as a leading performer while also developing a skill for dancemaking that transformed him into the Joffrey Ballet's chief choreographer and associate director.

In 1966, following **New York City Ballet**'s transfer to the Lincoln Center, Joffrey's company was invited to become the City Center Joffrey Ballet. The next year, he choreographed the multimedia duet *Astarte*. Its rock music, films, projections and strobe lighting caused a furore and ended up on the cover of *Time* magazine. The American ballet boom had been born. The youth image became a trademark, especially in Arpino's works such as *Trinity* (1970), which celebrated the energies and verve of modern young America, and his 1972 flower-child ritual *Sacred Grove on Mount Tamalpais*. Arpino's works can be sleek and sensual, but are often thin and transparent (a trait shared with **Maurice Béjart**). It was left for other more radical modernists such as **Twyla Tharp**, **Laura Dean** and **Pilobolus Dance Theatre** to prove that the Joffrey youth market could be captured without talking down or resorting to thinly disguised show business tricks.

In the same year as *Astarte*, the Joffrey produced the first American production of **The Green Table**, aptly marketed to the Vietnam generation as an 'anti-war' ballet. From this point onwards, the Joffrey began to consolidate its custodial position with an unprecedented run of major revivals: **Petrushka**, **Parade**, **L'Après-midi d'un faune**, the largest repertory of **Frederick Ashton** works outside the Royal Ballet, modern American classics like **Rodeo** and several 1950s works by **Jerome Robbins**. This lovingly preserved repertory was crowned in 1987 when, after some decades of trying, Robert Joffrey was finally able to unveil a reconstruction of Nijinsky's **Le Sacre du printemps**.

The Joffrey went on its first US State Department Tour as early as 1962 and has twice visited the USSR (1963 and 1974). In 1983, the company officially became bi-coastal when it was appointed as the first resident dance company at the Music Center in Los Angeles.

Lineage

Like **Antony Tudor**, Robert Joffrey choreographed few ballets of his own, but during the first quarter-century of his company's existence he commissioned an astonishing 103 new ballets (more than a third from Arpino). Joffrey's legacy will be in the diligent way he set out to raise the profile of dance in America through a catholic mix of modern classics and experimental works. His belief in the future of ballet led him to expand his school to incorporate a touring company known as Joffrey II. This group of sixteen young dancers takes ballet to small theatres across the USA. Many of its dancers are eventually invited to join the first company. **London Festival Ballet**'s second troupe, LFB, and **Sadler's Wells Royal Ballet** are other examples of smaller scale versions of a parent company.

Follow-up

The Joffrey Ballet inaugurated the Dance in America television series in 1976 (with *Parade* and *The Green Table*) and appeared in the series again in a 1981 *Homage to Diaghilev* with guest artist Rudolf Nureyev. The 1966 film *Robert Joffrey Ballet* includes excerpts from *Pas de Déesses* and *Gamelan* (both choreographed by Joffrey), *Opus 65* (Anna Sokolow) and *Incubus* and *Viva Vivaldi!* (both Gerald Arpino).

Gelsey Kirkland

Born: 29th December 1952/ Bethlehem, Pennsylvania

Gelsey Kirkland will be remembered in the history books as one of the most profligate of talents. She was one of the glories of the ballet boom years, the perfect partner for **Mikhail Baryshnikov** and the supreme **Giselle** of her generation. However, because of personal and emotional problems, her brilliant career took a precipitous nosedive just at the moment it had reached its peak. She was fired from **American Ballet Theatre** and eventually institutionalised for cocaine addiction, all of which is recounted in her autobiography *Dancing on my Grave*.

Following her elder sister Johnna into the School of American Ballet, Kirkland was taken into **New York City Ballet** at the age of sixteen, and in 1970 **George Balanchine** staged a new version of **The Firebird** for her. When Baryshnikov came to the West he sought out Kirkland as a partner. She joined American Ballet Theatre in 1975, and together they generated the sort of adulation once reserved for **Margot Fonteyn** and **Rudolf Nureyev**.

In addition to the classics, Kirkland created the leading roles in **Antony Tudor**'s last two ballets, *The Leaves are Fading* and *The Tiller in the Fields*. She also played Ophelia in **John Neumeier**'s turgid *Hamlet Connotations* (1976). This was meant to have been a blockbuster with Baryshnikov as Hamlet, **Erik Bruhn** as Claudius and Marcia Haydée as Gertrude. Instead it turned out to be a perfect illustration of the truism that great dancers do not always inspire concomitantly great choreography.

Kirkland has become well-known for an obsessive perfectionism which drives her to spend months rehearsing what other dancers would do in a week or even days. She worked for years on **Swan Lake** and then only gave a single performance before deciding she was still not satisfied with her interpretation. This compulsion also led to a series of cosmetic surgery corrections ranging from her upper lip to her ankles. She could have been the greatest ballerina of the century; instead she has become the Judy Garland of the dance world – unmatched but totally erratic.

Over the years, Kirkland has maintained a special guest relationship with the **Royal Ballet**. She has been one of its finest Juliets and in 1986/87 danced **The Sleeping Beauty** in London.

Lineage

Gelsey Kirkland dances with the same airy delicacy as **Natalia Makarova**, the same innate musicality as **Margot Fonteyn**; yet, like **Suzanne Farrell**, who was Kirkland's first role model, her dancing can be idiosyncratic and filled with unpredictable surprises. She is one of those gamine dancers who appear to be all legs and arms until they start moving, whereupon they are transformed from colts into champions.

Follow-up

The video of Mikhail Baryshnikov's *The Nutcracker* captures Kirkland at the height of her radiance. Her autobiography *Dancing on my Grave* (1986), a nightmare saga of misunderstood needs and sad deprivations, has become one of the best-selling dance books of all time.

Kirov Ballet

Formed: 1738, as the St Petersburg School of Ballet by Jean-Baptiste Landé and Empress Anna Ivanovna

The Kirov Ballet has a history even longer and more distinguished

than the **Bolshoi Ballet**, and a contrasting performance style. Whereas the Bolshoi throws an extrovert mantle around its muscular, Muscovite shoulders, the Kirov wears its pedigree with an elegant, aristocratic and sometimes academic cool.

From the outset, Russian ballet was both designed to entertain and be controlled by the Tsar and his court. The company that performed in the mid-eighteenth century in the royal residences of St Petersburg and Moscow grew out of the school instituted by French dancing master Jean-Baptiste Landé. Under royal patronage, ballet flourished, growing stronger throughout the nineteenth century due to a stream of French and Italian choreographers, teachers and virtuoso dancers who poured into Russia (including **Jules Perrot**, **Arthur Saint-Léon** and Marie Taglioni). It was **Marius Petipa**, however, who most firmly built the classical structure of ballet as the Kirov practises it today. During his directorship, the Maryinsky Theatre, the Kirov's home since 1860, staged the premieres of **The Sleeping Beauty**, **Raymonda**, **La Bayadère** and the now standard version of **Swan Lake**.

The Kirov (re-named after an assassinated Communist Party leader in 1935) was called the Maryinsky State Theatre in 1917, when ballet's function in a new socialist state had to be re-thought. Dance was to be an art for the people rather than a diversion for monarchs, an expression of collective spirit represented by ballets based on either Russian literary heritage or narratives centred on the workers' struggle. **Michel Fokine**, active at the Maryinsky at this time, was offered the post of chief ballet master and choreographer, but he finally left Russia in 1918 when agreement could not be reached.

In the twenties and early thirties, the company, called the State Academy Theatre for Opera and Ballet (or GATOB), entered a period of experimentation typified by Fyodor Lopokov's influential

1923 symphonic ballet *Dance Symphony*, with a cast that included a young **George Balanchine**. The most important new Soviet ballets premiered in what was now Leningrad, culminating in the 1940 production of **Romeo and Juliet**. During this time, the former dancer Agrippina Vaganova consolidated her position as the premier pedagogue of the Soviet style, developing a system of dance instruction that has spread throughout the Russian territories.

Under Oleg Vinogradov's direction (since 1972), today's Kirov dancers are known for their dazzling and assured technique, purity of line, dignified stage manners and a light, lyrical mobility that in ex-Kirov dancers **Rudolf Nureyev** and **Mikhail Baryshnikov** reached gravity-defying standards. The company is also graced with one of the world's most precise and musical corps de ballet. And yet, since the early 1950s, the Kirov has suffered from a creative sterility imposed by its own insularity. Although the company has appeared sporadically in the West since 1961, Western ballets rarely enter the repertory (works by **Maurice Béjart** and **Roland Petit** are exceptions), and Kirov dancers are rarely lent out. This isolation prompted first Nureyev (1961) and then **Natalia Makarova** (1970) and Baryshnikov (1974) to defect. After two years' struggle, dancers Valeri and Galina Panov were finally granted permission to emigrate to Israel in 1974. However, the spirit of *glasnost* allowed Altynai Asylmuratova and Faroukh Ruzimatov (the company's newest star couple) to dance two performances with American Ballet Theatre in 1988.

Lineage

The creative blood of the French, Italian and Danish schools continues to course through the Kirov's refined veins. Its tradition, filtered through the Russian temperament, was then redistributed as **Serge Diaghilev** lured away **Michel Fokine**, **Anna**

Pavlova, **Vaslav Nijinsky** and many others to the Ballets Russes. Their further dispersal has spread the benefits of St Petersburg training worldwide. Dancer, ballet master and one-time Kirov director Nicholas Sergeyev left Russia after the Revolution, taking Vladimir Stepanov's dance notations with him; these were instrumental in helping the **Royal Ballet** mount their first productions of the Russian classics in the 1930s.

Follow-up

Nicolai Legat's *The Story of the Russian School* (1932) is an account of the Imperial Ballet's golden age, while Natalia Roslavleva's *Era of the Russian Ballet* (1966) continues the story. A 1964 film of the Kirov's *Sleeping Beauty* features Natalia Makarova and Valeri Panov in the *Bluebird* pas de deux. There are later versions of this ballet on video, as well as *Giselle* and *Don Quixote*. An hour-long video, *Magic of the Kirov Ballet* (1988), spotlights some of the company's best dancers in excerpts from Petipa's most famous classical ballets; the 1983 *Backstage at the Kirov* focusses on preparations for *Swan Lake*.

Jirí Kylián

Born: 21st March 1947/Prague

In the late 1970s, Jirí Kylián burst into the international dance scene like a rocket. He has yet to burn out. His approach to dance is neither avant-garde nor revolutionary, but rather a synthesis of the smooth academics of classical ballet and the emotional power of modern dance. Punctuated by impressive feats of choreographic stuntwork and the rhythms and patterns of folk dance, his works tend to be buoyant, undemanding parades of flying bodies which execute sweeping runs, buckling leaps and tricky lifts. All of this vitality is

Bryony Brind in a pas de trois from the 1984 Royal Ballet staging of *Return to the Strange Land* by Jirí Kylián

underpinned by a musicality so innate that Kylián's dancers, and the music they move to, seem to spring from the same impulse.

Kylián's training (from the age of nine) incorporated classical ballet, folk dance and **Martha Graham**-style modern dance. In 1967, he won a scholarship to the **Royal Ballet** School, where **John Cranko** spotted him, inviting him to the **Stuttgart Ballet** the following year. Kylián stayed on as both dancer and dancemaker until 1975, but he found his true choreographic outlet at the **Netherlands Dance Theatre**. He made his first piece for them in 1973, joining as co-artistic director two years later and taking sole charge in 1978.

In the ensuing decade, Kylián turned his dancers into one of the tightest and most unaggressively glamorous troupes in Europe. His own ballets feature prominently in the repertory. An ability to stage large, religious choral works is typified by the company's signature piece *Sinfonietta* (1979): set to his compatriot Leos Janácek's score, this is an exuberant hymn to life's joys and sorrows. *Symphony of Psalms* (1978, to Stravinsky) and the all-male *Soldier's Mass* (1980) tread similar

territory. One of his most popular dances, also inspired by Janácek, is *Return to the Strange Land* (1975), a lyrically sculpted series of pas de deux and trois (the latter a Kylián speciality) that has entered the repertories of many companies, including the Royal Ballet and the **Joffrey Ballet**.

Lately, Kylián has moved towards longer, even more theatrical ballets such as *L'Enfant et les Sortilèges* (1984), after Colette's poem about the inanimate objects in a child's room coming to life, and *Kaguya-Hime* (1988), an allusively narrative spectacle based on a Japanese folk legend. His fascination with Australian aboriginal culture led to the creation of a trilogy – *Nomads* (1981), *Stamping Ground* (1982) and *Dreamtime* (1983) – which translates authentic aboriginal movements, rituals and themes into Kylián kinetics.

Lineage

Jirí Kylián is the most celebrated Central European choreographer since **Kurt Jooss**, and shares with **John Neumeier** and **Robert Cohan** a penchant for quasi-religious expression. Many of his dances are abstract on the surface, and neo-classical in terms of actual movement, but at the core there is intended to be a significant statement about mankind. His gift for swirling invention aligns him with **Jerome Robbins** and **Eliot Feld**, although like Feld he is too fond of self-quotation, sometimes lifting whole segments of his own choreography in dance after dance. Deeply influenced by Kylián, **Christopher Bruce** has often grafted folk dance traditions onto a strong classical base.

Follow-up

More than a dozen Kylián ballets have been filmed or made available on video, including *Sinfonietta, Symphony of Psalms*, the 1975 *Transfigured Night* and *Svadebka*, a 1982 variation on Igor Stravinsky's *Les Noces. Road to the Stamping Ground* is a documentary on one of Kylián's aboriginal ballets, and a record of the largest gathering of aboriginal tribal dancers ever assembled, which Kylián attended.

Kenneth MacMillan

Born: 11th December 1929/ Dunfermline, Fife

One of the most popular of contemporary ballet choreographers, Kenneth MacMillan debuted as a dancer with the new Sadler's Wells Theatre Ballet (now **Royal Ballet**) in 1946. The inaugural performance of The Choreographic Group, instituted in 1953 as a platform for young dancemakers, featured his first ballet *Somnambulism*, to a jazz score by Stan Kenton. From the start, he showed a flair for using the classical vocabulary in unorthodox ways, and as early as 1958 began exploring historical fact as the basis for a ballet. This work, *The Burrow*, was inspired by the plight of Anne Frank; he has repeatedly returned to historical figures throughout his career. In 1960, a major breakthrough

occurred with **The Invitation**, establishing both MacMillan and his favourite ballerina **Lynn Seymour** as the most daring talents of the day.

Tackling Stravinsky's **Le Sacre du printemps** in 1962, MacMillan produced a pulsating group ritual which has since lost its edge of startling originality, but at the time seemed revolutionary. His first full-length ballet, **Romeo and Juliet**, was a triumph and became a favoured vehicle for **Rudolf Nureyev** and **Margot Fonteyn**, who made a feature film of it the following year.

MacMillan's major 1965 project, **Song of the Earth**, was his first for the **Stuttgart Ballet**, then run by his friend **John Cranko**. The following year, MacMillan, with Seymour as his principal ballerina, moved to Berlin to take over as artistic director of the Deutsches Oper's ballet company. During his three seasons there (1966 to 1969), he staged the plotless *Concerto* (to Shostakovich's Piano Concerto No.2) and began work on *Anastasia*. The one-act Berlin version became the finale to a full-evening ballet created after returning to the Royal Ballet, where he succeeded **Frederick Ashton** as artistic director in 1970. Based on the case history of a mental patient who claimed to be the sole survivor of the slaughtered Russian ruling family, *Anastasia* juxtaposed differing eras, musics and even movement styles and even incorporated historical newsreel footage. MacMillan's third full-length ballet, *Manon*, was immediately followed by the broad comedy of *Elite Syncopations*, set to the ragtime music of Scott Joplin (both 1974). He returned to Stuttgart in 1976 to stage the Fauré *Requiem* in tribute to Cranko's untimely death.

In 1977, wanting to concentrate on choreography rather than administration, MacMillan resigned his post at the Royal to Norman Morrice. His next work, the blazing **Mayerling**, showed how deeply he had become involved in his intention to make ballet speak in a new adult manner. Next came (again for Stuttgart) his controversial and brutal depiction of incest and murder, *My Brother, My Sisters*.

He combined his interests in history and religious music in 1980 with Poulenc's *Gloria*, a paean to the lost generation senselessly slaughtered in the trenches during the First World War. It is too amorphously handled to be top rank, but, as with all of MacMillan's works, there are flashes of exceptional movement invention.

MacMillan's creativity went into a slump which led to such unsatisfying works as the full-length *Isadora* (1980), based on the life of American pioneer **Isadora Duncan**. *Wild Boy* (made for **Mikhail Baryshnikov** in 1981) is both sadistic and confusing. *Valley of Shadows* (1982), inspired by Giorgio Basani's *The Garden of the Finzi-Continis*, is a tragic story of a wealthy Jewish family in Mussolini's Italy. His revisions of *Woyzeck* as *Different Drummer* (1984) and *Hamlet* as *Sea of Troubles* (1988) are mannered silent movies rather than valid dance-theatre experiment.

Accepting a 1984 offer to join **American Ballet Theatre** as an artistic associate, MacMillan staged *Romeo and Juliet*, a new production of **The Sleeping Beauty** and a poorly received version of Andrew Lloyd Webber's *Requiem*. His latest muse, the young Alessandra Ferri, followed him to New York in much the same way as Seymour had gone to Berlin nearly two decades earlier. MacMillan has retained his position as chief choreographer for the Royal, although **David Bintley** is now the official resident choreographer. In 1986, he was working in London again, staging his second version of *Le Baiser de la Fée* (the first had been in 1960) and is scheduled to produce his sixth full-length Royal Ballet production, Benjamin Britten's *The Prince of the Pagodas*, in 1989. He has worked as a theatrical director, staging plays by Ionesco, Strindberg and Tennessee Williams, and was knighted in 1983.

Lineage

No one could ever accuse Kenneth MacMillan of playing it safe. One of the most inquisitive of modern ballet choreographers, he has repeatedly risked failure and derision by plunging into unknown territory and unorthodox movement styles. He knows that choreography, the most public of arts, must be exposed to an audience in order to exist. There are no ballet masterworks stored away in trunks like unpublished novels or unfinished symphonies. MacMillan, who has never been content with a single successful formula, has repeatedly courted disaster with his experimentations, and several of his ballets quickly disappeared. In this he is far from unique; even the greatest choreographers all produced their share of flops. What continues to keep MacMillan such an intriguing figure is his restless insistence on expanding the accepted perimeters of ballet through drama, religious music, historical fact and even dialogue.

Along with his lifelong friend **John Cranko**, MacMillan is the choreographer most responsible for the resurgence of full-evening ballets. The Bolshoi's **Yuri Grigorovich**, Hamburg's **John Neumeier** and Basel's **Heinz Spoerli** are other choreographers who have once again taken up the notion (abandoned by the Ballets Russes under **Serge Diaghilev**) of classically-based three-act works.

Follow-up

The 1966 Fonteyn/Nureyev version of MacMillan's *Romeo and Juliet* was the most popular dance film of its time. In 1984, MacMillan created a television adaptation of Brecht and Weill's *The Seven Deadly Sins* for Alessandra Ferri. Edward Thorpe's effusive *Kenneth MacMillan: The Man and the Ballets* (1985) ignores much of MacMillan's negative (particularly American) press coverage.

The Invitation

One act
Choreography: Kenneth MacMillan
Music: Matyas Seiber
Design: Nicholas Georgiadis
Premiere: 10th November 1960/ New Theatre, Oxford

The Invitation was the work which consolidated Kenneth MacMillan's burgeoning reputation as the most dramatic young dance talent Britain had seen since the early days of **Antony Tudor**. MacMillan devised his own scenario from a pair of novels, Colette's *Le Blé en herbe* (The Ripening Seed) and *House of the Angel* by the Argentinian author Beatriz Guido. He set the ballet – premiered by **Sadler's Wells Royal Ballet** on tour – in an unspecified country in the tropics some time just before the First World War. Its action takes place during a weekend house party. The story contains the seeds of his later, larger works: innocence betrayed; the rot behind the social mask; and the disastrous consequences of selfish and venal sexual appetites.

The story is one of double seduction. A pubescent girl and

Desmond Kelly and Marion Tait of Sadler's Wells Royal Ballet in MacMillan's *The Invitation*

her equally virginal boy cousin are innocently attracted to one another. Their youth turns into a fatal lure for a worldly and cynical couple who are part of the house party. The Wife, choosing her moment with accuracy, initiates the young man. The girl is not so lucky. Flattered by the attentions of The Husband, she flirts with him in the same coltish and unsophisticated way she had played with her cousin. The Husband, unable to control his desires, rapes the girl.

The ballet ends with the older couple leaving together. The boy, sensing that something is wrong, tries to comfort the girl, but she pulls away from him in fear. Forever scarred by the violence she has just experienced, she remains alone, trapped in eternal frigidity. She has become that recurrent MacMillan symbol of 'the outsider'.

The story is reinforced with some needlessly heavy symbolism. The ballet opens with a big to-do being made about the nude statues in the garden, and an entertainment for the guests features a trio of acrobats who play at being two cocks fighting over a hen. With the central choreography as strongly graphic as it is, these added signposts are hardly necessary.

Lineage

The exploration of sexual violence and its repercussions became MacMillan's main theme. As early as 1956 he had playfully touched on 'the outsider' in *Solitaire*, and later pushed it to extremes in the incest of *My Brother, My Sisters* and the full-length **Mayerling**. The fatality of repression is the central focus of *Las Hermanas* (based on Lorca's *La Casa de Bernarda Alba*). This thread in MacMillan's work draws from **Antony Tudor**, particularly **Pillar of Fire**. Flemming Flindt exposed sexual obsession and rape in *The Lesson* (based on Ionesco), as did **Birgit Cullberg** in *Miss Julie* (Strindberg). MacMillan also created a version of *Miss Julie* for Marcia Haydée in 1970, and directed Ionesco's *La Leçon* as a play.

Staging

1 Berlin Opera Ballet/1966

Song of the Earth

One act
Choreography: Kenneth MacMillan
Music: Gustav Mahler
Design: Nicholas Georgiadis
Premiere: 7th November 1965/ Württemburg State Theatre, Stuttgart

Often regarded as a MacMillan masterwork, *Song of the Earth* is a quasi-formalist recreation of Mahler's 1910 song symphony *Das Lied von der Erde*, which in turn is an evocation of thousand-year-old Chinese poetry. The central theme of the music, poetry and choreography tells us that our brief individual lives are only a minute part of a grand scheme. Life is short, but the earth is in a continual process of renewal. MacMillan's major character is a Messenger of Death who wears a white mask and, in each of the six scenes, comes to claim other characters. The two other main roles – the Man and the Woman – are humanity's representatives. Their final duet (turning into a trio with the Messenger) takes up nearly half of the ballet's sixty-five minutes.

The first five songs range from rollicking drunkenness for the men, to lads riding by on frisky (mimed) horses as a group of geisha-like maidens pick (mimed) lotus flowers. One of the poems tells of a pavilion by a pool. The choreography evokes this with some of the dancers on their backs mimicking the water's reflections. MacMillan is trying to have things both ways: he suggestively replicates the text when it suits him and ignores it when it does not. It is as if he does not want to illustrate the text, but cannot prevent himself from doing otherwise.

The ballet's immense popularity in Germany and Britain must originally have been partly based on the impact of a virtually bare stage and dancers in the simplest of costumes. The stark setting is just a uniformly dark cyclorama, the costumes are rehearsal clothes in white, grey or black. There are no props except the Messenger's mask. Yet for all its simplicity, the ballet is a distressing halfway house between true abstraction (á la **George Balanchine**) and the story ballets which MacMillan can do so effectively. It is only when he gets to the final song and reverts to what he can do best, the pas de deux, that the work really soars. Here, the words are less explicit, so he is forced back on his own lively sense of theatre rather than on images derived directly from the text.

Song of the Earth suffers from the dilemma common to all dances set to songs. How is the choreographer to use the lyrics: should he illustrate, comment on, enhance or ignore them? Whatever decision the choreographer takes, a part of the audience will never be satisfied, because words possess a concrete meaning which dancing, at its best, surmounts.

Lineage

Continental and American critical opinion is strongly divided over this work – and MacMillan's career in general. Though not as reviled in America as **Maurice Béjart** or **John Neumeier**, MacMillan is often viewed by US critics as a neo-expressionist romantic out of sync with the times. Americans often fail to see MacMillan's simplification of ballet as a liberating process from the bombast of the old opera house mentality. They tend to view his works as a dehydration of classical purity. This was particularly true during the 1970s, when the American classical aesthetic of **George Balanchine** was being equally enforced by the pure abstractions of **Merce Cunningham** and such leading post-modern choreographers as **Twyla Tharp**, **Trisha Brown**, **Laura Dean** and **Lucinda Childs**.

Follow-up

Natalia Makarova writes about performing *Song of the Earth* in *A Dance Autobiography* (1979).

Stagings

1 **Royal Ballet**/1966
2 **Australian Ballet**/1987
3 **National Ballet of Canada**/1988

Mayerling

Three acts
Choreography: Kenneth MacMillan
Libretto: Gillian Freeman
Music: Franz Liszt, arranged by John Lanchbery
Design: Nicholas Georgiadis
Premiere: 14th February 1978/ Royal Opera House, London

Kenneth MacMillan has always wanted ballet to do more than most choreographers believe it is capable of. Nowhere is he more successful in pushing the dramatic boundaries of the art form outwards than in *Mayerling*. Here he achieves a kind of nervous balance between sprawling grandiosity and compelling choreographic invention. It is as if (like the historical story on which the plot is based) things have gone as far as they can.

The Hollywood glamourisation of the 1889 suicide pact at Mayerling between Crown Prince Rudolf of the Austro-Hungarian Empire and his seventeen-year-old mistress Mary Vetsera is not for MacMillan. Instead, he and librettist Gillian Freeman set out to create an historically accurate portrait that exposes Rudolf's world as a place of degenerate depravity where sex is both a weapon and a last resort. The last eight years of his life are compressed into just over three hours which follow a relentless downward spiral of torrid sex, political intrigue, drugs and murder.

MacMillan's Rudolf is a womaniser, a syphilis-ridden morphine addict, a hedonist with a macabre passion for guns who (Hamlet-like) skulks around with a skull. At the beginning of the ballet, he is politically married off to a cousin he neither knows nor loves. Before he virtually rapes her on their wedding night, he has both blatantly tried to seduce her sister, and had a very Oedipal encounter with his mother. In the next act, he further degrades his wife by dragging her off to his favourite brothel, where he flaunts one former mistress and intrigues with another. This latter woman (Rudolf's 'evil genius') is the Countess Larisch, who connives for him to meet the teenaged Mary. As fervidly neurotic as Rudolf, she is smuggled into the palace for a violent liaison (one of the most acrobatic and steamy of all MacMillan's pas de deux). Less than two weeks later, he persuades Mary to die with him. After another sordid and obsessive duet, Rudolf murders her and then shoots himself.

This steamy and morbid story would perhaps make more sense in operatic or theatrical terms, and, as it is, many of the plot incidents and most of the minor characters are intelligible only through programme notes. Yet the intensity of the central characters is so vividly depicted in graphic movement that the ballet bursts with undeniable life. MacMillan openly acknowledges sex as his prime theme, and as he repeatedly does in so many other ballets, seems to affirm that everything else is mere window dressing.

Lineage

Sex, even when not so blatantly depicted as in *Mayerling*, has always been a major dance subject. As **Antony Tudor** did in the generation before him, MacMillan has frequently stressed ballet's need to grow up into an adult art form capable of dealing with complex subject matter. This work marked the peak of his own exploration to date; hereafter his ballets fall away in power and relevance. The late works can look like mediocre imitation MacMillan in the bloated **John Neumeier** manner. The new approach to sexuality in the excoriating works of **Pina Bausch**, **William Forsythe** and other young choreographers takes the same quantum leap beyond MacMillan which he himself took when he left fairy tales behind.

Follow-up

A BBC film crew was on the spot during the creation of this ballet: the result, *MacMillan's 'Mayerling'*, includes both rehearsals and large sections of the opening night performance. It became the first ballet programme ever to win the Prix d'Italia.

Natalia Makarova

Born: 21st October 1940/Leningrad

Already a major **Kirov Ballet** star when she chose to defect to the West, Natalia Makarova went on to become the great international ballerina of the ballet boom decade. Her performances are distinguished by an acute musical sensitivity supported by exceptional acting. Her delicate musical phrasing, always one of her strong suits, is something which was too often over-indulged. There were performances of **Swan Lake** with **American Ballet Theatre** when her adagio moments, though astonishingly heartrending from a movement sense, had become so drawn out and dewy that Tchaikovsky's score all but ground to a halt. No one who witnessed these performances will ever forget them, but Makarova's interpretation is something which fans of *Swan Lake* (as opposed to fans of Natalia Makarova) often found irksome.

Makarova did not start her training until she was thirteen, when she became part of an experimental class which was put through the Kirov programme in a pressurised six (rather than the usual nine) years. She had already scored triumphs as **Giselle** and in *Swan Lake* before her decision to stay in the West during the Kirov's London season in 1970. As with **Rudolf Nureyev** before her, and **Mikhail Baryshnikov** later, her motives were those of artistic freedom rather than politics.

She immediately became associated with American Ballet Theatre, making her Western debut in *Giselle* and continuing to dance the classics (adding **La Sylphide** and **The Sleeping Beauty**). She also began to explore the modern repertory, notably the works of **Antony Tudor**, **George Balanchine** (in *Apollo*) and **Glen Tetley**. In 1976, **Jerome Robbins** choreographed his *Other Dances* for her and Baryshnikov. Four years earlier, Makarova had made her debut with the **Royal Ballet**. Among her London roles have been **Kenneth MacMillan**'s **Romeo and Juliet**, *Manon* and **Song of the Earth**.

Makarova gave a new life and consistency to the corps de ballet at American Ballet Theatre when she staged 'The Kingdom of the

Natalia Makarova partnered by Martin James of London Festival Ballet

Shades' from **La Bayadère** in 1974; six years later, she mounted a unique Western staging of the entire ballet. Her work as a producer continued with **London Festival Ballet**: 'The Kingdom of the Shades' (1985) and *Swan Lake* (1988).

Makarova's sense of comedy, seen on the ballet stage in **La Fille mal gardée** and **Coppélia**, reached a new audience when she appeared on Broadway and in London in the revival of the 1930s musical *On Your Toes*, which ends with the famous 'Slaughter on Tenth Avenue' production number (restaged by **Peter Martins** from the original choreography by George Balanchine).

During the mature years of her career, Makarova has been particularly effective as Tatiana in **John Cranko**'s *Onegin* and as Natalia in **Frederick Ashton**'s *A Month in the Country*. In August 1988, Makarova's career (and ballet history) came full circle when she once again danced with the Kirov for a single performance in London.

Lineage

With **Galina Ulanova** and **Margot Fonteyn**, Makarova represents the supreme expression of the ballerina. Makarova was neither as idiosyncratic as Marcia Haydée nor as inconsistent as either **Lynn Seymour** or **Gelsey Kirkland**. Her only true rival for musicality during the ballet boom years was **Suzanne Farrell**, who chose to devote her career to the modern repertory of **George Balanchine** and left the realm of the nineteenth-century classics virtually untouched.

Follow-up

Ballerina, a BBC series (on video) featuring Makarova as narrator, was published in book form in 1987. Her *A Dance Autobiography* appeared in 1979 and includes nearly 200 pages of photos. Among the many Makarova videos are a Royal Ballet production of *Swan Lake* with Anthony Dowell, and *Natasha*, which includes excerpts from *A Month in the Country* and *Romeo and Juliet*.

Peter Martins

Born: 27th October 1946/ Copenhagen

In person, dancers invariably turn out to be considerably smaller than they appear on stage. A small, compact physique is ideal for ballet and even the most statuesque of ballerinas, such as Bryony Brind of the Royal Ballet and American Ballet Theatre's Cynthia Gregory and Martine van Hamel, are only around five foot seven. Peter Martins is an exception to the rule: at six foot two, he was one of the few tall ballet performers able to project the gracious elegance of classical line even though his body was more naturally suited to the playing fields.

A student at the Royal Danish Ballet School from the age of eight, Martins became a company member ten years later. In 1967, he was flown to Edinburgh at short notice to replace an injured Jacques d'Amboise in a **New York**

City Ballet performance of **Apollo** (which he had already danced in Copenhagen). Only two months later, he was in New York appearing as an NYCB guest, partnering **Suzanne Farrell** initially in **The Nutcracker** and then in 'Diamonds', the final act of **George Balanchine**'s *Jewels*. For the next two seasons, Martins commuted across the Atlantic. Ironically, just at the point that he decided to join NYCB full time, Farrell began her self-imposed five-year exile from the company.

The first roles created specifically by Balanchine for Martins were in *Stravinsky Violin Concerto* and *Duo Concertant* (both for the 1972 Stravinsky Festival and both danced with Kay Mazzo). Farrell's 1975 return to New York marked the 'golden age' in Martins' career.

The pair became one of the most exciting partnerships of the decade; both had an instinctual approach to music that lifted choreography into unpredictable realms. Together they were like a pair of consummate jazz improvisers who took Balanchine's neo-classicism into a sphere all their own.

Martins returned to Copenhagen for two guest stints, performing James in **La Sylphide** (1976) and Ove in the 1979 revival of **A Folk Tale**. He created his first piece of choreography for NYCB in 1977 (*Calcium Light Night*, to Charles Ives). In 1983, after partnering Farrell in New York City Ballet's 1000th performance of *The Nutcracker*, Martins retired as a performer to concentrate on choreography.

Following Balanchine's death that same year, he and **Jerome Robbins** were appointed co-heads of the company. In 1988, Martins not only organised the American Music Festival, but also choreographed several new works, chief among these the *Barber Violin Concerto*. Like Balanchine's *Episodes* (1959), it mixed ballet dancers (Merrill Ashley and Adam Lüders) with modern dance performers (David Parsons and Kate Johnson from the **Paul Taylor** stable).

Lineage

Like fellow Dane **Erik Bruhn**, Peter Martins was a regal dancer. He had none of the compactness of **Mikhail Baryshnikov** and never indulged in the flamboyant excesses that have marred periods of **Rudolf Nureyev**'s career.

Follow-up

The Farrell-Martins partnership is captured in several ballets of the Dance in America Balanchine series. His first choreography, *Calcium Light Night*, was filmed in 1980, and several short pieces were featured in the video *A Choreographer's Notebook: Stravinsky Piano Ballets by Peter Martins*. His autobiography *Far From Denmark* was published in 1982.

National Ballet of Canada

Formed: 1951

The development of ballet in Canada has been a distinctly post-war phenomenon. In 1946, there were no professional ballet companies in Canada. Ten years later there were three, all still active and important.

The creation of the National Ballet of Canada was a direct response to the founding of the oldest of these companies, the Winnipeg (later Royal Winnipeg) Ballet, which had begun in 1934 but only switched to full-time professional status in 1949. A group of art patrons in Toronto, reluctant to allow Winnipeg (in the province of Manitoba) to establish itself unchallenged as Canada's ballet capital, invited Celia Franca to create a new company.

Franca, recommended for the job by **Ninette de Valois**, was a British dancer who had studied with **Antony Tudor**, and danced with **Ballet Rambert** and **Sadler's**

Wells Royal Ballet. Her starting point for the establishment of the new company was an insistence on a solid base of the Russian classics, augmented by the Ballets Russes works and the contemporary British repertory – **Frederick Ashton's** *Les Rendezvous*, Antony Tudor's **Lilac Garden** and *Dark Elegies*, and **John Cranko**'s **Pineapple Poll**. This backbone supported the National Ballet's growth as it became the largest classical ballet company in Canada, now some sixty dancers strong.

The British connection was reinforced by the appointment of British artist and writer Kay Ambrose as artistic adviser from 1952 to 1961, and the arrival after Franca's retirement in 1974 (and a brief stay by David Haber) of the Royal Ballet character dancer Alexander Grant, who significantly expanded the company's Ashton repertory and added **Kenneth MacMillan's** ever popular *Elite Syncopations*. Nevertheless, local talent was cultivated in the shape of ex-National Ballet soloists, particularly James Kudelka (now artistic director of Les Grands Ballets Canadiens) and Constantin Patsalas.

Rudolf Nureyev enhanced the NBC profile with guest appearances in his own stagings of **The Sleeping Beauty** and **Romeo and Juliet**. In 1981, **Peter Schaufuss** had a major success with North America's first full-length version of **August Bournonville**'s Danish treasure **Napoli**, and John Cranko's **Onegin** entered the repertory in 1984.

Erik Bruhn, whose links with the National Ballet extended back to his 1965 staging of **La Sylphide**, and a controversial **Swan Lake** (in which von Rothbart was transformed into a Black Queen), took over from Grant in 1983. Although he died only three years later, he made a significant impact. His work was carried on by Lynn Wallis and Valerie Wilder, until the spring of 1989. They asked **Glen Tetley** to become artistic adviser: his new works for NBC include *Alice* (1986) and *La Ronde* (1987).

Much of the National Ballet's success is a product of its excellent school, run by the company's ballet mistress Betty Oliphant. Its style – a mix of English precision and Russian flair, with a rangy but forceful North American accent – has led to international acclaim for dancers like Karen Kain and Veronica Tennant and emerging stars such as Kimberly Glasco and Rex Harrington.

Lineage

Whereas the National Ballet of Canada has primarily based itself around the nineteenth-century classics, the Royal Winnipeg Ballet and Les Grands Ballets Canadiens, which are both considerably smaller companies, focus on original works. The National Ballet of Canada was clearly modelled on the **Sadler's Wells Royal Ballet**, and has much in common with the **Australian Ballet** in its approach.

Follow-up

Ken Bell and Celia Franca reviewed the history of the company in *The National Ballet of Canada* (1979). A National Film Board of Canada production features the work of all three Canadian companies in *For the Love of Dance* (1981), while the National Ballet has filmed *Romeo and Juliet* (1966), *Cinderella* (1970), *The Sleeping Beauty* (1973) and *Onegin* (1986).

National Ballet of Cuba

Ballet Nacional de Cuba
Formed: 1948, as Ballet Alicia Alonso

Cuban ballet revolves around one pre-eminent figure, the prima ballerina Alicia Alonso. It is through her personal efforts and persistence that dance in post-revolutionary Cuba has been elevated to world status.

When Alonso (born Alicia Martinez in 1921) was in her early teens, ballet in Cuba was confined to the activities of the Sociedad Pro-Arte Musical, an essentially amateur organisation run by society patrons. Cubans had seen Fanny Elssler during her two-year tour of the Americas in the early 1840s, and one admirer even presented her with a box of Havana cigars – each one solid gold. **Anna Pavlova** had stopped in Havana in 1917 on one of her long tours, but opportunities to see ballet were few and far between. Ballet was deemed a diversion, not a career. The young Alicia Martinez's desire to become a fulltime dancer was a potential disgrace, so – aged fifteen – she eloped to the USA with her first husband Fernando Alonso.

There, she was to become a major figure at a time when ballet in America, let alone Cuba, was still unformed. After training at the School of American Ballet and appearing on Broadway in the musical *Stars in Your Eyes* (along with Nora Kaye), Alonso joined Ballet Caravan, and later Ballet Theatre. Small, dark, slender, with a strong technique, and despite debilitating eye problems, she developed a famous **Giselle** and created the guilt-ridden murderess Lizzie Borden in **Agnes de Mille**'s *Fall River Legend*. **George Balanchine** choreographed his scintillating and technically demanding *Theme and Variations* (1947) for Alonso and her principal partner Igor Youskevitch.

Back in Cuba, she founded the country's first professional company as Ballet Alicia Alonso in 1948, and launched her school two years later. A sense of national identity was strengthened when the company was renamed Ballet de Cuba in 1955. After the 1959 Revolution it became the National Ballet, and has since acted as a showcase and international ambassador for the Castro government. Alonso's classical repertory (with *Giselle* still a firm favourite) was offset by the growth

of Cuban choreography, particularly the work of Alberto Alonso (Alicia's brother-in-law) who created a 1967 treatment of the **Carmen** story as *Carmen Suite* (for **Maya Plisetskaya** and the **Bolshoi**). The Cubans' homegrown choreography is often overtly populist, culled from Afro-Caribbean folklore and resorting to the larger-than-life polemics of the modernist Soviet style. A few company works, such as Alberto Mendez's *Tarde en la Siesta*, have garnered international praise. This 1984 work is for a quartet of ballerinas as turn-of-the-century sisters whose conflicts and unfulfilled aspirations boil over one hot afternoon.

Touring widely throughout the world and building up an international reputation, the National Ballet of Cuba was only allowed to perform in the US for the first time in 1978, and made its British debut at the Edinburgh Festival the following year. The ballet school has created a generation of gifted dancers (notably Jorge Esquivel), but Alonso remains *numero uno*. Her style of intense, technically strong classicism is the Revolution's finest example of cultural propaganda.

Lineage

More than figures like Celia Franca of the **National Ballet of Canada** or Sonia Gaskell at the **Dutch National Ballet**, Alicia Alonso is genuinely the single person responsible for establishing and sustaining ballet in Cuba. During the decade before the Revolution, she personally funded the company through her own international guest appearances.

Follow-up

Walter Terry has written on *Alicia and Her Ballet Nacional de Cuba* (1981). Charles Payne's 1977 *American Ballet Theatre* includes Alonso's essay on 'Performing Giselle'. The Cuban Film Institute has produced *Alicia* (a 1976 documentary with interviews and excerpts) plus a 1964 *Giselle* with Alonso in her prime and in her prime role.

John Neumeier

Born: 24th February 1942/
Milwaukee, Wisconsin

Neumeier is regarded as one of
the gods of European
contemporary ballet, certainly in
Germany, and especially in the
city of Hamburg, where he has
been artistic director and chief
choreographer of the Hamburg
Ballet since 1973. He is no stranger
to German opera house institutions,
having danced for **John Cranko** at
the **Stuttgart Ballet** from 1963 to
1969, where he also composed his
first professional choreography,
and directed the Frankfurt Ballet,
where his most important creations
included **Romeo and Juliet** and
The Nutcracker (both 1971).

As a ballet producer, Neumeier
tends to think big, favouring
heavyweight composers (Mahler,
Stravinsky, Tchaikovsky, Bach),
lofty themes and imposing literary,
legendary or religious sources. His
opera house sensibility is further
reflected in his choreography,
which tends towards high-flown,
overemphatic classicism. The
dancing can be acrobatically

Gigi Hyatt and Kevin Haigen of the Hamburg
Ballet performing John Neumeier's *St Matthew
Passion*

expressive, demonstrating
Neumeier's superficial command
of the genres he trades in, but
invariably it takes second place to
the choreographer's intellectual
and philosophical pretensions. For
instance, Neumeier's 1977 ballet
The Legend of Joseph is a
grandiose variation on **George
Balanchine**'s **The Prodigal Son**,
while the choreographer himself
has sometimes portrayed Jesus
Christ in a four-hour-plus version of
Bach's complete *St Matthew
Passion* (1981). In 1976, he made
Illusions – Like Swan Lake,
presenting **Lev Ivanov**'s second act
lakeside scenes as a ballet within
the ballet, entered by King Ludwig
of Bavaria, who assumes
Siegfried's role. Neumeier has
rethought the classics before and
since, including both a science-
fiction **The Firebird** and a time-
machine version of **The Sleeping
Beauty**, in which the Prince is clad
in 1970s denim.

While his detractors brand him
as one of the most unmusical major
choreographers of his generation,
others credit his originality in
illustrating musical form and
structure, recalling the (now
forgotten) symphonic ballets of
Léonide Massine. He started
working his way through the
Mahler canon with the *Third
Symphony* (1975), and subsequently
added ballets based on the 4th,
6th, 1st and 10th Symphonies.
Although the 4th, created for the
Royal Ballet, failed to last, many of
Neumeier's ballets have made it
into the international repertory.
One of the best travelled is *A
Midsummer Night's Dream* (1977),
an interpretation combining
slapstick mime, character dance,
modern dance and classical ballet.
The smorgasbord choreography is
matched by the ballet's score, a
coarse collage of György Ligeti,
Felix Mendelssohn and popular
barrel organ tunes. Neumeier's
Freudian, full-length *Othello* (1985)
is similarly kaleidoscopic.

Dance-theatre conceived and
executed on such a swollen scale
and striving so conscientiously to
underline its own seriousness can
be perceived as either exalting or

exhausting. Suffice to say that Neumeier's efforts to turn the Hamburg company into one of the Continent's most popular troupes have been successful. In 1988, he received a German Dance Award from the Society for Dance Teachers for his twenty-five years' service in the country as dancer, choreographer and teacher.

Lineage

The echoes of other choreographers in Neumeier's work are practically deafening. He is as extravagant as **Maurice Béjart** (and as fanatically admired), exhibits the dramatic leanings of **John Cranko** and **Kenneth MacMillan**, and goes in for a kind of cosmic neo-classicism, like **Jirí Kylián**. Neumeier shares with these and other choreographers a penchant for treating ballerinas like statuary, to be lifted and transported about the stage.

Follow-up

Published in 1983 to commemorate Neumeier's first decade as Hamburg's leader, *Zehn Jahre: John Neumeier und Das Hamburger Ballett* includes an essay by British critic John Percival. *John Neumeier*, a 1987 video profile, records the man at work in Hamburg, Paris and Pompeii. A 1988 BBC documentary about Maurice Béjart's ballet *The Chairs* features Neumeier and Marcia Haydée in interviews and on stage.

Rudolf Nureyev

Born 17th March 1938/Near Irkutsk, USSR

Chances are that more people have heard of Rudolf Nureyev than of any other dancer, living or dead. His name evokes a fierce, glamorous, seemingly ageless potency, based on his sensational vulpine looks, man-about-globe lifestyle and astounding gift for dramatic movement expression. His 'invasion' of the Western world in the early 1960s was the best advertisement for dance in the second half of the twentieth century.

He was born on a train, a fitting start given his later bewilderingly peripatetic schedule, and grew up in poverty in Ufa, a town at the foot of the Urals. Because his father, a military man, wanted him to join the army or take up engineering, the teenaged Nureyev began his ballet studies in secret. In Moscow for a folk dance festival, he auditioned for the **Bolshoi Ballet**, was accepted, but instead bought a one-way ticket to Leningrad where he successfully sought entry into the **Kirov Ballet** school. The young prodigy graduated within three years, after cultivating a reputation as a defiant maverick. His transgressions included learning English and trying to see every foreign dance company he could. He joined the Kirov as a principal in 1958, dancing in his first official performance opposite Natalia Dudinskaya, a prima ballerina twice his age, at her request. This was a taste of things to come.

Blessed with titanic stamina and a sponge-like curiosity about all kinds of dance (he reputedly knows more than eight dozen roles), Nureyev compensated for his late start in ballet by being a quick learner. His independent (though strictly apolitical) attitude did not endear him to the authorities. In Paris during the company's 1961 European engagements, he made his famous 'leap to freedom' at the airport, receiving political asylum in the West.

Within a week he was dancing again, keeping up the same demanding calendar of international performance he has sustained for nearly three decades. For dance fans and professionals, the effect was shattering.

As classical ballet's first contemporary superstar, he ensured that the supremacy of the ballerina was over and that the male dancer was given equal, and even greater, footing. Not since **Vaslav Nijinsky** had anyone witnessed such dancing: virile yet feline, febrile yet controlled, full of space-devouring leaps and Dionysian energy.

At **Margot Fonteyn**'s invitation, Nureyev became a permanent guest artist with the **Royal Ballet** in 1962. Fonteyn had danced her first **Swan Lake** in the year of Nureyev's birth; her vulnerable, polished maturity dovetailed beautifully with his youthful, impetuous bravura in such ballets as **Frederick Ashton**'s *Marguerite and Armand* and **Kenneth MacMillan**'s *Romeo and Juliet*.

But Nureyev is anything but a one-company man. He has appeared onstage with virtually every major ballet company in the Western world (and some lesser ones). In the 1970s, he entered the modern dance arena in works by **José Limón**, **Paul Taylor**, Murray Louis and **Martha Graham**, whose technique he learned from the ground up. Other choreographers who have made dances for him include Rudi van Dantzig, **Roland Petit**, **Glen Tetley** and **Maurice Béjart**. In 1979, the first of several star-laden touring groups dubbed 'Nureyev and Friends' made its Broadway debut.

Nureyev began staging his versions of the Kirov's **Marius Petipa** repertory in 1963. In these productions – including **La Bayadère**, **The Sleeping Beauty**, *Swan Lake*, **Don Quixote** and **Raymonda** – he has invariably augmented the leading male role. His first complete original ballet, *Tancredi* (1966), was a muddled Jungian meditation on sacred and profane love set to a Hans Werner Henze score. It was followed by *Manfred* (1979) after Byron, **The Tempest** (1982), an overblown adaptation of Henry James' novel *Washington Square* (1985) and **Cinderella** (1986). These ambitious ballets, though stuffed with ideas and production details, lack choreographic distinction.

In 1983, Nureyev became artistic director of the **Paris Opéra Ballet**.

One result of his appointment was a restoration of that company's world status. His improvements have included the development of a more varied repertory; balancing the classics with commissioned works from the likes of **William Forsythe**, **Karole Armitage**, **Lucinda Childs** and **Michael Clark**; and a streamlining of the company star system so that younger dancers have the chance to take centre stage. In 1987, he accepted the Soviet government's invitation to visit his homeland briefly for the first time since his defection.

While age has only underlined the power of his stage presence, Nureyev's physical abilities and what he can do with them have seriously declined. However, his voracious appetite for performing keeps attracting audiences keen to see the dancer once described as 'a wild animal let loose in a drawing room'.

Lineage

Nureyev, the **Vaslav Nijinsky** of the jet age, has been even more influential on his particular era and infinitely better documented. He belongs to that elite group of contemporary dancers (**Mikhail Baryshnikov**, **Peter Martins**, **Patrick Dupond**, **Michael Clark**) who command the dance equivalent of a pop star following. Both Nureyev and fellow **Kirov Ballet** defector Baryshnikov were pupils of Alexander Pushkin, renowned for his training of male dancers. Risking oversimplification, Nureyev dominates his roles whereas Baryshnikov slips into his, a case of dancer as star versus star as dancer.

Follow-up

In *An Evening with the Royal Ballet* (1963), the young Nureyev dances the complete *Les Sylphides* and *Le Corsaire* pas de deux with Margot Fonteyn. There are excellent full-length films of MacMillan's *Romeo and Juliet* (1966) and Nureyev's own *Don Quixote*, co-directed in 1973 by Robert Helpmann. The documentary *I Am a Dancer* (1973) juxtaposes backstage footage with performances of *La Sylphide*, *The Sleeping Beauty* and *Marguerite and Armand*. Nureyev suffers from under-direction in both of his non-dance films, the pseudo-biography *Valentino* (1977) and the arty thriller *Exposed* (1983). John Percival's 1975 biography is complemented by Clive Barnes' more subjective version from 1984; Nureyev himself authored *An Autobiography with Pictures* in 1962. *Observer of the Dance* by critic Alexander Bland (the joint pseudonym for the dancer's close friends, the late Nigel Gosling and Maude Lloyd) traces Nureyev's career through reviews.

Ashley Page

Born: 9th August 1956/Rochester, Kent

A student at the **Royal Ballet** Schools from the age of twelve, Ashley Page joined the company in 1975 and was promoted to principal dancer in 1984. Never a traditional prince, he is an intense and fervent performer with a wide-ranging modern repertory that includes **Jerome Robbins**' duet *Afternoon of a Faun*, Beliaev in **Frederick Ashton**'s **A Month in the Country**, and the amoral Lescaut, the pimping brother in **Kenneth MacMillan**'s *Manon*, plus works by **Glen Tetley**, **David Bintley**, **Jiří Kylián** and **Richard Alston**'s sole piece for the Royal, *Midsummer*.

Although continuing to dance, Page has increasingly focussed on choreography. As early as 1982, his workshop production *Seven Sketches* won the first Frederick Ashton Choreographic Award. His ballets for the Royal include *A Broken Set of Rules* (1984, to Michael Nyman) and *Pursuit* (1987, Colin Matthews) with a third scheduled for 1989. As both titles imply, Page is searching for ways of using the classical vocabulary in a fresh, invigorating and modern manner. Rather than jettisoning

ballet altogether or further exploring the dramatic vein so prevalent in the works of Continental choreographers, it is almost as if Page is trying to wed the classic to the post-modern by completely cutting out the intervening dramatics (from **Michel Fokine** to Kenneth MacMillan). His works are astringent, clean-lined, fast-paced and as tightly regulated as clockworks. He may up-end a ballerina on her head, but her feet will continue to execute recognisable ballet steps.

Page has also made several works outside the confines and dictates of his own company. He has been a regular participant in London's Dance Umbrella festival (an annual showcase of new dance from around the world) and in 1986 choreographed *Carmen Arcadiae Mechanics Perpetuum* (to an eponymous Harrison Birtwistle score) for **Rambert Dance Company**, for whom he produced *Soldat*, a new version of Stravinsky's *The Soldier's Tale*, minus the narrative, in late 1988.

Lineage

Page is one of the most promising of the emerging British choreographers. Like the American **Karole Armitage**, he is trying to fuse the rules of classicism to the hectic and unruly world of the 1980s. His work does not possess the lyrical finesse of **David Bintley**, whose ballets are more clearly part of an evolutionary process than Page's often unpredictable outbursts. Page is not chasing novelty for its own sake or shock value in the manner of young English superstar **Michael Clark**; his dances all have a clean sense of economy even when the designs are glaringly bright or eccentric. Fellow Royal dancer Wayne Eagling has also turned his hand to choreography. His *Frankenstein* (1985) and *Beauty and the Beast* (1987) are the exact antithesis of Page's work: long, elaborate pageants that rely on flashy stage effects, cunning costumes and pop classical scores for their undeniable box office appeal.

Paris Opéra Ballet

Ballet de l'Opéra de Paris
Formed: 1669, by Louis XIV

Louis XIV, an avid dancer, established the Académie Royale de Danse in 1661, and eight years later extended his patronage to the Académie Royale de Musique (now known as the Paris Opéra). In 1672, a dancing school was added; its purpose was to train artists - men only until 1681 - for a new hybrid series of opulent opera-ballets. In this way, ballet began its evolution from an elaborate aristocratic pastime to professional entertainment.

The Paris Opéra can boast a virtually unbroken line of dancers, ballet masters, aesthetic reformers and personalities from the Italian musician Jean-Baptiste Lully onwards (see Origins, page 8). By the time Filippo Taglioni and his daughter Marie arrived in 1828 artistic quality at the Opéra had slumped after several decades of cold, formal ballets and pervasive mediocrity. Taglioni's landmark **La Sylphide** was the archetypal product of the Romantic movement and ushered in one of the Opéra's golden eras, when **Giselle** and **Coppélia** were first staged, and **Arthur Saint-Léon**, **Marius Petipa**'s father Lucien, Jean Coralli and **Jules Perrot** were among the outstanding choreographers and ballet masters.

As Russia's strength as a dance centre grew towards the end of the century, Parisian dance activity again declined. The Opéra's creative stagnation was emphasised by the 1909 Paris premiere of the Ballets Russes. **Serge Diaghilev**'s success was such a stimulant that the Opéra's standards began to improve once more. **Anna Pavlova** and Olga Spessivtseva were engaged to dance, and **Michel Fokine** and

Bronislava Nijinska to produce dances. After Diaghilev's death in 1929, his protégé **Serge Lifar** undertook a complete revitalisation of the Opéra as its new ballet master and principal dancer. During his nearly thirty-year tenure, Lifar stabilised the company and restructured its training, in addition to creating over one hundred ballets. Under his guidance, Yvette Chauviré became the first French ballerina to win international recognition this century.

The Opéra lost some of its punch with Lifar's resignation in 1959. Subsequent company directors like Danish choreographer Harald Lander and ballerinas Violette Verdy and Rosella Hightower were unable to equal Lifar's inspiration and drive. During this uncertain period, the repertory expanded wildly, encompassing both **Yuri Grigorovich**'s and **John Cranko**'s **Romeo and Juliet**, as well as works from **Glen Tetley**, **Roland Petit**, **Maurice Béjart**, **Paul Taylor**, **Heinz Spoerli** and even **Merce Cunningham**.

The 1983 appointment of **Rudolf Nureyev** as artistic director has signalled another rejuvenation at the Opéra. He has promoted young star talent like the star ballerinas Sylvie Guillem and Isabelle Guérin, and bolstered the repertory of classics, among them his stagings of **Raymonda**, **The Nutcracker**, **Swan Lake** and **Cinderella**. Nureyev has also continued the company's progress into the contemporary dance arena, initiated in 1974 when **Carolyn Carlson** took up her specially created post as *danseuse étoile chorégraphique*. Carlson stayed for six years, her efforts formalised with the 1981 founding of the GRCOP (Groupe de Recherche Chorégraphique de l'Opéra de Paris) under the direction of Jacques Garnier. This small, experimental modern troupe has presented commissioned pieces by Carlson herself, **Lucinda Childs**, **Karole Armitage**, **Michael Clark** and French 'new wave' choreographers like **Maguy Marin** and François Verret.

Lineage

Of France's many provincial companies, the one nearest in clout to the Opéra is **Roland Petit**'s Ballet National de Marseille. In 1947, **George Balanchine** created *Palais de Cristal* (subsequently known as *Symphony in C*) at the Opéra during a six-month residency, an influence on his later, temperamentally French ballets *Gounod Symphony* (1958), *La Source* (1968) and *Chaconne* (1976).

Follow-up

Historian Ivor Guest's books about the Opéra include the two-volume *Ballet of the Second Empire* (1953/55) and *The Romantic Ballet in Paris* (1966). Actress Odette Joyeux's *Child of the Ballet: Memoirs of an Opéra 'Rat'* is a minor autobiographical classic, translated and introduced by British ballet authority Arnold Haskell. *The Paris Opéra Ballet* (1975), a two-part video, covers thirteen excerpts from the repertory. In 1987, the BBC broadcast Colin Nears' film of Nureyev's *Cinderella*, a sumptuous Hollywood fantasy.

Peter Schaufuss

Born: 26th April 1949/Copenhagen

Peter Schaufuss, one of the finest virtuoso dancers of his generation, has been in the theatre since childhood. His parents, ballerina Mona Vangsaae and dancer/ballet master Frank Schaufuss, were principals with the Royal Danish Ballet. Peter, who began training at age seven, made his professional debut within the year, accompanying his mother. A 1964 visit to the **National Ballet of Canada**, where his father was guest-starring, led to Schaufuss being offered a soloist's contract there once he had graduated back home.

Eager to broaden his technique

and disengage himself from what he regarded as an overprotective, nepotistic creative environment, he left Denmark for Canada in 1967. Leading roles in **Don Quixote** and **The Nutcracker** followed, but so did a period of unhappiness. Schaufuss was simply too young and inexperienced, personally and professionally, to handle the rigours of working in a major foreign country. He returned to Copenhagen after fifteen months, continued dancing and began choreographing; in the latter capacity, he helped organise and contributed to the first workshop performance in Royal Danish Ballet's history.

Schaufuss has a reputation for restless independence nearly equal to that of **Rudolf Nureyev**. He spent more than a decade moving between companies either as a 'permanent' member or guest artist. In 1970, he became a principal with **London Festival Ballet**, greatly expanding his classical repertory while developing the stamina necessary to fulfil a heavy touring schedule. His sense of musicality and phrasing were reinforced by his seasons with **George Balanchine** at **New York City Ballet** (from 1974 to 1977).

As a producer, his award-winning staging of **La Sylphide** for London Festival Ballet in 1979 was capped by his version of **Napoli** for National Ballet of Canada two years later. His 1984 appointment as artistic director has given London Festival Ballet a new lease of life. By the end of his second year there, the company had at least a dozen additional works in its repertory. His commitment to contemporary ballet is underlined by the choice of **Christopher Bruce** as associate choreographer. He was also responsible for the formation of LFB, a small, more portable offshoot of the main company. Guest artists like **Natalia Makarova**, Nureyev and **Patrick Dupond** have been imported, but not at the expense of company talent. To ensure the future, Schaufuss opened the LFB School in 1988.

Lynn Seymour in one of her most successful roles as Kenneth MacMillan's Juliet

Lineage

Schaufuss has resisted being typecast as a representative of a particular dance style, as have both **Rudolf Nureyev** and **Mikhail Baryshnikov**. The buoyant ballets of **August Bournonville** are undoubtedly the source of his spirit, but he has gone beyond the Bournonville technique by adding astounding physical embellishments to the given steps. Only dance superstars can get away with this. Schaufuss's grafting of a showy Russian style onto his Danish background is as uncommon among the Danes as **Peter Martins**' acquisition of **George Balanchine**'s neo-classical cool.

Follow-up

Roland Petit's 1980 ballet *Phantom of the Opera* was created on Schaufuss and broadcast by French television; the Schaufuss version of *La Sylphide* was presented by the BBC in 1980. In 1984, his career and working habits were used to illustrate the salient points of twentieth-century male dancing in the four-part BBC series *Dancer*, available on video; a book version of the programme is by Clement Crisp and Mary Clarke. The 1986 volume *Peter Schaufuss: Dancer* is a mainly pictorial appreciation by photographer David Street and writer Craig Dodd.

Lynn Seymour

Born: 8th March 1939/Wainwright, Alberta

An actress of rare dramatic potency, Lynn Seymour is a ballerina whose performances couple a ripe amplitude of movement with a striking lack of inhibition. Trained in Vancouver, she spent two years at the **Royal Ballet** School before making her 1956 debut with the Sadler's Wells branch of the company. She first worked with **Kenneth MacMillan** in *The Burrow* (1958), a ballet inspired by Anne Frank. Both choreographer and ballerina made a breakthrough into the limelight with **The Invitation**; this was the first ballet where Seymour was teamed with Christopher Gable. They were to become frequent partners, notably in **Frederick Ashton**'s *The Two Pigeons* (1961) and MacMillan's **Romeo and Juliet**. The trauma of creating the latter features prominently in Seymour's autobiography *Lynn*. She had an abortion and lost a husband in order to create this 'role of a lifetime', and then discovered just before the premiere that she and Gable were losing the first performance to superstars **Margot Fonteyn** and **Rudolf Nureyev**. To add insult to injury, Seymour then had to teach the role to Fonteyn and the four other ballerinas who would all be dancing it on stage before she could.

Only a year later, she migrated to Berlin with MacMillan, when he took over as director of the ballet company of the Deutsches Oper. Seymour's career (like her weight, an up and down affair) was at its nadir in the early seventies, but she was pulled back into shape by Ashton and given two of her most impressive roles in the evocative *Five Brahms Waltzes in the Manner* of *Isadora Duncan* and **A Month in the Country** (both 1976).

In 1978, she spent a chaotic season as director and principal ballerina of the Bavarian State Opera in Munich. The company was at a low ebb when she arrived, and Seymour was able to do little to better its position. She officially retired from dancing the next year, but in 1987 rejoined her old partner Gable (now director of Northern Ballet Theatre) to play the pinch-souled mother of painter L.S. Lowry in Gillian Lynne's bio-ballet *A Simple Man*. In 1988 she rejoined the ranks of major 'senior' ballerinas such as Marcia Haydée and **Natalia Makarova** by adding Tatiana in **Onegin** to her repertory.

Seymour has the distinction of being the only world-class ballerina who has consistently worked as a choreographer. She made her first ballet as early as 1973. Her best known works are the intensely dramatic *Rashomon* (1976) and her camp comedy on the death of Mozart, *Wolfi* (1987).

Lineage

Lynn Seymour has a voluptuous vulnerability which is unusual in dramatic ballerinas. Dancers such as **Martha Graham**, Nora Kaye, **Maya Plisetskaya** and Marcia Haydée work from a core of steel. The pliant Seymour is more like **Galina Ulanova** with her libido let off the leash.

Follow-up

Seymour's 'tell all' autobiography *Lynn* (1984) is not as harrowing as Gelsey Kirkland's *Dancing on my Grave*, but it leaves no doubts about the anguish and traumas Seymour has lived through. Film footage of Seymour at her best includes a BBC video of *A Month in the Country* and the docu-mentary about the making of MacMillan's *Mayerling*. She is seen at her most disadvantageous in *The Sleeping Beauty* pas de deux at the end of Rudolf Nureyev's *I Am a Dancer*, but few videos can match the transcendent *Isadora Waltzes* included in the Dance in America segment *Trailblazers*.

Antoinette Sibley

Born: 27th February 1939/ Bromley, Kent

The cool English beauty who smoulders with an inner fire, Antoinette Sibley is a ballerina of pristine presence who can go a step beyond and become a Circe. Her **Royal Ballet** triumphs, Titania in **Frederick Ashton**'s **The Dream** and the title role in **Kenneth MacMillian**'s *Manon*, stretch beyond the bounds of polite good manners into an abandoned sensuality. She gets away with it by being extra-terrestrial in the former, while Manon pays for her illicit pleasures with her life.

Sibley joined the Royal Ballet in 1956 and had her big break three years later, when she was called upon as a last-minute substitute for an indisposed ballerina. This was the first time in history that a Royal Ballet dancer not yet promoted to the leading rank of ballerina had ever performed **Swan Lake** at Covent Garden. The next day she was front-page news, and by the end of that season was also dancing **Giselle**, **Coppélia** and **The Sleeping Beauty**.

For *The Dream*, Ashton teamed her with young soloist **Anthony Dowell**, and a perfect partnership was born. Few dancers have ever been so ideally suited. Whereas **Margot Fonteyn** and **Rudolf Nureyev** were a combustible meeting of opposites, Sibley and Dowell were a sublime combination of similar rhythms and sensibilities. Together they became the ideal Royal Ballet couple, known as 'The Golden Pair'.

A major knee operation in 1976 was followed by five years in retirement. Everyone, including Sibley, assumed her career was over, but in 1981 Ashton persuaded her to perform in a gala. Bouncing back with surprising ease, she has been a regular guest artist with the Royal ever since. During this second phase of her career she

has been especially lauded for **A Month in the Country**.

Lineage

Antoinette Sibley donned the **Margot Fonteyn** mantle as the ideal Royal ballerina of her generation. Her wide repertory included virtually all the classics as well as many roles created for her by **Frederick Ashton** and **Kenneth MacMillan**. Like Fonteyn, Sibley is one of those rare ballerinas whose arms and shoulders are as vividly expressive as their legs and feet. Ashton, in particular, was a choreographer who frequently highlighted this in his subtle, understated and intricate manipulation of both women's upper bodies.

Follow-up

Distressingly little film footage exists of Sibley in action, though there is a 1976 television studio recording of *The Dream*. Barbara Newman's *Antoinette Sibley, Reflections of a Ballerina* (1986) is essentially her autobiography, created in interview format with Sibley, friends and colleagues.

Heinz Spoerli

Born: 8th July 1941/Basel, Switzerland

Heinz Spoerli is a classic case of 'local boy makes good'. Born and bred as a dancer in his hometown, he pursued an international career for ten years before returning to Basel to assume control of the company that gave him his start. In a sense, Spoerli *is* the Basel Ballet, since he is directly responsible for shaping this troupe of just under forty dancers into one of Switzerland's leading cultural exports.

He joined the company as a dancer in 1960, engaged by Vaslav Orlikowsky, a Russian-born ballet master who ran Basel Ballet very much along classical lines. After three years, Spoerli left to work in Köln, followed by stints with the Royal Winnipeg Ballet and Les Grands Ballets Canadiens. Having danced a wide range of works by twentieth-century choreographers, he cut his own choreographic teeth in 1967.

When he took over at Basel in 1973, it was a strictly provincial ballet attached to the city's municipal theatre and at the service of the more lucrative opera company. In essence, Spoerli, his perspective broadened by his experience abroad, had to fashion an ensemble almost from scratch. Although the company has danced works by choreographers such as **George Balanchine**, **William Forsythe** and especially Hans van Manen (for whom Spoerli created the lead role in his 1984 *John Falstaff*), Spoerli's ballets are predominant. In the early days this was largely due to economic necessity: Spoerli's eager young dancers needed to dance and the Stadttheater could not afford to hire guest choreographers.

A prolific dancemaker, he has staged admirable versions of older and more recent classics (**Swan Lake**, **Giselle**, **Romeo and Juliet**, **La Fille mal gardée**, *Ondine*) as well as producing a vast body of original ballets, both evening-length and mixed bills, and receiving frequent commissions on the Continent. Several companies have tried to lure him away on a permanent basis, but so far all comers have been rejected because Spoerli's heart belongs to Basel.

Not everything Spoerli choreographs is gold, yet he has a generous and versatile talent, favouring a neo-classical style often imbued with a lyric romanticism and a highly developed sense of theatre. The latter qualities are evident in *Orpheus and Eurydice* (1983), a dance version of Gluck's opera, in which hell is a complex of ducts and flues connected by ladders and catwalks; the entrance is a mammoth culvert equipped with a backwards-moving treadmill

that drags the mythic lovers to their sad separation. *La Belle Vie* (1987) is an opulent narrative ballet in which a theme of individual destiny is set against the backdrop of Paris during the Second Empire. *Chäs* (Cheese, 1978), a company signature piece, demonstrates his ability to create a light, enjoyable crowd-pleaser. This bubbling, good-humoured dance, set to Swiss folk music, ingeniously combines traditional Swiss wrestling moves and point work.

Lineage

There are ballet companies attached to opera houses in six major Swiss cities. Patricia Neary, formerly one of **George Balanchine**'s dancers, was artistic director first at Geneva and then Zurich. But it is Spoerli who has done most to move a Swiss dance company out from the shadow of its opera counterpart. His efforts in establishing a solid ensemble primarily representing the work of one choreographer parallel **John Neumeier**'s ascendancy at Hamburg Ballet and **Jiří Kylián**'s at **Netherlands Dance Theatre**. The dances themselves bear comparison with those of **Kenneth MacMillan** and **John Cranko.**

Follow-up

Heinz Spoerli: Ballett-Faszination, an illustrated, coffee-table guide to the man's career (untranslated), was published in Zurich in 1983.

Stuttgart Ballet

Formed: 1759

Today the city of Stuttgart is on the dance map because of **John Cranko**, but it has been an important centre at other key moments in the history of ballet. The earliest court ballets date back to 1609, but its first truly renowned ballet master was Jean-Georges Noverre, who was brought to Stuttgart by Duke Carl Eugen of Württemberg. In 1759, the year he arrived, the Frenchman published his thought-provoking and far-reaching *Lettres sur la danse et sur les ballets*, which he dedicated to the Duke. Noverre was dismissed in 1767 because his spectacles were costing too much (he had a company of fifty-eight dancers by that point, approximately the same number Cranko was to work with).

Stuttgart shone again when the Viennese Taglioni family was in residence (from 1824 to 1828). Father Filippo and his dancing children Marie and Paul would give birth to the Romantic era with **La Sylphide** at the Paris Opéra four years after leaving Germany. A century later, **Oskar Schlemmer**'s *Triadic Ballet* was premiered in Stuttgart; his amazing geometric costumes now have a room of their own in Die Neue Staatsgalerie directly behind the Opera House.

The Württemberg State Theatre Ballet, to give the company its official name, acquired an English director in 1961. John Cranko led the company to acclaim on a par with the great companies of the world. He amassed dancers from twenty-one different countries, dancers ironically often considered rejects from major troupes. Cranko was not interested in the sort of uniform look favoured in the great classical ensembles. Instead, he preferred individuals such as the exotic Brazilian ballerina Marcia Haydée, and turned all her eccentricities into dramatic assets. Her partner Richard Cragun was an unknown American kid whom Cranko pushed forward when his first leading man, Ray Barra, suffered a crippling injury. He also promoted the elegant Dane Egon Madsen and local girl Birgit Keil. This quartet became the nucleus for the Cranko team, and in ballets such as **Romeo and Juliet**, **Onegin** and *The Taming of the Shrew*, he showed them off to perfect imperfection. Cranko could never have pulled off his revolution in style in a major capital, yet by the time the company made its first

American tour in 1969, the dancers were so confident with their dramatically theatrical repertory that they were able to sweep aside all the traditional criticisms and ride to triumph on huge box office popularity, the first ballet company to tap into the mass market.

Following Cranko's sudden death, the company invited **Glen Tetley** to be the next director. He choreographed *Voluntaries* (1973), one of his most compelling works, in memory of Cranko. Guest choreographer **Kenneth MacMillan**, who had staged several works during the Cranko years, devised another eulogy in his Fauré *Requiem* (1976). Tetley stayed for only two seasons and Haydée has been the artistic director since his departure. The Cranko repertory is still the mainstay but there is also a continuing relationship with guest choreographers such as **Heinz Spoerli**, **Maurice Béjart** and **John Neumeier**.

Lineage

One of Jean-Georges Noverre's dictums was that dances should be suited to the personalities and skills of the performers. There could hardly be a more pertinent description of Cranko's method, and this is what both **Michel Fokine** and **Kurt Jooss** were aiming at as well. Like the **Joffrey Ballet**, Stuttgart has a loyal following more devoted to the company itself than to the artform in particular. During the Cranko regime, future choreographers **John Neumeier**, **Jiří Kylián** and **William Forsythe** were all dancers with the company and created some of their first works.

Follow-up

Leslie Spatt's photo book *The Stuttgart Ballet* (1978) has a brief text by German critic Horst Koegler. *John Cranko und das Stuttgarter Ballett 1961–73* has no English translation, but the pictures are impressive. Marcia Haydée, Birgit Keil and Richard Cragun all have photographic chronologies of their careers; Walter Terry, the American dance critic, wrote the biography *Richard Cragun* in 1982.

Glen Tetley

Born: 3rd February 1926/ Cleveland, Ohio

A pre-medical student before turning to dance, Glen Tetley holds a unique place in the development of contemporary ballet. He was the first choreographer to attempt a blend of modern dance and ballet. His pioneering works have a fervid intensity and non-stop propulsion coupled with a voluptuous physicality and an open sensuality. The standing he enjoys in Europe has often been derided by American critics, who find his work too mannered and strenuous.

Tetley trained with **Hanya Holm**, danced in Broadway musicals, and performed with **Martha Graham** from 1957 to 1959. He ultimately moved into the ballet world, performing with **American Ballet Theatre** and as an original member of the **Joffrey Ballet**.

His first major work, *Pierrot lunaire* (1962, to Schönberg), uses a trio of commedia dell'arte archetypes in a series of ribald, sometimes wistful, sometimes brutal sex games. Here he defined his style of mixing ballet and modern idioms without paying strict allegiance to the *école* conventions of either.

Working with **Netherlands Dance Theatre** throughout the 1960s, Tetley also maintained a close association with **Ballet Rambert**, culminating in a full-evening version of **The Tempest**. After a two-year stint with the **Stuttgart Ballet**, Tetley operated as a freelance choreographer, creating works for virtually every major Western ballet company. In 1986, he choreographed *Alice* for the **National Ballet of Canada**. This hour-long evocation of Lewis Carroll's Wonderland was so popular that he was asked to join the company as an artistic associate. This led to *La Ronde*, a series of interlocking pas de deux based on Schnitzler's *fin de siècle* play.

Augustus van Heerden and Yvonne Hall in a
Dance Theatre of Harlem staging of Glen Tetley's
Voluntaries

Lineage

Tetley's works use a vocabulary
combining the flexed feet and
supple backs of modern dance
with the speed and elongated
precision of classical technique,
and draw on the mythic intensity of
Martha Graham. Ritualism is always
a strong element in Tetley's ballets.
Sometimes his works can be
overloaded with symbolic weight
and arcane intentions. The
sensuous style of his movement
and his love of large-scale themes
aligns Tetley with European opera
house choreographers (**Kenneth
MacMillan**, **John Cranko** and
Maurice Béjart) rather than his
fellow Americans of the same age
such as **Jerome Robbins**, **Robert
Joffrey**. Tetley's English influence is
best seen in the ballets of
Christopher Bruce, who performed
the role of Prospero in the original
production of **The Tempest**.

Follow-up

Nureyev and Tetley are seen in
rehearsals for the Royal Ballet's
production of *Field Figures* in the
1973 film *I Am a Dancer*. Tetley's
version of *The Firebird* and a
documentary on its creation for the
Royal Danish Ballet (1982) are both
available on video.

The Tempest

Two acts
Choreography: Glen Tetley
Music: Arne Nordheim
Design: Nadine Baylis
Premiere: 3rd May 1979/
Schwetzingen, Germany

The only full-length ballet yet
created by Glen Tetley, *The
Tempest* is the outcome of a
special commission from the
Schwetzingen Festival, held

annually on a former baronial estate near Stuttgart. Each season, the Festival commissions a single work, usually an orchestral composition or chamber opera. The stage of this tiny rococo theatre is on the small side, and large ballets or full-blown operas tend to be too expansive for the space.

Tetley chose **Ballet Rambert** as the company to perform *The Tempest*. Working with his regular designer Nadine Baylis, Tetley incorporated a variety of theatrical effects drawn from Kabuki theatre, Renaissance masques and even the exotic **Denishawn** era. Without ignoring the Shakespeare text, Tetley goes beyond its boundaries. The ballet opens with two interpolated incidents (both merely described in the play). Sea creatures, naiads and mermaids are discovered below a billowing silken sea that flutters over the entire stage. Then Sycorax, the sorceress and mother of the half-animal, half-man Caliban, storms onto the island. She is a hideously pregnant Kabuki demon trailing red streamers of 'blood' that spurt from her elaborate costume as she gives birth to her devil's offspring.

In this version of *The Tempest*, both Ariel and Caliban seem to have equal claim on Prospero, as if they are the light and dark personifications of his own inner feelings. These three central figures form the heart of the ballet. The comedy characters, broad and often rude, are less successfully drawn; the physical jokes are somewhat strained.

The central pas de deux for the lovers (the chess-playing scene from Shakespeare) is turned into a love duet of sexual awakening for both Ferdinand and Miranda. Choreographed in Tetley's slow, sinuous style, it is a *Kama Sutra* transfigured by innocence.

During its initial season, Ballet Rambert gave nearly a hundred performances of the work; it subsequently entered the repertory of the Norwegian National Ballet, quickly becoming that company's most popular piece and chosen for their US debut in 1982.

Lineage

Throughout his career, **Frederick Ashton** toyed with the idea of making a ballet on *The Tempest*, but each time he got close he changed his mind. In the end, *Ondine* was as near as he ever came. In 1980, Michael Smuin devised a flashy Hollywood-elaborate version for **San Francisco Ballet**, and in 1982 **Rudolf Nureyev** created a one-act version for the **Royal Ballet**. Now dropped from the London repertory, Nureyev's version can still be seen at the **Paris Opéra Ballet**.

Staging

1 **Norwegian National Ballet**/1980

THE
DANCE
EXPLOSION

6th July 1962. At Judson Church on Washington Square in New York's Greenwich Village, a three-hour co-operatively produced dance performance was presented free of charge. The public debut of the loosely organised group of choreographers who would come to be known as the Judson Dance Theatre gave birth to post-modern dance, although it would be another fifteen years before that brand name could be affixed.

The Judson collective grew out of a choreographic workshop led by musician Robert Dunn. These wide-ranging exploratory sessions, held at the Merce Cunningham Studio, attempted to apply to dance the extremities of John Cage's compositional ideas about music.

For any choreographer at that point, Cunningham and Cage, collaborators since 1944, represented the brightest beacon of the avant-garde. Cunningham's ideals – not the least of which is that dance is about nothing but dancing – remain untarnished, and even today are capable of disturbing an audience who likes dance to be predictable, and, if not pretty, at least tidy.

Judson became a home base for new ideas, a fertile, disruptive point of liberation. In retrospect, it now appears that the Judsonites were more unanimous in what they did not want than in what they were striving to achieve. High on their list of positions to be defied was the creeping codification which, by the late 1950s, had turned modern dance into a formulaic, even opulent spectacle more akin to ballet than stringent radicalism. For the Judsonites, stultification was to be avoided at all costs and they created their rupture by re-thinking, sometimes eliminating, the very framework of dance. They travelled beyond even Cunningham by refusing to accept the notion that someone

became a dancer through mastering a dance technique. They wanted to chop dance down to size, and the size they were after was exactly that of both the dancers and their audiences. Stripping dance of its flounces, cutting out character, and abandoning technique in favour of everyday movement, the Judsonites attempted to shock their audiences awake and to jar them into seeing things from a new perspective. In replacing organisation with the haphazard reality of the moment, these choreographers eventually stepped across the boundaries into improvisation: with the formation of the Grand Union (from 1970 to 1976), dance was turned into a philosophical playground.

The dust had hardly begun to settle on all the broken rules when several of the new choreographers started creating counterpoints to the rumbustiousness of the Grand Union. Twyla Tharp, Lucinda Childs and Trisha Brown developed highly structured geometrics of movement which were manipulated with mathematical precision. These glacial edifices of pure calculation demanded the strictest of concentration from the performers; they could no longer be danced by 'the man on the street' who had been the initial Judson ideal.

Having accomplished their groundbreaking, Judson itself broke up. The demise of the Grand Union turned the last remnants of the collective into history, but the questions the Judsonites asked have continued to exert an influence (both pro and con) on virtually all new dance created since.

The Judson Dance Theatre's first performance was just months after Rudolf Nureyev's debut with the Royal Ballet and seven years before the Stuttgart Ballet's phenomenal first season in New York led to the coining of the phrase 'ballet boom'. The two realms of unstinting experimentation and modern ballet seemed separated by an unbridgeable gap of mutual distrust and misunderstanding. No one, not even the most ambitious of the Judson choreographers, would have predicted that they would grow up into the 1980s establishment, invited to make works for some of the great ballet companies. However, it is the very unpredictability of dance that keeps it eternally fascinating, forever veering off in unexpected directions.

The catalyst for the explosion was Robert Joffrey. The bombshell he chose was Twyla Tharp. Her 1973 creations for the Joffrey Ballet, and *Push Comes to Shove* for Mikhail Baryshnikov and American Ballet Theatre three seasons later, found some of her peers angrily accusing her of selling out. What she was really doing was storming the citadel. Tharp grabbed dance – experimental, classical, jazz, pop and Americana – by the scruff of the neck, tossed it up into the air and let it fall back onto the stage in a shower of confetti that resisted any attempts at labelling. The dance world is still reaping the benefits.

Jamie Bishton, Erzsebet Foldi, Shelley Washington and John Carrafa of Twyla Tharp Dance performing Tharp's 1987 work *In The Upper Room*.

Alvin Ailey

Born: 5th January 1931/Rogers, Texas

Alvin Ailey was one of the first choreographers to open up dance to a new, broad-based audience. His heartfelt celebration of black America became as popular as a musical comedy and as charged with energy as a rock concert. His dancers, skilled in a wide range of techniques (from classical to Broadway) handle the company's eclectic repertory with great aplomb. Ailey's dances dominate a roster of works by both black and white choreographers, including **Anna Sokolow**, **José Limón**, Lester Horton, Pearl Primus and Ulysses Dove. Consequently, the Alvin Ailey American Dance Theatre – the first modern dance troupe to be completely multi-racial – has become a repository for contemporary dance history. This would be of purely academic interest were it not for the company's striking theatricality and infectious energy. Unlike the austere, often tormented work devised by pioneers in the field, Ailey's troupe demonstrates that modern dance can be terrific entertainment.

Ailey, a large but graceful dancer, joined his teacher Lester Horton's California-based company in 1950, and choreographed for it after Horton's death in 1953. Subsequently, he studied with **Martha Graham**, **Doris Humphrey** and **Hanya Holm** (among others) while dancing and acting on and off Broadway. He retired from dancing in 1965 to devote himself to his company and his choreography.

Ailey's twin creative sources are the urban body language of black America and the spirit of the rural churchgoing community in which he was raised. His breakthrough piece *Blues Suite* (1958), a series of slice-of-life scenes, is set in a backwater brothel. The company's signature work *Revelations* (1960) is a masterly dance equivalent cf revivalist testimony, charting a communal journey from baptism through despair to salvation. This work significantly boosted the public profile of the choreographer and his dancers Dudley Williams and Judith Jamison (for whom Ailey created the solo *Cry* in 1971).

His dances tend to be direct, emotionally provocative and topical. The music accompanying them is familiar and accessible: spirituals, blues and jazz (Ailey is a Duke Ellington aficionado), contrasted with the works of Benjamin Britten, Samuel Barber and Ralph Vaughan Williams. The dancers are vividly costumed and lit; their onstage manner is flamboyant and confident. They sashay and strut with a loose-hipped electricity, head, neck and torso pulled up high, their arms held up and out. This formula has worked successfully throughout the world, although more demanding dancegoers might feel that something essential has been sacrificed on the altar of commercialism. Ailey has occasionally choreographed for outside companies, including the **Joffrey Ballet**, **Paris Opéra Ballet** and **American Ballet Theatre** (*The River*, 1970). His work is also in the repertories of the Royal Danish Ballet and **London Festival Ballet**.

Lineage

Like **Denishawn** and Lester Horton, Alvin Ailey has few qualms about making the maximum use of a theatrical format to bring serious dance to a wide audience. His blend of classical steps, **Martha Graham**-style contractions and distinctly black rhythms has been developed by the equally prolific **Garth Fagan**.

Follow-up

Moira Hodgson's *Quintet* (1976) contains a useful overview of Ailey's career, and Joseph H. Mazo has written *The Alvin Ailey American Dance Theatre* (1978). The video *Alvin Ailey – Memories and Visions* includes excerpts from all of his best work up to 1974. *Three by Three* (1985) features

Ailey's *Blues Suite*, Bill T. Jones'
Fever Swamp and Donald
McKayle's 1959 chain gang classic
Rainbow 'Round My Shoulder.

Richard Alston

Born: 30th October 1948/
Stoughton, Sussex

One of the most highly regarded of
contemporary choreographers,
Richard Alston is a confirmed
modernist whose choreography is
infused with a particularly English
style of lyricism.

Educated at Eton, Alston went to
art school before starting his dance
training at the then new London
Contemporary Dance School.
Quickly moving towards choreography, he created his first works
in 1968, and a year later *Something
To Do* became the first of nine
pieces devised for **London
Contemporary Dance Theatre**.
A 1972 grant from the Gulbenkian
Foundation allowed him to form the
experimental company Strider
(which would eventually become
the model for Second Stride). Alston
disbanded his troupe in 1975 and
moved to New York for two years
to study with **Merce Cunningham**.
This visit culminated in the 1977
UnAmerican Activities, an evening
of his own choreography
presented at the Cunningham
Studio.

After his return to London, Alston
spent three years working freelance. His first piece for **Ballet
Rambert**, *Bell High* (to a score by
Peter Maxwell Davies), premiered
in January 1980. Five months later,
he was appointed the company's
resident choreographer, a position
he held until February 1986, when
he was named Rambert's artistic
director. It was at Alston's
suggestion that the troupe was
re-christened Rambert Dance
Company in 1987.

Alston's choreographic style
generally eschews stories, concentrates on speed and lightness

rather than on weight, and is more
akin to the ideas of Cunningham
than the drama of **Martha Graham**.
One of the distinguishing features
of Alston's work – at variance with
Cunningham's approach – is his
sensitivity to music (although
several of his early works,
including *Soda Lake*, a solo
created for **Michael Clark** in 1981,
were danced in silence). Alston
particularly favours working with
modern, especially English,
composers such as Nigel Osborne,
who has written four commissioned
scores for him. He supports this
interest in English music with an
equal enthusiasm for British art:
painters Howard Hodgkin, Richard
Smith and John Hoyland, and
sculptor Nigel Hall have all
contributed designs for Alston
works.

Since joining Rambert, Alston has
turned down most offers to choreograph for other companies, but in
1982 he worked with the Royal
Danish Ballet (*Dances from the
Kingdom of the Pagodas*, to Britten)
and the following year used the
music of Michael Tippett for
Midsummer, his only work to
date for the **Royal Ballet**.

Lineage
Although **Merce Cunningham** is
the single most vivid influence on
Alston's work, his choreography
also bears strong links to the
greatest of all English dancemakers, **Frederick Ashton**. He
shares Ashton's easy sense of
fluidity and has the same well-
mannered and balanced outlook.
Even at its most rhythmically
intricate moments, Alston's work
has a lightness of touch and spirit
that seems to spring from Ashton.

Follow-up
The BBC series *Dancemakers* is
now on video: in one segment,
Alston, Richard Smith and Nigel
Osborne discuss the creation of
Wildlife (1984), followed by a
performance of the work. In 1988,
Alston and director Peter Mumford
completely reworked *Strong
Language* for the camera: the
result is one of the finest dance-for-
television videos ever produced.

Trisha Brown

Born: 25th November 1936/
Aberdeen, Washington

Trisha Brown, who was to become
one of the leading post-modern
choreographers, had an orthodox
modern dance background, but in
1960, during a summer school with
West Coast experimentalist Anna
Halprin, she met **Yvonne Rainer**.
Brown moved to New York in 1961
and, with Rainer, became one of
the original members of the
experimental Judson Dance
Theatre in 1962 – and later a
founder of the improvisational
Grand Union (from 1970 to 1976).

During the sixties and early
seventies, Brown created a series
of 'equipment pieces' that changed
both the way a dancer needed to
move and how the audience
perceived dancing. Among the
most infamous were a group of
dances where the performer was
rigged into a block and tackle
harness to perform his or her own
task cantilevered out from the wall,
parallel to the ground. *Walking on
the Walls* took place at the Whitney
Museum, New York, *Man Walking
Down the Side of a Building* outside
a lower Manhattan warehouse.
Spiral, performed in a park in
Minneapolis, had the dancers
walking down the trunks of trees
until they were lying flat on their
sides on the grass.

Roof Piece (1973) scattered fifteen
dancers across the roofs of
Manhattan buildings. In an
overlapping sequence of 'monkey
see, monkey do', they telegraphed
a series of movements from one
person to the next. The audience,
stationed on an adjacent rooftop,
watched as the movements
travelled across the sky.

Accumulation (1971) is perhaps
the most compelling and visually
satisfying work from this period.
As the title implies, the dance is a
build-up of simple gestural movements repeated again and again in
a growing chain.

In the late 1970s, Brown began to
loosen the strictures of her
rigorous work and to incorporate
design and music into her pieces.
It was at this point that she started
working in traditional theatres
rather than in lofts, galleries or
outdoors. *Glacial Decoy* (1979)
marks a turning point in her
career. Designed by major
American artist Robert Rauschenberg, it featured a backdrop of
black and white photographs. The
movement, like Rauschenberg's
projections, travelled laterally
across the stage. This dance
seemed to have begun before the
viewer could see it, and to be
continuing after it had passed out
of view. *Son of Gone Fishin'* (1981)
added music, by Robert Ashley.
Set and Reset (1983) featured
costumes and film projections by
Rauschenberg and a score by
Laurie Anderson: this lively,
visually exciting and often very
funny work completed Brown's
transition from fringe to mainstream artist.

Brown's current movement style
is composed as a continuous series
of liquid movements that ripple
through the dancers' bodies like
fish darting through a stream. The
deliberately pedestrian gestures of
the early works have evolved into
a silky, supple and highly personalised brand of virtuosity. *Lateral
Pass* (1985, designed by sculptor
Nancy Graves) features a dancer
in a harness, but now he uses the
equipment to allow him to cross the
stage in a single leap, to hover in
the air and to do a kind of
superman replication of the movement of the other dancers.

Lineage

Deeply influenced by the theories
of **Yvonne Rainer**, Trisha Brown
built up her current loose-limbed
style through years of patient
questioning and testing. Along with
Twyla Tharp, Brown and her works
demonstrate a gradual evolution
towards a brand of dance that can
be enjoyed by a general public
without sacrificing any of its
creator's artistic convictions.
Stephen Petronio and Randy
Warshaw, who were the first men

Trisha Brown giving a public demonstration of her dance style at Avignon in 1983

to join Brown's company (in 1980), have both gone on to launch their own troupes.

Follow-up

Trisha Brown (1987) is a dual-language French publication with essays by Lise Brunel, the leading Parisian critic of the avant-garde, plus interviews with Brown and her dancers. Brown also contributed an essay to Anne Livet's *Contemporary Dance* (1978); see also Sally Banes' *Democracy's Body* (1983) and *Terpsichore in Sneakers* (1980), and the 'Iconoclasts of the Sixties and Seventies' section of Deborah Jowitt's *The Dance in Mind* (1985). Brown's videos include *Set and Reset* and *Newark*.

Christopher Bruce

Born: 3rd October 1945/Leicester

Christopher Bruce's reputation as one of Britain's outstanding dancer-turned-choreographers is based partly on his mix of classical and modern dance idioms, and partly on his commitment to socially conscious themes. He joined **Ballet Rambert** in 1963, after studying at the company's school. In 1967, he danced the title role in a revival of **Glen Tetley**'s *Pierrot lunaire*. Overnight, the ballet, once described as a **Petrushka** for the 1960s, made him a star: he was even dubbed 'the **Rudolf Nureyev** of modern dance'. Subsequent roles have included Prospero in Tetley's **The Tempest**, the Faun in **L'Après-midi d'un faune** and, as recently as 1988, the title role in *Petrushka* for **London Festival Ballet**.

Rambert lasted seventeen years, during which time he became an associate director and choreographer. He created his first piece for the company in 1969 (*George Frideric*, to Handel). Like several of his ballets, it was an abstract dance with strong emotional undercurrents. Two of his finest works were derived from the writings and life of Federico García Lorca: *Ancient Voices of Children* (1975), the first of three Bruce ballets using a George Crumb score, and the massive hit *Cruel Garden* (1977), a full-length collaboration with **Lindsay Kemp**, successfully revived by London Festival Ballet in 1988. *Ghost Dances*, Bruce's most popular and most widely travelled ballet to date, was made for Rambert in 1981. An everyman parable set to haunting South American folk music, it is his response to political oppression.

Sometimes his insistence on imparting a significant message

can outweigh the value of the dancing. For example, he pours an exhausting amount of over-explicit choreographic power into *The Dream is Over*, a 1987 portrait of the life and times of John Lennon, only to have his earnest efforts overshadowed by Lennon's music.

In 1985, the success of Bruce's *Land*, for London Festival Ballet, led to his appointment there as associate choreographer; the post will have allowed him to produce six new ballets for the company over a three-year period.

Lineage

A **Marie Rambert** discovery, Bruce paid her tribute in the 1976 portrait *Girl in a Straw Hat*. Like **Glen Tetley** and **Jirí Kylián**, Bruce filters contemporary influences through a classical technique and, with Kylián, has a common interest in grafting folk dance onto a balletic movement vocabulary. His penchant for dance as a vehicle for social criticism places him in the tradition of choreographers like **Kurt Jooss**, **Anna Sokolow**, **Mary Wigman** and Rudi van Dantzig.

Follow-up

A filmed version of *Cruel Garden* was winner of the 1982 Prix Italia. Numerous Bruce ballets are available on video, including *Intimate Pages*, *Sergeant Early's Dream*, *The Dream is Over* and *Silence is the End of Our Song*. The BBC recorded Bruce's classic performance in Tetley's *Pierrot lunaire* in 1978.

Carolyn Carlson

Born: 7th March 1943/Oakland, California

Carolyn Carlson is a new age, post-Woodstock, version of **Isadora Duncan**. The notion of free expression is implicit in her dream-like, ritualistic dance spectacles, which she tends to assemble instinctually.

From 1966 to 1971, Carlson was a member of the **Alwin Nikolais** company; with her long, thin, flexible body, she was unmatched by anyone except fellow Nikolais disciple Murray Louis in her ability to isolate individual parts of her body into lively, singing expression. She was devising her own dances well before she left Nikolais to join (briefly) the Compagnie Anne Béranger in France. Invited to create a piece for **Paris Opéra Ballet** in 1973, she opted for a solo. *Densité 21.5*, to music by Edgard Varèse, was so well received that Carlson was asked to assume a post – *danseuse étoile chorégraphique* – invented expressly for her.

The Opéra provided Carlson with the facilities and the independence to make new work while evolving a small modern company called the Groupe de Recherches Théâtrales de l'Opéra. Free of union and in-house politics, she and her dancers set up shop in the Opéra's rotunda, an area accessible only through the orchestra pit. The results of this eagerly awaited experiment were far-reaching. Thanks partly, if not exclusively, to Carlson, there are now probably more modern dance troupes in Paris than anywhere else in the world outside New York City. In addition to GRCOP (the Groupe de Recherche Chorégraphique de Paris, formed in 1981), the choreographic flowering she inspired continues to grow through the work of such post-Carlson companies as Jean-Claude Gallotta's Grenoble-based Groupe Emile Dubois and Dominique Bagouet's troupe in Montpellier.

In 1980, Carlson was engaged by Venice's Teatro Fenice to fashion some inexperienced but eager young dancers into a performance unit for her own work. There, she produced a single full-evening piece annually; *Underwood* (1982), a memory-collage partly prompted by the birth of her son the previous year, dates from this period. By the middle of the decade, however, she was back in Paris, at the Théâtre de la Ville, where she is creating most of her new work, including both solos (*Blue Lady*, 1985) and ensemble pieces (*Still Waters*, 1986, and *Dark*, 1988).

Lineage

Carlson derives her particular sense of dance-theatre from **Alwin Nikolais**. Games, nostalgia, Zen philosophy, allusions to nature and non-dance movement are all part of the poetics of her pieces. Like **Isadora Duncan**, **Martha Graham** and such post-modern magicians as **Meredith Monk** and **Robert Wilson**, she is building a private mythology onstage. Her dances represent the more amorphous, less hostile flip side of the works of **William Forsythe** and **Pina Bausch**.

Follow-up

Luckily, Carlson's evanescent oeuvre has been well documented on film and video, as she has never been interested in amassing a permanent repertory. She also appeared in Ed Emshwiller's short *Film with Three Dancers* in 1970. Guy Delahaye's book *Carolyn Carlson* was published in 1988.

Lucinda Childs

Born: 26th June 1940/New York City

Lucinda Childs streamlined the post-modern ideas of the Judson Dance Theatre experimentalists into a sleek minimalism marked by a clean, cool restraint. Her works are deployed in elementary, even elemental, stage-wide patterns of skips, cantering, rhythmic walks, hops and little jumps which, repeated over and over, gradually reveal the diagrammatic scheme at their root. Her dancers, wearing sneakers or jazz shoes, perform with a passive expression and an upright carriage that focusses on their footwork. Like **Laura Dean**, Childs tends to keep the torso neutral and, also like Dean, her dancers are always democratic

individuals who duplicate movements simultaneously or in canon, but are never involved in any kind of partnering.

Soon after graduating from Sarah Lawrence College with a dance degree, Childs met **Yvonne Rainer** during a class at the **Merce Cunningham** Studio, and Rainer invited her to join the Judson group. Childs went on to create nearly a dozen pieces during the heyday of the Judson Dance Theatre from 1962 to 1964. These works were generally solos and often used dialogue (Childs' first goal had been to become an actress).

After a five-year hiatus, Childs returned to performing in 1973 with *Calico Mingling*, the first of the reductionist pattern pieces she has been creating ever since. During 1976, she danced in the **Robert Wilson**/Philip Glass opera *Einstein on the Beach*, for which she choreographed her own solos. The following year, she joined Wilson in a two-character play, *I Was Sitting On My Patio This Guy Appeared I Thought I Was Hallucinating*. Both pieces had major international tours.

Until 1979, Childs' dances had all been performed in silence, but thereafter she began adding music to her work. The first and still best known of these was called simply *Dance*, and featured a five-part, ninety-minute score by Glass. The production was augmented by a film from minimalist sculptor Sol Le Witt, which consisted of giant blow-ups of the live action projected simultaneously on a stage-wide scrim hung between audience and dancers. Another major work, *Relative Calm* (1981), had lighting designs by Wilson and music by John Gibson. *Available Light* (1983, music by John Adams) split Childs' patterns onto two levels through a two-tiered stage design from post-modern architect Frank Gehry.

In 1984, Childs was invited by **Rudolf Nureyev** to stage *Premier Orage* for the **Paris Opéra Ballet**. Like *Cascade*, made for the Pacific Northwest Ballet (also 1984, to Steve Reich's *Octet*), it marked Childs' first use of point shoes. She has also worked with Berlin's

Deutsches Oper (*Lichtknall*, 1987) and the Italian company Aterballetto (again using Reich's *Octet*).

Lineage

The cerebral quality in Childs' work links her directly to the minimalist movement in sculpture and painting of the 1970s. The patterning and repetition are superficially close to the work of **Laura Dean**, but with an austerity not found in Dean's choreography. There is nothing cosy, folk-like or communal in Childs' attitude or method of presentation.

Follow-up

There is an interview with Childs in Anne Livet's *Contemporary Dance* (1978); she is discussed in Sally Banes' *Democracy's Body* (1983) and *Terpsichore in Sneakers* (1980); see also *Further Steps* (1987, edited by Connie Kreemer).

Robert Cohan

Born: 27th March 1925/Brooklyn, NY

A long-time associate of **Martha Graham**, Robert Cohan was instrumental in liberating Britain from the academic traditions of classical dance by helping to create an indigenous modern dance movement.

His original intention to be a research naturalist was interrupted by the Second World War. As a soldier stationed in England, he saw **Robert Helpmann**'s *Miracle in the Gorbals* at Sadler's Wells Theatre while on leave. The impact of the ballet caused Cohan to switch careers, and back in New York a single class at Graham's school confirmed his decision. Within four months he had become a company member and was later Graham's regular partner, creating roles in *Diversion of Angels* (1948) through to *Cortege of Eagles* (1969).

During a five-year absence from her company (1957 to 1962), he taught, developed his choreography and headed his own short-lived modern dance group, before returning to the Graham fold and becoming co-director in 1966. While touring in Britain in the mid-1950s, Cohan had met a wealthy dance fan (particularly of Graham's work) called Robin Howard, who in 1967 invited Cohan to become the founding artistic director of **London Contemporary Dance Theatre** (LCDT). Using students from the newly formed London Contemporary Dance School, Cohan's task was to select and train dancers in the Graham technique, build a contemporary repertory and generate audience interest.

LCDT has been Cohan's creative anchor ever since, although in 1983 he began to loosen some of his ties. The troupe's first leading male dancer and principal teacher, he has also supplied much of its repertory. Another significant contribution, both to LCDT's reputation and to the acceptability of modern dance in Britain, was the organisation of company residencies, in which dancers visit communities to teach and demonstrate their art.

Like the LCDT teaching methods, Cohan's choreography is a development from Graham, with additional influence from American jazz dance. His work is emotionally cooler than Graham's, with a tendency towards thematic vagueness. Concern for social issues is a Cohan hallmark. A recent opus like *Video-Life* (1987) makes use of modern technology and special effects to create a superficial image of contemporary apocalypse. His best received dances include *Cell* (1969), a philosophical study on the loss of individuality; *Stages* (1971), a highly acrobatic multi-media allegory set in the space age; and *Class* (1975), which exalts the rejuvenating ritual of daily dance exercise.

Lineage

Cohan's pragmatic dedication to furthering the cause of dance and nurturing new talent in Britain has

been as important as the work of **Ninette de Valois** and **Marie Rambert**. Throughout his career he has generously fostered a whole generation of dancers and choreographers, including **Richard Alston**, Micha Bergese, **Siobhan Davies** and **Robert North**.

Follow-up

Cohan can be seen in film versions of Graham's *Acrobats of God* and *Cortege of Eagles* (both 1969), and the documentary *A Dancer's World* (1957). His TV ballet *A Mass for Man* was commissioned by the BBC in 1985.

Merce Cunningham

Born: 16th April 1919/Centralia, Washington

Merce Cunningham is the choreographer who liberated dance from its historical restraints; by cutting through conventions, he showed that dance could be about 'just' dancing. No one else, not

The Merce Cunningham Dance Company in a performance of his 1986 work *Points in Space*

even **George Balanchine**, has so relentlessly pushed and prodded at the very idea of dance. Through his revolutionary work, he has irremediably altered how audiences perceive, mentally organise and emotionally respond to movement.

Cunningham intended to become an actor, but opted for dance instead, studying everything from folk to tap to ballroom dance before **Martha Graham** asked him to join her company. During her 1939-45 seasons he created such important roles as the Revivalist in **Appalachian Spring**. He was (and still is) a remarkable performer, blessed in his prime with a combination of acute concentration and airborne elasticity.

In 1938, he met composer John Cage in a Seattle dance class. Their subsequent collaboration has been long and extremely influential on all art forms. Thanks largely to their perpetual experimentation, dance was given the option of becoming an activity governed by its own distinct rules and unpredictable, internal logic. They refute the accepted notion that music must support movement while the decor frames and

THE DANCE EXPLOSION

illustrates it. On the contrary, Cunningham fashions his steps independently of both designer and composer (who in turn work independently). In general, all the elements of a Cunningham performance meet up for the first time on the opening night. All have potentially equal value, as does every inch of the performing space, a contradiction of traditional ballet structure in which everything of significance tends to happen downstage centre.

Furthermore, Cunningham's dances are free of the dramatic baggage that is such a part of dance's heritage. Although his work encompasses as wide a range of emotions as any body of choreography – from bleak to playful to absurd – the audience must interpret the meanings and moods of the dances for themselves, becoming in a sense the choreographer's collaborator.

Cunningham began presenting solo concerts with music by Cage while he was still dancing for Graham. In 1953, he formed his own company at Black Mountain College, a progressive school in North Carolina where he and Cage were in residence. So was painter Robert Rauschenberg, their constant collaborator during the next decade, and the first in a long line of visual artists with whom Cunningham has worked, including Jasper Johns, Frank Stella and Andy Warhol.

By the early 1950s, first Cage, then Cunningham had begun to use chance operations to create music and dance, drawing up elaborate charts indicating qualities of time, sound, space and movement, and tossing coins to determine their choice and order in performance. This gained them notoriety; more importantly, it was the start of the so-called postmodern aesthetic, an interest in the creative process for its own sake.

The Merce Cunningham Dance Company's New York City debut in late 1953 was unattended by a single critic. The small company (then seven, today fifteen strong) survived through grant money, extensive touring and, above all, a communal belief in the value of what they were doing. A turning point occurred in 1964, when the attention lavished on the company during its first European tour raised Cunningham's creative profile. During that tour, he devised the first in a series of 'Events', uninterrupted, one-off evenings of dance composed of a mix of new and existing material shuffled, overlaid and performed to an original, often improvised soundscore. This format, initially a pragmatic way of dealing with unorthodox venues, has become another of his creative innovations.

Cunningham's radical ideas have been gradually absorbed into (but not diluted by) the cultural mainstream. Since the early 1970s he has created and taught at his studios and school in the lower Manhattan artists' complex Westbeth. The clear, clean lines of his dances mark him as perhaps the most balletic of post-modern choreographers; yet the shifts of weight and focus, the rapid rhythmic and directional changes and the dense, permutating patterns of his choreography reflect the fragmentation of contemporary life. Despite nearly fifty years of dancemaking, his thirst for discovering new movement possibilities remains unquenched, while the fact that he pulls no artistic punches still puts some noses out of joint. Limitations of age have in no way hindered his expressive mastery on stage. He continues to make usually brief but magnetic appearances in both his live and filmed work.

Cunningham has been a pioneer in the field of dance on video, inventively manipulating the restrictions of space and scale imposed by the film medium. In a reversal of conventional practice, several dances originally created for the camera (with film-makers Charles Atlas and Elliot Caplan) have subsequently been re-worked for the stage, including *Locale* (1979), *Channels/Inserts* (1982), *Coast Zone* (1983) and *Points in Space* (1986).

Cunningham has created more than seventy dances for his

company. Some have been revived, but mostly Cunningham is intent on making new pieces. His influence is founded on the cumulative impact of his methods, rather than on any specific work. His dances have been added to the repertories of **New York City Ballet** (*Summerspace*, created in 1958), **American Ballet Theatre** (*Duets*, 1980) and **Paris Opéra Ballet**, who commissioned Cunningham to choreograph *Un Jour ou deux* (1973). In 1988, **Rambert Dance Company** staged *Septet*, a 1953 dance set to Satie (one of Cunningham's favourite composers) and the last piece he choreographed directly to music. Cunningham is too revolutionary a figure ever to have pursued popular success, yet in recent years he has received both the Kennedy Center Honor and the MacArthur Foundation Fellowship in the USA, and the Olivier Award in London for his 1984 dance *Pictures*.

Lineage
As the father of post-modern dance, Merce Cunningham has spawned two generations of dancer-choreographers who can revere or rebel against him. Ex-company members who have gone on to become important dance-makers in their own right include Viola Farber, **Paul Taylor**, Remy Charlip, **Steve Paxton**, Douglas Dunn and **Karole Armitage**. The Cunningham technique is the major modern dance alternative to the movement theories of **Martha Graham**.

Follow-up
Cunningham's film/video output is broad, from *Westbeth* (1974) onwards. Klaus Wildenham made a feature-length documentary (1968) about the making of the dance *Scramble*; the 1979 documentary *Merce Cunningham* is available on video and features interviews with him and dancer Carolyn Brown (his major muse until her 1973 retirement). *Merce Cunningham* (1975), edited by photographer James Klosty, is an invaluable collection of images,

with essays and recollections by many of Cunningham's collaborators. Jacqueline Lesschaeve's conversations with Cunningham, *The Dancer and the Dance* (1985), are his only extended published interviews (The book includes a full list of works); he also worked with Frances Starr on the hard to find 1968 volume *Changes: Notes on Choreography*.

Siobhan Davies

Born: 18th September 1950/London

The understated intensity at the heart of Siobhan Davies' choreography has a quiet integrity which some viewers find deeply moving and others pallid or remote.

One of the original students at the London Contemporary Dance School, Davies was also one of the founding members of the **London Contemporary Dance Theatre** in 1967. She began choreographing in 1971, was appointed assistant choreographer three years later, and in 1983, the year she retired as a dancer, was named resident choreographer. By the time she resigned from LCDT in 1987, she had created seventeen works for the company.

She formed her own part-time company, Siobhan Davies and Dancers, in 1981, and a year later was instrumental in the foundation of Second Stride, a group based on the original Strider (a collective organised by **Richard Alston**). She created six pieces for Second Stride before travelling to America on a Fulbright Arts Fellowship; on her return she formed Siobhan Davies Company, which had its premiere during the tenth Dance Umbrella festival in 1988.

Davies has worked in close collaboration with lighting designer Peter Mumford and her husband, photographer/designer David Buckland. *New Galileo* (LCDT, 1984), is an impressive example:

Buckland's backdrop features huge blow-ups of the satellites of Jupiter; Mumford's lighting consists of a pair of overhead strips of light running from front to back of the stage. Davies' choreography begins with small movements which gradually expand to stage-wide patterns as the overhead lights imperceptibly move apart and begin to fill the stage with an ever brighter radiance.

Bridge the Distance (LCDT, 1985) is danced to Benjamin Britten's last string quartet. As with many of Davies' works, this is filled with implied relationships among the various pairs of dancers. There is often a peripheral drama in her dances that is never spelled out in a story format (à la **Robert Cohan**); instead, these emotional under-tones float suggestively just beneath the surface.

Davies has made a number of works for **Rambert Dance Company**: *Celebration* (1979); a 1987 revival of *Rushes* (first devised for Second Stride in 1982); and *Embarque* (1988) to Steve Reich's *Octet*. She has also worked with such contemporary composers as Michael Nyman, Brian Eno and John Adams.

Lineage

Robert Cohan has made a big impact on Davies, even if her works seem to resist his **Martha Graham**-based sense of theatricality. She has also been deeply influenced by **Merce Cunningham** and **Richard Alston**; she went to New York to perform with Alston at the Cunningham Studio in his *UnAmerican Activities*. The polarities of these styles have sometimes thrown Davies' work off kilter, but now, working on her own, away from LCDT's populist and dramatic artistic policy, she is free to develop in her own right.

Follow-up

Bridge the Distance, with Davies talking about the way she works and her goals, is included in the four-part BBC *Dancemakers* series on modern British choreographers. *Silent Partners* (1985) has also been filmed.

Laura Dean

Born: 3rd December 1945/Staten Island, NY

One of the key figures of the New York post-modern revolution, Laura Dean's choreographic profile is based on the most simple of physical movements, particularly the act of spinning. Dean's tech-nique is not that used by ballet dancers for their pirouettes, but a more natural way of spinning aligned to Turkish dervishes and found in other ethnic dance forms.

Dean, who attended New York's High School of Performing Arts, spent a year in the **Paul Taylor** Dance Company (from 1965 to 1966), where she replaced **Twyla Tharp**. In 1968, she travelled to San Francisco and began a two-year process of stripping all her dance knowledge back to basics. Returning to New York, she performed a series of minimalist works based on repetitions of simple, even transparent movement patterns. They had such self-descriptive titles as *Stamping Dance*, *Square Dance*, *Jumping Dance* and *Spinning Dance* (all 1971 to 1974). In 1975, she began collaborating with composer Steve Reich; their first work together was the ninety-minute *Drumming*.

Her company, Laura Dean Dancers and Musicians, was formed in 1976. Their debut piece, *Song*, had the dancers vocalising as they performed. From this point onwards, her dances have usually involved scores by Dean herself: *Spiral* (1977), *Dance* (1978), *Music* (1980) and *Tympani* (1981). All are based on stage-wide geometric patterns performed with deliberate repetitiveness by groups of six, eight or twelve dancers. Often everyone is doing the same movement in unison or in canonic sequences.

Dean's music is based on a steady rhythmic pulse that is mirrored count for count in the bright, lively, small-scale steps of the choreography. The focus is on feet and hands, with the dancers' torsos remaining upright and relatively neutral. These rudimentary steps, augmented by the lengthy periods of spinning, are not actually those of authentic folk dances, but the flavour of Dean's works is closer to the celebratory aspects of dancing for the sheer fun of it than that of any other contemporary choreographer.

Dean created her first work for the **Joffrey Ballet** in 1980. *Night*, to her own two-piano score, shows how her technique is enhanced when the spinning is transposed to ballerinas in point shoes. This resounding success was followed by *Fire* (1982) and *Force Field* (1986, to a Reich score). Dean and Reich collaborated again on *Space* for the **New York City Ballet**'s 1988 American Music Festival. One of her largest works to date, it was staged for a quartet of principal dancers augmented by a corps de ballet of thirty-four.

Lineage

Laura Dean's use of repetition and gradually evolving sets of patterns are akin to the work of **Lucinda Childs** and **Molissa Fenley**. Andrew deGroat, who worked with **Robert Wilson**, has used spinning as a motif in his *Rope Dances*. Charles Moulton created works that used repetition, but without the travelling patterns favoured by Dean and Childs. His *Nine Person Precision Ball-Passing* was just what the title says. Like Dean, **Meredith Monk** is a choreographer who composes her own scores.

Follow-up

Tympani was recorded on video for American television in 1981. Dean discusses her work and ideas in a chapter of *Contemporary Dance*, edited by Anne Livet (1978).

Laura Dean Dancers and Musicians performing the 1981 work *Tympani,* with music and choreography by Dean

Douglas Dunn

Born: 19th October 1942/Palo Alto, California

The most quixotic of post-modern choreographers, Douglas Dunn has an idiosyncratic sense of humour. This sometimes gives his work deadpan comic overtones that recall his mentor **Merce Cunningham** at his zaniest. Lanky and long-limbed, Dunn physically resembles Cunningham in both these elfin bursts of sardonic wit, and the ferocious concentration that wraps him in a hermetically sealed cocoon of air.

After two years of classical ballet studies, Dunn went to New York in 1968, and immediately began working with **Yvonne Rainer** and studying with Cunningham, in whose troupe he performed from 1969 to 1973. He was also a member of the improvisational Grand Union before forming his own company in 1977.

As with all the post-modern generation, Dunn is acutely concerned with the outer boundaries of dance. He took this to an ultimate, unnerving conclusion in 1974 with *101*. Subtitled 'A Performance Exhibit', it turned the viewer into the active participant, with the performer (Dunn) as passive object. The event took place in his studio, which was open four hours a day, six days a week for some two months. During this time, visitors were free to wander through a fifteen-foot high structural maze of wooden beams which Dunn had built. The observant 'audience member' would eventually find the inert Dunn lying like some Viking corpse at the top of the maze. The 'dancer' never moved, and it was the visitor who determined the length of the performance by how long he or she chose to remain in Dunn's environment.

Gestures in Red, an hour-long solo from 1975, methodically explored movement from a slow crab-like crawl round the edges of the space to an eventual explosion of sharp, percussive phrases. Filled with a subtle, subliminal sense of drama, this solo was the opening performance of London's first Dance Umbrella festival in 1978.

Taking a cue from Yvonne Rainer's *Continuous Project – Altered Daily*, Dunn began creating *Lazy Madge* in 1976 (the title is a bastardisation of Claude Debussy's *Les Images*). This work, for anywhere from eight to ten participants, continued to be danced over several seasons with new material incorporated into each performance. It was composed of solos and duets which Dunn choreographed in isolation from each other. Only during performances were these pieces spliced together, and each time the work was presented, the dancers had great freedom in how, when and where they would execute the sections they had been taught.

Highly respected in France, Dunn created an abstract version of Stravinsky's *Pulcinella* for the **Paris Opéra Ballet** in 1980; he has also choreographed for that company's small experimental troupe GRCOP, and for the Ballet de Nancy.

Lineage

Merce Cunningham and the revolutionary aesthetics of the Judson Dance Theatre era have both been major influences on Dunn. Like other alumni of the Cunningham company such as Viola Farber, **Karole Armitage** and the San Francisco-based Margaret Jenkins, Dunn has evolved a personal choreographic style filled with individual virtuosity, but devoid of the bravura often found in ballet or more traditional modern dance.

Follow-up

Douglas Dunn's video projects in collaboration with film-maker Charles Atlas include *Mayonnaise* (1973) and *Secret of the Waterfall* (1983). Dunn is one of the seven post-modern choreographers featured in Michael Blackwood's 1980 film *Making Dances*, and his work is discussed in a chapter of Sally Banes' *Terpsichore in Sneakers*. Dunn talks about his approach in *Further Steps* (1987, edited by Connie Kreemer), and in *The Vision of Modern Dance* by Jean Morrison Brown (1979).

Garth Fagan

Born: 3rd May 1940/Kingston, Jamaica

The evolution of Garth Fagan's Bucket Dance Theatre is one of the dance world's success stories of the 1980s, but it did not happen overnight. Fagan's career began when he left Jamaica as a teenager to tour Latin America with Ivy Baxter and Rex Nettleford's Jamaican National Dance Company. While attending college in the USA, he took master classes with **Merce Cunningham**, **José Limón**, **Martha Graham** and **Alvin Ailey**, and later danced and choreographed for several companies in Detroit.

Soon after joining the faculty of the State University of New York at Brockport in 1970 (a post he still holds), Fagan began teaching a handful of untrained young adults at the University's inner-city centre in nearby Rochester. In ironic apology, he dubbed them The Bottom of the Bucket But...Dance Theatre. A decade later the name was shortened to Bucket Dance Theatre – the time was right for a more dignified title. Functioning as both guru and benevolent patriarch in the tradition of leading mainstream dance figures, Fagan has worked at developing a distinctive movement vocabulary and a disciplined, devoted ensemble able to perform it.

Long-limbed and muscular, proud of carriage and flexible of spine, Fagan's dancers are notable for their often rapturous concentra-tion onstage. They dance with a combination of physical solidity and an almost spiritual sense of airy aspiration. They are super-lative exponents of the Bucket style, an amalgam of modern and jazz dance styles, with Afro-Caribbean roots and an overlay of balletic flair.

'Discipline is Freedom' is both the subtitle and the message of *Prelude* (1981), Bucket's signature piece. *Never Top 40 (Juke Box)* (1985) is an impressively coherent grab-bag of movement set to a selection of some of Fagan's favourite music, from Puccini to reggae, an eclecticism which he also applied to *Easter Freeway Processional* (1983) and *Mask Mix Masque* (1986). In the former, Fagan resists visualising Philip Glass's cyclical score, opting for slow, lyrical partnerings and sculptural poses rather than constant repetitious motion. *Mask Mix Masque* is an exploration of the mystique of Fagan's fellow Jamaican, pop icon Grace Jones.

Although Fagan's primary commitment is to Bucket, he has taken time out to direct a stage version of Duke Ellington's unfinished musical *Queenie Pie* and to choreograph *Footprints Dressed in Red* for **Dance Theatre of Harlem**.

Lineage
Fagan distils a range of sources into a strong, supple style. As well as Ivy Baxter, he was influen-ced by Pearl Primus and Lavinia Williams, two other famed dancer-teachers from the Caribbean. Although most of his dancers are black, their movement is not ethnic per se, even if their windmilling arms and syncopated footwork come from African dance. The emphasis on contraction and isolation is derived from **Martha Graham**, the show business spirit from **Alvin Ailey**.

Follow-up
The Bucket Dance Theatre was featured in the *Dance Black America* programme of US public television's Great Performances series.

Bob Fosse

Born: 23rd June 1927/Chicago, Illinois
Died: 23rd September 1987/ Washington, DC

Fosse was an acknowledged master of the American musical-comedy genre. The son of vaudeville performers, he was hoofing in burlesque at thirteen; four years later, he was the opening act for striptease shows. After the Second World War, he graduated to nightclubs and stage musicals, making his Broadway debut in 1950. The 1953 musical *The Pajama Game* (filmed four years later) established his choreographic reputation, particularly the witty, mock-cool number 'Steam Heat'. This was an early demonstration of Fosse's trademarks: angled limbs, locked ankles and knocked knees, provocative hip thrusts, shoulder rolls and backward leans, all set to syncopated rhythms.

Sweet Charity (1966) was the first musical that Fosse controlled from the start. A New York transplant of Frederico Fellini's non-musical film *Nights of Cabiria*, about the up-and-down fortunes of a waif-like prostitute, it was a vehicle for Fosse's then wife Gwen Verdon. The show's classic 'Big Spender' number, set in a sleazy dance hall, was a throwback to Fosse's youth in burlesque and a precursor of *Cabaret* (1972), his electrifying film version of the stage musical directed by Harold Prince. *Cabaret* accentuated the acidic razzle-dazzle of Fosse's work. It freed him from the old-style musical comedy form and pushed him into the field of 'concept' musicals that extends from **Jerome Robbins**' *West Side Story* to Michael Bennett's *A Chorus Line* and Andrew Lloyd Webber's *Cats*.

After *Cabaret*, Fosse's work became an even more stylised reflection of urban urgency and angst. *Chicago* (1975) was a cynical development of the decadence of *Cabaret*'s Berlin, while *Dancin'*

(1978) consisted of a string of gimmicky routines. The 1979 film *All That Jazz* was the frank, autobiographical saga of a workaholic Broadway director addicted to nicotine, pills, sex and intimations of his own mortality. Based on Fosse's own heart attack during the making of *Chicago*, it featured 'Airotica', his most aggressively sexual dance number. Other non-dance films and a few Broadway shows followed before Fosse's death en route to a theatrical revival of *Sweet Charity*.

Lineage

During his lifetime, Bob Fosse acknowledged the influence of **Fred Astaire**, Gene Kelly and **Jerome Robbins** (one of his mentors), as well as jazz and tap performers like the Nicholas Brothers and the director George Abbott, who taught Fosse how to structure and pace a show. Fosse's early choreography was similar to that of Jack Cole, a former student of **Denishawn** and **Doris Humphrey** who specialised in angular, athletic, night-club style dances with steps that had an ethnic edge. Like Cole and the equally innovative **Agnes de Mille**, Fosse became a leading figure in American popular entertainment. Prominent among his peers was Gower Champion, whose death backstage on the opening night of his production of *42nd Street* (1980) was even more 'the show must go on' than Fosse's. Neither Champion, Michael Bennett or Harold Prince ever achieved Fosse's movie success.

Follow-up

In addition to his film musicals, Fosse can be seen as a dancing actor in *Kiss Me Kate* (1953) and *My Sister Eileen* (1955). His 'snake in the grass' number is the high point of the 1974 musical film of Antoine de Saint-Exupéry's *The Little Prince*. Although Fosse's debut as a film director (*Sweet Charity*, 1969) was a flop, it contains some of the best onscreen dancing of the era. Martin Gottfried's book *Broadway Musicals* (1979) includes a well-informed essay on Fosse's work.

David Gordon

Born: 14th July 1936/Brooklyn, NY

David Gordon baulks at being called a choreographer. His programme credit, whether for **American Ballet Theatre** or his own small touring troupe, the Pick-Up Company, lists him as the 'constructor'. No one can claim his work is not choreography because he has beat them to the punch with the 'constructor' disclaimer. That may all be a question of semantics, but then wordplay is one of Gordon's proclivities. He has always loved puns, verbal and physical, and his work is strewn with word games and cross-references. (In the early 1980s, the emerging generation of young choreographers went through a phase of talking about themselves in their work. Typically, Gordon chose this moment to shut up.)

He was studying painting when he began dancing with the witty and eccentric James Waring, a generally unsung influence on the post-modern movement. Gordon started making his own works in 1960, was part of the Judson Dance Theatre, and danced in many **Yvonne Rainer** pieces, including the premiere of the seminal *Trio A*. He was also a principal member of the improvisational Grand Union in the early 1970s, a company that grew out of Rainer's insistence that dance could be performed without a choreographer at the helm. In 1966, Gordon's purposely gross solo *Walks and Digressions* was universally lambasted and he was so affected by the reaction that he did not create another theatre work of his own until 1971. This was called *Sleepwalking*, and featured a large number of dancers travelling back and forth across the stage while gradually increasing their tempo from a slow walk to running as fast as possible. Each performer was free to set their own increasing speed, so the work became a layered over-lapping of varied rhythms which

fluctuated at each performance.

Chair (1974), a minor-scaled major event, was a simultaneous double solo for Gordon and his English-born wife Valda Setterfield. Here Gordon devised a series of unemphatic movements performed in, on, around and through a metal folding chair. The same sequence was repeated five times with variations in tempo, direction and accompaniment (including a send-up of the chance procedures favoured by composer John Cage and the Judson group). Chairs have been a recurring motif in Gordon's work: his first creation for American Ballet Theatre, *Field, Chair and Mountain* (1985), had music by John Field, ballerinas on point promenading atop chairs, and a panoramic landscape by Santo Loquasto, which like all of the movement, unrolled left to right like an Oriental scroll (or the vision scene in **The Sleeping Beauty**).

In 1974, Gordon formed his own company. *Not Necessarily Recognizable Objects* four year later continued his interest in incidents that the audience might misread as accidents – trips, stumbles, seemingly spontaneous dialogue. In *TV Reel* (1982), he began experimenting with video as another component of the performance process. Many of his works still use language, but now as part of the pre-recorded soundscore.

There is a matter-of-fact camaraderie to Gordon's works and a laid-back sense of casualness where nothing is ever strained. The emotions that surface now and again are those of an urban romantic who knows how fleeting such moments tend to be.

Lineage

David Gordon's sense of humour, more appreciated in the USA and France than in Britain, marks him out from his post-modern colleagues. Both **Trisha Brown** and **Twyla Tharp** have filled some of their works with visual jokes, but Gordon's verbal high jinks are distinctly his own. Upfront gay choreographer Tim Miller is the person doing most to extend verbal dance in new directions.

Follow-up

The video *Made in USA* includes *Murder*, a mock Edwardian murder mystery created for ABT, with Mikhail Baryshnikov playing a gallery of very funny characters, and a made-for-television duet with talking for Baryshnikov and Valda Setterfield. Sally Banes' 1980 *Terpsichore in Sneakers* includes a chapter on Gordon.

London Contemporary Dance Theatre

Formed: 1967, as the Contemporary Dance Group

Now in its third decade, London Contemporary Dance Theatre (LCDT) has had a decisive impact on Britain's modern dance scene. In 1954, businessman Robin Howard met **Martha Graham**, whose company was making its London debut. A decade later Howard set up a trust to assist British dancers interested in studying the Graham technique. This was officially designated the Contemporary Dance Trust in 1966, when Howard also established the London Contemporary Dance School, the only European institution authorised to teach the Graham method.

Long-time Graham dancer and associate **Robert Cohan** was chosen as director of both the school and the company subsequently formed from its students. Under his leadership LCDT made its debut in 1967, followed two years later by a first full season at The Place, the company's home near London's Euston Station, now identified as one of Britain's major dance education centres and a prime alternative performance venue.

LCDT consists of about twenty

Linda Gibbs and Darshan Singh Bhuller of London Contemporary Dance Theatre

dancers who perform extensively throughout Britain and abroad. Their demanding touring schedule, coupled with the need to fill large performance spaces, has sometimes forced Cohan to produce choreography just to give the company more to perform. A large repertory of over 150 dances is augmented by at least four premieres each year, many featuring commissioned scores. Several prominent British choreographers have emerged from within the company ranks, but it is Cohan's Graham-based, socio-theatrical style which dominates the repertory. LCDT's twenty-first anniversary season marked the end of his artistic directorship; he finally passed on control to **Dan Wagoner** in early 1989.

Lineage

London Contemporary Dance Theatre has exerted the greatest influence on British dance since the formation and development of the **Royal Ballet** and **Ballet Rambert**. **Richard Alston**, **Siobhan Davies**, **Robert North** and Micha Bergese were students, dancers and choreographers of LCDT before each became artistic director of their own company. Current company members Christopher Bannerman, Jonathan Lunn and Darshan Singh Bhuller have all contributed to the repertory.

Follow-up

Much of LCDT's repertory has been filmed for television or video distribution, including Cohan's *Forest* and *Waterless Method of Swimming Instruction* (both filmed 1980), *Cell* and *Nympheas* (both 1983). The company performed Siobhan Davies' *Bridge the Distance* and Tom Jobe's *Rite Electrik* and *Liquid Assets* as part of the BBC's 1986 Dancemakers series. Mary Clarke and Clement Crisp's *London Contemporary Dance Theatre* was published in 1988.

Netherlands Dance Theatre

Formed: 1959

Always in the vanguard of experimentation, Netherlands Dance Theatre (NDT) was founded in 1959 as a rebellion against Sonia Gaskell's Nederlands Ballet (a precursor of **Dutch National Ballet**). Ringleaders included Carel Birnie and Benjamin Harkavy (NDT's first artistic director), plus dancer-choreographers Jaap Flier, Hans van Manen and (for a brief period) Rudi van Dantzig.

NDT started out producing some ten new, classically-based modern ballets a year. The troupe's interest in American modern dance was underlined by works from John Butler, **Glen Tetley** and **Anna Sokolow** in their first decade, Jennifer Muller and Louis Falco in the second. Tetley's input was particularly valuable: as resident choreographer he staged over sixteen ballets and for a short time served as co-director. His first piece, *The Anatomy Lesson* (1964), was inspired by Rembrandt's eponymous painting and choreographed for Flier; in 1970 Tetley collaborated with van Manen on *Mutations*, which gained notoriety for its non-exploitative nude sequences.

NDT suffered a period of decline after Tetley and van Manen resigned in the early 1970s. Then **Jirí Kylián** made his first piece for NDT in 1973, and two years later ended his career as a dancer with **Stuttgart Ballet** to become the Dutch company's full-time choreographer. As sole artistic director from 1978, he transformed NDT into a one-choreographer company and broadened its standing through a synthesis of classical ballet and modern dance.

The ensemble is tight-knit and very American in its energy and speed, but the no-star policy means the dancers sometimes lack individuality. NDT2, a second junior company, functions partly as a feeder of new talent into the main company. Both receive work from Kylián, van Manen (officially back on the staff from late 1988), Nacho Duato, Graeme Watson and Philip Taylor. Outside choreographers include **William Forsythe**, **Daniel Larrieu** and Graeme Murphy (of **Sydney Dance Company**). In 1987, NDT moved into its own, specially built, 1000-seat theatre in The Hague.

Lineage

NDT has had a major influence on European modern dance, particularly on the reforms instituted by **Ballet Rambert** in the mid-1960s. In the 1970s, founding artistic director Benjamin Harkavy returned to his native America and joined the directorial staff of Pennsylvania Ballet, a leading regional company. The offshoot NDT2 can be compared with the small second companies formed by the **Joffrey**, **Paris Opéra** and **London Festival Ballets**. Dansproduktie and Dansgroep Krisztina de Chatel top the list of younger Dutch modern dance exponents.

Follow-up

NDT ballets on film include the Kylián works *Symphony in D, Transfigured Night* and, most recently, *L'Enfant et les sortilèges*. Nacho Duato's *Jardi Tancat* (Catalan for 'Closed Garden') is also available. *The Anatomy Lesson* was filmed in 1968.

Alwin Nikolais

Born: 25th November 1910/ Southington, Connecticut

Alwin Nikolais is a theatrical magician, whose sleight of hand works are a dazzling amalgam of light, sound, props and bizarre costumes which transform his performers into other-worldly creatures inhabiting a strange and colourful universe. All the elements are of his own creation, and it is not incidental that Nik (as he is called) spent two years in the mid-1930s working as a puppeteer. He continues to manipulate depersonalised dancers as if they were controlled by invisible strings. In one of his most famous early pieces, *Tensile Involvement* (1953), the dancers do indeed have visible strings, pieces of elastic, attached to their hands and feet and stretching up into the flies and out into the wings. The dancers' movements, accentuated by these lines, seem to angle into infinity.

A 1933 performance by **Mary Wigman** led Nik to study with **Hanya Holm** at Bennington College and at her summer school in Colorado. He moved to New York in 1948 and became associated with the Henry Street Playhouse, first producing children's theatre and then founding the company which would become Nikolais Dance Theatre. He remained as director of the Playhouse until 1970.

In the age before performances could include almost any sort of effect thanks to the advances of technology, Nikolais was ahead of his time, a backyard prestidigitator who painted his own slide projections, created impressive lighting out of bits of cellophane and tin cans punched with holes, and even composed his own sound scores by splicing bits of tape. Then, in 1963, he became the first artist to make use of a Columbia University invention, the Moog Synthesizer. There is something awesome, and also something childlike, about the world as seen by this (now) grand old master of the theatre.

The major complaint about his work is that he turns dancers into automatons devoid of emotion. In *Noumenon* (1953), the performers are completely encased in stretch jersey shrouds and spend the dance standing on pedestals, contorting themselves into shapes that recall Henry Moore sculptures. In *Gallery* (1978), the dancers become bodyless heads which vanish and pop back up again to the pinging electronic score, like treadmill ducks in a fun-fair shooting gallery. In *Imago* (1963) and other works, the costumes extend the dancers' bodies into shapes that suggest everything from amoebas to visitors from outer space – anything but human beings.

Nikolais Dance Theatre first toured Europe in 1965. The troupe's 1968 Paris debut was a sensation and a decade later Nikolais was chosen by the French Ministry of Culture to form the Centre National de Danse Contemporaine at Angers (where he was succeeded by Viola Farber). For the **Paris Opéra Ballet**, he has created *Schema* (1980) and *Arc-en-Ciel* (1987).

Lineage

The experiments carried out at the turn of the century by Loie Fuller with fabric and electric light (she danced on a glass floor with coloured lights shining up from beneath) and **Oskar Schlemmer**'s radical Bauhaus works both pre-figure the theatre of Alwin Nikolais. His major dancer, Murray Louis, formed his own troupe in 1969; both men continue to share rehearsal space, and Nikolais is often the lighting designer for Louis, whose work is a witty and more humane reflection of the Nikolais style. Former Nikolais dancers **Carolyn Carlson** and Susan Buirge influenced Parisian modern dance in the 1970s. **Pilobolus Dance Theatre** made its New York debut after being discovered by Louis.

Follow-up

There are several Nikolais videos, including the documentary *Nik and Murray* (1987). *Aviary: A Ceremony for Bird People* was created specifically for video, and one of Nik's strongest stage works, *Tent* (1968), was re-worked for German television. Marcia B. Siegel's *Nik: A Documentary* was published in 1971 by the US quarterly *Dance Perspectives*; excerpts appear in *The Vision of Modern Dance* edited by Jean Morrison Brown (1979).

Robert North

Born: lst June 1945/Charleston, South Carolina

Robert North's father was a sculptor, and this may have influenced him to study art and design full time in London, only taking dance classes on the side. In 1965, he started a two-year course at the **Royal Ballet** School, and the following year began attending classes at the newly opened London Contemporary Dance School under **Robert Cohan**. By the end of the decade he had become a founding member of **London Contemporary Dance Theatre**, as well as joining **Martha Graham**'s company in New York. But his main allegiance was to LCDT, and he returned in 1969, staying for twelve years as both performer and choreographer.

North dances naturally and straightforwardly ('as if he were mending fences or building barns', according to one observer), but as a choreographer he is more difficult to categorise. His pre-dominantly modern work clearly reflects his classical training and keen interest in jazz dance. He has earned a reputation as a popular craftsman, a sometime experi-mentalist and a collaborator with painters, film-makers and other dancers, such as **Wayne Sleep** (*David and Goliath*) and **Lynn Seymour** (*Gladly, Sadly, Badly,*

Madly, both 1975). Early dances include *Still Life* (1975), a piece that incorporated film; the balletic *Scriabin Preludes and Studies* (1978); and *Troy Game* (1974), a cheerful, tongue-in-cheek men's display that underlines the jocularity in jock competitiveness (his best received work to date).

He began making dances for **Ballet Rambert** as early as 1967, and in 1981 was taken on as artistic director. Among the dances from this period are *Pribaoutki* (1982), a playfully jumbled tribute to Picasso's art and the Ballets Russes era; *Colour Moves* (1983), in collaboration with artist Bridget Riley; the lyrical **Antony Tudor**-style *Death and the Maiden* (1984); and *Entre Dos Aguas* (1984), a jazzed-up, show-stopping piece of flamenco entertainment.

In 1986, North was dismissed from his post. It was suggested that he had not been encouraging new talent or outside choreographers, or perhaps that his works had become too populist. Certainly, North's choreography was more easily digestible than that of the other members of the Rambert triumvirate, **Christopher Bruce** and **Richard Alston**. He now operates on a freelance basis.

North is married to the dancer-choreographer Janet Smith, for whose company (disbanded 1988) North made a number of dances, the best known being *Lonely Town, Lonely Street* (1980, remounted for Rambert the following year).

Lineage

Like **Christopher Bruce**, his contemporary at **Ballet Rambert**, North was a central creative figure for a long period at one company, in his case **London Contemporary Dance Theatre**; both choreographers blend classical and modern dance idioms with ease. And like other former LCDT members **Siobhan Davies**, Micha Bergese and Tom Jobe, North is a fine dancer as well as dancemaker.

Follow-up

Several Robert North works – *Death and the Maiden*, the award-winning *For My Daughter* (1983), *Entre Dos Aguas* and *Lonely Town, Lonely Street* – are on video. He also choreographed the dance sequences in the 1979 film *Slow Dancing in the Big City*.

Pilobolus Dance Theatre

Formed: 1971

The unique, hybrid performing style of Pilobolus is a mixture of gymnastics, mime and spectacle, as well as dance. Playfully named after a species of phototropic fungus that thrives in barnyards, the company began modestly as an outgrowth of Alison Chase's modern dance classes at Dartmouth College. Within two years founders Moses Pendleton and Jonathan Wolken had been joined by two more men (Robby Barnett and Lee Harris) and then two women (Chase and **Martha Clarke**). The troupe's penchant for striking body sculpture (*Ocellus*, 1972), surreal whimsy (*Untitled*, 1975) and good low humour (*Walklyndon*, 1971) was the foundation for its continuing success on the international dance touring circuit.

Pilobolus has always choreographed collectively, developing new pieces through the refinement of group improvisations. A fortuitous thunderstorm was the inspiration for *Day Two* (1980); one of the company's sexiest, most hypnotic dances, its smashing watersports finale never fails to bring down the house. Although their work sometimes lacks focus and structure, there is nevertheless something like a consistent Pilobolean vision, a freewheeling tableau of dream-logic imagery at once childlike and sophisticated.

The company's creative catchwords are metamorphosis and illusion, ambiguous states that enable the pretzel-bodied performers to transform themselves into creatures and organisms from some hallucinatory bestiary.

While Pilobolus's later offerings favour dramatic and psychological

Day Two, performed by Pilobolus Dance Theatre at Sadler's Wells in 1985

themes (the quasi-religious *Stabat Mater*, 1983, and the mock-Gothic *Land's Edge*, 1986), the company retains its proclivity for joyous, offbeat invention and the capacity to astonish (especially first-time) audiences.

Lineage

The original members of Pilobolus have all drifted into a range of other performance pursuits, yet four of them still assume company artistic directorship with long-time member Michael Tracy. In 1980, Pendleton and Chase formed MOMIX, a collaborative unit whose members have included Daniel Ezralow, once a dancer with **Paul Taylor** and a choreographer for both **London Contemporary Dance Theatre** and Israel's Batsheva Dance Company. MOMIX itself has subdivided into a further Pilobolean spore called ISO (founded 1987). **Martha Clarke** left Pilobolus in the late 1970s to head the dance-theatre group Crowsnest with Robby Barnett.

Follow-up

Pilobolus was the subject of Dance in America videos in 1977 and 1980. The video *Pilobolus on Broadway* dates from 1982, while photographer Tim Matson's 1978 book *Pilobolus* features images from seven productions supplemented by the dancers' comments. *Moses Pendleton Presents Moses Pendleton* is a 1983 documentary on the man's work and philosophy.

Yvonne Rainer

Born: 24th November 1934/San Francisco, California

Had Yvonne Rainer ever been comfortable with the traditionally authoritative role of the choreographer as 'boss lady' (to use her own words), she could have become one of the major artists of the era. Instead, she opted for a democratic relationship with her dancers that first led to a collective process of creation and finally found her dropping out of the field completely. Yet, before she moved on to film-making in 1973, she had posed so many questions and sparked off so many ideas among her contemporaries that her influence on the evolving post-modern movement can rightly be seen as both pervasive and crucial.

When she arrived in New York in 1956, Rainer began to study acting. She took her first dance classes the next year, and by 1959 was up to three sessions every day (two at the **Martha Graham** School, plus a ballet class). In the summer of 1960, she returned to California for Anna Halprin's experimental summer course, where she first met **Trisha Brown**. Halprin's notions about using everyday movements and tasks as the basis for dancing had a deep impact on Rainer. Back in New York, she began studying with **Merce Cunningham**, and performing with the eccentric James Waring. She enrolled in Robert Dunn's pioneering composition class, as did Brown, **Steve Paxton**, **David Gordon** and later **Lucinda Childs**. Using the radical ideas of composer John Cage as a starting point, these sessions explored new and alter-native ways of making dances, and were the genesis of the radical Judson Dance Theatre. During the seasons that the Judson collective was at its peak (from 1962 to 1964), Rainer was its most prolific choreo-grapher. Dissatisfied with the mythic grandeur of Graham and her followers, Rainer and the other Judson members moved in exactly the opposite direction. Rainer consciously attempted to eliminate all sense of learned technique and polish from her movement. Her famous dictum about performing begins: 'NO to spectacle no to virtuosity no to transformations and magic and make-believe . . .'

Trio A (1966), which is part of a larger work, *The Mind is a Muscle*, became her signature piece. It was first danced by Paxton, Gordon and the choreographer, but she maintained that anyone – young,

old, trained or not – could do it. She neutralised her control even further by stating that anyone who had ever danced *Trio A* was free to teach it to anyone else. The idea was that in whatever manner it was performed, *Trio A* would be 'right', because it would reveal each individual's unique sense of movement. *Trio A* is not simplistic, although it appears to be simple (walking, running, falling, lifting). It is what it is and nothing more. This would become the basic idea within the work of Paxton, Brown, Childs and many other post-modern choreographers.

Continuous Project – Altered Daily was started in 1970. Here Rainer attempted to blur the barrier between creation and performance. She set herself the task of inventing and teaching new choreography as a part of each performance. *Grand Union Dreams* was devised in 1971. By the time the piece was finished Rainer had all but handed over the reins to the individual performers including Brown, Gordon, Paxton and **Douglas Dunn** who were all then working collectively in an improv-isational format as the Grand Union (1970 to 1976).

Lineage

Rainer's wide-ranging ideas, which led her to experiment with dialogue, using props (she had an affinity for people hurling themselves onto mattresses) and the integration of film with live dancers, plus her radical concepts about the role of the choreo-grapher, helped to stimulate (both positively and negatively) virtually every member of the experimental dance scene during the sixties and seventies.

Follow-up

A performance of *Trio A* and a short interview with Rainer is part of the 1980 video *Beyond the Main-stream*. In 1974, Rainer published *Work 1961-73*. Sally Banes has written two books on the artists and the period: *Democracy's Body* (1983) is focussed specifically on Judson Dance Theatre, *Terpsichore in Sneakers* (1980) features a detailed physical and philosophical analysis of Rainer's *Trio A* and a chapter on the Grand Union.

Rambert Dance Company

Formed: 1987, from Ballet Rambert

Although Ballet Rambert did not change its name to Rambert Dance Company until 1987, it shifted its profile away from ballet to modern dance in a single decisive move on 17th July 1966. Faced with mounting financial difficulties and a general crisis of identity, Marie Rambert took the bold and forward-looking decision to abandon the classical repertory amassed over four decades of performance. She turned over the day-to-day responsibilities of the company to her final choreographic protégé Norman Morrice, who had created his first ballets for Rambert in 1958. He immediately began to formulate a new approach which strove to return the company to the heady days of the Ballet Club and the early seasons at the Mercury Theatre, when the focus had been on producing original choreography.

The impetus for this shift came from American modern dance, but the model was the **Netherlands Dance Theatre** which, at the time, was dynamically blending modern and classical techniques into a new European hybrid. Old works were dropped and the company was streamlined down to a group of eighteen soloists. Morrice invited the American **Glen Tetley** to work with Rambert on a regular basis (from 1967 to 1971). Other Americans who helped to shape the new image included **Anna Sokolow**, Louis Falco and Lar Lubovitch. The big British discovery during these years was dancer **Christopher Bruce**, who

began choreographing in 1969.

Feeling that he had achieved what he had set out to do, Morrice left in 1974, when dancer and choreographer John Chesworth took over as director, and Bruce was appointed resident choreographer. Two full-length successful works date from this period: *Cruel Garden*, choreographed by Bruce and **Lindsay Kemp** in 1977, and Tetley's **The Tempest**.

Chesworth, in turn, moved on in 1980, and the company spent a season with no official artistic director (Bruce refused to accept the post); however, it was in 1980 that **Richard Alston** first began working with Rambert. He was almost immediately appointed resident choreographer. The American-born **Robert North** was appointed director in 1981; the next five years saw major new works from the triumvirate of North, Bruce and Alston. In 1982, Rambert added the lyrical *Airs*, first choreographed by **Paul Taylor** for his own company in 1978. Two **Merce Cunningham** pieces, *Fielding Sixes* (1980) and *Septet* (1953) entered the repertory in 1983 and 1987 respectively. A final Tetley work, *Murderer Hope of Women* (1983), failed to adequately blend Oskar Kokoschka's 1907 Expressionist text with the choreography. Another American, **Dan Wagoner**, created *An Occasion for Some Revolutionary Gestures* for Rambert in 1985.

The 1986 Diamond Jubilee season saw further radical change. North was replaced by Alston. Bruce, after creating a final new work for the Jubilee gala, an animal-under-the-skin probing of Elizabethan manners ironically titled *Ceremonies*, switched to **London Festival Ballet**. Alston's own changes to the company profile were as profound as those of 1966. The dramatic works of Bruce and North were dropped and replaced by a new repertory based on the sleek, articulate Merce Cunningham technique. Less overtly emotive than North and Bruce, Alston's own dances were augmented by works from **Ashley Page**, **Michael Clark** and

Siobhan Davies. Other choreo-
graphers ranged from ballerina
Lynn Seymour to experimentalist
Ian Spink and company dancer
Mary Evelyn. Alston's policy was a
definite shift away from dramatic
modern dance towards a plotless
neo-classicism which was more
aligned to Cunningham and
Graham or **Robert Cohan**. For
Ballet Rambert, see entry in
Modern Ballet, page 99.

Lineage

Netherlands Dance Theatre, which
had been the model for the 1966
Rambert policy change, also
underwent an overnight shift in
direction when **Jirí Kylián** was
appointed artistic director and
jettisoned the existing repertory in
favour of his own new creations.
Few other companies have experienced (and survived) such radical
and sudden turning points.

Follow-up

Ballet Rambert: 50 Years and On
(1976, revised 1981) features
interviews with Morrice and
Chesworth.

Wayne Sleep

Born: 17th July 1948/Plymouth

Wayne Sleep spent his childhood
acquiring and developing his
skills: tap training at the age of
five, ballet at eight, a scholarship
to the **Royal Ballet** School when he
was twelve. Audiences took a
shine to him even then, at the
School's annual public displays.
After graduating into the Royal
Ballet in 1966, Sleep scored an
immediate double hit as the
virtuoso Blue Boy in **Frederick
Ashton**'s *Les Patineurs*, and Dr
Coppelius in **Coppélia**. He was
promoted to principal dancer in
1973, inheriting a rich roster of
character roles. Although he was
too small to portray conventional
princely heroes, he was able to
capitalise on his extrovert
personality and buoyant technical
brilliance in ballets by Ashton

(notably as the original Kolia in **A
Month in the Country**, and ideally
cast as Puck in **The Dream**) and
Kenneth MacMillan (who created a
comic pas de deux for Sleep and
the company's tallest woman in the
1974 *Elite Syncopations*).

In addition to appearing in the
original productions of the West
End smashes *Cats* (1981), *Song and
Dance* (1983) and the 1986 revival
of *Cabaret*, Sleep has taken on non-
dancing roles on stage, screen and
radio. In 1980, he launched his own
touring group, Dash, which has
continued to perform periodically.
His 1983/4 television series *The
Hot Shoe Show* was subsequently
adapted for the stage. Sleep's most
unabashedly commercial work,
which these last two projects
represent, are fast-paced fusions of
classical, modern, jazz, tap and
disco dancing wrapped up in
sheer show biz pizazz.

Lineage

Niels Kehlet of the Royal Danish
Ballet and Gen Horiuchi of **New
York City Ballet** are just two of
several male dancers who have
made maximum use of their small
stature. Sleep himself moves as
easily between dance and straight
theatre as **Robert Helpmann** did.
The wide public acceptance of his
all-dance revues *Dash* and *The Hot
Shoe Show* parallels choreographer Arlene Phillips' success
with her various pop-dance
groups, all named Hot Gossip.

Follow-up

Variations on Wayne Sleep, the
word-and-picture diary on the
making of *Song and Dance*, dates
from 1983, when Sleep was named
Show Business Personality of the
Year. He danced the roles of
Squirrel Nutkin and one of the two
Bad Mice in the delightful 1971 film
Tales of Beatrix Potter, choreographed by Frederick Ashton. Sleep
himself choreographed the dance
sequences in the 1978 film *Death
on the Nile*. His non-dancing films
include *The Virgin Soldiers* (1969)
and *The First Great Train Robbery*
(1979). *Dash* and *Song and Dance*
are both available on video.

Sydney Dance Company

Formed: 1971, as the Dance Company (New South Wales)

The present high standing in the dance world of Sydney Dance Company is principally due to the efforts of artistic director Graeme Murphy, the first major Australian choreographer since **Robert Helpmann**.

The troupe grew out of Ballet in a Nutshell, an educational touring unit formed by erstwhile **Australian Ballet** soloist Suzanne Musitz. Its transition into a contemporary company, suitable for permanent residence at Sydney's newly opened Opera House, took place in 1971. During his brief term as artistic director (from 1975 to 1976), Dutch dancer-choreographer Jaap Flier introduced the works of **Glen Tetley** and **Anna Sokolow** into the repertory. He was succeeded by Murphy, a young Melbourne-born dancer and choreographer who had trained at the Australian Ballet School.

From the start of his 1976 appointment, Murphy emphasised Australian choreography (notably his own), music and design. Assisted by dancer Janet Vernon, he has since fostered an enthusiastic following for his company by creating more than thirty ballets, many full-length, in a pungent, eclectic style. He is unabashed about supplementing his core classical vocabulary with whatever he deems necessary to make a production work: elements of musical-comedy, lighting effects and props, film and video, gymnastics, mime, even tap shoes and – in the 1980 pop-punk ballet *Daphnis and Chloe* – skateboards.

Murphy's subjects include the life and world of Jean Cocteau (*Poppy*, 1978), outdoor life (*Rumours*, 1979), the effect of the past on the present (*Homelands*, 1985), and black tie/dinner gown eroticism (*Shining*, 1986). The theme of sexuality is one of Murphy's recurrent choreographic drawing cards. Set in a Dantesque dreamworld of ever-changing locales, *Some Rooms* (1983) deals cleverly with romantic fantasy and sexual ambiguity, while *After Venice* (1984) uses Thomas Mann's novella *Death in Venice* as a springboard for Murphy's own meditations on youth, lust and death.

Murphy's *Beyond Twelve* (1980) and *Gallery* (1987) are in the repertory of the Australian Ballet, from whom he regularly receives commissions. A measure of the esteem in which he is held in his homeland was his creation of the nation's bicentennial birthday dance *Vast* in 1988. This commission brought together the full companies of four ensembles: Australian Dance Theatre, Queensland Ballet, West Australian Ballet and Murphy's own group.

Lineage

No one since **Robert Helpmann** has done so much to raise the profile of Australian dance as Murphy, whose flamboyant, sexy productions for Sydney Dance Company are the Antipodean answer to the work of **Maurice Béjart**. He is as unafraid to mix and match theatrical devices and movement styles as **William Forsythe** and **Lindsay Kemp**. The Melbourne-based Dance Works, formed in 1983 and headed by dancer-choreographer Nanette Hassall, is a smaller, more easy-going, post-modern version of Sydney Dance Company.

Follow-up

Sydney Dance Company appeared in a Channel 4 production of Murphy's *Daphnis and Chloe*; his *Boxes*, *Rumours* and *After Venice* have also been filmed. Much as Twyla Tharp, Peter Martins, Kenneth MacMillan and others have choreographed for John Curry and his Dance Theatre of Skating, Murphy devised *Fire and Ice*, a mythological television special, for Olympic skating champions Torvill and Dean.

Members of the Paul Taylor Dance Company in Taylor's *Arden Court*

Paul Taylor

Born: 29th July 1930/Pittsburgh, Pennsylvania

One of the most influential of modern dance choreographers, Taylor studied painting at college while on an athletic scholarship as a swimmer. His early performance career included dancing with **Merce Cunningham** (1953/4) and **Martha Graham** (from 1958 to 1962). Taylor's first choreography – notably an infamous static, minimal movement 'anti-dance' concert in 1957 – was often rebellious and sometimes incongruously funny. His *Three Epitaphs* (1956) features a sad-sack gaggle of slumped figures in head-to-toe black fabric and with tiny mirrors in their palms (design by Robert Rauschenberg). They huddle and shuffle around to a brass band playing Dixieland funeral music.

Starting in 1962 with *Aureole* (to Haydn), Taylor has evolved a sunny and generous neo-classical style of athletic, but essentially lyric movement. Dancers bound along on the momentum of the music (Bach, Beethoven, Elgar). Taylor's male dancers in particular are totally unlike ballet performers. They tend to be big,

even bulky (Taylor himself is a muscular six foot three). Their size gives his choreography a weighty bounce, a gracious solidity. In his masterwork *Esplanade* (1975), Taylor evokes a series of contrasting moods out of nothing but walking, running, skipping and hopping steps. The effect, as the speed mounts in response to the fleet energies of a Bach score, craftily belies the pedestrian genesis of the steps.

In stark contrast, Taylor has a bleak, bitter, even maniacal streak. He creates social satires of man the animal on the edge of self-inflicted destruction. In *Big Bertha* (1971) he decimates an all-American family on an amusement park outing that leads to incestuous rape and death. In *Cloven Kingdom* (1976), animalistic debaucheries bubble up from beneath polite stuffed shirts. Taylor's iconoclastic version of **Le Sacre du printemps** (1980) is the most successful rendition since the ballet's 1913 premiere.

Lineage

Taylor broke with the symbolic grandeur of **Martha Graham**'s dramatics, while at the same time choosing to stay more connected to traditional music values than experimentalists such as **Merce**

Cunningham. His works have entered the repertories of major modern and ballet companies throughout the world: *Aureole*, *Esplanade*, *Airs* (1978) and *Arden Court* (1981) have been the most popular. Among the many dancers who appeared with Taylor before founding their own companies are **Twyla Tharp**, **Laura Dean**, **Dan Wagoner** and **Pina Bausch**; more recently Daniel Ezralow and David Parsons have left to pursue their own choreographic careers.

Follow-up

The Taylor company features in three programmes of the Dance in America video series. His chatty, autobiography, *Private Domain*, was published in 1987.

Twyla Tharp

Born: 1st July 1941/Portland, Indiana

Twyla Tharp became *the* dance phenomenon of the 1970s. Her peripatetic career has ranged across an astounding spectrum: from the most stringent of conceptual choreography to works for all three of America's major ballet companies, from original creations for television and Broadway to Hollywood films.

The key to Tharp's popularity is her canny ability to make dances that are enjoyable and challenging in the same breath. She knows how to entertain audiences without pandering or condescending to them; she also knows that choreography does not have to be dour and dreary to be serious. This double edge, something **George Balanchine** also understood, makes her works (even her excoriating explorations of urban chaos) immensely watchable.

Tharp was an early achiever. As a child, she studied piano and violin, before switching, at the age of six, to viola and acrobatics. When her family moved to

California she added ballet, tap, modern, jazz, drums, baton-twirling and even took gipsy dance classes from Rita Hayworth's uncle. Moving to New York in 1961, she studied with every important dance teacher in town and after graduating with a degree in art history from Barnard College, spent a season with the **Paul Taylor** Dance Company.

Given her omnivorous appetite, her own choreography would come to embrace a similarly eclectic mélange of influences, but first she went through a cold, almost belligerent period of rigorously structured, mathematically based works usually performed in silence. Her first choreography was given to an audience of twelve in 1965; the entire evening lasted under four minutes. Like **Meredith Monk** and **Laura Dean**, she just missed the initial outburst of Judson Dance Theatre radicalism, but in 1966 *Re-Moves* premiered there. This complex gridwork trio had a setting which gradually blocked the audience's sightlines until, in the final segment, all the viewers could do was hear the choreography. This phase reached its zenith in *The Fugue* (1970), a series of percussive phrases performed by three women in boots on a floor amplified by microphones (Tharp was never a barefoot dancer).

The Fugue took her structural studies as far as they could go. In 1971, she began a series of dance suites set to American popular music with *Eight Jelly Rolls* (to the New Orleans piano music of Jelly Roll Morton). Other works in what is Tharp's most popular genre include *The Bix Pieces* (1971, to trumpeter Bix Beiderbecke); *Sue's Leg* (1976, to original recordings of Fats Waller's songs); *Baker's Dozen* (1979, to tunes by Harlem pianist Willie 'The Lion' Smith); and *Nine Sinatra Songs* (1982). These dances, with their casual floppiness and tossed-off scrambles and squiggles, are packed with physical comedy and sassy bravado. They are never sentimental and are nostalgic only in the most allusive way: as

illustrations of the rumbustious, high-spirited fun which no longer seems available to us.

In 1973, Tharp accepted an invitation to work with the **Joffrey Ballet**. The outcome, *Deuce Coupe*, performed by both Joffrey and Tharp dancers to a collage of California crooning by the Beach Boys, was a box office sensation. Eight months later, again for the Joffrey, she turned to Haydn for *As Time Goes By*. In 1976, she became the first American choreographer to showcase the talents of **Mikhail Baryshnikov** at **American Ballet Theatre** in *Push Comes to Shove*. Tharp sends the Russian's comedic talents on a headlong spree as he flirts with ABT ballerinas and cavorts with a tricky corps de ballet. It is all topped off by an elusive bowler hat that bounces through the ballet like a mascot in search of its lost owner. This joyous composition was the most popular ballet of the decade and ABT's biggest original success since **Jerome Robbins**' **Fancy Free**. Several subsequent ABT works, notably the full-scale neo-classical *Bach Partita* (1984), followed. In 1988, Tharp became an ABT artistic associate; to date her sole work for **New York City Ballet** has been *Brahms/Handel*, choreographed with Robbins in 1984.

Exploring new ways of integrating emotional content into dance (a new Tharp focus in the early 1980s) led to two full-length Broadway works. *When We Were Very Young* (1980) bounced furiously off a narration by playwright Thomas Babe. Vitriolic, confusing and too unformed to achieve success, it was followed by *The Catherine Wheel* (1983, to music by David Byrne). Here Tharp pushed out the boundaries of conventional dance storytelling, creating a gallery of characters (an archetypal American family) who love, hate, fight and destroy one another and then disappear into a radiantly apocalyptic finale known as 'The Golden Section'. In between, she refined this technique with the 1980 *Short Stories* (casual violence to music by Supertramp and Bruce Springsteen) and *Bad Smells* (1982,

to Glenn Branca), a holocaust of movement intensified by a gigantic live video shot by a cameraman worming his way through the dancers like a newsman reporting a disaster.

Consolidating her interest in ballet as her future format, Tharp's own company has given their first performances of her Joffrey work *As Time Goes By* and premiered the propulsive *In the Upper Room* (1987, music by Philip Glass).

Lineage

Like **George Balanchine** before her, Twyla Tharp is intent on proving that classical technique does not need to ossify into dead traditions. Other ballet choreographers such as **Peter Martins**, **William Forsythe**, **Eliot Feld** and **Karole Armitage** continue to explore the field, while modernists **Lucinda Childs** and **Laura Dean** have created works which extend their personal post-modern styles into the realm of ballet.

Follow-up

One of the first choreographers to embrace video wholeheartedly, Tharp's output is well documented: *The Fugue* and *Eight Jelly Rolls* (1974); *Sue's Leg* (part of the inaugural Dance in America series in 1976); *Confessions of a Cornermaker*, which includes *Baker's Dozen*, the *Bach Duet* and *Short Stories* (1981); *The Catherine Wheel* (rechoreographed for video in 1983); and *Baryshnikov by Tharp* (1985), with *Push Comes to Shove*, *The Little Ballet* and *Sinatra Suite*. Tharp's original video productions include *Making Television Dance* (1977) and *Twyla Tharp Scrapbook* (1982), a video assembly of her work from 1965 to 1982. Tharp's feature films include the dances for *Hair* (1979) and *White Nights* (1985), the opera sequences in *Amadeus* (1984) and the period dances in *Ragtime* (1980). Arlene Croce has written in depth on Tharp in her three volumes of criticism, and there is a survey of her career in Robert Coe's *Dance in America* (1985). Paul Taylor's autobiography *Private Domain* includes a vivid portrait of Tharp circa 1965.

Dan Wagoner

Born: 31st July 1932/Springfield, West Virginia

There is a personable nature about the dancers in Dan Wagoner's choreography which makes them seem to be a community, a clan who have come together to perform for the sheer joy of it. His communities may be heading for disintegration, cut adrift from their origins and lost in the modern world, but Wagoner optimistically continues to search for inner harmony.

Born on a farm, the last of ten children, Wagoner began dancing for fun, with no intention of making a career out of performing (he has a degree in pharmacy). He only became a full-time dancer in his mid-twenties, after receiving scholarships to study first at the Connecticut College summer dance school, and then with **Martha Graham** in New York. He performed with Graham's company from 1958 to 1962 and also appeared with the **Merce Cunningham** Dance Company during its 1959/60 season, but his longest, strongest association was with **Paul Taylor**. He joined the company in 1962 (although he had danced with it previously) and created dozens of new roles, notably in the classic *Aureole* and Taylor's masterpiece to the late Beethoven string quartets, *Orbs*. Wagoner formed his own small-scale troupe (Dan Wagoner and Dancers) in 1969 and has been choreographing works for them ever since. In autumn 1988, he was appointed to succeed **Robert Cohan** as artistic director of **London Contemporary Dance Theatre**.

The sense of community found in Wagoner's work often stems from the way he uses music. This can range from the 'change partners and dance' couples in *Spiked Sonata* (1981) and *Taxi Dances* (1974) to the shared sorrows in *Seven Tears* (1979, to John Dowland's Elizabethan *Lachryme*). He has used traditional American country music in several pieces, and his 1985 commission for **Ballet Rambert**, *An Occasion for Some Revolutionary Gestures*, was performed to a set of intricate piano variations on *Yankee Doodle Dandy*. One of his most formal and low-key works, it is danced in front of a pale, faded backdrop of an almost hidden American flag.

Throughout his career, Wagoner has repeatedly worked with poet George Montgomery. His 1969 solo *Brambles* was performed without music on a bare stage. As Wagoner danced, Montgomery described in detail the imaginary setting which the audience was supposed to envisage.

Wagoner has staged a number of works for British companies. In addition to his Rambert piece, he created *Flee as a Bird* (1985, American blues songs) for the now defunct Janet Smith and Dancers, staged *Spiked Sonata* for **Extemporary Dance Theatre** and worked with the now disbanded Mantis Dance Company. As early as 1974, *Changing Your Mind*, a quirky and challenging work with a Montgomery text and dialogue for the dancers, entered the repertory of London Contemporary Dance Theatre.

Lineage

Paul Taylor, **Merce Cunningham** and **Martha Graham** have all helped shape Wagoner's choreography. The influences of these three ebb and flow through his works. Cunningham's approach to random structure and Taylor's sardonic view of modern urban life are supplemented by Wagoner's love of his rural roots.

Follow-up

George's House (1985), an outdoor piece set in and around George Montgomery's New Hampshire farmhouse, was devised for video. Wagoner plays an important role in Paul Taylor's autobiography *Private Domain* (1987) and is one of fifteen American choreographers who discuss their work in *Further Steps* (1987, edited by Connie Kreemer).

ALTERNATIVES

3rd December 1975. Tons of damp, rich-smelling earth transformed a theatre in the Ruhr valley into the setting for Pina Bausch's new version of Stravinsky's *Le Sacre du printemps*. By the end of the first night, her performers were streaked and caked in the mud they had churned up. Bare-breasted, sweating and exhausted from flinging themselves compulsively onto the ground, the dancers of the Wuppertal Tanztheater had brought a messy but fertile sense of life back to modern dance.

Bausch the choreographer is an important creator but Bausch the trailblazer is a revolutionary whose vision of dance-theatre provided the first genuine alternative to the American post-modernists. She achieved this by devising a dramatic form of dance that has the emotional involvement of theatre but which never resorts to straightforward narrative. She and her dancers set in motion a trend that has given European dance a sense of freedom and independence from an American domination which goes back not just to Martha Graham, but all the way to Isadora Duncan.

During the 1960s and early 1970s, the American post-modern generation had stripped dance down to its basics in an effort to rediscover the integrity which was being buried by heavy theatricality and an increasing accumulation of clichés. The outcome was a radical art form that pared away all vestiges of storytelling. But even as they were working out their goals, it became clear that the only way for this new pure dance to survive was by moving back towards deeper implications. The clarity of the skeleton had been exposed; now some of the post-modernists wanted to put flesh back onto the bones. Pina Bausch beat them to it.

Bausch's alternative to American coolness was eagerly picked up by artists all over the Continent and quickly gained the kind of mass popularity that new dance in America had never known. Bausch broke down the barrier between audience and artist by seeming to transform the dancer into the actual subject matter of the performance. This was something that Bill T. Jones and Arnie Zane had already done in America, but on smaller, more intimate terms. The impact of Bausch came from her ability to make this approach work on a grand scale.

Other European artists have altered her dance-theatre to suit their own temperaments. Martha Clarke (an American who has created much of her work in Europe) and Maguy Marin provide a more polished, sometimes even surreal, alternative to Bausch's deliberately raw edges. Anne Teresa De Keersmaeker in Belgium, DV8 Physical Theatre in Britain and the American-born, Frankfurt-based William Forsythe have all used her blunt, direct manner as a base for their own creativity. Michael Clark sugar-coats the controversial and confessional aspects of Wuppertal-style dance-theatre by turning it into a three-ring circus. Yet his outrageous antics cloak some serious, genuinely subversive ideas about how to accommodate the pressures of life in the late twentieth century.

What will happen next, or where the next trends will spring up is anybody's guess. It is also one of the reasons why we all keep going to see dance.

Mechtild Grossmann and Christian Trouillas in the Pina Bausch work *Blaubart*

Karole Armitage

Born: 3rd March 1954/Madison, Wisconsin

Karole Armitage's choreography explodes like a Molotov cocktail hurled defiantly at the audience. The title of her first major work, *Drastic Classicism* (1981), is a bald statement of her credo: to take the rigour and virtuosity inherent in classical dance and reshape it for the contemporary world. The result is sharp, jagged, invigorating and controversial, and is often danced to the sort of art-rock music that makes the loudest of discos seem as docile as a nursery at twilight.

As a teenager, Armitage moved to Europe with her family and from 1972 to 1974 danced with the Ballets de Genève, a company whose repertory was then over-flowing with **George Balanchine** ballets. In 1976, back in the USA, she became a member of the **Merce Cunningham** Dance Company. During her five years there, Cunningham created several important roles for her. *Squaregame* (1976) includes a languorous duet for the choreographer and Armitage, who looked like an exotic, long-legged wading bird fearful of falling over. In *Channels/Inserts* (1981), he gave her a pivotal, percussive role in one of his masterworks.

Armitage began her own choreography while still dancing with Cunningham, and had a breakthrough with *Drastic Classicism*, a raw-edged cork-screwing of classical dance techniques performed in sharp, brittle bursts of movement. This skewering of the ballet lexicon immediately attracted the French, and Armitage's next works were created there, for her own dancers (who included the young **Michael Clark**) as well as for **Paris Opéra Ballet**.

The Watteau Duet (1985) originally had a physics equation as its title. It is quintessential

'Outrageous wonder woman': Karole Armitage in her favoured dance footwear

Armitage: full of loud, compelling music, outré costume changes and a series of confrontations. These encounters find Armitage performing both in point shoes and her favoured five-inch stiletto heels. Her footwear is used like weaponry. She jabs her toes into the floor, swings her legs in battering-ram extensions and swivels them into lancing arabesques. As she stamps and prowls the stage with punk-majestic elegance, her male partner (Joseph Lennon) becomes a subservient consort to Armitage's outrageous wonder woman.

In 1986, she was invited to make a ballet, *The Mollino Room*, for **Mikhail Baryshnikov** and **American Ballet Theatre**. That same year, she renamed her own company the Armitage Ballet.

Lineage

Merce Cunningham and **George Balanchine** are Karole Armitage's mentors. Using their innovations as a jumping-off point, she is striving for the same sort of aesthetic advances which those two giants achieved in the 1950s. She has not so far been as successful at this fusion as **Twyla Tharp**: Armitage's chaotic ferocity is devoid of Tharp's calibrated logistics. **Michael Clark** (who shares the services of designer Charles Atlas) and **Ashley Page** have both been influenced by Armitage.

Follow-up

Armitage is featured in two Cunningham videos: *Locale* (1978) and *Channel/Inserts*. Her own original dances for video include *Parafango* (1983, where she performs in duets with four exceptional male dancers) and the fractured, modernist, often very funny love story *Romance* (1986).

Les Ballets Trockadero de Monte Carlo

Formed: 1974

The Trocks, as they are affectionately known, are the dance world's funniest balleto-maniacs. This all-male satire troupe was formed by a trio of ballet enthusiasts who had split off from another, lesser drag dance company, Larry Ree's Gloxinia Trockadero Ballet. They began on a shoestring budget, playing occasional late-night gigs in lofts, off-off-Broadway theatres and church basements. Soon they caught on with press VIPs like *New Yorker* dance critic Arlene Croce, acquired an agent and started to amass a cult following. Within a few years they were an established attraction, steadily performing concert dates across the United States and beyond (including Monte Carlo).

Much of the Trocks' appeal lies in the juxtaposition of frilly tutus and hairy chests, the incongruity of dying swans and silly sylphs with bulging biceps and personalities to match stage names like Olga Tchikaboumskaya ('The White Rhinestone of Russian Ballet'), Nina Enimenimynimova and Margaret Lowin-Octeyn, D.B.E. Skilful and loving parodists of everything from the classical ballet repertory to the works of **George Balanchine**, **Martha Graham** and **Jerome Robbins**, the Trocks do not knock down so much as send up the conventions and pretensions of the dance world. Their witty, pitiless mockery extends as far as the ritual of fulsome curtain calls and gushing programme notes.

The group's gleeful good humour is grounded in accomplished technique. The dozen dancers, all of whom take ballet class daily, could not be so hilarious without being serious about their craft: their version of the 'Four Cygnets' sequence from **Swan Lake** is step-perfect. Some of their ballets have even been staged by the former **Kirov Ballet** dancers Alexander Minz and Yelena Tchernichova. Clearly the Trocks both satisfy and transcend the demands of knockabout drag.

Lineage

Ballet in drag (*en travesti*) has been around for centuries. There was even a period at the end of the Romantic era when the pendulum swung to the opposite extreme: Parisian ballet in the 1870s was so obsessed with the female form that a ballerina's partner was another woman dressed as a man. Peter Anastos, co-founder and star ballerina of the Trocks, has, since leaving, co-choreographed **Cinderella** with **Mikhail Baryshnikov** for **American Ballet Theatre** and Pennsylvania Ballet. His *Yes, Virginia, Another Piano Ballet* is a brilliant burlesque of **Jerome Robbins'** **Dances at a Gathering**. Several contemporary dancemakers, including **Michael Clark**, **Lindsay Kemp** and **Mark Morris**, sometimes bend genders with a similarly anarchic spirit.

Pina Bausch

Born: 27th July 1940/Solingen, West Germany

She has little curiosity about the work of her contemporaries and is utterly disinterested in the legion of younger dance artists who claim her as a mentor. She does not teach and refuses all offers of commissions or pleas to restage her works on other companies. Even so, Pina Bausch and her Wuppertal Tanztheater (dance-theatre) have exerted the most pervasive influence on European dance since **Serge Diaghilev** and his Ballets Russes.

Bausch's spectacles (four hours is not an unusual length for her works) are brutal representations of modern man's isolation - not only from other human beings, but even from his own inner self. Desolate, funny, violent, grand and messy, her creations polarise people: audiences are either captured by the mystique or driven away in loathing. The only reaction Bausch never elicits is indifference.

Bausch began studying with **Kurt Jooss** at his Essen Folkwang School. She had been there three years when a tour performance by the **José Limón** company fired her desire to go to New York. She spent a year at the Juilliard School of Music, where she worked with Limón and **Antony Tudor**, a season in the Metropolitan Opera's ballet company (then directed by Tudor), and then one season dancing with **Paul Taylor**. In 1963, she returned to work with Jooss.

A decade later she staged her first works for Wuppertal's opera house. These individualistic opera stagings led to an invitation to found a Wuppertal dance company. Since choreographing Stravinsky's **Le Sacre du printemps** and the Brecht/Weill *The Seven Deadly Sins* in the mid-1970s, Bausch has focussed on her own original creations.

Her works weld dialogue, dance, elements of psychoanalysis, comedy and sheer terror into grandiose, outsized epics. Her international company of twenty-six performers seem to use the innermost secrets of their lives as the springboard into these performances. They spew out their guts both physically and emotionally with an honesty that has become a byword for all of the Bausch imitators.

This sense of truthfulness and reality is heightened by Bausch's designs. Her works have taken place on stages strewn with dead leaves (*Bluebeard*, 1977), grass (*1980*), earth churned into mud (*Le Sacre du printemps*, 1975), or ankle-deep in water (*Arien*, 1979). In *Nelken* (Carnations, 1982) the stage is entirely covered in a field of fifteen thousand pink and white flowers. This bucolic landscape is patrolled round the edges by uniformed guards (the real thing, not actors), each with an Alsatian on a leash. Early on in the piece, the male dancers, in bright, ill-fitting party frocks, come sneaking into this field on hands and knees. Giggling, they erupt into a game of leapfrog, at which point the dogs go crazy, barking furiously, straining against their chains in an effort to get at the dancers. A black-suited man begins to chase the jumpers, who leapfrog out of his reach like scared rabbits. The one he catches is looking suitably embarrassed at being caught out in a lady's dress when the comedy suddenly flip-flops. Coldly, the man in black demands 'Passport', and the laughing audience is pulled up short, caught in a primal nightmare where fun must be paid for, where authority figures have the power to punish any deviation from a set of imposed rules.

Bausch is even less hopeful about the possibility of relationships between men and women. In piece after piece, her women are eternal victims who are used, battered and scorned by manipulative, thick-skinned men. In turn, their taunting humiliation of the men is no more charitable or optimistic.

One of the quintessential Bausch images comes from her shortest work, the thirty-five minute *Café Müller* (1978, the only piece in the repertory in which Bausch herself still appears). She plays a sleep-walker in a flimsy white shift who shuffles amongst the chairs and tables while other characters (implicitly figments of her imagination, memories from her childhood) suffer all forms of rejection. A woman repeatedly throws herself into a man's arms, but he does not bother to catch her. Instead, he lets her slip through his arms and fall to the ground. This fails to stop her from repeating the same action again and again with the same predictable results, but she either will not learn or is incapable of learning. Instead, she simply grows more frantic, increasing her speed until by the end of this long sequence, she is no longer even trying to jump into his arms, but throwing herself at his feet, clambering up and tossing herself down again as fast as she can. Small wonder that Bausch's theatre of despair both mesmerises and repels.

Lineage

Anna Sokolow explored brutality back in the 1950s. She also used realistic movements rather than conventional dance steps, but she stopped short of the autobiographical tone which permeates Bausch's work to its core. **Kei Takei**'s bleak vision shares Bausch's techniques of repetition and violent action. Bausch's influences, **Kurt Jooss** and **Antony Tudor** (together with **Paul Taylor** in his blackest moods), sought for truth and psychological depth. She has extended their acute focus into what *New Yorker* critic Arlene Croce has dubbed the 'pornography of pain'.

A list of German, Dutch, French, Belgian and Italian choreographers who have been influenced by Bausch would amount to a catalogue of half the Continent's dancemakers. The major, though by no means only, British exponent of Bausch's methods is **DV8 Physical Theatre**.

Follow-up

There are several Pina Bausch performance videos including *Café Müller* and *1980*. Film-maker Chantal Ackerman's award-winning documentary, *Pina Bausch and Her Company*, includes brief excerpts from several works. The two critical poles are summed up in the laudatory Norbert Servos volume, *Pina Bausch Wuppertal Dance Theatre or The Art of Training a Goldfish* (1984) and in Arlene Croce's scathing 'Bad Smells' article from *Sight Lines* (1987). *Pina Bausch* (1986) is a collection of performance shots by French photographer Guy Delahaye. The most succinct and human encapsulation of Bausch comes from Paul Taylor's autobiography, *Private Domain* (1987): 'At Juilliard she was one of Tudor's favorite students, and he seemed to enjoy seeing her go up on point. Besides causing her a sorrowful expression, this made her look even skinnier.'

Tim Buckley

Born: 12th December 1953/Indiana

Although he lives and works in New York City much of the time, Timothy Buckley has a country boy's distrust and dislike of the big city and its pressures. This does not prevent his rollicking dances from being packed with dynamic activity that zings along at a pace more suited to Manhattan streets than wide-open fields. Even when he evokes middle-America hearth-and-home values, he does so with a far from innocent irony. The tics, traumas and arguments that infuse his dances are a long way from the ideal of mom, pop and the kids on a Sunday picnic.

After graduating from Ohio State University, Buckley moved to New York and was soon dancing with Nina Wiener; he and **Bebe Miller** were among Wiener's earliest

229

company members. At first glance, Wiener (a three-year veteran of **Twyla Tharp**'s company in its most austere days) seems an unlikely mentor for Buckley. Her work is precise, cerebral, even fastidious, but, with both Buckley and Miller on board, she quickly discovered that she also had a liking for speed. Moving fast and moving a lot are the things Buckley likes to do best. He started to create his own choreography while still dancing with Wiener: his *Irish Jumping Songs* was performed by her company.

Buckley formed his own troupe of four (Tim Buckley and the Troublemakers) after leaving Wiener in 1982. Works such as *How to Swing a Dog* and *Barn Fever* are a mix of down-home scruffiness, echoes of square dances and explosions of supersonic speed. The steps are big, bold, brash and intricately constructed.

The sunny surface appeal of the Troublemakers quickly led to European engagements, and in 1984 the troupe spent five months working out of Düsseldorf's Werkstatt and touring through West Germany. For eight weeks of the next season, Buckley was in London creating *Breakneck Hotel* for the now defunct Mantis Dance Company. This piece had all the Buckley hallmarks – the speed, the sense of a bickering family (in this case a dance troupe out on the road), the use of strong, sharply honed movements culled from his country roots – but, as usual, Buckley pushed things to a funny, ironic and near chaotic overload. He wants his audiences to have a good time, but he is also warning them not to forget that rural day-dreams stand little chance in the real world.

In 1986, Buckley disbanded his company and suffered a serious knee injury which seemed to mark the early end of a promising career. He spent some time working in the costume shop of Joseph Papp's Public Theatre in New York and underwent experimental laser surgery. After nearly two years of remedial exercises, Buckley was able to perform and choreograph again, returning to Europe for an Amsterdam-based project in the autumn of 1988.

Lineage

Steve Paxton and **Dana Reitz** are just two of the major American dancers who have broken the stranglehold of New York City by heading for more salubrious environments. Like Buckley, Tim Miller is a choreographer who splits his time between New York and other locations, and one of the first things **Mark Morris** did after his company became successful was to move back to his hometown of Seattle. Buckley's love of Americana is something he shares with **Dan Wagoner**, but neither of them can match another country boy, **Paul Taylor**, at finding, digging into and exposing the rot beneath the dream.

Rosemary Butcher

Born: 4th February 1947/Bristol

For years Rosemary Butcher inhabited a secret garden. Her choreography has a self-contained, quiet assurance that is often difficult to describe and even more difficult to see. She has shunned theatres in favour of performances on beaches, atop Scottish mountains, in art galleries and other unorthodox settings. Although she has choreographed more than thirty pieces since 1976 and has taken part in seven of the first ten Dance Umbrella festivals, it is only recently that her work has begun to receive broad-based attention.

The first contemporary dance graduate from Dartington College in Devon (1969), Butcher went to New York where post-modernists **Trisha Brown**, **Steve Paxton** and **Lucinda Childs** and their stripped-

Tim Buckley (on right of picture) with Frank Conversano

to-essentials choreography exerted a strong influence on her development. Butcher's pristine regard for the process of creativity means that her works are a continuing exploration of ideas about performance. One of the main expressions of this process is the way she collaborates with artists, film-makers and composers. All are equal contributors to the eventual outcome. Artist Dieter Pietsch (who has been collaborating with Butcher since 1981) and the choreographers both firmly insist that their works are mutually incomplete without the other's.

Butcher's choreography falls into two distinct modes, each related to different minimalist tenets. *Flying Lines* (1985), with a solo piano score by Michael Nyman and an installation by Peter Noble, is akin to Childs' work. It is filled with cantering, repetitive patterns that skim along with a bouncy spring. In contrast, *Touch the Earth* (1986) is a meditative piece supported by a delicate Nyman score (for violin, viola and two female voices) and Pietsch's attenuated sculptural poles, which the dancers move around the space. This work is as quiet as *Flying Lines* is speedy. The actions in *Touch the Earch* are measured, contemplative, ritualistic. Seen side by side, these two works reflect the major strands of Butcher's attempts to produce a personal form of dance with the sort of compelling focus and integrity found in the choreography of **Merce Cunningham**.

Lineage

Martha Graham incorporated sculptor Isamu Noguchi's settings into her dances, but unlike Butcher's work with artists, one always has the sense that Noguchi's set pieces (brilliant and imaginative though they may be) were there to fulfil Graham's ideas rather than interact with them. **Merce Cunningham** has been equally intent on working with major artists, but he gives them such total independence that their work can actually obstruct the dancing. **Trisha Brown**'s collaborations probably come closest to the symbiotic give-and-take which Butcher strives to create.

Follow-up

A video of *Touch the Earth* was filmed in 1988 for inclusion in the second BBC *Dancemakers* series; the locale is an abandoned tobacco warehouse on the Bristol docks.

The Cholmondeleys

Formed: 1984, as The Cholmondeley Sisters

The British female quartet The Cholmondeleys (pronounced, like the surname, chum-leez) are endowed with the kind of quirky originality that inspires cult followings. They are expert practitioners of a dry-humoured, succinct performance style. Bucking the trend towards evening-length extravaganzas, chief choreographer and dancer Lea Anderson has created a sharp repertory of short pieces that have the brevity and punch of pop songs, minus the clichés.

An art school drop-out who later dabbled in the rock business, Anderson met fellow dancers Teresa Barker and Gaynor Coward while all three were studying at the Laban Centre for Movement and Dance in London. They formed themselves into a group whose name is derived from a double portrait of Elizabethan sisters in the Tate Gallery. Rossana Sen joined them in 1986, after they had cut their performing teeth in small clubs, cabarets, outdoors and, once, in a tunnel under the Thames.

None of the Cholmondeleys has a ballerina's body; they are built instead for precision, impact and speed. Their material is solidly rooted in code-like gestures: Anderson can get more mileage out of a little finger or jabbing fist than any English choreographer since **Frederick Ashton**. She colours basic movements with a fresh, stereotype-challenging style that raises idiosyncrasy to a fine art. Her strong, almost obsessive use of unison and repetition never negates the dancers' individual qualities, even in *Dragon* (1985), a fierce pressure-cooker of blunt motions performed as a canon.

The Cholmondeleys can be accomplished deadpan dance comediennes, as in *Baby, Baby, Baby* (1985), a signature work set to a Nina Simone recording, which is like seeing what goes on in the heads of a 1960s all-girl group got up in 1940s garb. In *The Clichés and the Holidays* (1985), they use the wail of Catalan folk music as the source of straight-faced pseudo-Spanish camp. Constructed around a shipping forecast soundtrack, *Fish Wreck* (1987) finds the group conducting a relay race on the high seas; the tone is similarly aquatic in *Marina* (1986), a witty and oddly moving piece danced to opera extracts by Bizet, Verdi and Rossini.

Beneath the droll comedy are some serious observations about human behaviour and attitudes. In *No Joy* (1987), Anderson uses deaf and dumb sign language to create a dark, claustrophobic realm in which one dancer's manipulation of another's face speaks volumes about passivity and dominance.

In 1988, Anderson officially expanded her choreographic repertory to include the opposite sex: men had previously only made brief cameo appearances. Her male sextet called The Featherstonehaughs (again, like the surname, pronounced fan-shaws) engage in slightly rougher interpretations of her co-ordinated aggressions and peculiarities. *Clump* is a tight, terse and trickily timed examination of the male herd instinct; in *Slump*, based partly on the iconographic body language of James Dean, the dancers shift between poses as buddies, rival and loners. Anderson has also taken the inevitable next step: to performances with men and women sharing the stage.

Lineage

Lea Anderson has choreographed for other companies, including Transitions, the Laban Centre's performing unit (other Laban alumni include Adventures in Motion Pictures and Jacob Marley). She often makes dances that are seriously witty, as **Merce Cunningham**, **David Gordon** and **Mark Morris** sometimes do. Her humour has none of the anarchy of **Michael Clark** — her dances only imply incongruities and outlandish situations.

Michael Clark in the 'dinosaur' outfit designed by Bodymap for the 1987 production *Because We Must*

Michael Clark

Born: 2nd June 1962/Aberdeen, Grampian

The vigorous vitality perpetuated by Michael Clark often approaches anarchy. Up-ending nearly every conceivable rule, he careers through the urban world of clubs, pubs, pop music and rebellious attitudes towards sex and society — all in search of the ultimate good time. His performances have featured cross-dressing, nudity, bagpipes, life-sized spouting teapots, purring pornographic soundtracks and rock music loud enough to make your teeth vibrate. This would add up to nothing more than an underground cabaret were it not for the fact that somewhere at the centre of all this hectic activity there lurks a prodigiously inventive choreographer who can, when he bothers to do so, create lean, abstract and totally satisfying movement rich in its own invention. His critics would prefer more choreography and fewer shenanigans, but Clark subversively chooses to gear his dance-theatre events to a mass, mostly young, audience.

At the age of four, Clark asked to start taking Scottish dance lessons. He was brought into the **Royal Ballet** School when he was thirteen and was quickly recognised as one of the most promising dancers of his generation. Four years later, he decided to walk out because he could no longer reconcile his real life with the ivory-tower mentality of ballet. He danced with **Ballet Rambert** from 1979 to 1981, where **Richard Alston** created several works for him, including *Dutiful Ducks* and the solo in silence, *Soda Lake*. After a summer school with **Merce Cunningham**, Clark began devising his own choreography and working as a dancer with **Karole Armitage**.

Clark's own company was launched in 1984 as a duo with the Dutch-born Ellen van Schuylenburch. The troupe quickly became a quartet and has been expanding steadily ever since. His major evening-length creations include *our caca phony H. our caca phony H.* (1985), *No Fire Escape in Hell* (1986) and *Because We Must* (1987). All have integrated non-dancers, hoards of extras and, wherever feasible, live music. *I Am Curious Orange* (1988), a commission from the Holland Festival, marked a turning point in his output. For the first time Clark created a piece where dance (albeit dolled up in a variety of out-landish guises) was the central focus of the evening. Without abandoning his party atmosphere, Clark crafted his sense of fun into a cascade of non-stop dancing which even included his first serious use of point shoes. Van Schuylenburch performed a languorous lament (supported by a pair of men disguised as lavender windmills, complete with battery-powered sails on their heads). There were hints of both **Merce Cunningham** and **George Balanchine** here, but after finishing her ballet turn, van Schuylenburch flopped to the floor, tore off her shoes, flung them into the wings and launched into a fast and furious solo reminiscent of no one but Clark himself.

Other companies who have commissioned works from Clark include the **Paris Opéra Ballet** (both the main company and the experimental GRCOP), Scottish Ballet and **London Festival Ballet**. His most enduring work for another company, *Swamp*, was created for Ballet Rambert's Diamond Jubilee season in 1986. It is dark, compelling and free of all campy clutter.

Lineage

Michael Clark's scattershot approach sets out to spoof self-important attitudes in the dance world, but also attempts to find a legitimate new format for enter-tainment. There are influences of both **Merce Cunningham** and **Richard Alston** in his choreo-graphy, but his use of fractured phrasing, outrageous designs and love of speed are more closely linked to **Karole Armitage**. Both Clark and Armitage have worked repeatedly with Charles Atlas, an American film-maker, designer and lighting specialist who has also worked with Cunningham. Clark's other principal designers are Leigh Bowery and Bodymap.

Follow-up

Clark appears as a dancer in Karole Armitage's videos *Parafango* and *Romance*, filmed by Charles Atlas. Clark and his company collaborated with Atlas on *Hail the New Puritan* (1986), a 'day in the life of' fantasy biography which is sparked off by a running parody of Richard Lester's film *A Hard Day's Night* (1964). There is also a half-hour documentary, *Michael Clark's 'No Fire Escape in Hell'* (1987).

Martha Clarke

Born: 3rd June 1944/Baltimore, Maryland

One of the first female members of **Pilobolus Dance Theatre**, Martha Clarke has since emerged as a major alternative theatrical visionary. Her productions are like lovingly prepared stews of tableaux, dance and movement, text and music.

Clarke started dance classes at the age of six; seven years later, while at a riding camp in Colorado, she was cast by the classically-trained dancer-choreographer Helen Tamiris in her *Ode to Walt Whitman*. She also spent summers at the American Dance Festival in Connecticut, studying with **José Limón**, **Alvin Ailey**, Charles Weidman, **Anna Sokolow** and Louis Horst, an associate of **Martha Graham** (after whom Clarke had been named). Clarke subsequently trained under Horst at the Juilliard School of Music, creating dance movements which

were based on impressionist paintings and primitive and medieval art.

She joined Sokolow's company for a few years before moving to Rome with her sculptor husband. There the couple immersed themselves in Italian art. On their return to Connecticut, Clarke's husband became resident artist at Dartmouth College, where the relatively untrained male quartet Pilobolus was just beginning to sprout. Clarke and the men's teacher Alison Chase joined the group in 1972, expanding its scope and bringing a shot of technical polish.

Within Pilobolus's mutating onstage universe, Clarke was often cast as a gorgeous clown. Her darker, more dramatic side was best revealed in Crowsnest, the company she founded with the Frenchman Félix Blaska and Pilobolus member Robby Barnett. She co-choreographed *The Garden of Villandry*, about a woman caught between two men, as a tribute to **Antony Tudor**, her choreographic role model. In the solo *Nocturne*, she portrayed a bare-breasted woman in a Romantic tutu, her face wrapped in gauze. This pathetic creature's dance is a haunting metaphor for loss, showing that Clarke, like **Paul Taylor**, could mine the vitality inside the grotesque.

Clarke expanded the creative scope of her work via an ingenious 1984 staging of Hieronymus Bosch's famous phantasmagorical triptych *The Garden of Earthly Delights*. Like all her spectacles, this allegory of Heaven and Hell was created collectively through months of carefully documented improvisations at her farmhouse.

In 1986 she made *Vienna: Lusthaus*, a deliberately fragmentary evocation of the atmosphere of the city before the First World War. Here Clarke drew on the paintings of Gustav Klimt and Egon Schiele and (indirectly) the writings of Freud and Wittgenstein for inspiration. Her next piece, a response to the life and literature of Kafka, was entitled *The Hunger Artist* (1987) and shared with its predecessors the transitory vividness of dreaming. In 1988, she staged the controversial multi-media production *Miracolo d'Amore*, based on a collection of Italianate fairy tales; the same year, she produced her early Crowsnest trio *The Garden of Villandry* for **American Ballet Theatre**.

Lineage

Clarke credits Louis Horst with teaching her how to use pre-existing art to make new art, and from **Anna Sokolow** she learned how to harness her natural predilection for emotion-based movement. Although she shares with **Pilobolus Dance Theatre** the ability to straddle the boundaries between dance and theatre, she differs in her **Antony Tudor**-like interest in sub-text. Once called 'the Federico Fellini of theatre-dance', she cites film-makers Ingmar Bergman and Luchino Visconti as equally valuable influences. Like **Pina Bausch**, **Lindsay Kemp**, **Maguy Marin** and others, Clarke concocts epic collages from a variety of performance disciplines.

Follow-up

Clarke is one of the dancers in an incomplete 1966 film of Anna Sokolow's *Rooms*. Joyce Choppra's 1981 documentary *Martha Clarke, Light and Dark: A Dancer's Journal/Journey* chronicles her transitions after leaving both her husband and Pilobolus.

Anne Teresa De Keersmaeker

Born: 11th June 1960/Mechelen, Belgium

The choreography of Anne Teresa De Keersmaker fuses the rigours of American minimalism (built on repeating patterns in the style of **Lucinda Childs**) with the emotive European expressionism spawned by **Pina Bausch**. The outcome is a compelling, exhaustive display of relentless energy deepened by De Keersmaeker's invitation to see her dancers from a dramatic point of view. American pattern-makers, such as Childs and **Laura Dean**, approach movement with an aesthetic distance and focus almost exclusively on acts of doing. De Keersmaeker, while following this path choreographically, deliberately engages our sympathies by colouring the movement with overtones that half emerge, disappear, or spark off ideas of oppression, violence and despair.

De Keersmaeker studied for two years at Mudra, the school in Brussels founded by **Maurice Béjart**, where she created her first piece *Asch* in 1980. She then spent a year in America at New York University's School of the Arts. The first two sections of *Fase* were performed there and were later expanded to four parts for a Belgian debut. This duet was set to four pieces of music by Steve Reich, one of the minimalists' most popular composers.

Rosas, De Keersmaeker's own company, was formed in 1983 and launched with the single-act, evening-length *Rosas Danst Rosas*. The next year she switched from minimalist music to recordings by Caruso for *Elena's Aria*, which also included her first use of both spoken text and film fragments. *Bartók/Aantekeningen* followed in 1986. These works, all quartets, often performed at gruellingly high speed, are for identically dressed women working in tight unison patterns. They begin the Bartók in tight black dresses and high heels and are soon forced to hitch up their skirts to hip level in order to accomplish the wide-stepping patterns. Eventually they abandon their high heels and later (in full view of the audience) change into loose, full-skirted dresses and lace-on ankle-high boots. The change seems to transform them from highly-strung modern women into schoolgirls cavorting in their gym uniforms. Snippets of text and film are interspersed with the music of Bartók's Fourth String Quartet; these elements flesh out the vigour and astonishing precision of the dancers. The way in which the four women alternate the text (Charlotte Corday's monologues from Peter Weiss's *Marat/Sade*) makes them appear to be differing facets of a single consciousness, a view reinforced by their unison movements.

In 1987, De Keersmaeker took her growing interest in text even further, with a dance-theatre production of *Verkommenes Ufer Medeamaterial Landschaft mit Argonauten* (by East German writer Heiner Müller). Like Müller's *Hamletmachine* (staged by **Robert Wilson**), this uses *Medea* only as a starting point for modern ruminations. She also staged Bartók's *Mikrokosmos*, seven pieces for two pianos, as a solo for Rosas member Johanna Saunier.

Lineage

Anne Teresa De Keersmaeker's individual synthesis of seemingly opposing styles is one of the most original choreographic concepts of the 1980s. Obviously influenced by **Lucinda Childs**, and often devising choreography that demands as much physical stamina as the works of **Molissa Fenley**, De Keersmaeker is just as clearly bringing a European sense of drama into play. Like so many choreographers, from **Martha Graham** to **Trisha Brown**, **Twyla Tharp** and **The Cholmondeleys**, she first began making dances with an all-female ensemble. She maintains that this is not a political statement so much as a desire to retain a unison appearance of style. One of De Keersmaeker's first dancers, the Italian Adriana Borriello, has started a company which playfully toys with this sense of precision; the Amsterdam-based Krisztina de Chatel achieves a sense of theatre in her pattern pieces by pitting the dancers against the settings: a row of powerful industrial fans or a square of glass walls relentlessly closing in on the performers.

DV8 Physical Theatre

Formed: 1986

Lloyd Newson's choreography for DV8 Physical Theatre pulls no punches, either physically or emotionally. Rather than providing pat answers or pretty pictures, DV8 aims at probing issues and exposing the ways real people love and hurt one another. This deliberately bald approach is an attempt at coming to grips with raw emotions and their implications – not only in a dance context, but also in everyday life. How the dancers perform is meant to make the viewer wake up to how he or she may be performing as well. There is no holding back, no playing safe, no faking it.

Newson, the company's founder and choreographer, did not start dancing until he was in college, and he already had a post-graduate degree in psychology from the University of Melbourne before he had his first professional dance job in 1979. Unlikely as it may seem, this was with the New Zealand Ballet (he had been the only man to turn up at the audition). Newson came to Britain in 1980 and spent a year at London Contemporary Dance School before joining **Extemporary Dance Theatre** (from 1981 to 1985). While dancing with the company he choreographed the prophetically titled *Breaking Images* (1982) and *Beauty, Art and the Kitchen Sink* (1984), a piece of fanciful dance-theatre as large and even as unwieldy as its name. By the time he left Extemporary, he was earning extra money choreographing pop videos.

Newson formed DV8 in 1986 with Nigel Charnock and Michelle Richecoeur; they were soon joined by Liz Ranken. As with Second Stride and Extemporary, this DV8 core group works on a flexible project-by-project basis. Some works have been swelled by huge numbers of extras, while the company's first big hit *My Sex, Our Dance* (1987) was a duet for Charnock and Newson. This work is filled with daring physical risks which parallel the emotional risks that occur when two men attempt to go beyond polite surface conventions and genuinely try to relate to each other. *Deep End* (also 1987) is a quartet where the two women struggle to assert their own identities and needs in relation to both the men and to each other. These works were choreographed by Newson, but all the performers had strong input during the working process.

My Body, Your Body (1987) is DV8's most disturbing creation to date. Its cast of eight women and eight men act out some of society's most blatant sexual stereotypes. The urgency and desperation boils over in confrontation after confrontation. In one long, brutal sequence, the women (hobbled by bandages tied round their knees) try to keep pace behind their men. This gradually builds into a horrific, self-destructive race.

Dead Dreams of Monochrome Men (1988) is a male quartet which deals with the conflicting poles of desire and loneliness. In December 1988, DV8 became the second London company to be included in the annual international Next Wave Festival at the Brooklyn Academy of Music. (In 1986, **Michael Clark**'s company was the first UK dance troupe to be invited to participate in this prestigious showcase.)

Lineage

Lloyd Newson's non-narrative, but dramatically emotional dance-theatre is linked to the work of **Pina Bausch**. The physical intensity of his choreography has its roots in contact improvisation techniques, but Newson also uses pedestrian movement, heightened to the point of stylisation through repetition and choice of emphasis. Like **Anne Teresa De Keersmaeker**, Newson is challenging assumptions rather than providing answers.

Follow-up

My Sex, Our Dance and *Deep End* were adapted for video by Newson in 1987.

Extemporary Dance Theatre

Formed: 1975, as Extemporary Dance Company

From its inception, Extemporary Dance Theatre's commitment to new dance has been reflected in a repertory which has gradually evolved in response to changing attitudes towards post-modern dance. Conceived by Geoff Powell, the company's first director, as a kind of half-way house to bridge the gap between London Contemporary Dance School and full-scale professional companies like **Ballet Rambert** and **London Contemporary Dance Theatre**, Extemporary has been instrumental in taking new dance to small theatres and out-of-the-way areas of the UK.

Initially the style was dominated by the **Martha Graham** technique, which is the foundation of both London Contemporary Dance Theatre and School (the first company were all recent graduates of LCDS). Paul Taras, a former Rambert dancer who took over as director in 1978, broadened the repertory, but it was the 1981 appointment of Emilyn Claid, an experimental dancer-choreographer, which moved the company away from contemporary dance towards the more adventurous ideas of post-modern choreography.

Claid immediately began to commission works from radical young choreographers such as **Michael Clark**, **Karole Armitage** and **Daniel Larrieu** (all of whom were just establishing themselves). In retrospect, Clark's *1 2 X U*,

Extemporary Dance Theatre's 1988 circus-inspired dance *Suddenly out of the Blue . . .*

Armitage's *It Happened at Club Bombay Cinema* and Larrieu's *Ombres Electriques* only hinted at what each would later produce, but that does not minimise their importance at the time. **Dan Wagoner** also contributed works, as did Lloyd Newson, then a dancer with the company and now director of **DV8 Physical Theatre**. Claid's interest in new trends can be seen in all of these works and particularly in the trio of pieces she commissioned from **David Gordon**: *Counter Revolution* (1981). *Field Study* (1985) and *Bach and Offenbach* (1987). The first is filled with counting games, the second uses the Gordon motif of chairs, the third plays off Bach cello against an Offenbach concerto. No other company in Britain was presenting such a diverse sampling of the latest trends in new dance. In 1986, the company produced a single evening-length work by Claid herself, *Pier Rides* (with a commissioned score from jazz composers Kate and Mike Westbrook). Extemporary's 1987 dance-theatre piece, *Grace and Glitter* explored the lives of three black and three white British women. This was followed in 1988 by *Suddenly Out of the Blue . . .*, created by a variety of choreographers and capped off by aerial dancing borrowed from the world of circus. Extemporary then announced a new policy for 1989 onwards, moving away from the 'abstract exploration of movement' towards 'dance as a theatrical tradition of performance'.

Lineage

Extemporary's repertory has offered more diversity than Second Stride's, but has never equalled that company's vital, trendsetting profile. One reason is that the Extemporary dancers tend to be young performers, while Second Stride's company includes some of the most experienced of British dancers. Several schools now have programmes aimed at providing similar performance experience. The Laban Centre in London has had great success with its company Transitions; 4D is an outgrowth of a class (number 4D) at London Contemporary Dance School; while Adventures in Motion Pictures is made up of Laban Centre graduates who have decided to stay together as an ensemble. As with the small ballet troupe **Dance Advance**, the value of Extemporary is in what the company is attempting to do rather than in the specific works they perform.

Molissa Fenley

Born: 15th November 1954/Las Vegas, Nevada

The high-energy propulsion at the centre of Molissa Fenley's choreography is based on a physical fitness regimen that includes a daily five-mile run, swimming and working out with weights rather than traditional dance classes. Her work is laid out in relentless patterns of curvaceous geometry wedded to a reverberating musical beat and designed in sweeping, swinging arcs and circles that jump, twist and fly across the stage.

Fenley grew up in Nigeria and spent two years in Spain (her father worked for the US State Department) before going to Mills College in California to study dance. She moved to New York in 1976 and began choreographing for herself a year later. Her Manhattan debut was at the **Merce Cunningham** Studio with *Planets* (1978). Other major works include the quartet *Energizer* (1980), the hour-long solo *Eureka* (1982) and the group work *Hemispheres* (1983, with a score by jazz pianist Anthony Davis and a set of commissioned drawings by Francesco Clemente which were handed out to the audience as a programme). All of these pieces stress the perpetual motion and energetic drive of her choreographic style.

In 1986, Fenley created *Feral* for the Ohio Ballet and was also commissioned by the Adelaide Festival to choreograph *A Descent into the Maelstrom* (music by Philip Glass) for the Australian Dance Theatre. After disbanding her ensemble, she returned to solo work in 1988 with *State of Darkness*, which was inspired by the **Joffrey Ballet**'s 1987 reconstruction of **Le Sacre du printemps**. Fenley turned the monumental Stravinsky score into a compelling solo that revealed a new direction in her

work. The dancing is still awesome in the physical demands it puts on her, but now it also involves the sort of nuances and changes of tempos that tended to be ridden over in her earlier pieces.

Lineage

The patternings and repetitions found in the works of **Laura Dean** and **Lucinda Childs** are obvious precursors to Molissa Fenley's choreography, but her style also has a sensuality – in the use of her arms and the rotating and thrusting of her pelvis – which reveals how deeply her childhood in Africa and Spain has influenced her dance-making.

Follow-up

Fenley is one of the fifteen contemporary American choreographers who discuss their works in *Further Steps* (1987), edited by Connie Kreemer.

William Forsythe

Born: 30th December 1949/New York City

The iconoclastic American expatriate William Forsythe is one of the *wunderkinder* of European contemporary ballet. Even before he became artistic director of the Frankfurt Ballet in 1984, he had already poured some explosive new wine into ballet's old choreographic bottles.

After training at the **Joffrey Ballet** School in New York City, Forsythe joined Joffrey II in the 1970s and also performed occasionally with the main company. **John Cranko** invited him to **Stuttgart Ballet** in 1973. A short while later, Forsythe proved useful in helping to fill the choreographic void left by Cranko's death. His first ballet, the lyrical pas de deux *Urlicht* (1976, set to Mahler), was devised by Forsythe and his wife, ex-Joffrey dancer Eileen Brady, in their New

York living room. That same season, Stuttgart artistic director Marcia Haydée danced the title role in his new *Daphne*.

It was not until 1978 that Forsythe's leanings towards highly stylised experimentation became evident in *Dream of Galileo* (for Stuttgart) and a radical piece called *Event* which he produced and funded independently. *Orpheus* (1979) was a collaboration with Hans Werner Henze, playwright Edward Bond and dancer Richard Cragun which finally put Forsythe on the international map. These early dances struck the notes of creative rebellion and unpredictability that he has continued to develop, first at Stuttgart, then Frankfurt, and in commissions.

His major productions include a revue-style work on popular culture called *Say Bye Bye* (1980); *Gänge* (Going, 1983), a dense three-act opus on dance, language and society; and *Artifact* (1984) a succession of *coups de théâtre*, the most notorious of which is a section where the curtain slams down, rises and plunges again and again during a vigorous ensemble dance. In each, Forsythe conducts an anarchic investigation into the formal elements of dance and theatre, pushing the classical dance vocabulary to its extremes while turning the conventions of dance stagecraft inside out.

As the plunging curtain in *Artifact* demonstrates, Forsythe is not above employing shock tactics. His lighting effects can be deliberately, irritatingly obscure so that the dancing itself is scarcely visible. He places overpowering emphasis on stage mechanics, for example in *LDC* (1985), a Frankfurt piece featuring a massive turbine, one wall of loudspeakers and another of lights, and use of the world's largest turntable stage. Consequently, the dancers are usually subordinate to Forsythe's vision. Yet since he often requires them to speak or shout words and phrases into microphones and bullhorns, they must also function like actors.

In 1983, the Joffrey imported

Forsythe's battle of the sexes dance *Love Songs* (1979) to their repertory. Set to a soundtrack of Aretha Franklin-Dionne Warwick pop songs, this violent piece is performed in a full-throttle manner of constant emotional attack and release. It is Forsythe's best known choreography in America. Although Forsythe has commissioned work from up-and-coming choreographers like **Daniel Larrieu** and **Stephen Petronio**, his own choreography still dominates the Frankfurt repertory.

Lineage

William Forsythe takes the self-referential fragmentation of post-modern art (à la **Merce Cunningham**) to extremes. He adds a nihilistic edge to the trendy, eclectic showmanship of **Maurice Béjart** and shares with **Pina Bausch** a penchant for grand-scale surrealism. Like **Michael Clark**, he subverts his classical background on stage. Forsythe's choreography contains allusions to **George Balanchine**'s neo-classical style, but his athletic approach is actually closer to **John Cranko**.

Antonio Gades

Born: November 1936/Province of Alicante, Spain

The leading Spanish dancer of his generation, Antonio Gades significantly widened his international audience in the 1980s by collaborating with director Carlos Saura on *Blood Wedding*, *Carmen* and *A Love Bewitched*, among the most successful renderings of dance on film ever achieved.

Gades was born to Republican parents in the first year of the Spanish Civil War. His circuitous route to dance included a brief stint as a bullfighter, a skill he likens to choreography. At sixteen, having already danced in cabaret, he joined Pilar Lopez's company

Ballet Español and stayed for nine years. Afterwards he performed and choreographed mainly in Italy, where he worked with both **Anton Dolin** and major Italian ballerina Carla Fracci, and staged dances at La Scala, Milan, including *L'Amour Sorcier* (to music by Manuel de Falla). Invited to participate in the 1964 New York World's Fair, he formed a fifteen-member troupe that caused a sensation; he has toured sporadically since, making his London debut in 1970. Gades is a fascinating dancer who happens to prefer choreography to performance. The form he uses is a distillation of authentic flamenco, shaped more for overall dramatic impact than to showcase individual talents.

The association with Saura came about after the film director watched the Gades company rehearsing the flamenco ballet *Bodas de Sangre* (Blood Wedding), a stripped-down version of Lorca's play. Saura was so impressed that he set their 1981 film adaptation in a rehearsal studio, where Gades and his dancers are first seen applying their make-up before warming up in fiery flamenco fashion. This develops into a ceremonially spare production in which the rhythm of thudding heels, the eerie wail of Spanish song and the swirl of gipsy costumes accentuate the power of Lorca's tragedy. There is no scenery and only minimal props. *Carmen* (1983) was an even bigger hit with audiences and critics; the choreographer-director Antonio (played by Gades), seeking a lead for his ballet version of *Carmen*, finds the volcanically regal Cristina Hoyos. The backstage set-up leads to a sizzling fictional performance. *Carmen* was followed by a third film, the ghostly melodrama *El Amor Brujo* (A Love Bewitched, 1986), after de Falla's 1915 score.

Lineage

Gades belongs to a rich line of superlative exponents of Spanish dance, which originated with La Argentina (born 1890), a classically trained dancer who transformed her native folkloric movement into artistic perfection. Others include Pilar Lopez and her elder sister La Argentinita, Vicente Escudero, Carmen Amaya and Antonio (an electric performer who was as responsible for restoring male supremacy in Spanish dance as **Rudolf Nureyev** was in classical ballet). These performers demonstrated what an adult dance form flamenco is, never as dependent on youthful practitioners as ballet.

Follow-up

Apart from the three Saura films, an earlier Gades ballet, *Los Tarantos*, was filmed in 1964. A large, mainly photographic boxed volume (1984) is based on the Gades/Saura *Carmen*.

Earl Lloyd Hepburn

Born: 8th July 1966/Gloucester

The speed and energy found in many of Earl Lloyd Hepburn's pieces are not just manifestations of *Mindless Matter* (a title he used in 1985). The propulsion and risk are meant to push back the boundaries of limitation, but Hepburn's interest does not stem from the exhaustive endurance-test school that can be traced back to **Pina Bausch** and which reaches apocalyptic fury in the raucous style of the Montreal-based La La La Human Steps. Hepburn questions the meaning and emotional context behind strong physical actions rather than showing off his dancers' willingness to risk broken limbs.

After leaving school, Hepburn took a two-year foundation course in dance and choreography at Thamesdown Dance Studios in Swindon. This was followed by three years (from 1983 to 1986) at the London Contemporary Dance School. In 1985, when *Mindless*

Earl Lloyd Hepburn's Images Dance Company in Hepburn's *Beneath the Bridge*

Matter won a London competition, Viola Farber, one of his instructors, encouraged him to enter the prestigious international choreographic competition held in the Paris suburb of Bagnolet. Hepburn and his newly formed Images Dance Company won the 1986 first prize, the first British troupe ever to do so. The next season he was appointed choreographer in residence at The Place, the building which doubles as a busy performance space and as the home of the **London Contemporary Dance Theatre** and School. His subsequent works, *Left of Centre*, *Filligree and Penumbra* (both 1987) and the evening-length *Tectonics* (1988) have premiered at the Dance Umbrella festival. Images-appeared at the Karachi Cultural Festival in 1988, the first modern company to perform in Pakistan.

Hepburn, who designs his own sets, has a fondness for props that can extend or challenge the dancers' range of physical possibilities: wooden scaffolding to clamber up and jump off or planks used as ramps to run up or rest against (while the plank is momentarily held vertical by another dancer).

Lineage

The drive in Earl Lloyd Hepburn's choreography is not as consistently high-speed as **Molissa Fenley**'s, nor as deliberately repetitive as that of Lloyd Newson's **DV8**

Physical Theatre. As a black man, Hepburn (who does not perform himself) has had to combat the stereotypes which have conditioned British audiences to associate black dance artists with the Afro-Caribbean styles exemplified by Irie! and Adzido, two of the most successful British troupes working in the field. The multi-racial Union Dance Company aims for a modern, urban social awareness, while both Hepburn and Phoenix, the all-male black company based in Leeds, stress dance rather than racial issues. Like black American choreographer **Bebe Miller**, neither Hepburn nor Phoenix director Neville Campbell shows much interest in soapboxing.

Bill T. Jones and Arnie Zane

Bill T. Jones
Born: 15th February 1951/Bunnell, Florida

Arnie Zane
Born: 26th September 1947/New York City
Died: 30th March 1988/New York City

The lives and careers of Bill T. Jones and Arnie Zane blended together to produce a radical brand of art that could both startle by its physical beauty and challenge the viewer's attitudes and assumptions about everything from racism and sexuality to faith and nuclear armageddon. Jones and Zane were striking opposites: Jones is tall, black and moves with a juicy amplitude; Zane was small, white and tended to be sharp-angled and feisty. Their demanding, even athletic duets sometimes looked like a leopard and a bull terrier playing, teasing and taunting one another. These duets always contained dialogue based on aspects of their personal lives – both together and apart – and much of the movement had the free flow of contact improvisation. The pieces ranged from sizzling expansiveness to a contained intensity where the most private of confidences were exchanged *sotto voce*. The duo's major trilogy of one-act works, *Monkey Run Road*, *Blauvelt Mountain* (both 1979) and *Valley Cottage* (1980, the name of the upstate New York town where they lived) are among the most evocative and autobiographical danceworks of the era. They led to a spate of confessional talking-dances in the experimental dance world of the early 1980s.

Jones, who intended to be an actor, was in college on a sports scholarship (as a runner) when he discovered dance, first Afro-Caribbean and then contact improvisation. Zane, a photographer, was encouraged by Jones to take contact classes. They became co-founders of American Dance Asylum, a collective based in Binghamton, New York. While working there (from 1974 to 1976), they pursued separate careers. However, it was the mesh of their talents, the chemistry and contrast in their performing relationship, which brought them widespread artistic recognition.

After touring internationally as a duo, they went on to form Bill T. Jones/Arnie Zane and Dancers in 1982 and began to move towards a brighter, bouncier style which never abandoned their original concerns, but did seem to sub-merge them within a flashy party atmosphere. *Secret Pastures* (1984) had settings by hip graffiti artist Keith Haring, an art-rock score by Peter Gordon and costumes by fashion designer Willi Smith. In this propulsive allegory, choreo-graphed for twelve dancers, a mad scientist (Zane) creates a Fab-ricated Man (Jones) who, trans-formed into an overnight celebrity, succumbs to the temptations of modern society. The piece was a big hit and brought them a new mass audience, but devotees of the duets were not always happy about the trade-off of the duo's former intimacy for box-office popularity.

A 1983 commission from the **Alvin Ailey** American Dance Theatre led to Jones' vibrant dance for six men, *Fever Swamp*. Jones and Zane collaborated on a second Ailey work, *Ritual Ruckus (How to Walk an Elephant)*, in 1985.

Zane's death will obviously have an impact on the future direction of the company. Jones' first sub-sequent work bravely attempted to transform the fact of Zane's death and its repercussions into a work of art/tribute.

Lineage

Contact improvisation, as formulated by **Steve Paxton**, played an important role in the development of the Jones/Zane style. Among Jones' other early influences were **Garth Fagan** and **Kei Takei**. The duo's penchant for dialogue goes back to the Grand Union and the works of **David Gordon**. Tim Miller is another dancer who uses every aspect of his personal life as fodder for the stage. Lloyd Newson's choreo-graphy for **DV8 Physical Theatre** also explores sexual politics as one of its major themes.

Follow-up

Fever Swamp is part of a 1985 video by the Alvin Ailey American Dance Theatre, *Three by Three*. The Jones/Zane duet *Rotary Action* was co-commissioned by Channel 4 in London and WGBH-TV in Boston. Each talks about his work in *Further Steps* (1987, edited by Connie Kreemer).

Lindsay Kemp

Born: 1939(?)/Isle of Lewis(?)

To call a Lindsay Kemp production 'dance' is something of a misnomer. For Kemp, dance is an umbrella term under which he gathers an astonishing array of cultural influences and performing styles.

A descendant of Shakespeare's clown William Kemp, his training included painting, classical and modern dance and mime. During his performing career he has worked in cabaret, musical chorus lines, straight and experimental theatre, films, television, fashion shows and rock spectacles (he mounted David Bowie's *Ziggy Stardust* concert in the early 1970s). He gained additional notoriety as the creator of two pieces for **Ballet Rambert**: the Hollywood parody *The Parade's Gone By* (1975), a light warm-up for his own company's *The Big Parade*, and *Cruel Garden* (1977), a dazzling fantasy derived from the life and writings of Federico García Lorca, conceived by Kemp and choreographed by **Christopher Bruce**.

Kemp formed his first company in the early 1960s; members came and went, but core performers included the Incredible Orlando. The group functions like a peripatetic circus family, although each production ultimately reflects Kemp's sensibility - a glittering, often erotic camp flamboyance.

There is no such thing as a definitive Kemp production; each show keeps evolving, not always for the better. *Flowers* (1973), based freely on the life and writings of Jean Genet, now comes across as the epitome of grandiose 1970s avant-garde by way of Las Vegas. Time has been kinder to *A Midsummer Night's Dream* (1979). This sweet-spirited and sensual combination of Elizabethan psychedelia, commedia dell'arte, Victorian panto and the *Arabian Nights* uses Shakespeare as a springboard to concoct its own hermaphroditic enchantment.

Lineage
Kemp studied classical dance with **Marie Rambert**, modern dance with Charles Weidman and mime with Marcel Marceau. **Michael Clark** shares with Kemp an understanding of how life and art intertwine, each spilling over into the other so that performing becomes an extension of the artist's offstage existence.

Follow-up
Kemp's company has been repeatedly filmed by Celestino Coronado in films such as *The Lindsay Kemp Circus* and *A Midsummer Night's Dream*. As an actor, Kemp can be seen in the Ken Russell films *Savage Messiah* (1972) and *Valentino* (1977), Derek Jarman's *Sebastiane* (1975) and *Jubilee* (1977), and the 1973 cult thriller *The Wicker Man*. *Lindsay Kemp and Company*, a book of photographic studies by Anno Wilms was published 1987.

Daniel Larrieu

Born: 23rd November 1957/ Marseille

The streak of impish humour in Daniel Larrieu's choreography is encapsulated in the way he began working. In 1982, four years after he started performing, Larrieu formed his own troupe and dubbed it Astrakan. He picked the name of this Persian lamb for its associations with luxury and early death. At the beginning there was scant luxury about. He did not have enough money to rent a rehearsal studio, so he and the two women who made up his first company began rehearsing in the gardens of the Palais Royal in Paris. To the left was the tradition-steeped Comédie-Française, behind them the windows of Jean Cocteau's former apartment, but more importantly, to their right were the offices of the Ministry of Culture. Such sly contextual showmanship has always been a Larrieu strong suit.

The dances his trio created there won a 1982 prize at the annual Bagnolet choreographic competion (named after the Paris suburb where it is held). In *Un Sucre ou deux* (1982), Larrieu strings together a series of natural gestures - bending, reaching, walking - that look as if they come from a post-modern primer. The work is a duet for Larrieu and Pascale Houbin, who often perform their tasks as one another's mirror image. Without tampering with the movement's basic neutrality, Larrieu turns the piece into theatre by performing it in atmospheric lighting to extracts from Prokofiev's **Romeo and Juliet**. At first this incongruous dichotomy of lush music and simple movement seems a fine joke. But once he has destabilised his audience with the juxtapositions, he makes his point: the two dancers execute a simple flat-backed stretch, each with a single outstretched arm; they pause, the tips of their fingers only inches away from touching. In that instant the 'star-cross'd lovers' come to life as the coincidence of gesture, music, lighting and implied emotion solidify and American post-modern ethics are turned into French dance theatre. It is a moment to take your breath away.

Waterproof (1986), commissioned by the Centre National de Danse Contemporaine at Angers is destined to become one of the most popular avant-garde creations of the era. Nearly two years in the making, this hour-long event for nine dancers takes place in an Olympic-sized swimming pool. The performers all wear identical black tank-top bathing costumes and goggles. They do not try to ape dance on dry land, nor do they indulge in synchronised aquabatics. Instead, Larrieu has devised a whole new realm of movement possibilities built around the notion of dancing in water. During the performance, giant video screens, on the opposite side of the pool from the audience, project images from an underwater perspective. Sometimes the video duplicates the live action, but more often it serves as a counterpoint that distorts, replays or even pre-figures what is happening in the water. *Waterproof* has very little to do with swimming; water simply happens to be the element in which the dancing, languorous and serene, is taking place.

Larrieu has accepted commissions to stage an opera in Lyon, and danceworks for **London Contemporary Dance Theatre**, **Netherlands Dance Theatre** and the Frankfurt Ballet.

Lineage
Daniel Larrieu's wit links him to the American post-modern punster **David Gordon** and London's Lea Anderson, the choreographer for **The Cholmondeleys**. Other emerging French artists such as Francois Verret, Jean-Claude Gallotta or Régine Chopinot (with whom Larrieu performed in 1982) all lack Larrieu's sense of irony.

Follow-up
A half-hour distillation of *Waterproof* has been shown on British and European television.

Maguy Marin

Born: 2nd June 1951/Toulouse

Maguy Marin is the most established member of the French new wave, both artistically and with the general public. Her creations, evening-length and for large groups, have the sweep and scope of dance-theatre, but Marin (more than other exponents of this genre) consistently makes choreographed movement the focus.

She began studying dance in Toulouse at the age of eight, had her first job with the Strasbourg Opéra Ballet, and then moved to

Brussels to study at **Maurice Béjart**'s school, Mudra. She joined his Ballet of the 20th Century, and choreographed *Yu-ku-ri* for the company in 1976. She won the 1978 first prize at the Bagnolet international choreographic competition and that same year founded her own troupe, originally Ballet Théâtre de l'Arche, now called Compagnie Maguy Marin. In 1981, they became the resident company in the 'future village' Parisian suburb of Créteil.

May B (1981), based on Samuel Beckett's writings, is peopled by slump-backed characters with white chalky faces who move with a worn-out, weary shuffle. This atmospheric work perfectly captures the physical comedy within Beckett's bleak vision of a lost, stumbling humanity with nowhere to go.

Babel Babel (1982) begins in a primordial dawn where a naked tribe slowly tramps across the grassy hillocked stage. Their weighted, rhythmic walk is loose and relaxed; their soft, flowing gestures are bucolic and reminiscent of **Isadora Duncan**. Gradually accruing clothes, a synthetic language and bundles of possessions, they become refugees searching through a dark night for an ideal homeland. Finally choosing their spot, they begin to construct their living quarters. This sequence, with its many rhythmic hammerings, sawings and poundings, is accompanied by expansive, repeated gestures that look like a lost form of folk dancing. Another dawn reveals that their tents are actually multi-coloured plastic and their new home a modern campsite. A hilarious bridge between these sections has the dancers grunting out a work chant, forming a coolie line and passing along heavy loads of lawn furniture, picnic tables and beer coolers.

What follows is an almost cinematic montage that transforms dancers into character actors and archetypal clowns. This peaks when the bandshell bursts open to reveal a rock'n'roll chanteuse (Marin herself) complete with all-

Compagnie Maguy Marin in a performance of her Beckett-inspired work *May B*

girl back-up trio and sequin-suited band. They zip through pop history from the 1950s to screaming punk. When Marin's music degenerates into nasty militancy (she is now in black leather rags and chains) the dancers sink to fistfights and cat-calling. As the tents collapse in disarray and all hope seems lost to the hooligans, the dance undergoes a transformation that takes us back to the original clean, grassy plain. Crawling and slith-ering out of their sunsuits and bermuda shorts, the dancers (once again nude) seem to re-invent the birth of humanity and *Babel Babel* ends in a gentle burst of shining exultation.

In addition to working with her own troupe, Marin has choreo-graphed two one-act pieces for the **Paris Opéra Ballet** (*Jaleo*, 1983 for the experimental GRCOP, and *Leçon de ténèbres*, 1988 for the main company). Her best known work is **Cinderella**, staged for the Lyon Opéra Ballet in 1985. She tells the fairy tale from a child's point of view and all the characters wear masks that make them resemble nineteenth-century dolls. A second work for Lyon, the Brecht/Weill *The Seven Deadly Sins* (1987), was performed as a joint project with her own company. In 1988 she created her first work for the **Dutch National Ballet**.

Lineage

Maguy Marin is the most significant modern choreographer now working in France. Her spectacles are not nearly as cryptic as those of **Carolyn Carlson**, and while there are similarities to **Pina Bausch**, **Meredith Monk**, **Lindsay Kemp** and **Robert Wilson**, Marin alone consistently links her extravaganzas to a choreographic pulse. Even at its most spectacular and situational, Marin's theatre never abandons dancing for propaganda or polemics.

Follow-up

May B, *Babel Babel* and *Calambre* (a 1985 blend of post-modern tactics and flamenco) are available on video. Marin's version of *Cinderella* is scheduled for release in 1989.

Susan Marshall

Born: 17th October 1958/Hershey, Pennsylvania

The work of New York-based Susan Marshall continually reveals her fascination with the vagaries of the human condition. Her smart, streetwise, unsentimental choreography is emphatically about people, men and women who react to each other and make decisions onstage.

Marshall began her performing career in gymnastics (in the 1984 *Routine and Variations*, she affectionately parodies this background). From high school displays, she moved to the Dance Department of the Juilliard School of Music in New York, before branching out on her own. She has been making dance pieces for herself and her small company since 1982, acquiring a reputation as a choreographer who is as compassionate as she is gifted and

receiving commissions from the GRCOP (the experimental wing of **Paris Opéra Ballet**) and the Boston and Dallas Ballets.

Marshall professes to have no fixed movement vocabulary, instead tailoring her choreography to the needs of each piece. She is fond of taking a theme - sibling rivalry or female bonding, for example - and developing it fully, yet succinctly, so that it abounds with resonance. She excels at dances for duos and trios. Her signature piece *Arms* (1984) is an intimate and accelerating five-minute duet for the upper body, or more precisely the upper limbs. This work suggests a range of feelings, from aggression to tenderness, with admirable economy. *Ward* (1983), a grimmer duet, details the fluctuating levels of dominance and submission in a relationship. In *Kiss* (1987), Marshall suspends two harnessed dancers from ropes to explore their intertwining passions, while the trio *Opening Gambits* (1985) captures the unbridled energies and clumsy lust of early teenage.

She is, however, equally adept at making ensemble dances. *Overture* and *The Aerialist* (both 1987) share lush movement, a melancholic mood and Marshall's favoured theme of the ambiguities of growing up and growing apart. *Arena* (1986), on the other hand, is a full-bodied, sophisticatedly comic send-up of human nature refracted through ballroom dancing, which demonstrates Marshall's knack for defining character and revealing a psychological sub-text.

Lineage

The use of shifting weight and mutual support in Marshall's choreography suggests the influence of contact improvisation as developed by **Steve Paxton**. Although her interest in so-called pedestrian movement links her to post-modern pioneers like **Trisha Brown** and **Yvonne Rainer**, she is just as keen to highlight everyday behaviour and to employ a sense of drama, humour and emotion deliberately absent from the work of her predecessors.

Bebe Miller

Born: 20th September 1950/New York City

There is nothing neutral about Bebe Miller. One of the strongest talents on New York's busy dance scene, she balances white-hot emotional expressiveness with a thorough-going commitment to her craft.

The young Miller took creative dance workshops from Murray Louis, **Alwin Nikolais**' star dancer, on Manhattan's Lower East Side. She met ex-**Twyla Tharp** dancer Nina Wiener while studying art and dance in the Midwest and, from 1976, was a member of Wiener's company in New York for six formative years. After touring with **Dana Reitz**, Miller formed her own company in 1984.

Active as a choreographer since 1978, Miller's interest in formal choreographic issues has gradually been superseded by what *Village Voice* critic Deborah Jowitt has called 'dancing that has the feel of living'. Intimate and intense, Miller's work is as emotionally involving as it is technically involved. The blistering *Two* (1986, co-choreographed with Ralph Lemon) cuts to the heart of human needs and rejections; her 1985 *Spending Time Doing Things* is a deft, 'doodling around in a dance studio' solo; and in the dynamic group piece *A Haven for Restless Angels of Mercy* (1986), she homes in on the fundamental drama inherent in most movement. In all these dances, her full-blooded approach produces choreography that, while neither exactly narrative nor purely abstract, promotes a definite atmosphere and set of feelings.

The dancers in Miller's company share her determined, yet often delicate, onstage energy. She has harnessed this power and applied it to *The Hell Dances* (1987), a trilogy about turbulent relationships, in which the dancers' physical entanglements parallel the intangible forces affecting their behaviour.

Lineage

While it would be inaccurate to say that the fact Miller is black and female is incidental to her art, she does not regard herself as a minorities representative. Her edgy, volatile work is closer to **Bill T. Jones** than to the packaged ethnic stance of mainstream companies like **Alvin Ailey**'s. Her dances sometimes suggest the playful eccentricities of **Twyla Tharp** via Nina Wiener, and she is linked to **Stephen Petronio** and **Susan Marshall** by her interest in high-speed, rhythmic complexity and physical interaction, and her emphasis on themes to do with human nature. Despite her attention to evocative gestures, she is neither a miniaturist like Lea Anderson of **The Cholmondeleys** nor a minimalist like **Dana Reitz**.

Meredith Monk

Born: 20th November 1943/Lima, Peru

The distinctly personal aura of Meredith Monk's choreography has been enriched by her parallel careers as composer and filmmaker. Dance is just one of the components in her work and, unlike her contemporaries, she has never jettisoned the concept of characters and emotional involvement in favour of the pure abstractions of minimalism.

Raised in Connecticut, Monk was able to sing before she could talk and was reading music before she could read words (her mother was a professional singer who had been on tour in South America when Monk was born). She began dance classes at three and formal music studies shortly afterwards. By sixteen she was composing seriously. Monk graduated from Sarah Lawrence College in 1964 and, after a brief association with the Judson Dance Theatre, began to devise her music/theatre/dance events. Her company, The House, was formed in 1968 and, often augmented by large groups of extras, started presenting her works in a variety of unconventional venues. *Juice* (1969) invited the audience to drift along with the eighty-five performers as they gradually ascended the spiral ramp of Manhattan's Guggenheim Museum. When they arrived at the top, the cast turned round and dashed back to the ground floor, leaving the audience behind to watch their activities in the central courtyard far below. *Vessel* (1971) drew on the mystery of St Joan and was set in three different locations: it concluded in a parking lot where Monk, who is petite and fragile-looking, ended the piece by disappearing into the night through a shower of sparks from a welder's torch.

Education of the Girlchild (1971) was her first international success. It conjures up a society which is both prosaic and exotic. The performers, mostly women, execute mundane tasks with an everyday frankness that achieves a homely dignity. The second half is a keening, ululating vocal and dance solo for Monk. She begins seated on a dais draped in white, an ancient sybil imparting deep knowledge in a foreign tongue. Gradually, as she moves down from her perch to travel a winding white fabric path, she disposes of her grey wig and glasses and trips back through time to childhood and a state of innocence. Her choreography, with its little steps, hops and spins, has the intentional naivety of fold dance.

Monk's search for a state of grace, a sense of knowledge that will free us from the terrors of modern life, is a recurrent theme. In *Quarry* (1976), a fevered child on her sickbed experiences the Second World War as a kaleidoscopic dream of displaced persons, mass rallies and anonymous streams of ghostly refugees who wend through the performance crooning a lullaby

and carrying cardboard cut-out clouds. *Specimen Days* (1981) is a panoramic dissection of the American Civil War revolving around a pair of families (one from each side) who suffer their anguish in mirror image. *The Games* (1983, created for the Schaubühne Theatre Ensemble in West Berlin) is set on a spaceship heading for an unspecified destination. The characters attempt to keep their links to twentieth-century civilisation alive through a series of ritual games that range from gladiatorial to war games and even quiz shows. Like a group of four one-act pieces collectively known as *The Travelogue Series* (1972-76), *The Games* was a collaboration with performance artist Ping Chong.

Lineage

Meredith Monk is more interested in choreographing time than in devising steps for dancers. Her evolution of new theatre forms is aligned to the work of **Kei Takei**, **Pina Bausch** and **Robert Wilson**. Japanese-born, New York-based Yoshiko Chuma also devises large-scale events for her company, The School of Hard Knocks, but she focusses on a rough-and-tumble speed and tends to use the driving rhythms of rock music. Blondell Cummings, who danced with Monk for nearly a decade, has since been creating an expressive, smaller-scale dance-theatre which incorporates black issues among a broad spectrum of ideas.

Follow-up

Recognised as a leading avant-garde composer, Monk has released half a dozen albums of her music and collected a variety of awards for these recordings. She has three Obies (the Off-Broadway theatre's version of the Oscar) as well as awards for her film/video works. These include *Quarry* (1978), *Ellis Island* (1981, about turn-of-the-century immigrants arriving in America) and *Turtle Dreams (Waltz)* (1983). Monk is one of the subjects in a four-part Peter Greenaway documentary on

American musical pioneers, and is one of the fifteen artists who talk about their work in the book *Further Steps* (1987, edited by Connie Kreemer). There is a chapter on Monk in Sally Banes' *Terpsichore in Sneakers* (1980).

Mark Morris

Born: 29th August 1956/Seattle, Washington

As one of the most universally praised dancer-choreographers of his generation, Morris combines an audacious talent with a shrewd sense of showmanship and a propensity for eclectic, off-beat invention.

Morris credits seeing José Greco's Spanish dance troupe as an early influence. He went on to study ballet and ethnic dance, became a member of a semi-professional Balkan folk troupe in his teens, and flirted with the idea of taking up professional flamenco dance. By his mid-twenties, he had danced in the companies of **Eliot Feld**, Lar Lubovitch, Hannah Kahn

Mark Morris in *One Charming Night,* a piece based on a book about vampires

and **Laura Dean**, and worked for **Twyla Tharp** on the 1979 film version of *Hair*. Morris's own dance group made a somewhat nonchalant debut at **Merce Cunningham**'s studio in 1980. Word spread that his work was consistently fresh, wide-ranging and often comic. His progression to international standing was clinched by high praise from *New Yorker* critic Arlene Croce (who had similarly elevated the profile of **Les Ballets Trockadero de Monte Carlo**).

Morris's dances spring from an all-embracing, openly gay sensibility and creative fearlessness. He moves easily from formality to slapstick in a single dance, extracting what he needs from ethnic, modern, ballet or jazz styles, yet making each piece whole and distinct. Subject matter runs from romantic love, depersonalised sex and spiritual suffering to championship wrestling, striptease and the metaphorical purity of soap powders. This last trio, collectively entitled *Mythologies* (1987), is based on essays by French semiologist Roland Barthes. Morris's choice of music is equally catholic: Brahms and Vivaldi, country and western, gospel and traditional Tahitian, Liberace and Yoko Ono. His sheer musicality has made him the post-modern heir apparent to **George Balanchine**.

Dedicated to dance and attracted to outrageous excess, he has no qualms about introducing nudity on stage, performing part of a dance with a paper bag over his head, or reversing gender roles so that women lift men. His own presence is striking: the body, large and voluptuous, topped by the face of a delicate-featured, slightly dissolute pre-Raphaelite angel.

Morris has staged the dances for, or directed in their entirety, several operas, including the choreography for *Nixon in China* (1987) with its canny re-working of the **Central Ballet of China**'s *Red Detachment of Women*. He has composed dances for the **Joffrey Ballet** (*Esteemed Guests*, 1986) and **American Ballet Theatre** (*Drink To

Me Only With Thine Eyes, 1988, a virtuoso semi-classical classroom exercise featuring **Mikhail Baryshnikov**). In late 1988, he premiered *Allegro, il Penseroso ed il Moderato*, after Handel, at the Théâtre de la Monnaie in Brussels, where his company has replaced that of **Maurice Béjart**.

Lineage

Morris draws on an extremely broad range of choreographic references. Apart from his interest in music visualisation, his Hindu solo *O Rangasayee* (1984) and the tongue-in-cheek *The Tamili Film Songs in Stereo Pas de Deux* both recall the work of **Denishawn** with a post-modern twist. His dances show some of the exuberance and wit of **Paul Taylor**, while his attention to form and musical appetite bears comparison with **George Balanchine**. His sense of humour places him in the company of **David Gordon** and **Michael Clark**. As a gay artist, he is as up-front as Tim Miller.

Follow-up

The Mark Morris Dance Group was the subject of a 1986 Dance in America programme that featured six dances, including *Songs That Tell a Story (Robe of White)*, *Dogtown*, *Gloria* and the solo *Jealousy*.

Steve Paxton

Born: 21st January 1939/Tucson, Arizona

An elusive grand master, Steve Paxton has honed his personal performance style to an incandescent flame where everything extraneous has been burned away.

The man who is credited with inventing the dance format known as contact improvisation was a high school gymnast who began taking dance classes to help polish the appearance of his chosen sport.

By 1958, when he moved to New York, he was concentrating on dance.

He studied with **Merce Cunningham**, spent a year with the **José Limón** Dance Company, and was a member of the Cunningham company from 1961 to 1964. An original participant in the Robert Dunn composition course which would lead to the Judson Dance Theatre, Paxton (in conjunction with **Yvonne Rainer**) was one of the people most instrumental in getting the Judson performances started. During this time he appeared in works by Rainer, **Trisha Brown** and others as well as choreographing his own pieces. He did not like the hierarchical structures inherent in established dance companies and opted to work instead with impromptu groups of varying sizes. Paxton was in the first performance of Rainer's seminal *Trio A* (with **David Gordon** and the choreographer) and was a founding member of the improvisational Grand Union.

It was in 1972, while leading a class for eight men during an extended residency at Oberlin College in Ohio, that Paxton's ideas about new dance finally gelled into contact improvisation. This style uses the performer's own weight as the fulcrum for his or her relationship to other dancers. It is based on give and take, on trusting someone to be there if you decide to fall or lean or bounce off them. A mix of martial arts, sports and ideas of freedom and sexual equality, the style stretches the principle of non-display dancing to its natural outcome: improvisational performing where the rules and the risks make dancers as responsible for their partners as they are for themselves.

Paxton has long since abandoned New York. He lives on a farm hidden away in Vermont and often teaches (and performs) at Workcentrum in Amsterdam and Dartington College in Devon. In recent years he has been performing less frequently and then usually alone. His solo to Glenn Gould's interpretation of Bach's

Goldberg Variations is one of the ideal 1980s distillations of the unemphatic, democratic 1960s. Paxton dances with a strength devoid of macho posturings and infused with a quiet, but also intricate, sense of fluid movement.

Lineage

Some of Paxton's ideas about contact improvisation have become a basic part of all contemporary dance languages. Paxton himself turned out to be the most anonymous of the Judson generation of post-modern choreographers. **Trisha Brown, Lucinda Childs, David Gordon, Laura Dean** and **Twyla Tharp** have all developed distinctly individual styles, whereas Paxton's way of moving has been absorbed into the very fabric of new dance. Among the choreographers who built on this base are **Rosemary Butcher**, English soloist Laurie Booth and the all-male San Francisco collective Mangrove.

Follow-up

Paxton talks about contact improvisation and performs with five others in a sequence from the 1980 Dance in America video *Beyond the Mainstream*. Sally Barnes writes about him in both *Democracy's Body* (1983) and *Terpsichore in Sneakers* (1980).

Stephen Petronio

Born: 20th March 1956/Nutley, New Jersey

One of the most promising of America's young choreographers, Stephen Petronio was a pre-medical student who became hooked on dance at college. He studied contact improvisation with **Steve Paxton** and exposed his natural talent to the likes of **Yvonne Rainer**, **Trisha Brown** and other important experimentalists from the

Judson Dance Theatre. He began choreographing while earning a reputation as one of Brown's finest dancers (from 1979 to 1986).

In performance, Petronio is loose and limber in the extreme, with a liquid, rag doll quality reinforced by an explosive attack and precision. His stated intention is to layer the body through space the way he layers ideas through the body. Petronio's dances are dense and intricate. They evolve though the gathering, filtering and collating of images and impressions from the media, reading and first-hand observations on the street. The stationary, yet convulsively active solo *#3* (1986) is built on the body language of public speakers and pop singers, while his group dance *Walk-In* (1986) is based on scenes of collision, impending disaster and rescue. Here the dancers' bodies have the elasticity and snap of rubber bands. They swoop, ripple and jolt their way about the stage in a kind of kamikaze ecstasy. The effect is ruthless and exhilarating.

Petronio's growing popularity led to a commission from **William Forsythe**'s forward-looking Frankfurt Ballet in 1987: the result was entitled *Simulacrum Court*.

Lineage

Stephen Petronio brings a luxuriant force to the flowing movement style he learned from studying with **Steve Paxton** and performing with **Trisha Brown**. The rigorous organisation and formal structures he applies to this style suggest the influence of **Merce Cunningham**.

Dana Reitz

Born: 19th October 1948/ Rochester, NY

Dana Reitz, primarily a soloist, is one of America's most quietly magical performers. Since she began her choreographic career in 1973, she has dedicatedly developed a technique uniquely her own.

Tall and thin, with a boyish figure and a swinging fringe of hair, Reitz moves like someone who studied meditation and martial arts but instead opted for a precise, idio-syncratic fusion of the two. She controls a battery of intuitive, vibratory gestures with radar-like concentration. Her movement style is at once mysteriously fluid and crystal clear, full of serious yet playful rhythms and odd, delicate phrasings. (She sometimes executes simple preparatory drawings in order to visualise the moves she will improvise on in performances.) Watching her, you sense what it might be like to observe fish dreaming that they are learning how to swim in the air: strange, enigmatic, utterly fascinating.

Reitz spent some of her teenage years in Japan before joining a four-year dance and theatre programme at the University of Michigan, Ann Arbor. After gradu-ating in 1970, she moved to New York and during the ensuing years studied classical ballet, the Chinese movement discipline t'ai chi chuan, the Indian dance-drama Kathakali, and contemporary dance with **Merce Cunningham**. She appeared (briefly) in the companies of **Twyla Tharp** and **Laura Dean**, and played a major role in the **Robert Wilson**/Philip Glass opera *Einstein on the Beach* (1976).

Her charismatic talent, however, is much more than the sum of these parts. There is nothing remotely glamorous or commercial about her dances; they may not be as instantaneously accessible as those of other choreographers, but they hold rich rewards. Reitz indulges in no great leaps or falls, totally shuns narrative and rarely depends on music. Yet her work is physically very active, and highly musical in a virtuoso manner similar to jazz artists who improvise and extend their themes (she originally wanted to be a musician). Juggling a myriad of minute impulses, she makes unusual, complex modulations of tempo, weight and focus appear as natural as breathing.

Reitz's kinetic stream of consciousness - visible in works like *Journey for Two Sides: A Solo Dance Duet* (1978) and *Solo in Silence* (1986) - is adaptable to ensemble pieces, where the dancing seems to flow in currents from one dancer to the next. *Quintet Project* (1981) and *Field Papers* (1983) are fine examples. In recent years, Reitz has been developing her interest in the inter-play between light and movement in such pieces as *Severe Clear* (1985) and *Circumstantial Evidence* (1987), collaborations respectively with lighting designers James Turrell and Jennifer Tipton.

Lineage

Like **Denishawn**, **Merce Cunningham** and **Erick Hawkins**, Reitz has absorbed Asian philo-sophy and art into her work. As a performer, she combines Hawkins' serenity with Cunningham's intensity. Unlike **Lucinda Childs**, Reitz the choreographer is a miniaturist whose busy minimalism does not cover vast spaces. Her movement can be as quirky as **Twyla Tharp**'s, and gestural detail is as integral to her dances as it is to those of **The Cholmondeleys**.

Follow-up

Reitz collaborated on film/video projects throughout the 1970s. Titles include *Airwaves* (1974), and *Two Sides: A Solo Dance Duet* (1978) with Eric Bogosian.

Sankai Juku

Formed: 1975

Butoh, or as it was originally called 'ankoku butoh' (dark soul dance), is one of the world's most radical performance art genres.
It developed in the 1950s and 60s under the joint leadership of the late Tatsumi Hijikata and Kazuo

Ohno (still performing in his eighties) as an angry, often sexually explicit alternative to the dominant Japanese and Western movement traditions. It was something of an underground movement addressing the concerns of the post-Hiroshima generation, and although at least forty troupes and individuals practise butoh today, it is still regarded in Japan with some suspicion.

As embodied by Sankai Juku (which translates as Studio of the Mountain and Sea), butoh is more about ceremonial metaphysics than political protest. The five-man group was formed out of intensive physical and psychic workshops conducted by company leader and choreographer Ushio Amagatsu, who with his fellow performers has forged a more spectacular and streamlined style of butoh than their predecessors.

A typical Sankai Juku performance offers a quintet of near-naked, hairless men caked from scalp to sole with grey rice powder. They resemble escapees from some post-holocaust horror film. Their movement is a blend of frenetic steps and precise, intro-verted gentures fraught with multiple meanings. Their bodies, like extraordinarily controlled plastic sculptures, are often prone or near to the ground. As their eyes roll back into their sockets, they writhe, twist and undulate. Much of the dynamic details arises from the use of hands locked into distorted positions or from extremely supple back muscles.

The company tours regularly. *Kinkan Shonen* (The Kumquat Seed, 1978), their first full-scale production, is still in many ways their strongest and most accessible; other works include the 1982 *Jomon Sho* (*Homage to Prehistory*) and *Unetsu* (*Eggs Standing Out of Curiosity*) from 1985. *Jomon Sho*, in which the performers dangle head first from ropes, has proved to push risk-taking in dance to fatal limits. During a September 1985 performance of the work on the outside of a Seattle office block,

A performance of Jomon Sho (Homage to Prehistory) by Sankai Juku at Sadler's Wells Theatre in 1983

company member Yoshiyuki Takada plunged to his death after his rope broke.

Sankai Juku perform in stage environments that feature sand or water, and symbolic geometric shapes. In these settings, Amagatsu's tableau-like images (sometimes supported by rock music or cool jazz) unfold with an immediacy that can induce awe or discomfort. The audience may not fully understand or accept what is experienced, but the impact of the performance expands in retro-spect.

Lineage

Butoh's stylistic and philosophical influences include Dadaism, Jungian psychology, Western pop music, nihilism and Japan's own performing heritage. Founder Ohno cites La Argentina (stage name of the great Spanish dancer Antonia Mercé) as a major source of inspiration: his most popular piece is entitled *Admiring La Argentina* (1977). Ohno studied with Takaya Eguchi, who had in turn studied with **Mary Wigman** in Germany, and there is a link with Wigman's stylised questioning of human suffering. Butoh's influence abroad is exemplified by perfor-mance artists Eiko and Koma and **Kei Takei** in the US, and emerging British-based soloist Lindsay John.

Ian Spink

Born: 8th October 1947/Melbourne

Frequent work with opera and theatre companies has opened up Ian Spink's choreographic methods into a fusion where dance, design, music and sometimes even dialogue come together on an equal footing. Spink's intelligent and highly original creations are laced with cross-references which give the finished product an extra resonance by sparking off a series of subliminal associations. His allusive version of post-modernism draws on ancient myths and world religions, other artworks, historical figures and even movie fantasies.

One of Spink's most successful pieces, *Further and Further into Night* (1984) bases both its intricate choreography and its sequences of repetitive natural gestures on incidents in Alfred Hitchcock's romantic spy thriller *Notorious*. The male trio *De Gas* (1981) is centred round the mundane, but strictly unison ablutions of gents in turn-of-the-century garb. Its genesis was the signature of Impressionist painter Edgar Degas, who signed his name as though it were two words. It is not essential to know this, nor to register that the four pianos on stage in *Bösendorfer Waltzes* (1986) are a wink at Stravinsky's four-piano **Les Noces**, or that much of the choreography stems from another Stravinsky ballet, **The Firebird**. All of Spink's works have an innate validity even if the references mean nothing to the viewer. Previous knowledge is a reward rather than a criterion of enjoyment.

Spink's traditional training led him to a five-year stay with the **Australian Ballet** from 1969 to 1974. It was here, during a 1972 choreographic workshop, that he devised his first works. After abandoning the ballet world, Spink performed with the Dance Company of New South Wales (now **Sydney Dance Company**) and also had an oppor-tunity to study with **Merce Cunningham** during an Australian tour.

Soon after arriving in England in 1977, he formed the Ian Spink Group, but it was only in 1982 that he found his ideal working format. At the suggestion of Val Bourne, director of the Dance Umbrella festival, Spink joined forces with **Siobhan Davies** and guest choreographer **Richard Alston** to launch Second Stride (the name is a pun on Alston's earlier company Strider, for which Davies had been a dancer). Alston contributed works during the first two seasons, while between them Davies and Spink have choreographed some twenty Second Stride premieres. When Davies formed her own troupe in 1987, Spink became sole artistic director of Second Stride, with designer Anthony McDonald as associate director.

Spink's latest works, *Further and Further...*, *Bösendorfer Waltzes* and *Weighing the Heart* (1987, all collaborations with McDonald and composer Orlando Gough) have firmly established the lively company as Britain's most innovative and adult dance-theatre troupe. In 1988, they began a three-year period as the company-in-residence at the Towngate Theatre, Basildon; their first premiere there was *Dancing and Shouting*.

Lineage

Ian Spink's dance-theatre works are in the same vein mined by other unclassifiable artists such as **Meredith Monk, Pina Bausch** and **Robert Wilson**. His movement vocabulary incorporates a range of styles from folk dance to classical ballet with stylistic tinges of **Merce Cunningham** and **Richard Alston**.

Follow-up

A Mouthful of Birds, a collaboration with playwright Caryl Churchill, led to the video *Fugue*, a 'play with movement' created for the 1988 Dancelines series. Two early Spink works, *De Gas* and *Canta*, were filmed in 1982.

Kei Takei

Born: 30th December 1939/Tokyo

Light, Kei Takei's magnum opus, was begun in 1969. To date there are twenty-five parts running to at least as many hours. Each section is based on a single ritualistic, often violent, image performed in a relentless, obsessive and overpowering style. Although it is now too huge to be performed in one sitting, it *is* a single entity; each part (capable of standing on its own) also comments on and extends the dramatic intensity of the other sections.

Anna Sokolow spotted Takei in a Tokyo dance class and recommended her for a 1967 Fulbright fellowship to study at the Juilliard School of Music, where Sokolow was on the dance department staff. Takei formed her own company, Moving Earth, in 1969 and began work on *Light*. In 1981, the company gave a single eleven-hour performance of the then completed fifteen parts.

Harsh and hard-hitting, each section is a struggle for survival. Started during the Vietnam War, the first parts are a dumb show of rage populated by 'refugees' doggedly trudging a road to nowhere. Sometimes they are weighed down by mammoth bundles strapped to their backs, at other times blindfolded and herded together. This culminates in *Light, Part 5* where a trio of bodies form a single pile of human debris. Sinking under their own weight, the trio is slowly dragged to the ground only to rise and fall and rise again and again. The inexorable slow motion of their struggle is like a funeral knell. Takei did not find such a consistently powerful image again until *Parts 10 to 13*, subtitled 'The Stone Field'. These parts begin with Takei, blinded by a black X painted across her face, fiercely defending her turf against a pair of intruders. Defiant, but clearly terrified, she prances and prowls the stage rapping a pair of rocks together over her head in a vain effort to frighten off the unseen (by her) intruders, who are methodically hurling handfuls of stones at her feet.

Gradually, as if she were an anthropologist who has discovered her own tribe, Takei transforms the stone field into a shrine. By *Part 13*, a group of dancers have joined her in organising the stones into a floor-wide mandala. While Takei squats at its centre, the others perform a prehistoric-looking stamping dance around the edges of their magic circle.

The longest and largest section to date, running for nearly two uninterrupted hours is *Light, Part 23* (1986). Subtitled 'Pilgrimage', it features more than twenty performers. All of them are struggling violently to reach some unspecified goal, but as the piece goes on their numbers dwindle until all of them (now ghosts perhaps) have been forced to the edges of the stage. There, they continue to move in a slow, dreamlike procession.

Lineage

Takei and **Meredith Monk** are the two major post-modern choreographers who never felt the need to make work deliberately devoid of emotional content. *Light* is a combination of **Anna Sokolow**'s bleak urban vision with butoh, the suggestively theatrical avant-garde Japanese dance style. Other Oriental artists popular in the West, such as husband and wife team Eiko and Koma, and **Sankai Juku**, also deal with the cultural implications of Hiroshima and its aftermath.

Follow-up

Kei Takei talks about her work in the book *Further Steps* (1987), a collection of fifteen interviews with leading contemporary choreographers. Her work is discussed and illustrated in *Contemporary Dance*, edited by Anne Livet (1978). She is one of the artists featured in the 1980 Dance in America segment *Beyond the Mainstream*.

Robert Wilson

Born: 4th October 1941/Waco, Texas

Robert Wilson's spectacles for the subconcious inhabit a world where intuition takes precedence over fact. A typical Wilson creation is a reverie of meditation, an idiosyncratic amalgam of pageantry, art and music, drifting along at sleepwalker's pace and filled with mystery, beauty and symbolism. Wilson's epics, devoid of linear progression or discernable stories, are a paradox: simultaneously hypnotic and boring, sophisticated and naive, unfathomable and shallow. His carefully designed imagery works like great paintings: the initial impact of the whole scene is followed by a lengthy period of repose, a time to explore and reflect upon the images in front of you.

One of the keys to Wilson's work is his training as a painter. He studied in Texas, spent a year in Paris, and in 1965 received a degree in architecture and design from Pratt Institute in New York. His work, which has never lost its painterly base, often resembles three-dimensional painting created with light, scenery and bodies.

His major stylistic device is the reshaping of time. Some of his productions have lasted longer than twelve hours and most of his scenes creep along with a snail's pace gradation of changing light and movement. He also reshapes the audience's conditioned expectations. In his mythic tableaux, ostriches prance across lunar landscapes and spaceships hover above fields; his is a dream world where characters can hang in mid-air, balanced on levitating chairs or dangling from a (harmless) noose, while other characters calmly read newspapers or just as calmly commit murder.

To anyone who resists Wilson's suggestiveness, his theatre will seem not only excruciatingly dull but also pompous and pretentious. It is impossible to meet him only half-way; as with much postmodern art, it has to be all or it is nothing at all.

His major productions include *The Life and Times of Sigmund Freud* (1969), *The Life and Times of Joseph Stalin* (1973, twelve hours with a cast of 144), *A Letter for Queen Victoria* (1974, on Broadway with choreography by Andrew deGroat), *Einstein on the Beach* (1976, an opera with music by Philip Glass, choreography by deGroat and **Lucinda Childs**), the two-character play *I Was Sitting On My Patio This Guy Appeared I Thought I Was Hallucinating* (1977, with Childs), *Death, Destruction and Detroit* (1979), *The Golden Windows* (1982), *Great Day in the Morning* (1983, with opera singer Jessye Norman) and *The CIVIL WarS*.

The latter is one of the biggest theatre events ever attempted. The different acts were created over four years in various locations around the world and were to have been assembled into a fourteen-hour extravaganza as part of the 1984 Olympics Arts Festival in Los Angeles. It proved too expensive to pull off and has yet to be staged as a single entity. In 1988, **Rudolf Nureyev** invited Wilson to stage *Le Martyre de Saint Sébastien* (music by Debussy) for the **Paris Opéra Ballet**.

Lineage

The ways in which Wilson warps time links him to both **Meredith Monk** and **Kei Takei**. His sense of spectacle is aligned to that of Monk, **Maguy Marin** and **Pina Bausch**, with whom he shares a propensity for guru-like master control. Wilson has designed lighting for **Lucinda Childs**' *Relative Calm*, directed operas and plays, and has drawings and sculptures (often props from his productions) in many major museum collections.

Follow-up

Robert Wilson: From a Theatre of Images (1980) includes essays by John Rockwell and Robert Stearns.

GLOSSARY

THE TERMS LISTED in this section of the Handbook are words used in the main text of the book which may require either clarification or amplification. For a complete list of technical terms used in ballet, we recommend either Gail Grant's *Technical Manual and Dictionary of Classical Ballet* (third edition 1982, Dover Publications) or Cyril W. Beaumont's *A French-English Dictionary of Technical Dance Terms* (1930, reissued in 1980 by ISTD).

ABSTRAKTERTANZ Bauhaus term coined by Oskar Schlemmer and confined to his constructivist creations, in which dancers were transformed into objects. Not to be confused with the generally used English phrase 'abstract dance', ie dance which abandons a narrative for pure movement.

ARABESQUE One of ballet's fundamental positions: standing on one leg, the dancer raises the other leg to the back at a 90° angle. See the photo from *La Bayadère* on pages 34-5. An attitude is an arabesque performed with the leg bent at the knee – this pose is derived from the famous statue of Mercury by Giovanni da Bologna.

BALLET MASTER The term originally referred to the person who actually staged the ballets, in other words the choreographer. In the nineteenth century it also meant the director of a company, such as Marius Petipa (George Balanchine always called himself the ballet master of New York City Ballet rather than its artistic director). Today's ballet masters are the people in charge of rehearsing works after they have been choreographed.

BARRE A wooden handrail used by dancers to maintain their balance while training. Dancers do not grip the barre for actual support, but use it to guide and steady themselves throughout the opening exercises of a class (as seen onstage in dances from August Bournonville's *Konservatoriet* to Martha Graham's *Acrobats of God*).

BRISÉS VOLES Like *cabrioles* and *entrechats*, *brisés* are fancy footwork steps performed while the dancer is in mid-air, and are meant to show off exceptional agility. *Entrechats*, performed in one place but off the ground, are a front, back, front crisscrossing of the feet. In *cabrioles* and *brisés*, the dancer beats his feet together while leaping forward or backward across the stage.

BUTOH Avant-garde Japanese dance form that emerged after the Second World War. Its central focus is emotional intensity rather than physical dexterity. Leading practitioners include the Paris-based Sankai Juku and New York-based Kei Takei.

CHARACTER DANCE In a ballet, anything which is not classically based is likely to be a character dance of one kind or another. The term can include everything from the hornpipes in *Pineapple Poll* to comedy characters such as Bottom in *The Dream*. Marius Petipa repeatedly used character dance (like the national dances in Act Three of *Swan Lake*) to provide a sense of exotic local colour. *Demi-caractère* refers to dances that are neither out-and-out character roles nor purely classical.

CONTACT IMPROVISATION This form of movement blends sports and everyday movement together into a loose, easy-going style of performance. For a fuller description, see the entry on Steve Paxton (page 251).

CORPS DE BALLET Nearly all the dancers in any ballet company are members of the corps de ballet. They dance together in group formations which create a backdrop to the main action. Several gradings exist within different companies, ranging from *artiste* through *coryphée* to *demi-soloist*. The corps can on occasion play a major role, as in the 'Kingdom of the Shades' act from *La Bayadère*.

DANCE-THEATRE This current trend in performance is an amalgam of all types of theatre, incorporating anything from singing and dialogue to film and other multi-media techniques.

Exponents of dance-theatre believe that by building a bridge between dance and theatre, they can achieve a broader, more immediate appeal than through the abstractions of pure dance steps. See the Alternatives chapter opener (page 224).

DIVERTISSEMENTS Literally 'diversions', these are suites of dances where the plot comes to a halt for a display of technical virtuosity. The last acts of *The Sleeping Beauty* and Balanchine's *A Midsummer Night's Dream* are prime examples.

ÉCOLE The French word for school can be used to describe any dancer or performer who follows a set of prescribed rules. It does not have to refer only to those who are classically trained ballet dancers.

ELEVATION Like *ballon*, elevation concerns a dancer's ability to fly through the air. Elevation usually refers to the height a dancer can attain, while *ballon* describes the springy and elastic quality with which it is achieved.

ENCHAÎNEMENT When steps are linked together in a series of moves, the entire sequence of the pattern is called an *enchaînement*.

FOUETTÉ A series of quick, whipping turns usually performed by a ballerina on a single spot. The Italian dancer Pierina Legnani was the first to popularise these devilish, crowd-pleasing turns in the third act of *Swan Lake*. Many a Swan Queen has since had reason to curse her.

MIME The code of gestures used to relate the story of a dance can range from the obvious to the near abstract. In classical ballet, the mime follows French grammatical structure, so that the gestures for 'I love you' are actually performed as 'I you love' ('Je vous aime'). Read Joan Lawson's *Mime* (1957, republished by Dance Horizons) for a detailed analysis with specific examples. See also the Classical Ballet chapter opener (page 26).

NEO-CLASSICISM The main point behind neo-classicism is to create a contemporary and vital dance language, but one firmly rooted in the classic principles of ballet which can be traced back through Marius Petipa to Louis XIV's Académie Royale de Danse. As with George Balanchine's American neo-classicism, the visually radical steps all reflect their four hundred years of dance heritage.

PAS DE DEUX Literally 'step for two', the pas de deux was codified by Marius Petipa into a specific format, called the grand pas de deux, that opens with the ballerina and her partner dancing together, continues with display solos (first for the man, then for the woman) and concludes with a coda where the two dance together again. These grands pas de deux are often excerpted and performed at galas. The pas de trois and pas de quatre (and come to that, the pas de sept) are variations on this form. Many choreographers have used the pas de trois, but Jiří Kylián has turned trios into a trademark.

POINT SHOES Today's point shoes are pieces of sophisticated equipment, always handmade and, in the case of leading ballerinas, individually and precisely tailored. They are of necessity flimsy creations made for flexibility rather than durability, and ballerinas performing *Swan Lake* or *The Sleeping Beauty* would expect a pair of toe shoes to maintain their peak condition for only a single act of a single performance (see also the Romantic Ballet chapter opener, page 12).

POSITIONS The five cardinal positions of the feet were invented in seventeenth-century France and are meant to allow the dancer maximum freedom and diversity of movement. There is a similar codification of arm gestures called *port de bras*. For fuller details, refer to the books recommended in the introduction above.

POST-MODERNISM This unsatisfactory, catch-all term covers experimental dance from the time of Merce Cunningham onwards. The movement away from 'classic' modern dance to a more radical approach began with the Judson Dance Theatre in New York (from 1962 to 1964) and can be loosely used of all new dance since. In the narrowest of definitions, post-modernism is the lean and cerebral movement in dance that parallels the minimalist movement in painting and sculpture during the 1960s and 1970s.

PREMIER DANSEUR The title which designates the male equivalent of the prima ballerina.

PRIMA BALLERINA Not all female dancers are ballerinas in the strict sense of the word. Members of the corps de ballet and solo dancers are often called ballerinas, of course, but technically the term really only applies to the principal female dancers of a company. The prima is the leading (and usually senior) ballerina. The honorary title *prima ballerina assoluta* has only been granted a few times in history; Margot Fonteyn, for example, was named the Royal Ballet's *assoluta* in 1979, the year of her sixtieth birthday.

PROMENADE During a promenade, a dancer holds a pose on one leg while turning (or being turned) in a complete circle. The idea is to show off the perfection of a single pose from every possible angle. George Balanchine's *Agon* contains a particularly inventive promenade.

SYMPHONIC BALLET A genre of ballet popularised in the 1930s by Léonide Massine and which includes a complete and already extant symphony as its score and source of inspiration. It is only the grandiosity of conception that marks out these works as different from shorter, essentially plotless ballets such as Frederick Ashton's *Symphonic Variations* or many of the works George Balanchine choreographed to Stravinsky scores.

EN TRAVESTI This tradition goes back to the very birth of professional dance. The first performances of the Académie Royale de Danse were exclusively male (with boys in feminine garb) playing the women's roles: at the time, it was considered improper for a woman to appear on the stage. Two hundred years later, Parisian tastes had so altered that the drag roles were reversed, and during the last decades of the nineteenth century women were dressed as men to partner the ballerinas (see the entry on *Coppélia*, page 24). Today almost all of the roles performed *en travesti* are for comic characters such as the ugly sisters in *Cinderella*. The all-male Les Ballets Trockadero de Monte Carlo is a hilarious satire troupe who spoof this tradition with great glee.

TUTU The name comes from French baby talk for 'bottom' and refers to the skirt worn by the ballerina. Tutus first became popular during the Romantic era; until then, women's stage costumes had been elaborations of contemporary fashions. The tutu took over as a standard costume with *La Sylphide*. At this point it was mid calf-length and composed of layers of tulle or tarlatan. Because it was so delicate, the costume tended to drift in the breeze and float in the air even after a ballerina had already completed a jump. This gave an extra dimension of airy magic to her every move. By the time of the more rigid and technically demanding choreography of Marius Petipa, the tutu had become shorter and stiffer in order to show off the demanding virtuosity of his choreography.

DANCE BOOKS

THE FOLLOWING LIST of books is a selection of titles covering various aspects of dance, including dictionaries, general histories and collections of criticism. Books which deal specifically with individual choreographers or dancers, works or dance companies are listed in the Follow-up section for the relevant main entry. Some titles may now be out of print, but available in secondhand bookshops.

AFTERIMAGES, GOING TO THE DANCE and **SIGHT LINES** – Three volumes of commentary by the dance writer of *The New Yorker*. Arlene Croce/Knopf/1977, 1982 and 1987 respectively.

BALANCHINE'S COMPLETE STORIES OF THE GREAT BALLETS – The Kobbé of the dance world: plots and short commentaries of over 400 major works, plus useful appendices. Also known as *Balanchine's Festival of Ballet*. George Balanchine and Francis Mason/Comet Books/1954, revised 1977 (2 volumes).

THE CONCISE OXFORD DICTIONARY OF BALLET – A reliable A-Z. Horst Koegler/Oxford University Press/Second edition 1982, updated 1987.

CONTEMPORARY DANCE – An anthology of lectures, interviews and essays by and with the most important post-1960s American choreographers, critics and scholars, plus fine photographs. Edited and with an introduction by Anne Livet/Abbeville Press/1978.

DANCE AS THEATRE ART – Original dance writing from 1581 to the present. Edited with commentary by Selma Jeanne Cohen/Dodd, Mead/1974.

DANCE IN AMERICA – The first decade of the PBS video dance series serves as the basis for this survey of the art form, including valuable documentation on companies, works and performers in the series' first forty programmes. Robert Coe/Dutton/1985.

DANCE WRITINGS – Perceptive, concise, even poetic pieces from the dean of American critics. Edwin Denby/Dance Books/1986.

FURTHER STEPS: FIFTEEN CHOREOGRAPHERS ON MODERN DANCE – Interviews with and statements of belief by contemporary American artists, with chronologies of their works. Edited by Connie Kreemer/Harper & Row/1987.

MAKING A BALLET – Covers all the stages of creating, rehearsing and mounting a dance performance, from the choreographer at work to the opening night. Mary Clarke and Clement Crisp/Studio Vista/1974.

THE MAGIC OF DANCE – A general history based on the BBC series. Margot Fonteyn/BBC Publications/1980.

MEN DANCING – A celebration of the re-emergence of the male dancer: analysis, historical background and a Roll of Honour of the greats. Alexander Bland and John Percival/Weidenfeld & Nicolson/1984. In the same vein:

DANCER and **BALLERINA** – Both taken from BBC series centred around Peter Schaufuss and Natalia Makarova respectively. Mary Clarke and Clement Crisp/BBC Publications/1984 and 1987.

MODERN BALLET – The title says it all. John Percival/Harmony Books/1970, revised 1980.

NEXT WEEK, SWAN LAKE – Wide-ranging observations on dance and dancers, theory and aesthetics. Selma Jeanne Cohen/Wesleyan University Press/1982.

OBSERVER OF THE DANCE 58-82 – Collected reviews by Nigel Gosling and Maude Lloyd for *The Observer*, written under their joint pseudonym. Alexander Bland/Dance Books/1985.

THE SHAPES OF CHANGE – An in-depth view of American dances from Denishawn to Twyla Tharp. Marcia B. Siegel/Houghton Mifflin/1979.

TERPSICHORE IN SNEAKERS and **DEMOCRACY'S BODY** – Overviews of post-modern dance. Sally Banes/Houghton Mifflin/1980 and 1983 respectively.

TIME AND THE DANCING IMAGE – Serious, but readable reflections on dance by the principal critic of *The Village Voice* for twenty years. Deborah Jowitt/William Morrow/1988.

WHERE SHE DANCED – A social history of the female dancer in the early twentieth century. Explains how changes in society affected the dancer and vice versa. Elizabeth Kendall/Knopf/1979.

THE WORLD OF SERGE DIAGHILEV – A general view (in colour) of the Ballets Russes. Charles Spencer/Paul Elek/1974.

Photograph books:

BARBARA MORGAN – Barbara Morgan/Morgan & Morgan Inc./1982.
THE FUGITIVE GESTURE – William Ewing/Thames & Hudson/1987
WALDMAN ON DANCE – Max Waldman/William Morrow/1977

= DANCE INFORMATION =

THIS SECTION lists selected information sources and contact points for the further exploration of dance. These include dance magazines, national and regional companies, festivals with a major dance element, dance organisations and specialist book or video sources. The listing is based on the latest information available at the time of going to press, but will inevitably be subject to change. Amendments and suggestions for inclusion should be sent to: The Dance Handbook, Longman Group UK Limited, Longman House, Burnt Mill, Harlow, Essex CM20 2JE.

UNITED KINGDOM

Magazines
DANCE & DANCERS
Monthly
Plusloop Limited
248 High Street
Croyden CR0 1NF
01 681 7817
Subscriptions:
Cloister Court
22–26 Farringdon Lane
London EC1R 3AU
01 253 3135

DANCE THEATRE JOURNAL
Quarterly
Laban Centre
Laurie Grove
London SE14 6NH
01 692 4070

DANCING TIMES
Monthly
Clerkenwell House
45–47 Clerkenwell Green
London EC1R OBE
01 250 3006

NEW DANCE
Quarterly
48 Ash Grove
Leeds LS6 1AY
0532 782464

Companies
COMMON GROUND
DANCE THEATRE
7 Kirchen Road
West Ealing
London W13 0TY
01 579 3626
Touring company of deaf and hearing dancers and actors

DIVERSIONS
(Welsh Repertory Dance Company)
30 Richmond Road
Cardiff CF2 3AS
0222 463751

ENGLISH DANCE THEATRE
Dance City
Peel Lane
Off Waterloo Street
Newcastle-Upon-Tyne NE1 4DW
091 261 0505
Mailing list

LONDON CITY BALLET
London Studio Centre
42–50 York Way
London N1
01 831 1137
Friends organisation

LONDON CONTEMPORARY
DANCE THEATRE
The Place
17 Dukes Road
London WC1H 9AB
01 387 0324

LONDON FESTIVAL BALLET
Festival Ballet House
39 Jay Mews
London SW7 2ES
01 581 1245

NORTHERN BALLET
THEATRE
11 Zion Crescent, Hulme Walk
Manchester M15 5BY
061 226 3309/5381
Friends/mailing list

RAMBERT DANCE
COMPANY
94 Chiswick High Road
London W4 1SH
01 995 4246/3996
Mailing list/newsletter

THE ROYAL BALLET
Royal Opera House
Covent Garden
London WC2E 9DD
01 240 1200
Friends/mailing list

SADLER'S WELLS ROYAL
BALLET
Sadler's Wells Theatre
Roseberry Avenue
London EC1R 4TN
01 278 8916
Friends/mailing list

SCOTTISH BALLET
261 West Princes Street
Glasgow G4 9EE
041 331 2931
Friends/newsletter

Organisations
BRITISH BALLET
ORGANISATION
Woolborough House
39 Lonsdale Road
London SW13 9PJ
01 748 1241

LABAN CENTRE FOR
MOVEMENT AND DANCE
Laurie Grove
London SE14 6NH
01 692 4070
Publishes Dance Theatre Journal (see Magazines above) and working papers in dance studies

NATIONAL ORGANISATION
FOR DANCE AND MIME
(NODM)
9 Rossdale Road
London SW15 1AD
01 788 6905
Represents all who work in and support dance and mime; administers the Digital Dance Awards

NATIONAL RESOURCE
CENTRE FOR DANCE
University of Surrey
Guildford GU2 5XH

Festivals
BRIGHTON FESTIVAL
May
Festival Office
Marlborough House
54 Old Steine
Brighton BN1 1EQ
0173 29801

DANCE UMBRELLA
October/November
Riverside Studios
Crisp Road
London W6 9RL
01 741 4040/9358

EDINBURGH
INTERNATIONAL FESTIVAL
August/September
Edinburgh Festival Society
21 Market Street
Edinburgh
031 226 4001

FOCUS ON DANCE –
GLASGOW
July
Assembly Theatre Limited
Assembly Rooms
54 George Street
Edinburgh EH2 2LR
031 226 2428/041 221 4911

Book Source
DANCE BOOKS
9 Cecil Court
London WC2N 4EZ
01 836 2314

Museum
ANNA PAVLOVA
MEMORIAL MUSEUM
Ivy House
North End Road
Golders Green
London
NW1

AUSTRALIA

Magazine
DANCE AUSTRALIA
Room 16, Level 3
1 City Road
South Melbourne, Victoria
3205
03 62 1444/62 1955

Companies
AUSTRALIAN BALLET
11 Mount Alexander Road
Flemington, Victoria 3031
03 376 1400

AUSTRALIAN DANCE
THEATRE
120 Gouger Street
Adelaide, SA 5060
08 212 2084

QUEENSLAND BALLET
COMPANY
129 Margaret Street
Brisbane,
Queensland 4000
07 229 3355

SYDNEY DANCE
COMPANY
Pier 4
Hickson Road
Walsh Bay
Sydney, NSW 2000
02 221 4811

WEST AUSTRALIAN BALLET
COMPANY
PO 7228 Cloister Square
Perth, WA 6000

Organisation
AUSTRALIAN CENTRE –
INTERNATIONAL THEATRE
INSTITUTE
PO 137
King's Cross, NSW 2011
02 357 1200

Research source
LIBRARY OF THE
PERFORMING ARTS
Sydney Opera House
Bennelong Point
Sydney, NSW 2001

AUSTRIA

Company
VIENNA STATE OPERA
BALLET
Opernring 2,
1010 Wien
0222 51444

Festivals
BREGENZ FESTIVAL
July/August
PO 119
6900 Bregenz

INTERNATIONAL
TANZWOCHEN – VIENNA
July/August
PO 155
1091 Wien
01 93 55 58

SOMMERSZENE
July/August
Szene, Waagplatz 1A
5020 Salzburg
0662 84 26 23

BELGIUM

Companies
BALLET ROYAL DE
WALLONIE
COMPAGNIE JORGE
LEFEBRE
Palais des Beaux-Arts
Place du Manège
6000 Charleroi
071 31 4420

ROYAL BALLET OF
FLANDERS
Keizerstraat 14
2000 Antwerpen
03 234 34 38

Festivals
FESTIVAL VAN
VLAANDEREN –
ANTWERPEN
October
Stadhuis de Directie
Grote Markt
2000 Antwerpen
03 231 16 90

FESTIVAL VAN
VLAANDEREN – GENT
September/October
Algemeen Secretariaat
Eugeen Flageyplein 18
1050 Brussels
02 648 14 84

CANADA

Companies
LES GRANDS BALLETS
CANADIENS
4816 rue Rivard
Montréal, Québec H2J 2N6
514 849 8681

NATIONAL BALLET OF
CANADA
157 King Street East
Toronto, Ontario
M5C 1G9
416 362 1041

ROYAL WINNIPEG BALLET
289 Portage Avenue
Winnipeg, Manitoba R3B 2B4
204 956 0183

Organisation
DANCE IN CANADA
ASSOCIATION
Association Danse au
Canada
#403–322 King Street West
Toronto, Ontario M6C 2K2
416 595 0165
Publish Dance in Canada
(quarterly)
Choreographic video
archives/mailing list

Festivals
FESTIVAL INTERNATIONAL
DE NOUVELLE DANSE
3575 St Laurent, Bureau 609
Montréal, Québec H2X 2T7
514 287 1423

FESTIVAL DANSE CANADA
DANCE FESTIVAL
June/July
Centre National des Arts
Ottawa, Ontario
613 996 5051

DENMARK

Company
ROYAL DANISH BALLET
PO Box 2185
1017 Copenhagen K
01 14 17 65/322020

Festival
BALLET FESTIVAL
May
Det Kongelige Teater
PO 2185
1007 Copenhagen K
01 322 020

EASTERN EUROPE

Magazine
TANECNI LISTY
Mrstíkova 23
100 00 Prague 10
02 781 4823

Companies
BRNO STATE THEATRE
BALLET
Státní divadlo
Dvořákova 11,
657 70 Brno
05 26311

HUNGARIAN STATE OPERA
BALLET
Vl. Népköztársaság. U. 22
Budapest PF 503
1373 Hungary
312 550

PRAGUE NATIONAL
THEATRE BALLET
Národni divadlo, Ostrovní 1
110 00 Praha, 1
02 269 744

SLOVAK NATIONAL
THEATRE BALLET
Slovenské národné divadlo
Gorkého ui 4
800 00 Bratislava
07 333 083

WARSAW BALLET
Teatru Wielkiego
Pl. Teatralny 1
00950 Warszawa
26 30 01

FINLAND

Magazine
TANSSI-LEHTI
Quarterly
Keskuskatu 6G
00 100 Helsinki
0660 570

Company
FINNISH NATIONAL
BALLET
Bulevardi 23–27
00180 Helsinki 18
012 921

Organisations
THE DANCE COUNCIL OF
FINLAND
Keskustatu 6G
00100 Helsinki
0174 907

DANCE GROUP OF THE
HELSINKI CITY THEATRE
Ensi Linja 2
00530 Helsinki
0353 071

Festivals
HELSINKI FESTIVAL
August/September
Unionkatu 28
00100 Helsinki
065 96 88

KUOPIO DANCE AND
MUSIC FESTIVAL
June
Tulliportinkatu 27
70100 Kuopio
071 221844/118103

FRANCE

Magazine
SAISONS DE LA DANSE
Monthly
Editions Arabesques
3 rue des Petits-Carreaux
75002 Paris
1 42 36 12 04/42 33 66 64

Companies
BALLET DU NORD
Le Colisée
33 rue de l'Epaule
59100 Roubaix
20 24 66 66

BALLET DE NANCY
Centre Chorégraphique
National
5 rue Henri Bazan
54000 Nancy
83 36 78 07

BALLET DE L'OPERA DE
LYON
Auditorium Maurice Ravel
149 rue Garibaldi
69003 Lyon
78 28 09 50/95 11 97

BALLET NATIONAL DE
MARSEILLE
1 place Auguste-Carli
13001 Marseille
91 47 94 88

COMPAGNIE MAGUY
MARIN
Maison des Arts
Place Salvador Allende
94000 Créteil
48 99 55 80

PARIS OPERA BALLET
GRCOP (Groupe de
Recherche Chorégraphique
de l'Opéra de Paris)
8 rue Scribe
75009 Paris
1 42 66 50 22

Festivals
BIENNALE
INTERNATIONALE DE LA
DANSE LYON
September/October (even
years)
127 rue Servient
69003 Lyon
78 60 85 40

FESTIVAL D'AVIGNON
July/August
8 bis rue de Mois
8400 Avignon
90 82 07 08

FESTIVAL DE
CHATEAUVALLON
Théâtre National de la Danse
et de l'Image
83190 Ollioules
94 24 11 76

FESTIVAL INTERNATIONAL
DE LA DANSE DE PARIS
October/November
Théâtre des Champs-Elysées
15 avenue Montaigne
75008 Paris
1 47 39 28 26

FESTIVAL INTERNATIONAL
MONTPELLIER DANSE
June/July
7 Boulevard Henri IV
3400 Montpellier
67 61 11 20

HONG KONG

Magazine
DANCE SHOWCASE
Premiere Showcase Limited
PO Box 11477
#303 Entertainment Building
30 Queen's Road, Central
Hong Kong
3 713 0649

Festivals
ASIAN ARTS FESTIVAL
Hong Kong Coliseum Annex
Kowloon, Hong Kong

HONG KONG ARTS
FESTIVAL
January/February
13th Floor
Hong Kong Arts Centre
2 Harbour Road, Wanchai
Hong Kong
5 295 555

REPUBLIC OF IRELAND

Companies
DUBLIN CONTEMPORARY
DANCE THEATRE
The Dance Centre
Digges Lane
Dublin 2
01 78 42 05

IRISH NATIONAL BALLET
18 Emmet Place
Cork
21 27 01 12

ISRAEL

Publication
ISRAEL DANCE
Yearly
c/o Dance Library of Israel
26 Bialik Street, Tel Aviv

Companies
BAT-DOR COMTEMPORARY
DANCE COMPANY
Batsheva Bat-Dor Dance
Society
30 Ibn Gvirol Street
Tel Aviv 64078
03 263175

ISRAEL BALLET
2 Hey Be'iyar Street
62093 Tel Aviv
03 266610

JERUSLAEM TAMAR
DANCE COMPANY
PO 71120
Jerusalem

Festival
JERUSALEM ISRAEL
FESTIVAL
May–June
Jerusalem Sherover Theatre
30 Marcus Street
Jerusalem

ITALY

Magazine
BALLETTO OGGI
Monthly
Editoriale Nuova Scena
Viale Emilio Caldara 35
20122 Milano
02 54 58 878/54 58 881

Companies
ATERBALLETTO
Piazza Martiri 7 Luglio
Reggio Emilia
0522 48296

LA SCALA OPERA BALLET
Teatro Alla Scala
20121 Milano

Festivals
ESTATE FIESOLANO
June/August
Ente Teatro Romano di
Fiesole
Villa La Torraccia
Via delle Fontanelle 24
S. Domenico di Fiesole
055 59 99 83

FESTIVAL DEI DUE MONDI -
SPOLETO
June/July
Via del Duomo 7
Spoleto
0743 28 120

NERVI FESTIVAL
INTERNAZIONALE DEL
BALLETTO
Teatro Communale
dell'Opera di
Genova
Via XX Settembre 37/7
16121 Genova
010 54 27 92T

JAPAN

Magazine
BAREE NO HON
Book of Ballet
Quarterly
Ongakuno-Tomo-Sha
6-30 Kagurazaka,
Shinjuk-ku
Tokyo 162
03 268 6151

DANCE MAGAZINE
Bi-monthly
Shinshokan Co. Ltd
1-21-7 Sengoku,
Bunkyo-ku
Tokyo 112
03 946 5331

DANCE NOW
Monthly
TES Shuppan
Nichibei-Shokai Building
1-6-3 Ohashi, Meguro-ku
Tokyo 153
03 463 2405

TOKYO SCENE
c/o Dancework Foundation
2-17-20 Ebisu, Shibuya-ku
Tokyo 150
03 433 2622

Organisations
JAPAN BALLET
ASSOCIATION
Nihon Ballet Kyokai
Shinyo Building, 33-8
Udagawa-cho
Shibuya-ku
Tokyo 150
03 462 5524

MODERN DANCE
ASSOCIATION
Gendai Buyo Kyokai
1-6-2 Shibuya, Shibuya-ku
Tokyo 150
03 400 4544

Festival
TOGA FESTIVAL
July/August
c/o The Japan Performing
Arts Center
1-20-10-103 Takatano Baba
Sinjuku-ku, Tokyo 160
03 202 2170

LATIN AMERICA

Magazines
CUBA EN EL BALLET
Quarterly
Calzada 510 e/D & E Vedado
Habana 4
Cuba
07 32 63 43/32 28 29

DANÇAR
Bi-monthly
Rua Rodolfo
Troppmair, 49
04001 São Paulo
Brazil
011 855 4599/7239

Companies
BALÉ DA CIDADE DE SÃO
PAULO
Rua João
Passalacqua, 66
01326 São Paulo
Brazil

BALLET NACIONAL DO
BRASIL
c/o Dalal Achcar
Rua Oitis, 20
22451 Rio de Janeiro
Brazil

BALLET NACIONAL DE
CUBA
Empresa Gran Teatro de La
Habana
Calzada 510 e/D & E Vedado
Habana 4
07 32 63 43/32 51 41

Organisations
FUNDACEN
Fundação Nacional de Artes
Cênicas
Av. Rio Branco, 257-130
20040 Rio de Janeiro
Brazil
021 220 9156

GRUPO AMALGAMA
c/o Anne U. V. Westphal
Rua Bambina 67/305
Rio de Janeiro
Brazil
021 286 9153

Festivals
FESTIVAL INTERNACIONAL
DE BALLET DE LA HABANA
October/November
(bi-annual)
Calzada 510 e/D and
E Vedado
Habana 4
Cuba
07 32 41 51/32 05 04

FESTIVAL NACIONAL DE
DANÇA
July
CBDD
Rua Francisco Serrador 2
20031 Rio de Janeiro
Brazil
021 262 5636

NETHERLANDS

Magazines
DANS
Monthly
Kroon Uitgevers bv
PO 3055
Zijpendaalseweg 51
6802 DB Arnhem
085 51 48 11

MUZIEK EN DANS
Vondelstraat 120
1054 GS Amsterdam
020 85 45 11

Companies
DUTCH NATIONAL BALLET
Het Muziektheater
Waterlooplein 22
PO 16486
1001 RM Amsterdam
020 551 89 11
Friends/mailing list

NETHERLANDS DANCE
THEATRE
Schedeldoekshaven 60
2511 EN s'Gravenhage
70 60 99 31
Friends/Bericht magazine
five times a year

Organisation
NEDERLANDS INSTITUUT
VOOR DE DANS
Herengracht 174
1016 BR Amsterdam
020 23 75 41

Festivals
CADENCE FESTIVAL
MODERNE DANS
April-May
John Reinders
Den Haag
070 543 202

HOLLAND FESTIVAL
June
Kleine-Gartmanplantsoen 21
1017 RP Amsterdam
020 27 65 66

SPRINGDANCE FESTIVAL
April
Lucas Bolwerk 24
3512 EJ Utrecht
030 331 343

NORWAY

Company
NORWEGIAN NATIONAL
BALLET
Den Norske Opera
Storgaten 23
0184 Oslo 1
02 42 94 75
Friends/newspaper guide to
the arts in Oslo (Stage)

SOUTH EAST ASIA

Magazines
MANILA ARTS BULLETIN
Cultural Center of the
Philippines
Roxas Boulevard, Manila
02 832 3875

PERFORMING ARTS
National Theatre Dance
Circle
National Theatre Trust
Clemenceau Avenue
Singapore 0923

Companies
BALLET PHILIPPINES
Presidential Commission on
the Arts
C/o Cultural Center of the
Philippines
Roxas Boulevard, Manila
02 832 1125

DANCE THEATRE
PHILIPPINES
College of Music
University of the Philippines
Diliman, Quezon City 1101
02 976 963

SPAIN

Magazines
MONSALVAT
Monthly
Plaza Gala Placidia 1, 16 -1B
08006 Barcelona
03 218 11 97
Covers classical, opera and
dance

EL PUBLICO
Monthly
Centro de Documentación
Teatral
Capitán Haya 44
28020 Madrid
01 270 57 49
Publishes annual Guía
Teatral

Company
BALLET DEL TEATRO
LIRICO NACIONAL DE LA
ZARZUELA
Plaza de Isabel II
28013 Madrid

DANCE INFORMATION

Organisations
INAEM
Instituto Nacional de Artes
Escénicas y Música
Plaza del Rey, 1, 3a planta
28071 Madrid
01 429 24 44

Festivals
FESTIVAL INTERNACIONAL
DE MUSICA Y DANZA -
GRANADA
June/July
Dirección del Festival
Ancha de Santo
 Domingo 1
18009 Granada
058 225 201

MAIATZA
DANTZAN/JORNADAS DE
DANZA CONTEMPORANEA
May
Departmento de Cultura de
la Diputación Foral de
Guipúzcoa
Plaza de Guipúzcoa s/n
2004 San Sebastian
043 29 00 11

DANSA A VALENCIA
February
Dirección de Cultura,
Educación y Ciencia
Avenida Campanar 32
46015 Valencia
06 347 01 44

TEMPORADA DE DANSA
DE LA CAIXA DE
TERRASSA
October/June
Centre Cultural Caixa de
Terrassa
Rambla d'Egara 340
08221 Terrassa
093 780 41 44

MADRID EN DANZA
May/June
Centro Cultural de la Villa
Jardines del Descubrimiento
s/n
28001 Madrid
01 275 45 51

LOS VERANOS DE LA
VILLA
July/August
Ayuntamiento de Madrid
Dirección general de
Servicios de Cultura
Calle Mayor 83,
1a Planta
28005 Madrid
01 242 35 42

FESTIVAL DE OTONO
September/October
Calle Zurbano 56
28010 Madrid
01 410 73 00

SWEDEN

Companies
CULLBERG BALLET
Ricksteatern
Rasundavägen 150
17130 Solna
08 730 52 20

ROYAL SWEDISH BALLET
PO 16094
103 22 Stockholm
08 22 17 40

STORA TEATERNS BALLET
Stora Teatern
PO 53116
400 15 Göteborg
031 17 47 45

Museum
DANSMUSEET
Laboratoriegatan 10
115 27 Stockholm
08 667 95 12
International museum
devoted to dance in all
aspects and cultures

SWITZERLAND
Companies

BASEL BALLETT
Basler Theater
PO 4010 Basel
061 22 11 30/22 19 76

BEJART BALLET LAUSANNE
Palais de Beaulieu,
CP 80
1000 Lausanne 22
021 45 11 11

ZURICH OPERA BALLET
Opernhaus Zürich
8001 Zürich
01 251 69 20

Festivals
BASEL TANZTAGE
September
Hochbergerstrasse 15
4002 Basel
061 66 14 88

BERNER TANZTAGE
September
Association 'Berner Tanztage'
PO 4061
3001 Bern
031 40 04 28

TURKEY

Festival
FESTIVAL INTERNATIONAL
ISTANBUL
June/July
Besiktas 1
Istanbul 80700
160 45 33

USA

Magazines
DANCE CHRONICLE
Three times a year
PO Box 331,
Village Station
NY 10014
212 242 4358
Studies in dance history and
aesthetics
Subscriptions:
Marcel Dekker Journals
PO 11305, Church Street
Station
New York NY 10249
212 696 9000

DANCE MAGAZINE
Monthly
33 West 60th Street
New York NY 10023
212 245 9050

Companies
ALVIN AILEY AMERICAN
DANCE CENTER
1515 Broadway, Minskoff
Theater Building
New York NY 10036
212 997 1980

AMERICAN BALLET
THEATRE
890 Broadway
New York NY 10003
212 477 30 30

BALLET WEST
50 West 200th South
Salt Lake City UT 84101
801 364 4343

CUNNINGHAM DANCE
FOUNDATION
463 West Street
New York NY 10014
212 255 8240

DANCE THEATRE OF
HARLEM
446 West 152nd Street
New York NY 10031
212 977 7751

MARTHA GRAHAM
CENTER OF
CONTEMPORARY DANCE
316 East 63rd Street
New York NY 10021
212 832 9166

HOUSTON BALLET
1916 West Gray
PO 13150
Houston TX 77219-3150
713 523 6300

JOFFREY BALLET
130 West 56th Street
New York NY 10019
212 265 7300
and
135 North Grand Avenue
Los Angeles CA 90012
213 972 7642

NEW YORK CITY BALLET
New York State Theater
Lincoln Center for the
Performing Arts
New York NY 10023
212 870 5500

PACIFIC NORTHWEST
BALLET
4649 Sunnyside Avenue
North
Seattle WA 98103
206 547 5900

SAN FRANCISCO BALLET
455 Franklin Street
San Francisco CA 94102
415 861 5600

TWYLA THARP DANCE
853 Broadway
New York NY 10003
212 475 7788

Organisations

AMERICAN DANCE GUILD
31 West 21st Street
New York NY 10010
212 627 3790
Promotes dance and needs
of dance artists
Newsletter/conferences

**CONGRESS ON RESEARCH
IN DANCE**
Dance and Dance Education
Department
New York University
35 West 4th Street,
Room 675
New York NY 10003
212 998 5410
Encourages scholarly study
of dance
Publishes Dance Research
Journal twice a year

**DANCE THEATER
WORKSHOP**
219 West 19th Street
New York NY 10011
212 691 6500
Co-ordinating organisation for
the National Performance
Network

**DANCE PERSPECTIVES
FOUNDATION**
c/o Curtis L. Carter,
President
Haggerty Museum of Art
Marquette University
Milwaukee WI 53233
414 224 7290
Promotes scholarship and
research in dance as a form
of art

DANCE/USA
777 Fourteenth Street NW
Suite 540
Washington, DC 20009
National service organisation
for professional dance in
USA
Monthly Journal (Update)

Festivals

**AMERICAN DANCE
FESTIVAL**
June/July
PO 6097
College Station
Durham NC 27708
919 684 6402
also
1697 Broadway, Suite 1201
New York NY 10019
212 586 1925

ASPEN MUSIC FESTIVAL
June/August
PO Box AA
Aspen CO 81612
303 925 3254

DANCEMOBILE
Winter, spring, summer
536 West 111th Street, Suite
76
New York NY 10025
212 662 0657
Indoor/outdoor
performances of dance

**JACOB'S PILLOW DANCE
FESTIVAL**
June-August
Box 287
Lee MA 01238
413 637 1322

PEPSICO SUMMERFARE
July
The International Performing
Arts Festival of the State
University
Purchase NY 10577-0410
914 253 5949

Research source

**THE DANCE COLLECTION
OF THE PERFORMING ARTS
RESEARCH CENTER**
New York Public Library
111 Amsterdam Avenue
New York
NY 10023
212 870 1655
Central reference collection
of the literature and
iconography of dance

Danceabilia

THE DANCE MART
Box 48
Homecrest Street
Brooklyn NY 11229
718 627 0477
Rare books, autograph
material

Book sources

**DANCE HORIZONS BOOKS
DANCE BOOK CLUB**
Princeton Book Co.
Publishers
PO 57
Pennington NJ 08534
609 737 8177

GOLDEN LEGEND INC.
7615 Sunset Boulevard
Los Angeles CA 90046
213 850 5520

Film/video sources

**DANCE FILMS
ASSOCIATION**
241 East 34th Street, Room
301
New York NY 10016
212 688 7019

DANCE IN AMERICA
WNET/13
356 West 58th Street,
7th floor
New York NY 10019
212 560 200

EYE ON DANCE
ARC Videodance
88 Lexington Avenue, #3K
New York NY 10016
212 725 5530

KULTUR
121 Highway 36
West Long Branch NJ 07764
201 229 2343

USSR

Companies

BOLSHOI BALLET
Bolshoi Theatre
Sverdlov Square
Moscow K9

KIROV BALLET
Kirov State and Academic
Theatre of Opera and Ballet
Leningrad

Festival

**LENINGRAD WHITE
NIGHTS**
June
via Intourist Moscow Limited
292 Regent Street
London W1
01 631 1252

WEST GERMANY

Magazine

BALLETT INTERNATIONAL
Monthly
PO Box 270 443
Richard-Wagner-Strasse 33
5000 Köln 1
0221 23 66 36
International editorial office:
Herengracht 174
NL 1016 BR Amsterdam
Netherlands
020 26 82 90

Companies

**DEUTSCHES OPER BALLET
– BERLIN**
Richard-Wagner-Strasse 10
1000 Berlin 10
030 34 38 264

FRANKFURT BALLET
Untermainanlage 11
6000 Frankfurt
069 25 62 335

HAMBURG BALLET
Hamburgische Staatsoper
Grosse Theaterstrasse 34
2000 Hamburg 36
040 356 800

STUTTGART BALLET
Oberer Schlossgarten 6
7000 Stuttgart 1
0711 20320

**WUPPERTALER
TANZTHEATER**
Spinnstrasse 4
5600 Wuppertal 2
0202 55 00 50

Festivals

**INTERNATIONALE
TANZWERKSTATT BONN**
PO 2467
5300 Bonn 1
0228 63 23 26

TANZWERKSTATT BERLIN
June
Spichernstrasse 15
1000 Berlin 30
030 213 33 32

INDEX

Page numbers in bold refer to main entries.

A

Abbott, George 208
Accumulation 196
Acrobats of God 18, 201, 258
Adagio Hammerklavier 158
Adam, Adolphe 20
Adams, John 199, 204
Admiring La Argentina 254
Adorations 18
Adventures in Motion Pictures 232, 238
Adzido 242
Aerialist, The 247
After Venice 219
Afternoon of a Faun 18, 57, 122, 182
Agon 40, 42, 95, **97-8**, 101, 154, 155, 159, 260
Ailey, Alvin 64, 83, 144, 154, 157, **194-5**, 207, 234, 243, 248
Airs 217, 221
Airwaves 253
Alexander, Rod 103
Alice 177, 189
All That Jazz 208
Allegro Brillante 96
Allegro, il Pensero ed il Moderato 251
Allegri Diversi 146
Alonso, Alberto 120, 121, 178
Alonso, Alicia 22, 88, 89, 103, 177, 178
Alonso, Fernando 178
Alston, Richard 42, 59, 79, 126, 182, **195**, 201, 203, 210, 214, 217, 233, 255
Amagatsu, Ushio 254
Amaya, Carmen 241
Ambrose, Kay 177
American Document 68
American Ballet 71, 117
American Ballet Company 160
American Ballet Theatre 16, 17, 22, 29, 30, 34, 35, 37, 47, 48, 49, 53, 54, 58, 68, 81, 87, **88-9**, 94, 103, 104, 106, 111, 112, 114-5, 116, 118, 121, 122, 123, 128, 129, 131, 138, 142, 143, 149, 155, 160, 165, 167, 170, 174, 175, 189, 193, 194, 203, 209, 210, 222, 226, 227, 235, 250
American Ballroom Theatre 63
American Dance Asylum 243
American Dance Machine 72, 103
American Genesis 43
American in Paris, An 110
Amor Brujo, El 241
Amour Sorcier, L' **see** *Amor Brujo, El*
Amsterdams Ballet 157
Anastasia 169
Anastos, Peter 93, 227
Anatomy Lesson, The 211, 212
Ancient Voices of Children 197
Andersen, Hans Christian 14, 110
Andersen, Ib 148
Anderson, Laurie 196

Anderson, Lea 231, 232, 245, 248
Angels of the Inmost Heaven 71
Anna Karenina 121
Antonio 241
Apollinaire, Guillaume 52
Apollo 40, **41-2**, 46, 96, 98, 113, 117, 128, 159, 174, 176
Appalachian Spring 66, **67-8**, 116, 201
Apparitions 48, 50, 107, 136
Après-midi d'un faune, L' 39, 49, 53, 55, **56-7**, 99, 164, 197
Arc-en-Ciel 213
Archer, Kenneth 58
Arden Court 220, 221
Argentina, La 241, 254
Argentinita, La 241
Arien 228
Armitage, Karole 88, 153, 181, 182, 183, 203, 206, 222, **226-7**, 233, 234, 237, 238
Arms 247
Armstrong, John 90
Arpino, Gerald 52, 150, 164, 165
Artifact 240
Artus-Sage 153
As Time Goes By 222
Asch 235
Ashley, Merrill 176
Ashley, Robert 196
Ashton, Frederick 17, 20, 23, 29, 33, 37, 47, 48, 50, 54, 55, 59, 60, 66, 75, 81, 87, **88-93**, 99, 100, 104, 105, 107, 109, 110, 112, 114, 116, 117, 124, 125, 126, 127, **136-40**, 143, 145, 147, 155, 156, 158, 159, 165, 169, 175, 177, 181, 182, 185, 186, 187, 191, 195, 218, 232, 260
Astafieva, Serafina 106
Astaire, Adele 62
Astaire, Fred **62-3**, 109, 115, 208
Astarte 164
Asylmuratova, Altynai 167
At Midnight 160
At the Edge of the Precipice 157
Aterballetto 200
Atlas, Charles 202, 206, 227, 234
Auld, John 49
Aureole 220, 221, 223
Australian Ballet 34, 37, 91, 100, 108, 109, 113, 138, 139, **140-1**, 152, 153, 173, 177, 219, 255
Australian Dance Theatre 141, 219, 239
Autumn Leaves 47
Available Light 199
Aviary: A Ceremony for Bird People 213

B

Babe, Thomas 222
Babel, Babel 246, 247
Babilée, Jean 119
Baby, Baby, Baby 232
Bach, Johann Sebastian 43, 60, 122, 144, 179, 220, 238, 251
Bach and Offenbach 238
Bach Duet 222

Bach Partita 222
Bad Smells 84, 222
Bagouet, Dominique 198
Baiser de la Fée, Le 107, 147, 170
Baker's Dozen 222
Bakst, Léon 39, 47, 56
Bal à la Cour de Louis XIV 10
Bal, Le 106
Balanchine, George 8, 17, 24, 25, 28, 30, 31, 33, 34, 35, 36, 37, 39, **40-3**, 44, 45, 46, 47, 48, 51, 54, 60, 62, 68, 69, 81, 86, 87, 88, 90, 91, 92, **93-8**, 101, 103, 110, 112, 116, 117, 118, 122, 126, 128, 130, 134, 139, 140, 143, 146, 147, 152, 154, 155, 158, 159, 161, 165, 167, 172, 173, 174, 175, 176, 178, 179, 184, 185, 187, 188, 201, 218, 221, 222, 226, 227, 233, 240, 250, 251, 258, 259, 260
Ballet Caravan 71, 114, 115, 116, 117, 128, 178
Ballet de la Délivrance de Renaud 8, 9
Ballet de Marseille 25, 30, 119, 120, 184
Ballet de Nancy 156, 206
Ballet Español 241
Ballet Gulbenkian **141-2**
Ballet Imperial **see** *Tchaikovsky Piano Concerto No. 2*
Ballet in a Nutshell 219
Ballet of the 20th Century 49, 52, 54, 58, 121, 144, 145, 246
Ballet Rambert 58, 66, 89, 91, **98-100**, 116, 142, 176, 189, 191, 195, 197, 210, 212, 214, 217, 223, 233, 237, 244 (see also Rambert Dance Company)
Ballet School 18
Ballet Society 87, 94, 97
Ballet Theatre **see** American Ballet Theatre
Ballet West 17, 128
Ballets de Génève 226
Ballets de Paris 118
Ballets des Champs-Elysées 118
Ballets Jooss 76
Ballet(s) Russe(s) de Monte Carlo 50, 87, 94, 103
Ballets Russes (de Serge Diaghilev) 33, 38-59, 76, 87, 91, 96, 99, 104, 106, 107, 112, 113, 114, 116, 119, 127, 164, 167, 170, 177, 183, 214, 228
Ballets Trockadero de Monte Carlo, Les 23, 125, **227**, 250, 260
Ballets: USA 122
Ballets 33, Les 40
Banda 154
Bannerman, Christopher 210
Barber, Samuel 194
Barber Violin Concerto 176
Bardon, Henry 138
Barker, Teresa 232
Barn Fever 230
Barnett, Robby 215, 234
Barra, Ray 188
Bartlett, Terry 147

Bartók, Béla 235, 236
Bartók/Aantekeningen 235
Baryshnikov, Mikhail 22, 29, 30, 34,
 37, 43, 47, 56, 62, 88, 89, 93,
 107, 109, 110, 112, 119, 120, 125,
 134, 136, 140, **142-3**, 156, 157,
 165, 166, 167, 170, 174, 176,
 181, 185, 193, 210, 222, 226,
 227, 251
Basel Ballet 22, 49, 98, 112, 138,
 170, 187
Batchelor, Michael 153
Batsheva Dance Company 215
Bauchant, André 41
Bausch, Pina 58, 76, 83, 120, 123,
 130, 142, 174, 199, 221, 224,
 228-9, 235, 237, 240, 241, 247,
 249, 255, 257
Bavarian State Opera Ballet 186
Baxter, Ivy 207
Bayadère, La 31, 33, **34-5**, 37, 114,
 145, 166, 175, 181, 258
Baylis, Lilian 104, 125
Baylis, Nadine 190, 191
Beach Boys 124, 222
Beauchamps, Piere 78
Beauty and the Beast 128 (Lew
 Christensen), 182 (Wayne Eagling)
Beauty, Art and the Kitchen Sink 236
Because We Must 232, 233
Beccari, Filippo 100
Beethoven, Ludwig Van 50, 60, 220,
 222, 158
Begichev, Vladimir 30
Béjart, Maurice 20, 48, 49, 51, 52,
 54, 56, 58, 64, 65, 70, 77, 118,
 119, 120, 121, 131, 141, **143-5**,
 150, 157, 159, 161, 164, 167,
 173, 180, 181, 183, 189, 190, 219,
 235, 240, 246, 251
Belasco, David 63
Bell High 195
Belle au bois dormant, La **see**
 Sleeping Beauty, The
Belle Vie, La 188
Beloved, The 155
Beneath the Bridge 242
Benesh, Rudolf and Joan 78
Benjamin, Leanne 146
Bennett, Michael 110, 122, 208
Benois, Alexandre 46, 48, 145
Béranger, Anne 198
Berg, Alban 83, 159
Bergese, Micha 201, 210, 214
Berlioz, Hector 12, 50, 112
Bernstein, Leonard 111, 122, 123
Bessmertnova, Natalia 21, 101, 111,
 159, 161, 162, 163
Beyond Twelve 219
Bhakti 144
Bhuller, Darshan Singh 210
Biches, Les 52, 53, **54-5**, 91, 126, 154
Big Bertha 220
Big City, The 76
Big Parade, The 244
Billy the Kid, 68, 103, 114, **115-6**, 117
Bintley, David 29, 42, 49, 126, 127,
 128, **145-7**, 170, 182
Birnie, Carel 211

Birthday Offering 23, 33, 92, 107
Birtwistle, Harrison 182
Bishton, Jamie 193
Bix Pieces, The 221
Bizet, Georges 51, 119
Björnsson, Fredbjörn 18
Blake, William 105
Blaska, Félix 234
Blauvelt Mountain 243
Bliss, Arthur 105
Block Play 81
Blood Wedding 240, 241
Blue Angel, The 119
Blue Lady 199
Bluebeard 106 (Michel Fokine), 224,
 228 (Pina Bausch)
Blues Suite 194, 195
Blum, René 50
Bocca, Julio 143
Bodas de Sangre **see** *Blood Wedding*
Bodymap 232, 234
Bogosian, Eric 253
Bolender, Todd 117
Bolero **145**
Bolm, Adolph 127
Bolshoi Ballet 10, 18, 22, 30, 31, 32,
 37, 88, 93, **100-1**, 107, 110, 111,
 119, 120, 121, 133, 143, 149, 150,
 161, 162, 166, 171, 178, 180
Bond, Edward 240
Bonnefous, Jean-Pierre 59
Booth, Laurie 252
Borchsenius, Valborg 18
Borovansky, Edouard 140
Borovansky, Xenia 140
Borriello, Adriana 236
Bortoluzzi, Paolo 49
Bösendorfer Waltzes 255
Boston Ballet 247
Bourne, Val 255
Bournonville, August 12, 13, **14-19**,
 22, 23, 32, 137, 148, 152, 177,
 185, 258
Boutique fantasque, La 25, 50
Bowery, Leigh 234
Bowie, David 244
Boxes 219
Bozzacchi, Giuseppina 24
Bozzoni, Max 156
Brady, Eileen 239
Brae, June 105
Brahms, Johannes 50, 160, 250
Brahms/Handel 122, 222
Branca, Glenn 222
Braunsweg, Julian 113, 114
Breaking Images 236
Breakneck Hotel 230
Brecht, Bertolt 170, 228, 246
Brenaa, Hans 16, 18
Bridge the Distance 204, 210
Brigadoon 103, 116
Brind, Bryony 168, 175
Britten, Benjamin 89, 127, 136, 150,
 194, 204
Broken Set of Rules, A 182
Brown, Carolyn 203
Brown, Trisha 35, 54, 84, 173, 193,
 196-7, 209, 216, 231, 236, 247,
 251, 252

Browne, Leslie 88
Bruce, Christopher 100, 114, 142,
 169, 184, 190, **197-8**, 214, 217,
 244
Bruhn, Erik 14, 16, 22, 25, 32, 81,
 88, 89, 102, 116, 128, 134,
 148-9, 155, 156, 165, 176, 177
Bubbles, John 62
Bucket Dance Theatre 154, 207
Buckland, David 203, 204
Buckley, Tim **229-30**
Bugaku 155
Buirge, Susan 213
Bujones, Fernando 88, 156
Burge, Lucy 60, 66
Burrow, The 169, 185
Burrows, Jonathan 153
Butcher, Rosemary **230-1**, 252
Butler, John 211
Byrne, David 222

C

Cabaret 208, 218
Café Müller 229
Cage, John 57, 113, 192, 201, 202,
 209, 216
Cage, The 122
Calambre 247
Calcium Light Night 176
Calico Mingling 199
Camargo, Marie 9, 10
Camargo Society 91, 106, 127
Camelot 72
Campbell, Neville 242
Canta 255
Cantate No. 51 144
Caplan, Elliot 202
Capriol Suite 89
Card Game, The 117
Carlson, Carolyn 183, **198-9**, 213,
 247
Carmen 33, 102, **119-20**, 148, 150,
 178, 240, 241
*Carmen Arcadiae Mechanics
 Perpetuum* 182
Carmen Suite 120, 121, 178
Carousel 103
Carrafa, John 193
Caruso, Enrico 235
Cascade 199
Castle, Vernon and Irene 62
Catherine Wheel, The 70, 222
Cats 208, 218
Cave of the Heart 69
Cecchetti, Enrico 112, 116
Celebration 204
Cell 200, 210
Central Ballet of China 106, **149-50**,
 163, 250
Ceremonies 217
Cerrito, Fanny 22, 23
Chabukiany, Vakhtang 35
Chaconne 43, 159, 184
Chadwick, Fiona 30
Chagall, Marc 47
Chair 209
Chairs 180
Champion, Gower 208
Chanel, Coco 39, 44

Changing Your Mind 223
Channels/Inserts 202, 226
Chant du rossignol, Le 116
Charlip, Remy 203
Charnock, Nigel 236, 237
Chäs 188
Chase, Alison 215, 234
Chase, Lucia 88, 89, 106, 143, 160
Chausson, Ernest 130
Chauviré, Yvette 21, 183
Checkmate 105, 109
Chesworth, John 217, 218
Chicago 208
Chicago City Ballet 159
Childs, Lucinda 35, 54, 145, 173,
   181, 183, 193, **199-200**, 205,
   216, 222, 230, 235, 236, 239,
   252, 253, 257
Cholmondeleys, The **231-2**, 236,
   245, 248, 253
Choo San Goh 153
Chopin Concerto 47
Chopin, Frédéric 46, 123, 124, 125,
   139
Chopiniana see *Sylphides, Les*
Chopinot, Régine 245
Choréartium 50
Choreographic Offering 144
Choros 146
Chorus Line, A 110, 208
Christensen, Harold 117, 127, 128
Christensen, Lew 115, 117, 123, 127,
   128
Christensen, William 117, 127, 128
Chuma, Yoshiko 249
Cinderella 29, 31, 89, **92-3**, 107,
   109, 137, 143, 145, 159, 181,
   183, 184, 227, 246, 247, 260
Circumstantial Evidence 253
Circus Polka 94
CIVIL WarS, The 52, 257
Claid, Emilyn 237, 238
Clark, Michael 114, 123, 181, 182,
   183, 195, 217, 224, 226, 227,
   232, **233-4**, 237, 238, 240, 244,
   251
Clarke, Martha 144, 215, 224, **234-5**
Class 200
Clavé, Antoni 119
Clegg, Peter 25
Clemente, Francesco 239
Clichés and the Holiday, The 232
Cloven Kingdom 220
Clump 232
Clytemnestra 69
Coast Zone 202
Cobras 63
Cochran, C.B. 112
Cocteau, Jean 39, 44, 51, 52, 118,
   156, 219
Cohan, Robert 67, 168, **200-1**, 204,
   210, 213, 217, 223
Cohen, Fritz 76
Cole, Jack 208
Coleman, Michael 124, 136, 137
Collier, Lesley 136, 137
Colour Moves 254
Concert, The 122, **123-4**
Concerto 169

Concerto Barocco 117
Consort Lessons 147
Continuous Project- Altered Daily
   206, 216
Conversano, Frank 231
Copland, Aaron 67, 74, 103, 115, 116
Coppélia 23, **24-5**, 27, 28, 29, 32,
   49, 82, 93, 99, 109, 119, 125,
   127, 148, 157, 175, 183, 186,
   218, 260
Coralli, Jean 20, 183
Corder, Michael 126
Corelli, Arcangelo 68
Corsaire, Le 157, 181
Cortège Hongrois 24, 37
Cortege of Eagles 200, 201
Counter Revolution 238
Coward, Gaynor 232
Cragun, Richard 49, 134, 150, 188,
   189, 240
Craig, Gordon 82
Cramér, Ivo 102
Cranko, John 81, 101, 104, 108, 112,
   118, 126, 134, 140, 146, 147,
   148, **150-3**, 159, 168, 169, 170,
   175, 177, 179, 180, 183, 188,
   189, 190, 239, 240
Creation of the World, The 142
Cross-Garter'd 129
Crow, Susan 127, 153
Crowsnest 215, 234, 235
Cruel Garden 114, 197, 198, 217, 244
Crumb, George 197
Cry 194
Cullberg, Birgit 53, **102**, 131, 141,
   148, 172
Cummings, Blondell 249
Cunningham, Merce 52, 57, 66, 67,
   68, 70, 71, 79, 88, 92, 113, 161,
   173, 183, 192, 195, 199, **201-3**,
   204, 206, 207, 216, 217, 220,
   223, 226, 231, 232, 233, 239,
   240, 250, 251, 252, 253, 255,
   259
Curry, John 219

D

Dai Ailian 149
Dallas Ballet 247
d'Amboise, Jacques 175
Dance 199 (Lucinda Childs), 204
   (Laura Dean)
Dance Advance 127, **153**, 238
Dance Symphony 110, 167
Dance Theatre of Harlem 21, 22, 48,
   55, 98, 116, 123, 134, **154-5**, 207
Dance Works 219
Dancers 110, 143
Dances at a Gathering 47, 122,
   124-5, 227
*Dances from the Kingdom of the
   Pagodas* 195
Dancin' 208
Dancing and Shouting 255
Dandré, Victor 59
Danilova, Alexandra 25, 40, 47, 94,
   107
Dansproduktie 212
Dantzig, Rudi van 110, 158, 181, 198,

211
Daphne 240
Daphnis and Chloe 148 (John
   Cranko), 219 (Graeme Murphy)
Dark 199
Dark Elegies 102, 129, 130
Dark Meadow 69
Darrell, Peter 22, 32
Dash 218
Dauberval, Jean 11, 138
David and Goliath 213
Davies, Peter Maxwell 195
Davies, Siobhan 201, **203-4**, 210,
   214, 217, 255
Davis, Anthony 239
Day on Earth 68, 73, **74-5**
Day Two 215
Dead Dreams of Monochrome Men
   237
Dean, Laura 164, 173, 199, 200,
   204-5, 220, 221, 222, 235, 239,
   250, 251, 252, 253
Death and the Maiden 214
Death, Destruction and Detroit 257
Death in Venice 136
Deaths and Entrances 66
de Basil, Colonel 50
Debussy, Claude 39, 56, 57, 206,
   257
de Chatel, Krisztina 212, 236
Deep End 237
de Falla, Manuel 50, 241
De Gas 255
deGroat, Andrew 205, 257
De Keersmaeker, Anne Teresa 224,
   235-6, 237
Delibes, Léo 24, 93
Delius, Frederick 111
Dello Joio, Norman 70
Delsarte, François 78
de Mille, Agnes 62, 68, 87, 88,
   102-4, 115, 116, 122, 129, 154,
   178, 208
Denard, Michaël 16
Densité 21.5 198
de Pulszky, Romola 44, 56
Derman, Vergie 124
Denishawn 60, **63-5**, 66, 73, 144,
   191, 194, 208, 251, 253
Descent into the Maelstrom 239
De Soto, Edward 81
Deuce Coupe 124, 222, 153
Deutches Oper Berlin 169, 172, 185,
   199
de Valois, Ninette 33, 36, 37, 43, 45,
   53, 87, 89, 90, 100, **104-6**, 107,
   108, 109, 125, 127, 136, 176,
   201
Diaghilev, Serge 16, 21, 33, 36, 38-9,
   40, 42, **43-5**, 47, 50, 51, 53, 55,
   56, 58, 59, 86, 87, 98, 106, 107,
   108, 112, 113, 116, 127, 140, 154,
   157, 164, 167, 170, 183, 228
Different Drummer 170
Dim Lustre 129
Dior, Christian 119
Display, The 141
Diversion of Angels 67, 200
Divertimento from 'Le Baiser de

la Fée' 147
Dlugoszewski, Lucia 71
Dogtown 251
Dolin, Anton 23, 43, 45, 62, **106-7**, 108, 109, 112, 113, 116, 117, 125, 141, 149, 150, 156, 241
Don Quixote **33-4**, 89, 101, 109, 121, 141, 143, 149, 159, 167, 181, 184
Donn, Jorge 145
Donovan, Karen 90
Dorazio, Ralph 71
Dougla 154, 155
Dove, Ulysses 194
Dowell, Anthony 30, 32, 88, 126, 139, 140, **155-6**, 158, 175, 186
Dowland, John 223
Dragon, The 232
Drastic Classicism 226
Dream, The 81, 136, **138-9**, 140, 145, 155, 186, 187, 216, 258
Dream is Over, The 198
Dream of Galileo 240
Dreams 77, 83
Dreamtime 168
Drink To Me Only With Thine Eyes 251
Drop Your Pearls and Hog it, Girl 114
Drumming 204
Duato, Nacho 212
Dubreuil, Alain 151
Dudinskaya, Natalia 180
Duets 203
Dukes, Ashley 99
Duncan, Isadora 9, 45, 47, 60, 64, **65-66**, 72, 85, 98, 101, 144, 170, 198, 199, 224, 246
Dunham, Katherine 64
Dunn, Douglas 203, **206-7**, 216
Dunn, Robert 192, 216, 251
Duo Concertant 176
Dupont, Patrick 43, **156-7**, 181, 184
Dutch National Ballet 58, 77, 154, **157-8**, 178, 211, 247
Dutiful Ducks 233
DV8 Physical Theatre 83, 84, 120, 224, 229, **236-7**, 238, 242, 243
Dvořák, Anton 129
Dying Swan, The 45, 59

E

Eagling, Wayne 112, 126
Early, Fergus 17
Easdale, Brian 110
Easter Freeway Processional 207
Echoing of Trumpets 77, 129
Education of the Girlchild 249
Eguchi, Takaya 255
Eight Jelly Rolls 221, 222
Eiko and Koma 254, 256
Einstein on the Beach 199, 253, 257
Ek, Mats 102
Ek, Niklas 102
Elena's Aria 235
Elgar, Edward 75, 220
Elite Syncopations 91, 124, 169, 177, 216
Ellington, Duke 194, 207
Ellis Island 249
Elssler, Fanny 21, 178

Embarque 204
Energizer 239
Enfant et les Sortilèges, L' 168, 212
Enigma Variations 75, 136
Eno, Brian 204
Entre Dos Aguas 214
Episodes 97, 117, 176
Epitaph 158
Ernst, Max 119
Errand into the Maze 69
Erté 119
Escudero, Vicente 241
Eshkol, Noa 78
Esmeralda, La 19, 23
Esplanade 220, 221
Esquivel, Jorge 178
Esteemed Guests 250
Etudes 18, 29, 113, 156
Eunice 45
Eureka 239
Evdokimova, Eva 25, 102
Event 240
Evil Queen, The 102
Extemporary Dance Theatre 17, 223, 236, **237-8**
Ezralow, Daniel 215, 220

F

Façade 55, 89, **90-1**, 116, 124
Fagan, Garth 153, 154, 194, **207**, 243
Falco, Louis 80, 142, 211, 217
Fall River Legend 88, 102, 103, 115, 178
Family Portrait 102
Fancy Free 52, 87, 88, 103, 115, 121, **122-3**, 154, 155, 160, 222
Far from Denmark 152
Farber, Viola 203, 206, 213, 242
Farrell, Suzanne 40, 43, 95, 155, **159-60**, 166, 175, 176
Fase 255
Faurè, Gabriel 43, 75, 94, 169, 189
Faust 19
Featherstonehaughs, The 232
Fedorovitch, Sophie 91
Feld, Eliot 88, 134, 151, **160-1**, 169, 222, 250
Fenley, Molissa 35, 205, 145, 236, **239**, 242
Feral 239
Ferri, Alessandra 22, 110, 112, 170
Fever Swamp 195, 243
Fiddler on the Roof 54, 122
Field, John (composer) 209
Field, John (dancer/director) 114
Field, Chair and Mountain 209
Field Figures 190
Field Papers 253
Field Study 228
Fielding Sixes 217
Fille mal gardée, La 11, 89, 126, 136, **137-8**, 145, 157, 175, 187
Filling Station, The 115, 123
Fire 205
Fire and Ice 219
Firebird, The 31, 38, 45, **47-8**, 77, 127, 144, 165, 179, 190, 255
Fish Wreck 232

Five Brahms Waltzes in the Manner of Isadora Duncan 60, 65, 136, 185, 186
Flee as a Bird 223
Flier, Jaap 211, 219
Flindt, Flemming 18, 172
Flowers 244
Flowers of the Forest 146
Fokine, Michel 16, 33, 35, 39, 40, 41, 43, 44, **45-9**, 50, 54, 59, 76, 82, 88, 99, 106, 107, 112, 113, 125, 130, 131, 139, 140, 144, 166, 167, 182, 183, 189
Foldi, Erzsebet 193
Folk Tale, A **18-19**, 176
Fonteyn, Margot 20, 31, 32, 36, 47, 67, 87, 105, **107-8**, 109, 112, 117, 125, 126, 127, 133, 134, 136, 141, 159, 165, 166, 169, 170, 175, 181, 185, 186, 187, 260
Footprints Dressed in Red 207, 154
For My Daughter 214
Force Field 205
Forces of Rhythm 155
Forest 210
Forsythe, William 83, 120, 123, 128, 142, 174, 181, 187, 189, 199, 212, 219, 222, 224, **239-40**, 252
Fosse, Bob 122, **208**
Fountain of Bakhchisaray, The 133
Four Saints in Three Acts 89
Four Schumann Pieces 155, 158
Four Temperaments, The 87, **96-7**, 98
Fracci, Carla 16, 21, 22, 49, 88, 89, 107, 149, 150, 241
Franca, Celia 100, 176, 177, 178
Franck, César 91
Frankenstein 182
Frankfurt Ballet 30, 48, 179, 239, 240, 245, 252
Franklin, Frederic 107, 116
Frankie and Johnny 115, 123
Freaks, The 112
Freeman, Gillian 173
French, Jared 115
Frontier 66, 68
Fugue 255
Fugue, The 221, 222
Fugue for Four Cameras 129
Fuller, Loie 60, 64, 213
Further and Further into Night 255

G

Gable, Christopher 185, 186
Gade, Niels W. 16, 18
Gades, Antonio 120, **240-1**
Gaîté Parisienne 50
Galanteries 146, 147
Galeotti, Vincenzo 10, 14
Gallery 213 (Alwin Nikolais), 219 (Graeme Murphy)
Gallotta, Jean-Claude 198, 245
Gamelan 165
Games, The 249
Gamson, Annabelle 65
Gänge 240
Garden of Earthly Delights, The 234
Garden of Villandry, The 234, 235

Garnier, Jacques 183
Gaskell, Sonia 157, 158, 178, 211
Gautier, Théophile 20, 21
Gehry, Frank 199
Geltser, Vasily 30
Gentlemen Prefer Blondes 103
George Frideric 197
George's House 223
Georgiadis, Nicholas 172, 173
Gershwin, George and Ira 62, 91
Gesture Dance 81
Gestures in Red 206
Geva, Tamara 40
Ghost Dances 142, 197
Gibbs, Linda 210
Gibson, John 199
Gielgud, Maina 37, 141
Gilbert, W.S. 151
Gilpin, John 107, 114, 156
Girl in a Straw Hat 198
Giselle 19, **20-1**, 22, 27, 31, 32, 46, 59, 88, 89, 99, 101, 107, 109, 110, 113, 116, 126, 127, 133, 142, 143, 149, 154, 156, 158, 165, 167, 174, 178, 183, 186, 187
Glacial Decoy 196
Gladly, Sadly, Badly, Madly 213
Glasco, Kimberly 177
Glass, Philip 122, 199, 207, 222, 239, 253, 257
Glass Pieces 122
Glazunov, Alexander 37
Gloria 75, 76, 170 (Kenneth MacMillan), 251 (Mark Morris)
Gnatt, Poul 17
Godunov, Alexander 88, 161
Goldberg Variations, The 122 (Jerome Robbins), 252 (Steve Paxton)
Golden Age, The 101, **163-4**
Golden Fleece, The 72
Golden Windows, The 257
Golovin, Alexander 47
Goncharova, Natalia 47, 53
Gordon, David 79, 88, 124, **209-10**, 216, 232, 238, 243, 245, 251, 252
Gordon, Gavin 105
Gordon, Peter 243
Gore, Walter 100, 141, 142
Gorsky, Alexander 101
Gosling, Nigel 129, 182
Gough, Orlando 255
Gould, Glenn 251
Gounod Symphony 184
Grace and Glitter 238
Graduation Ball 29
Graham, Martha 18, 50, 58, 59, 60, 64, **66-71**, 72, 73, 79, 83, 94, 102, 108, 116, 117, 118, 131, 158, 161, 168, 181, 186, 189, 190, 194, 195, 199, 200, 201, 202, 203, 204, 207, 210, 213, 216, 217, 220, 223, 224, 227, 231, 234, 236, 237, 258
Grahn, Lucile 12, 15, 22
Grand Canon 160
Grand Union, The 193, 196, 206, 209, 216, 217, 243, 251
Grand Union Dreams 216

Grands Ballets Canadiens, Les 128, 131, 177, 187
Grant, Alexander 177
Graves, Nancy 196
Great American Goof, The 115
Great Day in the Morning 257
Greco, José 250
Gregory, Cynthia 88, 175
Grey, Beryl 113, 114
Green Table, The 52, 75, **76-7**, 164, 165
Grigorovich, Yuri 30, 32, 37, 100, 101, 111, 153, 159, **161-4**, 170, 183
Grisi, Carlotta 12, 19, 20, 21, 22
Grosse Fuge 158
Grossman, Mechtild 224
Groupe de Recherche Chorégraphique de l'Opéra de Paris (GRCOP) 153, 183, 198, 206, 233, 246, 247
Groupe de Recherches Théâtrales de l'Opéra 198
Groupe Emile Dubois 198
Grüne Tisch, Der see *Green Table, The*
Guérin, Isabelle 183
Guillem, Sylvie 93, 183
Gusev, Pyotr 149, 150
Gypsy 122

H

Haber, David 177
Haigen, Kevin 179
Hail the New Puritan 234
Hall, Nigel 195
Hall, Yvonne 190
Halprin, Anna 196, 216
Halston 67
Hamburg Ballet 32, 36, 37, 153, 170, 179, 188
Hamel, Martine van 88, 175
Hamlet 53 (Bronislava Nijinska), 81, 108, 109 (Robert Helpmann)
Hamlet Connotations 165
Hamletmachine 236
Handel, George Frederick 197, 251
Harbinger 160
Haring, Keith 243
Harkavy, Benjamin 211, 212
Harlequinade 43
Harrington, Rex 177
Harris, Lee 215
Hartman, J.P.E. 18
Haven for Restless Angels of Mercy, A 248
Hawkins, Erick 64, 66, 67, 68, 71, 253
Haydée, Marcia 88, 134, 150, 152, 159, 165, 172, 175, 180, 186, 188, 189, 240
Haydn, Joseph 220, 222
Heckroth, Hein 76, 110
Heerden, Augustus van 190
Hell Dances 248
Helpmann, Robert 34, 36, 37, 43, 81, 92, 105, 107, **108-10**, 116, 125, 140, 141, 181, 200, 218, 219
Helsted, Edvard 16
Hemispheres 239
Henze, Hans Werner 89, 181, 240

Hepburn, Earl Lloyd **241-2**
Here and Now with Watchers 71
Hermanas, Las 34, 172
Hérold, Ferdinand 137
Hightower, Rosella 53, 183
Hijikata, Tatsumi 253
Hindberg, Linda 17
Hindemith, Paul 82, 96, 97
Hockney, David 156
Hodgkin, Howard 195
Hodson, Millicent 58, 59
Hoffman, E.T.A. 24, 28, 82
Hogarth, William 104
Holberg Suite 155
Holder, Geoffrey 48, 154, 155
Holm, Hanya 67, **72**, 73, 78, 122, 189, 194, 212
Homelands 219
Hoop Dance 81
Hopkins, Kenyon 83
Horiuchi, Gen 218
Horst, Louis 234, 235
Horton, Lester 64, 155, 194
Hot Gossip 218
Hot Shoe Show, The 218
Houbin, Pascale 245
House, The 249
Houston Ballet 150
How to Swing a Dog 230
Howard, Andrée 100
Howard, Robin 200, 210
Hoyland, John 195
Humphrey, Doris 60, 64, 67, 68, 72, **73-5**, 79, 80, 84, 161, 194, 208
Humpbacked Horse, The 23, 121
Hunger Artist, The 235
Hyatt, Gigi 179
Hynd, Ronald 25, 108, 114, 141

I

I Am Curious Orange 233
I Was Sitting on My Patio This Guy Appeared I Thought I Was Hallucinating 199, 257
Icare 113
Illuminations 89
Illusions - Like Swan Lake 179
I'm Old-Fashioned 62
Images Dance Company 242
Imago 213
In G Major 159
In Memory Of... 159
In the Night 125
In the Upper Room 193, 222
Incense 63
Incredible Orlando 244
Incubus 165
Informer, The 103
Ingres, Dominique 50
Intermezzo 160
Intermezzo No.2 160
Intimate Pages 198
Invitation, The 131, 169, 170, **171-2**, 185
Ionesco, Eugene 18
Irié 242
Irish Jumping Songs 230
Isadora 170
ISO 215

It Happened at Club Bombay Cinema 238
Ivan the Terrible 161, 163
Ivanov, Lev **28-32**, 34, 35, 138, 156, 179
Ivanovna, Empress Anna 166
Ives, Charles 75
Ivesiana 75, 97

J

Jackson, Jennifer 127, 153
Jacob's Pillow 64
Jaleo 246
Jamaican National Dance Company 207
James, Martin 175
Jamison, Judith 194
Janaček, Leos 168
Jaques-Dalcroze, Emile 64, 72, 78, 84, 98
Jardi Tancat 212
Jardin aux lilas **see** Lilac Garden
Jealousy 251
Jeanmaire, Renée 119, 120
Jenkins, Margaret 206
Jeu de Cartes 150, 152
Jeune Homme et la Mort, Le 119, 157
Jeux 56
Jewels 94, 96, 143, 159, 176
Jiang Zuhui 149
Job 43, 104, 106
Jobe, Tom 210, 214
Joffrey Ballet 18, 23, 49, 52, 53, 57, 58, 59, 68, 76, 77, 84, 91, 104, 114, 122, 134, 138, 150, 152, 155, **164-5**, 168, 189, 193, 194, 205, 212, 222, 239, 240, 250
Joffrey, Robert 58, 122, 139, **164-5**, 190, 193
John Falstaff 187
John, Lindsay 254
Johns, Jasper 202
Johnson, Kate 176
Johnson, Louis 155
Johnson, Virginia 21
Jomon Sho (Homage to Prehistory) 254
Jones, Bill T. 83, 194, 224, **242-3**, 248
Jones, Grace 207
Jones, Inigo 9
Jones, Marilyn 141
Jonson, Ben 9
Jooss, Kurt 52, **75-7**, 78, 102, 130, 149, 168, 189, 198, 228, 229
Joplin, Scott 91, 124, 169
Jour ou deux, Un 203
Journey for Two Sides: A Solo Dance Duet 253
Judson Dance Theatre 192, 196, 199, 206, 209, 216, 221, 249, 251, 252, 259
Jugement de Pâris, Le 23
Juice 249
Jumping Dance 204

K

Kabuki 144
Kaguya-Hime 168

Kahn, Hannah 250
Kain, Karen 177
Kalidasa 34
Kammermusik No. 2 97
Karsavina, Tamara 21, 48
Kasatkina, Natalia 101
Kaye, Nora 88, 89, 130, 132, 178, 186
Kehlet, Neils 218
Keil, Birgit 150, 188, 189
Kelly, Desmond 170
Kelly, Gene 62, 110, 123, 208
Kemp, Lindsay 114, 144, 197, 217, 219, 227, 235, **244**, 247
Kenton, Stan 169
Kern, Jerome 62
Khachaturian, Aram 162, 163
Khudekov, Sergei 34
Kinetic Molpai 64
King and I, The 122
Kinkan Shonen 254
Kirkland, Gelsey 21, 30, 88, 107, 129, 133, 142, **165-6**, 175, 186
Kirkland, Johnna 165
Kirov Ballet 16, 23, 34, 35, 45, 88, 93, 100, 101, 110, 111, 133, 134, 142, 143, 144, 149, 150, 161, 162, 163, **166-7**, 174, 180, 181, 227
Kirsova, Helene 140
Kirstein, Lincoln 40, 82, 87, 93, 94, 98, 114, 115, 117, 128, 154
Kiss 247
Kiss Me, Kate 72
Klimt, Gustav 234
Kochno, Boris 42, 45
Kokoschka, Oskar 217
Kolpakova, Irina 36
Konservatoriet **17-18**, 258
Kreutzberg, Harald 71, 79, 85
Kronstam, Henning 148
Kudelka, James 128, 177
Kylián, Jiri 42, 77, 131, 134, 142, 151, 161, **167-9**, 180, 182, 188, 189, 198, 212, 217, 259

L

La La La Human Steps 241
Laban, Rudolf von 72, 75, **78-9**, 84, 85, 149
Lacotte, Pierre 16, 24, 25
Lady From the Sea 102
Lady of the Camellias (Die Kamiliendame) 47, 153
Laing, Harold 129, 130, 132
Lament for Ignacio Sánchez Mejiás 73
Lamentation 66
Lancaster, Osbert 137, 151
Lanchbery, John 137, 138, 139, 173
Land 198
Landé, Jean-Baptiste 166
Lander, Harald 16, 18, 29, 113, 156, 183
Lander, Toni 88, 89
Land's Edge 215
Landscap 158
Larrieu, Daniel 238, 240, **244-5**
Larsen, Neils Bjørn 25
Last Look 84

Lateral Pass 196
Laurencin, Marie 54
Lavrovsky, Leonid 101, **110-2**, 121, 133, 163
Lavrovsky, Mikhail 111
Lawrence, Pauline 79, 80
Lazy Madge 206
LDC 240
Leaves are Fading, The 129, 165
LeClercq, Tanaquil 94
Leçon de ténèbres 246
Left of Centre 242
Legat, Nicolai 112
Legend of Joseph, The 43, 50
Legend of Love 161
Legnani, Pierina 26, 27, 31, 259
Lemon, Ralph 248
Lennon, John 198
Lesson, The 18, 172
Letter from Queen Victoria 257
Letter to the World 66, 68, 70, 71
Lewis, Daniel 81
Le Witt, Sol 199
Liberace 250
Lichine, David 29
Lichtknall 200
Liepa, Andris 101
Liepa, Maris 87
Lifar, Serge 41, 42, 44, 45, 85, 107, 109, **112-3**, 116, 118, 119, 141, 156, 183
Life and Times of Sigmund Freud, The 257
Life and Times of Joseph Stalin, The 257
Ligeti, György 179
Light, Parts 1-25 256
Lilac Garden 129, **130-1**, 177
Limón, José 64, 65, 68, 73, 74, 75, 77, **79-81**, 148, 181, 194, 207, 228, 234, 251
Liquid Assets 210
Liszt, Franz 50, 173
Little Ballet, The 222
Lloyd, Maude 129, 182
Lloyd Webber, Andrew 170, 208
Locale 202, 217
London Ballet 129
London City Ballet 13
London Contemporary Dance School 195, 200, 203, **210**, 213, 236, 237, 241, 242
London Contemporary Dance Theatre 67, 195, 200, 203, 204, 210, 213, 214, 215, 223, 237, 242, 245
London Festival Ballet 16, 17, 18, 22, 25, 29, 30, 32, 35, 37, 42, 49, 50, 51, 52, 57, 93, 100, 106, 112, **113-4**, 116, 120, 128, 136, 141, 142, 145, 149, 153, 165, 175, 184, 194, 197, 198, 212, 217, 233
Lonely Town, Lonely Street 214
Lopez, Pilar 241
Lopokov, Fyodor 162, 166
Loquasto, Santo 209
Lorca, Federico García 172, 197, 244
Loring, Eugene 68, 103, **114-6**, 154
Louis, Murray 181, 198, 213, 248

Loup, Le 119
Love Bewitched, A see *Amor Brujo, El*
Love, Kermit 103, 122
Love Songs 240
Løvenskjold, Herman 15Lubovitch,
   Lar 54, **141**, 217, 250
Lucifer 67, 108
Lüders, Adam 176
Lully, Jean-Baptiste 8, 11, 183
Lumbye, Hans Christian 16
Lumley, Benjamin 22
Lunn, Jonathan 210
Lustig, Graham 127, 153
Lynne, Gillian 186
Lyon Opéra Ballet 77, 93, 246
Lyric Suite 83
Lyric Theatre Company 83

M

McCall, Debra 82
McDonald, Anthony 255
Macero, Ted 83
McKayle, Donald 195
Mackerras, Charles 151
MacMillan, Kenneth 19, 32, 33, 37,
   58, 64, 75, 77, 88, 91, 98, 101,
   108, 111, 112, 119, 120, 124, 126,
   127, 131, 134, 136, 140, 143,
   147, 150, 153, 155, 159, **169-74**,
   177, 180, 181, 182, 185, 186,
   187, 188, 189, 190
Maddox, Michael 100
Madsen, Egon 150, 188
Mahler, Gustav 51, 75, 129, 172,
   179, 239
Mahler Symphonies 179
Maid of the Sea, The 149
Makarova, Natalia 21, 32, 35, 88,
   112, 114, 119, 125, 132, 133, 136,
   140, 142, 143, 153, 155, 166,
   167, 173, **174-5**, 184, 186
Malclès, Jean-Denis 92
Malinche, La 79
Maliphant, Russell 153
*Man Walking Down the Side of a
   Building* 196
Manen, Hans van 58, 120, 126, 142,
   150, 155, 158, 187, 211, 212
Manfred 181
Mangrove 252
Mann, Thomas 219
Manon 119, 155, 156, 169, 174, 182,
   186
Mantis Dance Company 223, 230
Marceau, Marcel 244
Marguerite and Armand 107, 108,
   126, 136, 181, 182
Marin, Maguy 93, 183, 224, 235,
   245-7, 257
Marina 232
Markard, Anna 76, 77
Markova, Alicia 21, 22, 45, 87, 88,
   106, 107, 109, 113, **116-7**, 125
Marley, Jacob 232
Marshall, Susan **247**, 248
Martins, Peter 14, 42, 43, 95, 118,
   122, 148, 159, **175-6**, 181, 185,
   222
Martyre de Saint Sébastien 257

Mask Mix Masque 207
Mass for Man, A 201
Massine, Léonide 25, 28, 33, 39, 40,
   41, 44, 45, 49, **50-2**, 58, 82, 88,
   104, 107, 110, 112, 113, 114, 116,
   126, 141, 162, 179, 260
Matisse, Henri 39
Matthews, Colin 182
May B 246, 247
Mayerling 120, 169, 172, **173-4**, 186
Mayonnaise 206
Mazzo, Kay 176
Meadowlark 160
Medea 102
Medium: Rare 160
Meehan, John 141
Mejia, Paul 159
Mendelssohn, Felix 138, 179
Merry Widow, The 108, 141
Messerer, Asaf 18
Metamorphosis 146, 147
Metropolitan Opera Ballet 52, 59,
   228
Midsummer Night's Dream, A 17, 81,
   94, 159, 179, 244, 259
Midsummer 126, 195, 182
Mielziner, Jo 131
Mikrokosmos 236
Miller, Bebe 230, 242, **248**
Miller, Tim 209, 230, 243, 251
Mind is a Muscle, The 216
Mindless Matter 241
Minkus, Ludwig 33, 34
Minz, Alexander 227
Miracle in the Gorbals 109, 200
Miracolo d'Amore 235
Miss Julie 53, 102, 131, 148, 172
Missa Brevis 77, 79
Mitchell, Arthur 21, 22, 134, 154,
   155
Mollino Room, The 226
MOMIX 215
Monk, Meredith 64, 82, 130, 199,
   205, 220, 247, **248-50**, 255,
   256, 257
Monkey Run Road 243
Monotones 92, 136, 155
Montgomery, George 223
Month in the Country, A 47, 136,
   139-40, 143, 175, 182, 186, 218
Monument for a Dead Boy 158
Moon Reindeer 102
Moor's Pavane, The 75, 79, **80-1**,
   148
Mordkin Ballet 88
Moreland, Barry 114
Morrice, Norman 100, 126, 156, 169,
   217, 218
Morris, Margaret 78
Morris, Mark 88, 227, 230, 232,
   250-1
Moscow Classical Ballet 101
Moulton, Charles 205
Movements for Piano and Orchestra
   97, 98
Moves 85, 122
Moving Earth 256
Mozart, Wolfgang Amadeus 43, 146
Mozartiana 96, 159

Mudra 144, 235, 246
Mukhamedov, Irek 101, 143, 162,
   163
Müller, Heiner 236
Muller, Jennifer 80, 211
Mumford, Peter 203, 204
Munich State Opera Ballet 58, 153
Murder 210
Murderer Hope of Women 217
Murphy, Graeme 141, 212, 219
Music 204
Musitz, Suzanne 219
Mussorgsky, Modest 44, 147
Mutations 211
My Body, Your Body 84, 237
My Brother, My Sisters 131, 170, 172
My Fair Lady 72
My Sex, Our Dance 237
Mythologies 250

N

N.Y. Export: Op. Jazz 122
Nabokov, Nicolas 34
Napoli **16-17**, 19, 23, 114, 155, 177,
   184
National Ballet of Canada 16, 17, 25,
   32, 37, 81, 100, 128, 131. 138,
   139, 141, 148, 152, 153, 173,
   176-7, 178, 184, 189
National Ballet of Cuba 22, **177-8**
Neary, Patricia 42, 188
Nederlands Ballet 157, 158, 211
Nelken 228
Netherlands Dance Theatre 131, 150,
   158, 188, 189, **211-2**, 217, 245
Nettleford, Rex 207
Neumeier, John 20, 30, 32, 36, 37,
   43, 47, 48, 51, 81, 101, 118, 139,
   144, 147, 151, 153, 156, 157,
   165, 168, 170, 173, 174, **179-80**,
   188, 189
Never Top 40 (Juke Box) 207
New Ballet School 160
New Dance 75
New Galileo 203
New Sleep 128
New Year's Sacrifice, The 149
New York Baroque Dance Company
   11
New York City Ballet 25, 28, 30, 31,
   33, 34, 42, 43, 47, 48, 53, 71,
   87, 88, 89, 93, 94, 95, 97, **117-8**,
   121, 122, 123, 124, 129, 131, 143,
   148, 149, 152, 154, 155, 159,
   164, 165, 176, 184, 203, 205,
   218, 222, 258
New Zealand Ballet 236
Newark 197
Newson, Lloyd 83, 84, 236, 238,
   242, 243
Nicholas Brothers 208
Night 205
Night Encounter 140
Night Journey **69-70**, 71
Night Shadow see *La Sonnambula*
Nijinska, Bronislava 39, 44, 46, 47,
   53-5, 89, 91, 106, 112, 126, 138,
   145, 183
Nijinska, Irina 53, 54, 55

Nijinsky, Clown de Dieu 56, 70
Nijinsky, Vaslav 21, 39, 44, 46, 49,
  50, 53, 54, **55-9**, 60, 70, 98, 112,
  113, 134, 144, 157, 164, 165,
  167, 181
Nikolais, Alwin 25, 72, 82, 157, 198,
  199, **212-3**, 248
Nine Person Precision Ball-Passing
  205
Nine Sinatra Songs 55, 62, 221
Ninth Symphony 51
Nixon in China 257
No Fire Escape in Hell 233, 234
No Joy 232
Noble, Peter 231
Noces, Les 46, **53-4**, 55, 122, 126,
  255
Nocturne 234
Noguchi, Isamu 67, 69, 70, 231
Nomads 168
Nordheim, Arne 190
Norman, Jessye 257
North, Robert 201, 210, **213-4**, 217
Northern Ballet Theatre 25, 77, 186
Norwegian National Ballet 191
Not Necessarily Recognizable Objects
  209
Notre Faust 144
Nuitter, Charles 24
Noverre, Jean-Georges 10, 188, 189
Noumenon 213
Nureyev, Rudolf 12, 16, 22, 29, 30,
  32, 34, 35, 36, 37, 43, 47, 49,
  56, 63, 64, 67, 68, 81, 88, 93,
  107, 108, 109, 112, 113, 114, 119,
  126, 127, 134, 136, 141, 142,
  148, 150, 156, 157, 158, 165,
  167, 169, 170, 174, 176, 177,
  180-2, 183, 184, 185, 186, 191,
  193, 197, 198, 241, 257
Nutcracker, The 24, 25, **28-30**, 31,
  33, 36, 43, 49, 89, 93, 94, 96,
  107, 119, 125, 127, 128, 143,
  156, 166, 176, 179, 183, 184
Nyman, Michael 182, 204, 231
Nympheas 210

O

O Rangasayee 251
Oakland Ballet 54
*Occasion For Some Revolutionary
  Gestures, An* 217, 223
Ocellus 215
Ode to Walt Whitman 234
Oedipus Rex 156
Offenbach, Jacques 238
Offenbach in the Underworld 124
Ohio Ballet 239
Ohno, Kazuo 253
Oklahoma! 62, 68, 103, 104, 116
Oliphant, Betty 177
Oman, Julia Trevelyan 30, 139
Ombres Electriques 238
On Your Toes 62, 94, 103, 175
Ondine 17, 20, 23, 89, 107, 108,
  127, 136, 156, 187, 191
One by Nine 153
One Charming Night 250
Onegin 140, 150, **152-3**, 175, 177,

  186, 188
Ono, Yoko 250
Our caca phony H. our caca phony H.
  233
Opening Gambits 247
Opus 19/The Dreamer 122
Opus 65 165
Orbs 223
Orfeo ed Euridice 117
Orpheus 69, 98 (George Balanchine),
  240 (William Forsythe)
Orpheus and Eurydice 187
Orlikowsky, Vaslav 187
Osborne, Nigel 195
Othello 140, 179
Other Dances 125, 143, 174
Outsider, The 145
Overture 247

P

Pacific Northwest Ballet 30, 128,
  154, 199
Page, Ashley 126, 153, **182**, 217, 227
Page, Ruth 79, 115, 123
Paint Your Wagon 68, 103
Painted Birds 158
Pajama Game, The 208
Palais de Crystal, Le see *Symphony
  in C*
Paloma Azul, La 83
Pan, Hermes 62
Panov, Valeri 112, 167
Panova, Galina 102, 167
Papp, Joseph 160, 230
Paquita 33, 37, 154
Parade 50, **51-2**, 82, 164, 165
Parade's Gone By, The 244
Paradise Lost 108
Parafango 227, 234
Paramour 153
Paris Opéra (Ballet) 8, 11, 19, 20, 25,
  27, 37, 38, 40, 43, 45, 48, 53,
  54, 67, 88, 93, 94, 98, 108, 112,
  113, 118, 119, 131, 137, 138, 145,
  153, 156, 181, **183-4**, 191, 194,
  198, 203, 206, 212, 213, 226,
  233, 246, 257
Parsons, David 176, 221
Pas de dix 37
Pas de quatre 19, **22-3**, 106, 117, 149
Pas des Déesses 23, 165
Pas des trois cousines 23
Pashkova, Lydia 37
Patineurs, Les 89, 91, 116, 218
Patsalas, Constantin 177
Paulli, Holger Simon 16, 17
Pavlova, Anna 25, 34, 39, 45, 47,
  59, 89, 108, 117, 127, 133, 140,
  167, 178, 183
Paxton, Steve 203, 216, 230, 231,
  243, 247, **251-2**, 258
Pendleton, Moses 215
Peer Gynt 153
Penitente, El 66, 68
Pennsylvania Ballet 154, 212, 227
Penumbra 242
Perrot, Jules **19-23**, 27, 32, 107,
  166, 183
Peter Pan 122

Petipa, Lucien 32, 183
Petipa, Marius 12, 17, 20, 23, 24, 26,
  28, 30, 31, **32-7**, 40, 43, 44, 45,
  86, 87, 90, 91, 98, 101, 138, 139,
  145, 147, 156, 166, 181, 183,
  258, 259, 260
Petit, Roland 20, 25, 30, 33, 102,
  108, **118-20**, 121, 131, 144, 148,
  157, 167, 181, 183, 184, 185
Petronio, Stephen 196, 240, 248,
  252
Petrushka 39, 45, 46, **48-9**, 54, 82,
  121, 145, 147, 164, 197
Phantom of the Opera 157, 185
Phillips, Arlene 218
Phoenix 242
Piano Concerto in G 122
Piano Variations 158
Picasso, Pablo 33, 39, 44, 50, 51, 52,
  67, 214
Pick-Up Company 209
Pictures 203
Pier Rides 238
Pierrot lunaire 189, 197, 198
Pietsch, Dieter 231
Pillar of Fire 19, 88, 89, 104, 129,
  130, **131-2**, 172
Pilobolus Dance Theatre 71, 153, 164,
  213, **215**, 234, 235
Pineapple Poll 104, 150, **151-2**, 177,
  213, 258
Ping Chong 249
Planets 239
Plisetskaya, Maya 10, 87, 101, 119,
  120, **121**, 144, 145, 178, 186
Poème de l'extase 108
Points in Space 201, 202
Pole Dance 81
Porter, Cole 62
Poulenc, Francis 39, 43, 44, 54, 55,
  75, 170
Powell, Geoff 237
Powell, Michael 110
Powell, Ray 141
Praagh, Peggy van 100, 109, 140
Prelude 207
Premier Orage 199
Présages, Les 50
Pressburger, Emeric 110
Pribaoutki 214
Price, Roland 146
Primitive Mysteries 66, 68
Primus, Pearl 194, 207
Prince of the Pagodas, The 127, 150,
  170
Prisoner of the Caucasus 110
Private Lesson, The see *Lesson, The*
Prodigal Son, The 40, **42-3**, 106, 113,
  122, 126, 134, 143, 179
Prokofiev, Sergei 39, 42, 81, 89, 92,
  93, 111, 122, 161, 245
Puccini, Giacomo 207
Pugni, Cesare 22
Pulcinella 206
Purcell, Henry 80
Pursuit 182
Push Comes To Shove 88, 142, 143,
  153, 193, 222
Pushkin, Alexander 142, 152, 181

Pygmalion 9

Q

Quarry 249
Quartet 70
Queenie Pie 207
Queensland Ballet 141, 219
Quintet Projects 253

R

Radha 63, 65
Rainbow 'Round My Shoulder 195
Rainer, Yvonne 196, 198, 206, 209, **215-7**, 247, 251, 252
Rake's Progress, The 105
Rambert Dance Company 182, 195, 203, 204, **217-8** (see also Ballet Rambert)
Rameau, Jean-Philippe 11
Rambert, Marie 45, 58, 78, 87, 89, **98-100**, 102, 117, 126, 127, 129, 133, 164, 198, 201, 217, 244
Ranken, Liz 237
Rashomon 186
Rauschenberg, Robert 52, 196, 202, 220
Ravel, Maurice 39, 48, 118, 122, 145, 159
Raymonda **37**, 141, 166, 181, 183
Raymonda Variations 37
R.B.M.E. 150
Red Detachment of Women 149, 163, 250
Red Poppy, The 101, 133, 163
Red Shoes, The 50, 109, **110**
Ree, Larry 227
Reich, Steve 160, 199, 200, 204, 205, 235
Reisinger, Julius 30
Reitz, Dana 71, 85, 230, 248, **252-3**
Relative Calm 199, 257
Rembrandt, Ryn 211
Re-Moves 221
Rendezvous, Les 91, 116, 177
Requiem 75, 169, 170, 189
Return to the Strange Land 168
Revelations 194
Rhapsody 92, 136, 143, 156
Richecoeur, Michelle 236
Riegger, Wallingford 72
Riley, Bridget 214
Rimbaud, Arthur 89
Ris et Danceries 10, 11
Rite Electrik 210
Rite of Spring, The **see** *Sacre du printemps, Le*
Ritual Ruckus (How to Walk an Elephant) 243
River, The 194
Robbins, Jerome 18, 28, 42, 43, 47, 52, 54, 57, 62, 83, 85, 87, 88, 103, 110, 111, 115, 117, 118, **121-5**, 126, 143, 154, 155, 159, 160, 161, 165, 169, 174, 176, 182, 190, 208, 222, 227
Robert Schumann's 'Davidsbündlertanze' 140
Rodeo 68, 87, 102, **103-4**, 115, 116, 165

Roerich, Nicholas 57
Rogers, Ginger 62
Romance 227, 234
Romeo and Juliet 63, 81, 88, 89, 92, 108, 110, **111-2**, 114, 117, 121, 127, 128, 129, 130, 133, 134, 144, 150, 153, 154, 159, 163, 167, 169, 170, 174, 175, 177, 179, 181, 183, 185, 187, 188, 245
Ronde, La 131, 177, 189
Roof Piece 196
Rooms **83-4**, 235
Rope Dances 205
Ropes of Time 158
Roriz, Olga 142
Rosas 235
Rosas Danst Rosas 235
Rose, Jürgen 152
Rose malade, La 119, 121
Ross, Bertram 70
Rossignol, Le 138, 156
Rotary Action 243
Rouault, Georges 42
Rouge et Noir 50
Routine and Variations 247
Royal Ballet, The 17, 22, 29, 30, 35, 37, 42, 43, 47, 54, 55, 58, 78, 88, 90, 91, 92, 97, 98, 100, 104, 105, 106, 107, 108, 109, 111, 112, 113, 114, 117, 124, **125-7**, 129, 131, 136, 137, 138, 140, 141, 145, 148, 150, 153, 155, 156, 158, 166, 167, 168, 169, 170, 173, 174, 175, 177, 179, 181, 182, 185, 186, 191, 193, 195, 210, 213, 218, 233, 260
Royal Danish Ballet 10, 12, 4, 17, 18, 40, 43, 89, 112, 120, 131, 138, 148, 175, 184, 194, 195, 218
Royal Swedish Ballet 10, 18, 29, 30, 32, 81, 102, 129, 132, 139, 144, 148, 153
Royal Winnipeg Ballet 22, 176, 177, 187
Rubinstein, Ida 89, 144
Rumours 219
Rushes 204
Russell, Francia 128
Ruzimatov, Faroukh 143, 167

S

Sacre du printemps, Le 31, 39, 50, 53, 54, 56, **57-9**, 98, 144, 147, 169, 220, 224, 228, 239
Sacred Grove on Mount Tamalpais 164
Sadler's Wells Royal Ballet 27, 43, 49, 89, 114, **125-7**, 136, 140, 141, 145, 146, 147, 151, 153, 165, 169, 170, 171, 176, 185
Sadoff, Simon 80
St Denis, Ruth **63-5**, 72, 73
Saint-Léon, Arthur **23-5**, 78, 166, 183
St Matthew Passion 179
Saint-Saëns, Camille 59
Salavisa, Jorge 141, 142
Salem Shore 68
Sallé, Marie 9, 10

Salome 157
Samovskaya, Capitoline 20
San Francisco Ballet 32, 112, 114, 117, **127-8**, 149, 191
Sankai Juku 144, **253-4**, 256, 258
Sansom, Bruce 138
Saroyan, William 115
Satie, Erik 39, 44, 50, 51, 92, 136, 203
Saunier, Johanna 236
Saura, Carlos 240, 241
Say Bye Bye 240
Scala, La 37, 112, 150, 241
Scanlon, Jennifer 81
Scènes de Ballet 92, 107
Schaufuss, Frank 184
Schaufuss, Peter 14, 16, 17, 29, 30, 114, 148, 157, 177, **184-5**
Schayk, Toer van 158
Schéhérazade 46, 48, 55, 154
Schema 213, 157
Schiele, Egon 234
Schlemmer, Oskar 25, 78, **81-2**, 85, 188, 213, 258
Schnitzler, Arthur 131, 189
Schönberg, Arnold 131, 189
School of American Ballet 87, 93, 94, 96, 117, 118, 154, 159, 160, 178
School of Hard Knocks 249
Schooling, Elisabeth 57
Schuman, William 69
Schuylenburch, Ellen van 233
Scott, Margaret 141
Scottish Ballet 16, 17, 22, 32, 142, 233
Scriabin Preludes and Studies 214
Sea of Troubles 153, 170
Seagull, The 121
Second Stride 195, 203, 204, 236, 238, 255
Secret of the Waterfall 206
Secret Pastures 243
Seiber, Matyas 171
Sen, Rossana 232
Sendak, Maurice 30
Septet 203, 217
Seraphic Dialogue **70-1**
Serenade 35, 93, **95-6**
Sergeant Early's Dream 198
Sergeyev, Konstantin 93
Sergeyev, Nicholas 87, 126, 167
Set and Reset 196, 197
Setterfield, Valda 209, 210
Seven Deadly Sins, The 170, 228, 246
Seven Sketches 182
Seven Tears 223
Seventh Symphony 50
Severe Clear 253
Seymour, Lynn 22, 66, 136, 140, 153, 159, 169, 170, 175, **185-6**, 213, 217
Shadowplay 129, 155
Shakers, The 68, 73
Shakespeare, William 80, 111, 138, 191, 244
Sharaff, Irene 123
Shaw, Brian 137
Shawn, Ted **63-5**, 73, 78

Shearer, Moira 107, 110
Shellman, Eddie J. 21
Sheriff, Stephen 153
Shook, Karel 154, 155
Short Stories 222
Shining 219
Shostakovich, Dmitri 50, 163, 169
Sibley, Antoinette 139, 155, **186-7**
Silence is the End of Our Song 198
Silent Partners 204
Simple Man, A 186
Simulacrum Court 252
Sinfonietta 168
Singin' in the Rain 122
Sitwell, Edith 90
Sizova, Alla 36
Skeaping, Mary 22
Sleep, Wayne 213, **218**
Sleeping Beauty, The 12, 25, 33,
    35-7, 44, 53, 88, 92, 93, 101,
    106, 107, 109, 114, 125, 148,
    158, 166, 167, 170, 174, 177,
    179, 181, 182, 186, 209, 259
Sleeping Princess, The see *Sleeping
    Beauty, The*
Sleepwalking 209
Slump 232
Smith, Janet 214, 223
Smith, Oliver 88, 103, 122
Smith, Richard 195
Smith, Willi 243
Smuin, Michael 112, 128, 191
Snow Queen, The 29, 146, **147**
Sokolow, Anna 64, 67, 75, 77, **82-4**,
    165, 194, 198, 211, 217, 219, 229,
    234, 235, 256
Soldat 182
Soldier's Mass 77, 168
Solitaire 172
Solo in Silence 253
Some Rooms 219
Something To Do 195
Somnambulism 169
Son of Gone Fishin' 196
Song 204
Song and Dance 218
Song for Dead Warriors, A 128
Song of the Earth 75, 169, **172-3**,
    174
*Songs That Tell a Story (Robe of
    White)* 251
Sonnambula, La 48
Sons of Horus, The 128, 146
Source, La 184
Space 205
Space Dance 81
Sparemblek, Milko 141
Spartacus 101, 153, 161, **162-3**
Specimen Days 249
Spectre de la rose, Le 46, 49, 55
Spending Time Doing Things 248
Spessivtseva, Olga 21, 107, 183
Spiked Sonata 223
Spink, Ian 217, **255**
Spinning Dance 204
Spiral 196 (Trisha Brown), 204
    (Laura Dean)
Spoerli, Heinz 22, 49, 81, 112, 137,
    138, 147, 151, 157, 170, 183,

187-8, 189
Spohr, Arnold 22
Springsteen, Bruce 222
Square Dance 68 (George
    Balanchine), 204 (Laura Dean)
Squaregame 226
Stabat Mater 215
Staff, Frank 100
Stages 200
Stamping Dance 204
Stamping Ground 168
Stanislavski, Konstantin 101, 133
State of Darkness 239
Steadfast Tin Soldier, The 25
Stein, Gertrude 89, 155
Stella, Frank 202
Stepanov, Vladimir 167
Stevenson, Ben 93, 149, 150
Stevenson, Hugh 130
Still Life 214
'Still Life' at the Penguin Café 146
Still Waters 199
Stolze Kurt-Heinz 152
Stone Flower, The 121, 161
Stowell, Kent 30, 128
Strasbourg Opéra Ballet 245
Strauss, Richard 43
Stravinsky, Igor 31, 38, 39, 40, 41,
    44, 47, 48, 53, 57, 58, 67, 92,
    94, 97, 98, 117, 118, 138, 147,
    156, 168, 176, 179, 182, 206,
    224, 228, 239, 255, 260
Stravinsky Violin Concerto 40, 176
Strider 195, 203, 255
Strindberg, August 102
Strong Language 195
Stuttgart Ballet 10, 53, 54, 58, 98,
    112, 134, 148, 150, 153, 168,
    169, 170, 179, **188-9**, 193, 212,
    239, 240
Styles, Sheila 153
Sucre ou deux, Un 245
Suddenly Out of the Blue... 238
Sue's Leg 124, 221, 222
Suite en Blanc 113
Sullivan, Arthur 151
Summerspace 203
Sunset 123
Supertramp 222
Svenska Danseatern 102
Swamp 233
Swan Lake 25, 26, 27, 28, **30-2**, 35,
    46, 101, 102, 107, 114, 116, 121,
    125, 127, 148, 149, 150, 156,
    157, 158, 166, 167, 174, 175,
    177, 181, 183, 186, 187, 227,
    258, 259
Swan of Tuonela, The 146
Sweet Charity 208
Sydney City Ballet 141
Sydney Dance Company 141, 212,
    219, 255
Sylphide, La 11, 12, 13, **15-16**, 19, 46,
    99, 107, 114, 134, 148, 174, 176,
    177, 182, 183, 184, 185, 188, 260
Sylphides, Les 16, 35, 39, 45, **46-7**,
    55, 99, 125, 181
Symphonic Variations 89, **91-2**, 107,
    136, 140, 260

Symphonie fantastique 50
Symphony in C 51, 94, 184
Symphony in D 124, 212
Symphony in Three Movements 40,
    97, 98
Symphony of Psalms 168

T

Taglioni, Filippo 15, 183, 188
Taglioni, Marie 12, 14, 15, 19, 22, 53,
    117, 133, 134, 166, 183, 188
Taglioni, Paul 188
Tait, Marion 151, 170
Takada, Yoshiyuki 254
Takei, Kei 229, 243, 249, 254, **256**,
    257, 258
Tales of Beatrix Potter, The 110, 136,
    218
Tallchief, Maria 94, 159
*Tamili Film Songs in Stereo Pas de
    Deux* 251
Taming of the Shrew, The 81, 150,
    152, 188
Tamiris, Helen 234
Tancredi 181
Tarantos, Los 241
Taras, John 48, 117
Taras, Paul 237
Tarde en la Siesta 178
Taxi Dances 223
Taylor, Paul 43, 55, 58, 67, 70, 75,
    79, 84, 88, 96, 118, 123, 176,
    181, 183, 204, 215, 217, **220-1**,
    223, 228, 229, 230, 234, 251
Taylor, Philip 212
Tchaikovsky Piano Concerto No. 2 96,
    117
Tchaikovsky, Pyotr Ilyich 27, 28, 30,
    31, 32, 35, 36, 50, 92, 93, 94,
    118, 152, 159, 174, 179
Tcherina, Ludmila 110
Tchernichov, Igor 112
Tchernichova, Yelena 227
Tectonics 242
Tempest, The 81, 128, 181, 189,
    190-1, 197, 217
Tennant, Veronica 37, 177
Tensile Involvement 212
Tent 213
Ter-Arutunian, Rouben 48
Tetley, Glen 58, 64, 67, 72, 81, 88,
    114, 120, 126, 131, 142, 150, 164,
    174, 177, 181, 182, 183, **189-91**,
    197, 198, 211, 212, 217, 219
Tharp, Twyla 42, 53, 55, 62, 70, 75,
    84, 85, 88, 122, 124, 134, 142,
    143, 153, 164, 173, 195, 204,
    209, 220, **221-2**, 227, 230, 236,
    248, 250, 252, 253
Theme and Variations 88, 94, 96,
    178
Theodore, Lee 72, 103
There is a Time 79
Thesmar, Ghislaine 16
Thomson, Virgil 89
Three Epitaphs 220
Three Preludes 149
Three Virgins and a Devil 102
Three-Cornered Hat, The 33, 50

Tiller in the Fields, The 129, 165
Tippett, Michael 195
Tipton, Jennifer 253
Tomasson, Helgi 32, 128, 149
Torvill and Dean 219
Touch the Earth 231
Tovey, Bramwell 147
Tracy, Michael 215 *Tragedy of Fashion, A* 89, 99
Train bleu, Le 52, 53, 106
Traitor, The 79
Transfigured Night 212
Transitions 232, 238
Travelogue 52
Travelogue Series, The 249
Trend 72
Triadic Ballet 25, 81, 82, 188
Trinity 52, 134, 164
Trio A 209, 216, 217, 251
Trouillas, Christian 224
Troy Game 214
Tudor, Antony 19, 32, 70, 76, 77, 81, 87, 88, 100, 102, 103, 104, 111, 112, 117, 124, **129-32**, 140, 155, 158, 165, 171, 172, 173, 174, 176, 177, 214, 228, 229, 234, 235
Turgenev, Ivan 139
Turner, Harold 105
Turning Point, The 88, 143
Turrell, James 253
Turtle Dreams (Waltz) 249
TV Reel 209
Twilight 158
Two 248
Two Pigeons, The 89, 185
Tyl Eulenspiegel 56
Tympani 204, 205
Tzigane 159

U

Ulanova, Galina 21, 22, 101, 112, 121, **133**, 175, 186
Ullmann, Lisa 78
UnAmerican Activities 195, 204
Undertow 104, 129
Unetsu (Eggs Standing Out of Curiosity) 254
Union Dance Company 242
Union Jack 152
Unsung, The 79
Untitled 215
Urlicht 239
Urusov, Prince 100

V

Vaganova, Agrippina 133, 167
Valley Cottage 243
Valley of Shadows 170
Valse, La 48
Valse nobles et sentimentales 136
Vangsaae, Mona 17, 18, 184
Varèse, Edgard 72, 83, 198
Variations for Four 106, 149
Variations for Orchestra 40
Vasiliev, Vladimir 87, 156, 163
Vasiliov, Vladimir 101
Vaslav 157
Vast 219
Vaughan Williams, Ralph 105, 194

Verdon, Gwen 208
Verdy, Violette 183
Veredon, Gray 52
Verkommenes Ufer Medeamaterial Landschaft mit Argonauten 236
Vernon, Janet 219
Vernoy de Saint-Georges, Jules Henri 20
Verret, François 183, 245
Vestris 142
Vestris, Auguste 14, 17
Vestris, Gaetano 17, 19
Vic-Wells Ballet 23, 28, 36, 88, 89, 91, 104, 106, 107, 116, 125
Video-Life 200
Vienna: Lusthaus 234
Vienna State Opera Ballet 32, 34, 43, 132
Vienna Waltzes 48, 159
Villella, Edward 43, 64
Villumsen, Arne 17
Vinogradov, Oleg 167
Violin Concerto 97, 98
Virsaladze, Simon 162, 163
Viva Vivaldi! 165
Vivaldi, Antonio 68, 250
Voluntaries 189
Vsevolojsky, Ivan 35

W

Wachmann, Abraham 78
Wagner, Richard 60
Wagoner, Dan 67, 210, 217, 220, **223**, 230, 238
Walbrook, Anton 110
Walker, David 92, 138
Walk-In 253
Walking on the Walls 196
Walklyndon 210
Walks and Digressions 209
Wallis, Lynn 177
Walton, William 90, 124
Ward 247
Warhol, Andy 202
Waring, James 209, 216
Warshaw, Randy 196
Washington National Ballet 93
Washington, Shelley 193
Washington Square 181
Water Study 73
Waterless Method of Swimming Instruction 210
Watermill 122
Waterproof 245
Watson, Graeme 212
Watteau Duet, The 226
Weaver, John 9, 10
Webern, Anton 117
Wedding Bouquet, A 89, 109, 155
Weeme, Mascha ter 157
Weidman, Charles 64, 73, 79, 234, 244
Weighing the Heart 255
Weill, Kurt 170, 228, 246
Weininger, Andreas 82
Welch, Garth 140
Wellenkamp, Vasco 142
West Australian Ballet 141, 219
West Side Story 110, 112, 122, 160,

161, 208
Westbeth 203
Westbrook, Kate and Mike 238
Western Symphony 68
When We Were Very Young 70, 222
Whims of Cupid and the Ballet Master, The 10, 11, 14
White Nights 119, 143, 222
Who Cares? 62, 91
Wiener, Nina 229, 230, 248
Wigman, Mary 60, 71, 72, 78, **84-5**, 198, 212, 254
Wild Boy 170
Wilder, Valerie 177
Wildlife 195
Wiley, Roland John 29, 30, 32, 37
Williams, Dudley 194
Williams, Lavinia 207
Wilson, Robert 52, 82, 144, 199, 205, 236, 247, 249, 253, 255, **257**
Wilson, Sallie 132
Witch Dance 84
With My Red Fires 73
Wolfi 186
Wolken, Jonathan 215
Woolliams, Anne 141
Wright, Peter 22, 29, 30, 37, 127
Wuppertal Dance Theatre 58, 224, 228

Y

Yes, Virginia, Another Piano Ballet 125, 227
Young Apollo 146
Youskevitch, Igor 178
Yu-ku-ri 246

Z

Zakharov, Rostislav 93, 133
Zane, Arnie 224, **242-3**
Zorina, Vera 94, 107
Zurich Opera Ballet 37

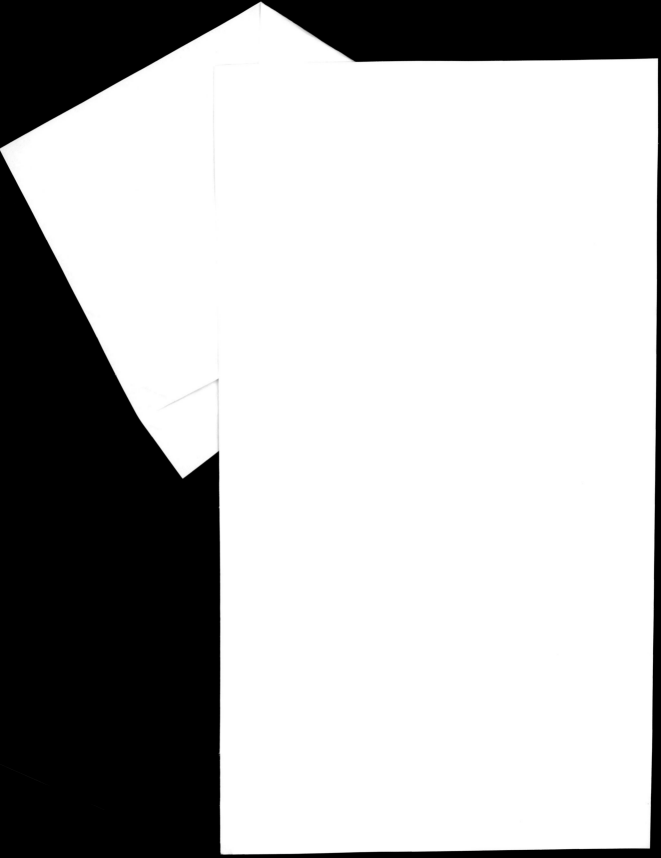

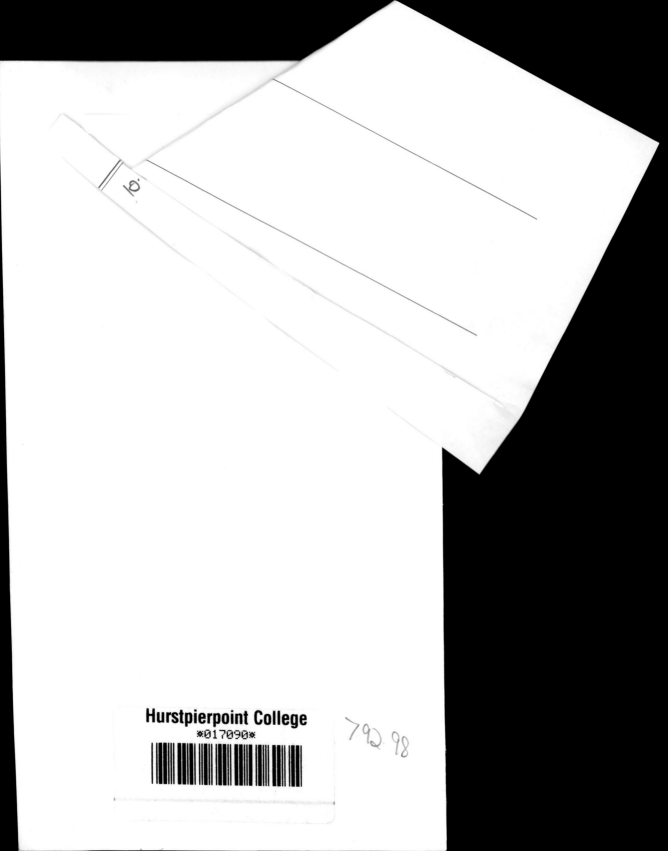